TABLE OF CONTENTS

[The page number at which the new material appears in this Supplement is indicated in the right column; the page number of the Casebook at which we suggest the new material should be considered appears in the left column. Many of the footnotes to the cases have been omitted; those retained have not been renumbered. Parallel citations to cases and statutes have also been omitted without so indicating.]

Page

PREFACE.. iii

Casebook		Supplement
Page		**Page**

Chapter 1

56   Update on the Dodd-Frank Act, the JOBS Act and the Decline in IPOs................1

Chapter 4

334   2. Initial Coin Offerings and Crypto-Currencies

     Securities Exchange Act Release No. 81207 (July 25, 2017) ("Report of Investigation Pursuant to Section 21(a) of the Securities Exchange Act of 1934: The DAO")............................7

Chapter 13

1037   4. Statutes of Limitations and Rules of Repose

     Cal. Pub. Employees' Ret. Sys. v. ANZ Sec. Inc. 25

     5.Concurrent Jurisdiction

     Cyan Inc. v. Beaver County Employees Retirement Fund 36

Chapter 14

1039   In re Petrobras Securities Litig. 50

Chapter 19

1447   3. Statute of Limitations

     Kokesh v. SEC 74

APPENDICES

App.		**Page**
I.	Prospectus, filed pursuant to Rule 424(b)(4), of Dropbox, Inc.	81
II.	Form of Underwriting Agreement for Dropbox, Inc., including Form of Lock-Up Agreement	330

UNIVERSITY CASEBOOK SERIES®

2018 SUPPLEMENT TO

SECURITIES REGULATION

CASES AND MATERIALS

THIRTEENTH EDITION

a. Dodd-Frank Downsizing and the Pending Changes in the Volcker Rule: 2018 is the tenth anniversary of the 2008 financial crisis, and both Congress and financial regulators appear to have decided that this anniversary should be celebrated through significant deregulation.

The best evidence of this shift towards deregulation is the "Economic Growth, Regulatory Relief, and Consumer Protection Act," which passed both Houses of Congress and was signed by President Trump at the end of May. Under Dodd-Frank, banks with assets of $50 billion or more were considered "systemically important financial institutions" (or "SIFIs"), and were subject to stricter oversight from the Federal Reserve. The new legislation increases the SIFI threshold from $50 billion to $250 billion, thereby exempting an estimated two dozen banks from closer supervision (although the Federal Reserve can order that banks with assets over $100 billion should remain subject to stress tests).

Equally important rulemaking changes are underway at the financial regulators. The Federal Reserve is rewriting its leverage-ratio rule (which requires U.S. banks to maintain a minimum level of capital against all their assets) to correspond to a lower level agreed to by the Basel Committee on Banking Supervision. This compromise raised the level for most European banks, but lowered it for U.S. banks. Also in the process of being relaxed is the Volcker Rule, which restricts large banks from engaging in "proprietary trading" or owning or sponsoring a hedge fund. The Dodd-Frank enacted this prohibition on the premise that banks could otherwise use customer deposits to support their risky trading. Five federal agencies -- the Federal Reserve, the Office of the Controller of the Currency, the Federal Deposit Insurance Corporation, the SEC, and the CFTC -- have to agree on any reform of the Volcker Rule, but press reports have indicated that they will permit banks significantly greater leeway in determining what constitutes "proprietary trading." No official draft of the proposed revisions has yet emerged, but one is expected to be released this summer.

It would be an overstatement to say that these changes repeal or even "cripple" the Dodd-Frank Act, but they do amount to a significant relaxation.

b. **The JOBs Act and IPOs**. Passed in 2013, the JOBs Act created a 5-year "on ramp" for "emerging growth companies" ("EGCs") under which EGCs that went public would be spared from having to comply with all the disclosure and governance rules to which other "reporting companies," were subject (for example, certain executive compensation disclosures and "say on pay" votes would not apply to them). The hope was that this would encourage more initial public offerings (or "IPOs").

What happened? As the diagram below shows, the annual number of IPOs (and their average first day returns) collapsed with the burst of the Hot IPO bubble in 2001 and have never recovered. In 2015 and 2016, the number of IPOs fell to levels below those at the time of the JOBs Act's passage in 2012, but there was a modest uptick in 2017. Although large high-tech IPOs still occur (including the Dropbox offering this year), smaller IPOs (measured in terms of companies with annual sales below $60 million) have become rare.

IPO volume has been very low in the U.S. since 2000

In 1980-2000, an average of 310 firms went public every year
In 2001-2017, an average of 108 firms went public every year

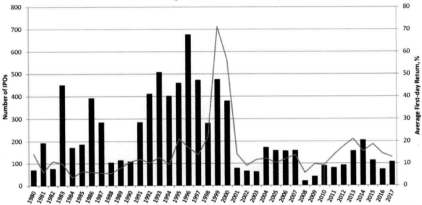

Number of Offerings (bars) and Average First-day Returns (line) on US IPOs, 1980-2017

This pattern has been even more pronounced for smaller firms, as next shown:

Exhibit Two

U.S. IPO Volume has been particularly low for small firms

Small firm IPOs are defined as IPOs with less than $60 million in LTM sales ($2016)

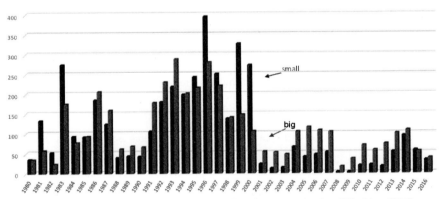

Number of U.S. IPOs with pre-IPO Annual Sales less than or greater than $60m/Year (2016)

Although, from 1995 to 2000, small IPOs generally outnumbered larger IPOs, this pattern has reversed, itself, since 2000.

This decline in IPO volume is not unique to the United States. The decline in Canada has been even more extreme (where the absence of a national securities regulator undercuts the argument that an overzealous national regulator is the cause): Similarly, IPO volume has fallen in Europe and Japan by amounts corresponding to the U.S. decline. If the decline in IPOs were the product of SEC overregulation, one would expect a decline in the U.S. only, but instead the pattern is a global decline.

What explains this decline and, in particular, the eclipse of smaller IPOs? Two explanations seem most plausible:

First, private companies find it easier, quicker, and generally cheaper to raise capital in robust private markets from venture capital and private equity funds. Also, the litigation risk is far more modest in private markets if the issuer does not prosper (for example, Section 11 of the Securities Act will not apply).

Second, because IPOs for smaller firms have been consistently unprofitable for a sustained period, investors and underwriters have come to shun them. In response, the sponsors of these smaller firms increasingly seek to exit through the "M&A" market, selling their firm to a large corporate buyer. Possibly because they are acquiring control, these corporate buyers tend to pay a higher price than does the IPO market. Academic research suggests that the decline in volume and relative unprofitability of smaller firm IPOs are because such firms cannot gain the economics of scope and scale that are increasingly necessary to compete successfully in global markets.[2] The corporate acquirer can give the smaller firm the scope and scale that it cannot achieve on its own.

A key premise to the JOBs Act was that if the costs of effecting an IPO were reduced (including the costs of becoming a "reporting company"), the number of IPOs would rise. But what are the real costs of an IPO? By most accounts, the largest cost is the underwriter's discount (which by custom comes to 7% of the offering on most IPOs in the medium-size range). Depending on the size of the IPO, the underwriter's discount ranges between 70 to 80% of the total costs of the IPO (with the fees to legal counsel and the issuer's auditor ranking second and third, respectively). The costs of SEC registration rank near the bottom at only 2 to 3% of total costs.

This may suggest that the logic of the JOBs Act was flawed. Only reducing the size of the underwriter's discount would have meaningful cost impact (and this is not likely). Nonetheless, in 2018, a group of securities industry organizations (including SIFMA and Nasdaq) released a report, entitled "Expanding the On-Ramp: Recommendations to Help More Companies Go and Stay Public," which called for extending the JOBs Act's 5-year "on ramp" to ten years and permitting large issuers-to stay "emerging growth companies." Legislation to preempt and downsize a series of SEC rules in keeping with these recommendiatons is currently being considered by the House Financial Services Committee.

Is there a crisis in that few companies are going public? If these companies are gaining easy access to capital on attractive terms in private equity markets, this may suggest not that public companies are overregulated but that private markets are very

---

2 See Xiaohui Gao, Jay R. Ritter, and Zhongyan Zhu, "Where Have All the IPOs Gone?" Journal of Financial and Quantitative Analysis (December 2013)(available on SSRN at https://ssrn.com/abstract=1954788).

successful. Investors in private markets can fend for themselves and negotiate terms that are satisfactory to them. Further, if smaller companies can command higher prices in the "M&A" market than in the IPO market, few will turn to IPOs, even if that market is significantly deregulated. Nonetheless, this debate will continue.

SECURITIES AND EXCHANGE COMMISSION

SECURITIES EXCHANGE ACT OF 1934

Release No. 81207 / July 25, 2017

Report of Investigation Pursuant to Section 21(a) of the Securities Exchange Act of 1934: The DAO

I. Introduction and Summary

The United States Securities and Exchange Commission's ("Commission") Division of Enforcement ("Division") has investigated whether The DAO, an unincorporated organization; Slock.it UG ("Slock.it"), a German corporation; Slock.it's co-founders; and intermediaries may have violated the federal securities laws. The Commission has determined not to pursue an enforcement action in this matter based on the conduct and activities known to the Commission at this time.

As described more fully below, The DAO is one example of a Decentralized Autonomous Organization, which is a term used to describe a "virtual" organization embodied in computer code and executed on a distributed ledger or blockchain. The DAO was created by Slock.it and Slock.it's co-founders, with the objective of operating as a for-profit entity that would create and hold a corpus of assets through the sale of DAO Tokens to investors, which assets would then be used to fund "projects." The holders of DAO Tokens stood to share in the anticipated earnings from these projects as a return on their investment in DAO Tokens. In addition, DAO Token holders could monetize their investments in DAO Tokens by re-selling DAO Tokens on a number of web-based platforms ("Platforms") that supported secondary trading in the DAO Tokens.

After DAO Tokens were sold, but before The DAO was able to commence funding projects, an attacker used a flaw in The DAO's code to steal approximately one-third of The DAO's assets. Slock.it's co-founders and others responded by creating a work-around whereby DAO Token holders could opt to have their investment returned to them, as described in more detail below.

The investigation raised questions regarding the application of the U.S. federal securities laws to the offer and sale of DAO Tokens, including the threshold question whether DAO Tokens are securities. Based on the investigation, and under the facts presented, the Commission has determined that DAO Tokens are securities under the Securities Act of 1933 ("Securities Act") and the Securities Exchange Act of 1934 ("Exchange Act").[1] The Commission deems it appropriate and in the public interest to issue this report of investigation ("Report") pursuant to

---

[1] This Report does not analyze the question whether The DAO was an "investment company," as defined under Section 3(a) of the Investment Company Act of 1940 ("Investment Company Act"), in part, because The DAO never commenced its business operations funding projects. Those who would use virtual organizations should consider their obligations under the Investment Company Act.

Section 21(a) of the Exchange Act[2] to advise those who would use a Decentralized Autonomous Organization ("DAO Entity"), or other distributed ledger or blockchain-enabled means for capital raising, to take appropriate steps to ensure compliance with the U.S. federal securities laws. All securities offered and sold in the United States must be registered with the Commission or must qualify for an exemption from the registration requirements. In addition, any entity or person engaging in the activities of an exchange must register as a national securities exchange or operate pursuant to an exemption from such registration.

This Report reiterates these fundamental principles of the U.S. federal securities laws and describes their applicability to a new paradigm—virtual organizations or capital raising entities that use distributed ledger or blockchain technology to facilitate capital raising and/or investment and the related offer and sale of securities. The automation of certain functions through this technology, "smart contracts,"[3] or computer code, does not remove conduct from the purview of the U.S. federal securities laws.[4] This Report also serves to stress the obligation to comply with the registration provisions of the federal securities laws with respect to products and platforms involving emerging technologies and new investor interfaces.

II.   Facts

A.   Background

From April 30, 2016 through May 28, 2016, The DAO offered and sold approximately 1.15 billion DAO Tokens in exchange for a total of approximately 12 million Ether ("ETH"), a

---

[2] Section 21(a) of the Exchange Act authorizes the Commission to investigate violations of the federal securities laws and, in its discretion, to "publish information concerning any such violations." This Report does not constitute an adjudication of any fact or issue addressed herein, nor does it make any findings of violations by any individual or entity. The facts discussed in Section II, *infra*, are matters of public record or based on documentary records. We are publishing this Report on the Commission's website to ensure that all market participants have concurrent and equal access to the information contained herein.

[3] Computer scientist Nick Szabo described a "smart contract" as:

> a computerized transaction protocol that executes terms of a contract. The general objectives of smart contract design are to satisfy common contractual conditions (such as payment terms, liens, confidentiality, and even enforcement), minimize exceptions both malicious and accidental, and minimize the need for trusted intermediaries. Related economic goals include lowering fraud loss, arbitrations and enforcement costs, and other transaction costs.

See Nick Szabo, *Smart Contracts*, 1994, http://www.virtualschool.edu/mon/Economics/SmartContracts.html.

[4] *See SEC v. C.M. Joiner Leasing Corp.*, 320 U.S. 344, 351 (1943) ("[T]he reach of the [Securities] Act does not stop with the obvious and commonplace. Novel, uncommon, or irregular devices, whatever they appear to be, are also reached if it be proved as matter of fact that they were widely offered or dealt in under terms or courses of dealing which established their character in commerce as 'investment contracts,' or as 'any interest or instrument commonly known as a 'security'.'"); *see also Reves v. Ernst & Young*, 494 U.S. 56, 61 (1990) ("Congress' purpose in enacting the securities laws was to regulate investments, in whatever form they are made and by whatever name they are called.").

virtual currency[5] used on the Ethereum Blockchain.[6] As of the time the offering closed, the total ETH raised by The DAO was valued in U.S. Dollars ("USD") at approximately $150 million.

The concept of a DAO Entity is memorialized in a document (the "White Paper"), authored by Christoph Jentzsch, the Chief Technology Officer of Slock.it, a "Blockchain and IoT [(internet-of-things)] solution company," incorporated in Germany and co-founded by Christoph Jentzsch, Simon Jentzsch (Christoph Jentzsch's brother), and Stephan Tual ("Tual").[7] The White Paper purports to describe "the first implementation of a [DAO Entity] code to automate organizational governance and decision making."[8] The White Paper posits that a DAO Entity "can be used by individuals working together collaboratively outside of a traditional corporate form. It can also be used by a registered corporate entity to automate formal governance rules contained in corporate bylaws or imposed by law." The White Paper proposes an entity—a DAO Entity—that would use smart contracts to attempt to solve governance issues it described as inherent in traditional corporations.[9] As described, a DAO Entity purportedly would supplant traditional mechanisms of corporate governance and management with a blockchain such that contractual terms are "formalized, automated and enforced using software."[10]

---

[5] The Financial Action Task Force defines "virtual currency" as:

> a digital representation of value that can be digitally traded and functions as: (1) a medium of exchange; and/or (2) a unit of account; and/or (3) a store of value, but does not have legal tender status (i.e., when tendered to a creditor, is a valid and legal offer of payment) in any jurisdiction. It is not issued or guaranteed by any jurisdiction, and fulfils the above functions only by agreement within the community of users of the virtual currency. Virtual currency is distinguished from fiat currency (a.k.a. "real currency," "real money," or "national currency"), which is the coin and paper money of a country that is designated as its legal tender; circulates; and is customarily used and accepted as a medium of exchange in the issuing country. It is distinct from e-money, which is a digital representation of fiat currency used to electronically transfer value denominated in fiat currency.

FATF Report, Virtual Currencies, Key Definitions and Potential AML/CFT Risks, FINANCIAL ACTION TASK FORCE (June 2014), http://www.fatf-gafi.org/media/fatf/documents/reports/Virtual-currency-key-definitions-and-potential-aml-cft-risks.pdf.

[6] Ethereum, developed by the Ethereum Foundation, a Swiss nonprofit organization, is a decentralized platform that runs smart contracts on a blockchain known as the Ethereum Blockchain.

[7] Christoph Jentzsch released the final draft of the White Paper on or around March 23, 2016. He introduced his concept of a DAO Entity as early as November 2015 at an Ethereum Developer Conference in London, as a medium to raise funds for Slock.it, a German start-up he co-founded in September 2015. Slock.it purports to create technology that embeds smart contracts that run on the Ethereum Blockchain into real-world devices and, as a result, for example, permits anyone to rent, sell or share physical objects in a decentralized way. *See* SLOCK.IT, https://slock.it/.

[8] Christoph Jentzsch, *Decentralized Autonomous Organization to Automate Governance Final Draft – Under Review*, https://download.slock.it/public/DAO/WhitePaper.pdf.

[9] *Id.*

[10] *Id.* The White Paper contained the following statement:

> A word of caution, at the outset: the legal status of [DAO Entities] remains the subject of active and vigorous debate and discussion. Not everyone shares the same definition. Some have said that [DAO Entities] are autonomous code and can operate independently of legal systems; others

9

B.   The DAO

"The DAO" is the "first generation" implementation of the White Paper concept of a DAO Entity, and it began as an effort to create a "crowdfunding contract" to raise "funds to grow [a] company in the crypto space."[11] In November 2015, at an Ethereum Developer Conference in London, Christoph Jentzsch described his proposal for The DAO as a "for-profit DAO [Entity]," where participants would send ETH (a virtual currency) to The DAO to purchase DAO Tokens, which would permit the participant to vote and entitle the participant to "rewards."[12] Christoph Jentzsch likened this to "buying shares in a company and getting … dividends."[13] The DAO was to be "decentralized" in that it would allow for voting by investors holding DAO Tokens.[14] All funds raised were to be held at an Ethereum Blockchain "address" associated with The DAO and DAO Token holders were to vote on contract proposals, including proposals to The DAO to fund projects and distribute The DAO's anticipated earnings from the projects it funded.[15] The DAO was intended to be "autonomous" in that project proposals were in the form of smart contracts that exist on the Ethereum Blockchain and the votes were administered by the code of The DAO.[16]

have said that [DAO Entities] must be owned or operate[d] by humans or human created entities. There will be many use cases, and the DAO [Entity] code will develop over time. Ultimately, how a DAO [Entity] functions and its legal status will depend on many factors, including how DAO [Entity] code is used, where it is used, and who uses it. This paper does not speculate about the legal status of [DAO Entities] worldwide. This paper is not intended to offer legal advice or conclusions. Anyone who uses DAO [Entity] code will do so at their own risk.

Id.

[11] Christoph Jentzsch, *The History of the DAO and Lessons Learned*, SLOCK.IT BLOG (Aug. 24, 2016), https://blog.slock.it/the-history-of-the-dao-and-lessons-learned-d06740f8cfa5#.5o62zo8uv. Although The DAO has been described as a "crowdfunding contract," The DAO would not have met the requirements of Regulation Crowdfunding, adopted under Title III of the Jumpstart Our Business Startups (JOBS) Act of 2012 (providing an exemption from registration for certain crowdfunding), because, among other things, it was not a broker-dealer or a funding portal registered with the SEC and the Financial Industry Regulatory Authority ("FINRA"). *See Regulation Crowdfunding: A Small Entity Compliance Guide for Issuers*, SEC (Apr. 5, 2017), https://www.sec.gov/info/smallbus/secg/rccomplianceguide-051316.htm; *Updated Investor Bulletin: Crowdfunding for Investors*, SEC (May 10, 2017), https://www.sec.gov/oiea/investor-alerts-bulletins/ib_crowdfunding-.html.

[12] *See* Slockit, *Slock.it DAO demo at Devcon1: IoT + Blockchain*, YOUTUBE (Nov. 13, 2015), https://www.youtube.com/watch?v=49wHQoJxYPo.

[13] *Id.*

[14] *See* Jentzsch, *supra* note 8.

[15] *Id.* In theory, there was no limitation on the type of project that could be proposed. For example, proposed "projects" could include, among other things, projects that would culminate in the creation of products or services that DAO Token holders could use or charge others for using.

[16] *Id.*

On or about April 29, 2016, Slock.it deployed The DAO code on the Ethereum Blockchain, as a set of pre-programmed instructions.[17] This code was to govern how The DAO was to operate.

To promote The DAO, Slock.it's co-founders launched a website ("The DAO Website"). The DAO Website included a description of The DAO's intended purpose: "To blaze a new path in business for the betterment of its members, existing simultaneously nowhere and everywhere and operating solely with the steadfast iron will of unstoppable code."[18] The DAO Website also described how The DAO operated, and included a link through which DAO Tokens could be purchased. The DAO Website also included a link to the White Paper, which provided detailed information about a DAO Entity's structure and its source code and, together with The DAO Website, served as the primary source of promotional materials for The DAO. On The DAO Website and elsewhere, Slock.it represented that The DAO's source code had been reviewed by "one of the world's leading security audit companies" and "no stone was left unturned during those five whole days of security analysis."[19]

Slock.it's co-founders also promoted The DAO by soliciting media attention and by posting almost daily updates on The DAO's status on The DAO and Slock.it websites and numerous online forums relating to blockchain technology. Slock.it's co-founders used these posts to communicate to the public information about how to participate in The DAO, including: how to create and acquire DAO Tokens; the framework for submitting proposals for projects; and how to vote on proposals. Slock.it also created an online forum on The DAO Website, as well as administered "The DAO Slack" channel, an online messaging platform in which over 5,000 invited "team members" could discuss and exchange ideas about The DAO in real time.

1. DAO Tokens

In exchange for ETH, The DAO created DAO Tokens (proportional to the amount of ETH paid) that were then assigned to the Ethereum Blockchain address of the person or entity remitting the ETH. A DAO Token granted the DAO Token holder certain voting and ownership rights. According to promotional materials, The DAO would earn profits by funding projects

---

[17] According to the White Paper, a DAO Entity is "activated by deployment on the Ethereum [B]lockchain. Once deployed, a [DAO Entity's] code requires 'ether' [ETH] to engage in transactions on Ethereum. Ether is the digital fuel that powers the Ethereum Network." The only way to update or alter The DAO's code is to submit a new proposal for voting and achieve a majority consensus on that proposal. *See* Jentzsch, *supra* note 8. According to Slock.it's website, Slock.it gave The DAO code to the Ethereum community, noting that:

> The DAO framework is [a] side project of Slock.it UG and a gift to the Ethereum community. It consisted of a definitive whitepaper, smart contract code audited by one of the best security companies in the world and soon, a complete frontend interface. All free and open source for anyone to re-use, it is our way to say 'thank you' to the community.

SLOCK.IT, https://slock.it. The DAO code is publicly-available on GitHub, a host of source code. *See The Standard DAO Framework, Inc., Whitepaper*, GITHUB, https://github.com/slockit/DAO.

[18] The DAO Website was available at https://daohub.org.

[19] Stephen Tual, *Deja Vu DAO Smart Contracts Audit Results*, SLOCK.IT BLOG (Apr. 5, 2016), https://blog.slock.it/deja-vu-dai-smart-contracts-audit-results-d26bc088e32e.

that would provide DAO Token holders a return on investment. The various promotional materials disseminated by Slock.it's co-founders touted that DAO Token holders would receive "rewards," which the White Paper defined as, "any [ETH] received by a DAO [Entity] generated from projects the DAO [Entity] funded." DAO Token holders would then vote to either use the rewards to fund new projects or to distribute the ETH to DAO Token holders.

From April 30, 2016 through May 28, 2016 (the "Offering Period"), The DAO offered and sold DAO Tokens. Investments in The DAO were made "pseudonymously" (i.e., an individual's or entity's pseudonym was their Ethereum Blockchain address). To purchase a DAO Token offered for sale by The DAO, an individual or entity sent ETH from their Ethereum Blockchain address to an Ethereum Blockchain address associated with The DAO. All of the ETH raised in the offering as well as any future profits earned by The DAO were to be pooled and held in The DAO's Ethereum Blockchain address. The token price fluctuated in a range of approximately 1 to 1.5 ETH per 100 DAO Tokens, depending on when the tokens were purchased during the Offering Period. Anyone was eligible to purchase DAO Tokens (as long as they paid ETH). There were no limitations placed on the number of DAO Tokens offered for sale, the number of purchasers of DAO Tokens, or the level of sophistication of such purchasers.

DAO Token holders were not restricted from re-selling DAO Tokens acquired in the offering, and DAO Token holders could sell their DAO Tokens in a variety of ways in the secondary market and thereby monetize their investment as discussed below. Prior to the Offering Period, Slock.it solicited at least one U.S. web-based platform to trade DAO Tokens on its system and, at the time of the offering, The DAO Website and other promotional materials disseminated by Slock.it included representations that DAO Tokens would be available for secondary market trading after the Offering Period via several platforms. During the Offering Period and afterwards, the Platforms posted notices on their own websites and on social media that each planned to support secondary market trading of DAO Tokens.[20]

In addition to secondary market trading on the Platforms, after the Offering Period, DAO Tokens were to be freely transferable on the Ethereum Blockchain. DAO Token holders would also be permitted to redeem their DAO Tokens for ETH through a complicated, multi-week (approximately 46-day) process referred to as a DAO Entity "split."[21]

2. Participants in The DAO

According to the White Paper, in order for a project to be considered for funding with "a DAO [Entity]'s [ETH]," a "Contractor" first must submit a proposal to the DAO Entity. Specifically, DAO Token holders expected Contractors to submit proposals for projects that could provide DAO Token holders returns on their investments. Submitting a proposal to The DAO involved: (1) writing a smart contract, and then deploying and publishing it on the

---

[20] The Platforms are registered with FinCEN as "Money Services Businesses" and provide systems whereby customers may exchange virtual currencies for other virtual currencies or fiat currencies.

[21] According to the White Paper, the primary purpose of a split is to protect minority shareholders and prevent what is commonly referred to as a "51% Attack," whereby an attacker holding 51% of a DAO Entity's Tokens could create a proposal to send all of the DAO Entity's funds to himself or herself.

Ethereum Blockchain; and (2) posting details about the proposal on The DAO Website, including the Ethereum Blockchain address of the deployed contract and a link to its source code. Proposals could be viewed on The DAO Website as well as other publicly-accessible websites. Per the White Paper, there were two prerequisites for submitting a proposal. An individual or entity must: (1) own at least one DAO Token; and (2) pay a deposit in the form of ETH that would be forfeited to the DAO Entity if the proposal was put up for a vote and failed to achieve a quorum of DAO Token holders. It was publicized that Slock.it would be the first to submit a proposal for funding.[22]

ETH raised by The DAO was to be distributed to a Contractor to fund a proposal only on a majority vote of DAO Token holders.[23] DAO Token holders were to cast votes, which would be weighted by the number of tokens they controlled, for or against the funding of a specific proposal. The voting process, however, was publicly criticized in that it could incentivize distorted voting behavior and, as a result, would not accurately reflect the consensus of the majority of DAO Token holders. Specifically, as noted in a May 27, 2016 blog post by a group of computer security researchers, The DAO's structure included a "strong positive bias to vote YES on proposals and to suppress NO votes as a side effect of the way in which it restricts users' range of options following the casting of a vote."[24]

Before any proposal was put to a vote by DAO Token holders, it was required to be reviewed by one or more of The DAO's "Curators." At the time of the formation of The DAO, the Curators were a group of individuals chosen by Slock.it.[25] According to the White Paper, the Curators of a DAO Entity had "considerable power." The Curators performed crucial security functions and maintained ultimate control over which proposals could be submitted to, voted on, and funded by The DAO. As stated on The DAO Website during the Offering Period, The DAO relied on its Curators for "failsafe protection" and for protecting The DAO from "malicious [sic] actors." Specifically, per The DAO Website, a Curator was responsible for: (1) confirming that any proposal for funding originated from an identifiable person or organization; and (2)

---

[22] It was stated on The DAO Website and elsewhere that Slock.it anticipated that it would be the first to submit a proposal for funding. In fact, a draft of Slock.it's proposal for funding for an "Ethereum Computer and Universal Sharing Network" was publicly-available online during the Offering Period.

[23] DAO Token holders could vote on proposals, either by direct interaction with the Ethereum Blockchain or by using an application that interfaces with the Ethereum Blockchain. It was generally acknowledged that DAO Token holders needed some technical knowledge in order to submit a vote, and The DAO Website included a link to a step-by-step tutorial describing how to vote on proposals.

[24] By voting on a proposal, DAO Token holders would "tie up" their tokens until the end of the voting cycle. *See* Jentzsch, *supra* note 8 at 8 ("The tokens used to vote will be blocked, meaning they can not [sic] be transferred until the proposal is closed."). If, however, a DAO Token holder abstained from voting, the DAO Token holder could avoid these restrictions; any DAO Tokens not submitted for a vote could be withdrawn or transferred at any time. As a result, DAO Token holders were incentivized either to vote yes or to abstain from voting. *See* Dino Mark et al., *A Call for a Temporary Moratorium on The DAO*, HACKING, DISTRIBUTED (May 27, 2016, 1:35 PM), http://hackingdistributed.com/2016/05/27/dao-call-for-moratorium/.

[25] At the time of The DAO's launch, The DAO Website identified eleven "high profile" individuals as holders of The DAO's Curator "Multisig" (or "private key"). These individuals all appear to live outside of the United States. Many of them were associated with the Ethereum Foundation, and The DAO Website touted the qualifications and trustworthiness of these individuals.

confirming that smart contracts associated with any such proposal properly reflected the code the Contractor claims to have deployed on the Ethereum Blockchain. If a Curator determined that the proposal met these criteria, the Curator could add the proposal to the "whitelist," which was a list of Ethereum Blockchain addresses that could receive ETH from The DAO if the majority of DAO Token holders voted for the proposal.

Curators of The DAO had ultimate discretion as to whether or not to submit a proposal for voting by DAO Token holders. Curators also determined the order and frequency of proposals, and could impose subjective criteria for whether the proposal should be whitelisted. One member of the group chosen by Slock.it to serve collectively as the Curator stated publicly that the Curator had "complete control over the whitelist ... the order in which things get whitelisted, the duration for which [proposals] get whitelisted, when things get unwhitelisted ... [and] clear ability to control the order and frequency of proposals," noting that "curators have tremendous power."[26] Another Curator publicly announced his subjective criteria for determining whether to whitelist a proposal, which included his personal ethics.[27] Per the White Paper, a Curator also had the power to reduce the voting quorum requirement by 50% every other week. Absent action by a Curator, the quorum could be reduced by 50% only if no proposal had reached the required quorum for 52 weeks.

3. Secondary Market Trading on the Platforms

During the period from May 28, 2016 through early September 2016, the Platforms became the preferred vehicle for DAO Token holders to buy and sell DAO Tokens in the secondary market using virtual or fiat currencies. Specifically, the Platforms used electronic systems that allowed their respective customers to post orders for DAO Tokens on an anonymous basis. For example, customers of each Platform could buy or sell DAO Tokens by entering a market order on the Platform's system, which would then match with orders from other customers residing on the system. Each Platform's system would automatically execute these orders based on pre-programmed order interaction protocols established by the Platform.

None of the Platforms received orders for DAO Tokens from non-Platform customers or routed its respective customers' orders to any other trading destinations. The Platforms publicly displayed all their quotes, trades, and daily trading volume in DAO Tokens on their respective websites. During the period from May 28, 2016 through September 6, 2016, one such Platform executed more than 557,378 buy and sell transactions in DAO Tokens by more than 15,000 of its U.S. and foreign customers. During the period from May 28, 2016 through August 1, 2016, another such Platform executed more than 22,207 buy and sell transactions in DAO Tokens by more than 700 of its U.S. customers.

---

[26] Epicenter, *EB134 – Emin Gün Sirer And Vlad Zamfir: On A Rocky DAO*, YOUTUBE (June 6, 2016), https://www.youtube.com/watch?v=ON5GhIQdFU8.

[27] Andrew Quentson, *Are the DAO Curators Masters or Janitors?*, THE COIN TELEGRAPH (June 12, 2016), https://cointelegraph.com/news/are-the-dao-curators-masters-or-janitors.

4. *Security Concerns, The "Attack" on The DAO, and The Hard Fork*

In late May 2016, just prior to the expiration of the Offering Period, concerns about the safety and security of The DAO's funds began to surface due to vulnerabilities in The DAO's code. On May 26, 2016, in response to these concerns, Slock.it submitted a "DAO Security Proposal" that called for the development of certain updates to The DAO's code and the appointment of a security expert.[28] Further, on June 3, 2016, Christoph Jentzsch, on behalf of Slock.it, proposed a moratorium on all proposals until alterations to The DAO's code to fix vulnerabilities in The DAO's code had been implemented.[29]

On June 17, 2016, an unknown individual or group (the "Attacker") began rapidly diverting ETH from The DAO, causing approximately 3.6 million ETH—1/3 of the total ETH raised by The DAO offering—to move from The DAO's Ethereum Blockchain address to an Ethereum Blockchain address controlled by the Attacker (the "Attack").[30] Although the diverted ETH was then held in an address controlled by the Attacker, the Attacker was prevented by The DAO's code from moving the ETH from that address for 27 days.[31]

In order to secure the diverted ETH and return it to DAO Token holders, Slock.it's co-founders and others endorsed a "Hard Fork" to the Ethereum Blockchain. The "Hard Fork," called for a change in the Ethereum protocol on a going forward basis that would restore the DAO Token holders' investments as if the Attack had not occurred. On July 20, 2016, after a majority of the Ethereum network adopted the necessary software updates, the new, forked Ethereum Blockchain became active.[32] The Hard Fork had the effect of transferring all of the funds raised (including those held by the Attacker) from The DAO to a recovery address, where DAO Token holders could exchange their DAO Tokens for ETH.[33] All DAO Token holders

---

[28] *See* Stephan Tual, *Proposal #1-DAO Security, Redux*, SLOCK.IT BLOG (May 26, 2016), https://blog.slock.it/both-our-proposals-are-now-out-voting-starts-saturday-morning-ba322d6d3aea. The unnamed security expert would "act as the first point of contact for security disclosures, and continually monitor, pre-empt and avert any potential attack vectors The DAO may face, including social, technical and economic attacks." *Id.* Slock.it initially proposed a much broader security proposal that included the formation of a "DAO Security" group, the establishment of a "Bug Bounty Program," and routine external audits of The DAO's code. However, the cost of the proposal (125,000 ETH), which would be paid from The DAO's funds, was immediately criticized as too high and Slock.it decided instead to submit the revised proposal described above. *See* Stephan Tual, *DAO.Security, a Proposal to guarantee the integrity of The DAO*, SLOCK.IT BLOG (May 25, 2016), https://blog.slock.it/dao-security-a-proposal-to-guarantee-the-integrity-of-the-dao-3473899ace9d.

[29] *See TheDAO Proposal_ID 5*, ETHERSCAN, https://etherscan.io/token/thedao-proposal/5.

[30] *See* Stephan Tual, *DAO Security Advisory: live updates*, SLOCK.IT BLOG (June 17, 2016), https://blog.slock.it/dao-security-advisory-live-updates-2a0a42a2d07b.

[31] *Id.*

[32] A minority group, however, elected not to adopt the new Ethereum Blockchain created by the Hard Fork because to do so would run counter to the concept that a blockchain is immutable. Instead they continued to use the former version of the blockchain, which is now known as "Ethereum Classic."

[33] *See* Christoph Jentzsch, *What the 'Fork' Really Means*, SLOCK.IT BLOG (July 18, 2016), https://blog.slock.it/what-the-fork-really-means-6fe573ac31dd.

who adopted the Hard Fork could exchange their DAO Tokens for ETH, and avoid any loss of the ETH they had invested.[34]

III. Discussion

The Commission is aware that virtual organizations and associated individuals and entities increasingly are using distributed ledger technology to offer and sell such instruments such as DAO Tokens to raise capital. These offers and sales have been referred to, among other things, as "Initial Coin Offerings" or "Token Sales." Accordingly, the Commission deems it appropriate and in the public interest to issue this Report in order to stress that the U.S. federal securities law may apply to various activities, including distributed ledger technology, depending on the particular facts and circumstances, without regard to the form of the organization or technology used to effectuate a particular offer or sale. In this Report, the Commission considers the particular facts and circumstances of the offer and sale of DAO Tokens to demonstrate the application of existing U.S. federal securities laws to this new paradigm.

A. Section 5 of the Securities Act

The registration provisions of the Securities Act contemplate that the offer or sale of securities to the public must be accompanied by the "full and fair disclosure" afforded by registration with the Commission and delivery of a statutory prospectus containing information necessary to enable prospective purchasers to make an informed investment decision. Registration entails disclosure of detailed "information about the issuer's financial condition, the identity and background of management, and the price and amount of securities to be offered … ." *SEC v. Cavanagh*, 1 F. Supp. 2d 337, 360 (S.D.N.Y. 1998), *aff'd*, 155 F.3d 129 (2d Cir. 1998). "The registration statement is designed to assure public access to material facts bearing on the value of publicly traded securities and is central to the Act's comprehensive scheme for protecting public investors." *SEC v. Aaron*, 605 F.2d 612, 618 (2d Cir. 1979) (citing *SEC v. Ralston Purina Co.,* 346 U.S. 119, 124 (1953)), *vacated on other grounds*, 446 U.S. 680 (1980). Section 5(a) of the Securities Act provides that, unless a registration statement is in effect as to a security, it is unlawful for any person, directly or indirectly, to engage in the offer or sale of securities in interstate commerce. Section 5(c) of the Securities Act provides a similar prohibition against offers to sell, or offers to buy, unless a registration statement has been filed. Thus, both Sections 5(a) and 5(c) of the Securities Act prohibit the unregistered offer or sale of securities in interstate commerce. 15 U.S.C. § 77e(a) and (c). Violations of Section 5 do not require scienter. *SEC v. Universal Major Indus. Corp.*, 546 F.2d 1044, 1047 (2d Cir. 1976).

---

[34] *Id.*

B.   DAO Tokens Are Securities

　　　　1.   *Foundational Principles of the Securities Laws Apply to Virtual*
　　　　　　　Organizations or Capital Raising Entities Making Use of Distributed
　　　　　　　Ledger Technology

Under Section 2(a)(1) of the Securities Act and Section 3(a)(10) of the Exchange Act, a
security includes "an investment contract." *See* 15 U.S.C. §§ 77b-77c. An investment contract
is an investment of money in a common enterprise with a reasonable expectation of profits to be
derived from the entrepreneurial or managerial efforts of others. *See SEC v. Edwards*, 540 U.S.
389, 393 (2004); *SEC v. W.J. Howey Co.,* 328 U.S. 293, 301 (1946); *see also United Housing
Found., Inc. v. Forman*, 421 U.S. 837, 852-53 (1975) (The "touchstone" of an investment
contract "is the presence of an investment in a common venture premised on a reasonable
expectation of profits to be derived from the entrepreneurial or managerial efforts of others.").
This definition embodies a *"flexible rather than a static principle*, one that is capable of
adaptation to meet the countless and variable schemes devised by those who seek the use of the
money of others on the promise of profits." *Howey*, 328 U.S. at 299 (emphasis added). The test
"permits the fulfillment of the statutory purpose of compelling full and fair disclosure relative to
the issuance of 'the many types of instruments that in our commercial world fall within the
ordinary concept of a security.'" *Id.* In analyzing whether something is a security, "form should
be disregarded for substance," *Tcherepnin v. Knight*, 389 U.S. 332, 336 (1967), "and the
emphasis should be on economic realities underlying a transaction, and not on the name
appended thereto." *United Housing Found.*, 421 U.S. at 849.

　　　　2.   *Investors in The DAO Invested Money*

In determining whether an investment contract exists, the investment of "money" need
not take the form of cash. *See, e.g., Uselton v. Comm. Lovelace Motor Freight, Inc.*, 940 F.2d
564, 574 (10th Cir. 1991) ("[I]n spite of *Howey's* reference to an 'investment of money,' it is
well established that cash is not the only form of contribution or investment that will create an
investment contract.").

Investors in The DAO used ETH to make their investments, and DAO Tokens were
received in exchange for ETH. Such investment is the type of contribution of value that can
create an investment contract under *Howey*. *See SEC v. Shavers*, No. 4:13-CV-416, 2014 WL
4652121, at *1 (E.D. Tex. Sept. 18, 2014) (holding that an investment of Bitcoin, a virtual
currency, meets the first prong of *Howey*); *Uselton*, 940 F.2d at 574 ("[T]he 'investment' may
take the form of 'goods and services,' or some other 'exchange of value'.") (citations omitted).

　　　　3.   *With a Reasonable Expectation of Profits*

Investors who purchased DAO Tokens were investing in a common enterprise and
reasonably expected to earn profits through that enterprise when they sent ETH to The DAO's
Ethereum Blockchain address in exchange for DAO Tokens. "[P]rofits" include "dividends,
other periodic payments, or the increased value of the investment." *Edwards*, 540 U.S. at 394.
As described above, the various promotional materials disseminated by Slock.it and its co-
founders informed investors that The DAO was a for-profit entity whose objective was to fund

projects in exchange for a return on investment.[35] The ETH was pooled and available to The DAO to fund projects. The projects (or "contracts") would be proposed by Contractors. If the proposed contracts were whitelisted by Curators, DAO Token holders could vote on whether The DAO should fund the proposed contracts. Depending on the terms of each particular contract, DAO Token holders stood to share in potential profits from the contracts. Thus, a reasonable investor would have been motivated, at least in part, by the prospect of profits on their investment of ETH in The DAO.

4. *Derived from the Managerial Efforts of Others*

a. The Efforts of Slock.it, Slock.it's Co-Founders, and The DAO's Curators Were Essential to the Enterprise

Investors' profits were to be derived from the managerial efforts of others—specifically, Slock.it and its co-founders, and The DAO's Curators. The central issue is "whether the efforts made by those other than the investor are the undeniably significant ones, those essential managerial efforts which affect the failure or success of the enterprise." *SEC v. Glenn W. Turner Enters., Inc.*, 474 F.2d 476, 482 (9th Cir. 1973). The DAO's investors relied on the managerial and entrepreneurial efforts of Slock.it and its co-founders, and The DAO's Curators, to manage The DAO and put forth project proposals that could generate profits for The DAO's investors.

Investors' expectations were primed by the marketing of The DAO and active engagement between Slock.it and its co-founders with The DAO and DAO Token holders. To market The DAO and DAO Tokens, Slock.it created The DAO Website on which it published the White Paper explaining how a DAO Entity would work and describing their vision for a DAO Entity. Slock.it also created and maintained other online forums that it used to provide information to DAO Token holders about how to vote and perform other tasks related to their investment. Slock.it appears to have closely monitored these forums, answering questions from DAO Token holders about a variety of topics, including the future of The DAO, security concerns, ground rules for how The DAO would work, and the anticipated role of DAO Token holders. The creators of The DAO held themselves out to investors as experts in Ethereum, the blockchain protocol on which The DAO operated, and told investors that they had selected persons to serve as Curators based on their expertise and credentials. Additionally, Slock.it told investors that it expected to put forth the first substantive profit-making contract proposal—a blockchain venture in its area of expertise. Through their conduct and marketing materials, Slock.it and its co-founders led investors to believe that they could be relied on to provide the significant managerial efforts required to make The DAO a success.

Investors in The DAO reasonably expected Slock.it and its co-founders, and The DAO's Curators, to provide significant managerial efforts after The DAO's launch. The expertise of The DAO's creators and Curators was critical in monitoring the operation of The DAO, safeguarding investor funds, and determining whether proposed contracts should be put for a

---

[35] That the "projects" could encompass services and the creation of goods for use by DAO Token holders does not change the core analysis that investors purchased DAO Tokens with the expectation of earning profits from the efforts of others.

vote. Investors had little choice but to rely on their expertise. At the time of the offering, The DAO's protocols had already been pre-determined by Slock.it and its co-founders, including the control that could be exercised by the Curators. Slock.it and its co-founders chose the Curators, whose function it was to: (1) vet Contractors; (2) determine whether and when to submit proposals for votes; (3) determine the order and frequency of proposals that were submitted for a vote; and (4) determine whether to halve the default quorum necessary for a successful vote on certain proposals. Thus, the Curators exercised significant control over the order and frequency of proposals, and could impose their own subjective criteria for whether the proposal should be whitelisted for a vote by DAO Token holders. DAO Token holders' votes were limited to proposals whitelisted by the Curators, and, although any DAO Token holder could put forth a proposal, each proposal would follow the same protocol, which included vetting and control by the current Curators. While DAO Token holders could put forth proposals to replace a Curator, such proposals were subject to control by the current Curators, including whitelisting and approval of the new address to which the tokens would be directed for such a proposal. In essence, Curators had the power to determine whether a proposal to remove a Curator was put to a vote.[36]

And, Slock.it and its co-founders did, in fact, actively oversee The DAO. They monitored The DAO closely and addressed issues as they arose, proposing a moratorium on all proposals until vulnerabilities in The DAO's code had been addressed and a security expert to monitor potential attacks on The DAO had been appointed. When the Attacker exploited a weakness in the code and removed investor funds, Slock.it and its co-founders stepped in to help resolve the situation.

b.   DAO Token Holders' Voting Rights Were Limited

Although DAO Token holders were afforded voting rights, these voting rights were limited. DAO Token holders were substantially reliant on the managerial efforts of Slock.it, its co-founders, and the Curators.[37] Even if an investor's efforts help to make an enterprise profitable, those efforts do not necessarily equate with a promoter's significant managerial efforts or control over the enterprise. *See, e.g., Glenn W. Turner*, 474 F.2d at 482 (finding that a multi-level marketing scheme was an investment contract and that investors relied on the promoter's managerial efforts, despite the fact that investors put forth the majority of the labor that made the enterprise profitable, because the promoter dictated the terms and controlled the scheme itself); *Long v. Shultz*, 881 F.2d 129, 137 (5th Cir. 1989) ("An investor may authorize the assumption of particular risks that would create the possibility of greater profits or losses but still depend on a third party for all of the essential managerial efforts without which the risk could not

---

[36] DAO Token holders could put forth a proposal to split from The DAO, which would result in the creation of a new DAO Entity with a new Curator. Other DAO Token holders would be allowed to join the new DAO Entity as long as they voted yes to the original "split" proposal. Unlike all other contract proposals, a proposal to split did not require a deposit or a quorum, and it required a seven-day debating period instead of the minimum two-week debating period required for other proposals.

[37] Because, as described above, DAO Token holders were incentivized either to vote yes or to abstain from voting, the results of DAO Token holder voting would not necessarily reflect the actual view of a majority of DAO Token holders.

pay off."). *See also generally SEC v. Merchant Capital, LLC,* 483 F.3d 747 (11th Cir. 2007) (finding an investment contract even where voting rights were provided to purported general partners, noting that the voting process provided limited information for investors to make informed decisions, and the purported general partners lacked control over the information in the ballots).

The voting rights afforded DAO Token holders did not provide them with meaningful control over the enterprise, because (1) DAO Token holders' ability to vote for contracts was a largely perfunctory one; and (2) DAO Token holders were widely dispersed and limited in their ability to communicate with one another.

First, as discussed above, DAO Token holders could only vote on proposals that had been cleared by the Curators.[38] And that clearance process did not include any mechanism to provide DAO Token holders with sufficient information to permit them to make informed voting decisions. Indeed, based on the particular facts concerning The DAO and the few draft proposals discussed in online forums, there are indications that contract proposals would not have necessarily provide enough information for investors to make an informed voting decision, affording them less meaningful control. For example, the sample contract proposal attached to the White Paper included little information concerning the terms of the contract. Also, the Slock.it co-founders put forth a draft of their own contract proposal and, in response to questions and requests to negotiate the terms of the proposal (posted to a DAO forum), a Slock.it founder explained that the proposal was intentionally vague and that it was, in essence, a take it or leave it proposition not subject to negotiation or feedback. *See, e.g., SEC v. Shields,* 744 F.3d 633, 643-45 (10th Cir. 2014) (in assessing whether agreements were investment contracts, court looked to whether "the investors actually had the type of control reserved under the agreements to obtain access to information necessary to protect, manage, and control their investments at the time they purchased their interests.").

Second, the pseudonymity and dispersion of the DAO Token holders made it difficult for them to join together to effect change or to exercise meaningful control. Investments in The DAO were made pseudonymously (such that the real-world identities of investors are not apparent), and there was great dispersion among those individuals and/or entities who were invested in The DAO and thousands of individuals and/or entities that traded DAO Tokens in the secondary market—an arrangement that bears little resemblance to that of a genuine general partnership. *Cf. Williamson v. Tucker,* 645 F.2d 404, 422-24 (5th Cir. 1981) ("[O]ne would not expect partnership interests sold to large numbers of the general public to provide any real partnership control; at some point there would be so many [limited] partners that a partnership vote would be more like a corporate vote, each partner's role having been diluted to the level of a single shareholder in a corporation.").[39] Slock.it did create and maintain online forums on which

---

[38] Because, in part, The DAO never commenced its business operations funding projects, this Report does not analyze the question whether anyone associated with The DAO was an "[i]nvestment adviser" under Section 202(a)(11) of the Investment Advisers Act of 1940 ("Advisers Act"). *See* 15 U.S.C. § 80b-2(a)(11). Those who would use virtual organizations should consider their obligations under the Advisers Act.

[39] The Fifth Circuit in *Williamson* stated that:

20

investors could submit posts regarding contract proposals, which were not limited to use by DAO Token holders (anyone was permitted to post). However, DAO Token holders were pseudonymous, as were their posts to the forums. Those facts, combined with the sheer number of DAO Token holders, potentially made the forums of limited use if investors hoped to consolidate their votes into blocs powerful enough to assert actual control. This was later demonstrated through the fact that DAO Token holders were unable to effectively address the Attack without the assistance of Slock.it and others. The DAO Token holders' pseudonymity and dispersion diluted their control over The DAO. *See Merchant Capital*, 483 F.3d at 758 (finding geographic dispersion of investors weighing against investor control).

These facts diminished the ability of DAO Token holders to exercise meaningful control over the enterprise through the voting process, rendering the voting rights of DAO Token holders akin to those of a corporate shareholder. *Steinhardt Group, Inc. v. Citicorp.*, 126 F.3d 144, 152 (3d Cir. 1997) ("It must be emphasized that the assignment of nominal or limited responsibilities to the participant does not negate the existence of an investment contract; where the duties assigned are so narrowly circumscribed as to involve little real choice of action ... a security may be found to exist ... . [The] emphasis must be placed on economic reality.") (citing *SEC v. Koscot Interplanetary, Inc.*, 497 F.2d 473, 483 n. 14 (5th Cir. 1974)).

By contract and in reality, DAO Token holders relied on the significant managerial efforts provided by Slock.it and its co-founders, and The DAO's Curators, as described above. Their efforts, not those of DAO Token holders, were the "undeniably significant" ones, essential to the overall success and profitability of any investment into The DAO. *See Glenn W. Turner*, 474 F.2d at 482.

C.   Issuers Must Register Offers and Sales of Securities Unless a Valid Exemption Applies

The definition of "issuer" is broadly defined to include "every person who issues or proposes to issue any security" and "person" includes "any unincorporated organization." 15 U.S.C. § 77b(a)(4). The term "issuer" is flexibly construed in the Section 5 context "as issuers devise new ways to issue their securities and the definition of a security itself expands." *Doran v. Petroleum Mgmt. Corp.*, 545 F.2d 893, 909 (5th Cir. 1977); *accord SEC v. Murphy*, 626 F.2d 633, 644 (9th Cir. 1980) ("[W]hen a person [or entity] organizes or sponsors the organization of

A general partnership or joint venture interest can be designated a security if the investor can establish, for example, that (1) an agreement among the parties leaves so little power in the hands of the partner or venture that the arrangement in fact distributes power as would a limited partnership; or (2) the partner or venturer is so inexperienced and unknowledgeable in business affairs that he is incapable of intelligently exercising his partnership or venture powers; or (3) the partner or venturer is so dependent on some unique entrepreneurial or managerial ability of the promoter or manager that he cannot replace the manager of the enterprise or otherwise exercise meaningful partnership or venture powers.

Williamson, 645 F.2d at 424 & n.15 (court also noting that, "this is not to say that other factors could not also give rise to such a dependence on the promoter or manager that the exercise of partnership powers would be effectively precluded.").

limited partnerships and is primarily responsible for the success or failure of the venture for which the partnership is formed, he will be considered an issuer ... .").

The DAO, an unincorporated organization, was an issuer of securities, and information about The DAO was "crucial" to the DAO Token holders' investment decision. *See Murphy*, 626 F.2d at 643 ("Here there is no company issuing stock, but instead, a group of individuals investing funds in an enterprise for profit, and receiving in return an entitlement to a percentage of the proceeds of the enterprise.") (citation omitted). The DAO was "responsible for the success or failure of the enterprise," and accordingly was the entity about which the investors needed information material to their investment decision. *Id.* at 643-44.

During the Offering Period, The DAO offered and sold DAO Tokens in exchange for ETH through The DAO Website, which was publicly-accessible, including to individuals in the United States. During the Offering Period, The DAO sold approximately 1.15 billion DAO Tokens in exchange for a total of approximately 12 million ETH, which was valued in USD, at the time, at approximately $150 million. Because DAO Tokens were securities, The DAO was required to register the offer and sale of DAO Tokens, unless a valid exemption from such registration applied.

Moreover, those who participate in an unregistered offer and sale of securities not subject to a valid exemption are liable for violating Section 5. *See, e.g., Murphy*, 626 F.2d at 650-51 ("[T]hose who ha[ve] a necessary role in the transaction are held liable as participants.") (citing *SEC v. North Am. Research & Dev. Corp.*, 424 F.2d 63, 81 (2d Cir. 1970); *SEC v. Culpepper*, 270 F.2d 241, 247 (2d Cir. 1959); *SEC v. International Chem. Dev. Corp.*, 469 F.2d 20, 28 (10th Cir. 1972); *Pennaluna & Co. v. SEC*, 410 F.2d 861, 864 n.1, 868 (9th Cir. 1969)); *SEC v. Softpoint, Inc.*, 958 F. Supp 846, 859-60 (S.D.N.Y. 1997) ("The prohibitions of Section 5 ... sweep[] broadly to encompass 'any person' who participates in the offer or sale of an unregistered, non-exempt security."); *SEC v. Chinese Consol. Benevolent Ass'n.*, 120 F.2d 738, 740-41 (2d Cir. 1941) (defendant violated Section 5(a) "because it engaged in selling unregistered securities" issued by a third party "when it solicited offers to buy the securities 'for value'").

D.   A System that Meets the Definition of an Exchange Must Register as a National Securities Exchange or Operate Pursuant to an Exemption from Such Registration

Section 5 of the Exchange Act makes it unlawful for any broker, dealer, or exchange, directly or indirectly, to effect any transaction in a security, or to report any such transaction, in interstate commerce, unless the exchange is registered as a national securities exchange under Section 6 of the Exchange Act, or is exempted from such registration. *See* 15 U.S.C. §78e. Section 3(a)(1) of the Exchange Act defines an "exchange" as "any organization, association, or group of persons, whether incorporated or unincorporated, which constitutes, maintains, or provides a market place or facilities for bringing together purchasers and sellers of securities or for otherwise performing with respect to securities the functions commonly performed by a stock exchange as that term is generally understood ... ." 15 U.S.C. § 78c(a)(1).

Exchange Act Rule 3b-16(a) provides a functional test to assess whether a trading system meets the definition of exchange under Section 3(a)(1). Under Exchange Act Rule 3b-16(a), an organization, association, or group of persons shall be considered to constitute, maintain, or provide "a marketplace or facilities for bringing together purchasers and sellers of securities or for otherwise performing with respect to securities the functions commonly performed by a stock exchange," if such organization, association, or group of persons: (1) brings together the orders for securities of multiple buyers and sellers; and (2) uses established, non-discretionary methods (whether by providing a trading facility or by setting rules) under which such orders interact with each other, and the buyers and sellers entering such orders agree to the terms of the trade.[40]

A system that meets the criteria of Rule 3b-16(a), and is not excluded under Rule 3b-16(b), must register as a national securities exchange pursuant to Sections 5 and 6 of the Exchange Act[41] or operate pursuant to an appropriate exemption. One frequently used exemption is for alternative trading systems ("ATS").[42] Rule 3a1-1(a)(2) exempts from the definition of "exchange" under Section 3(a)(1) an ATS that complies with Regulation ATS,[43] which includes, among other things, the requirement to register as a broker-dealer and file a Form ATS with the Commission to provide notice of the ATS's operations. Therefore, an ATS that operates pursuant to the Rule 3a1-1(a)(2) exemption and complies with Regulation ATS would not be subject to the registration requirement of Section 5 of the Exchange Act.

The Platforms that traded DAO Tokens appear to have satisfied the criteria of Rule 3b-16(a) and do not appear to have been excluded from Rule 3b-16(b). As described above, the Platforms provided users with an electronic system that matched orders from multiple parties to buy and sell DAO Tokens for execution based on non-discretionary methods.

IV. Conclusion and References for Additional Guidance

Whether or not a particular transaction involves the offer and sale of a security—regardless of the terminology used—will depend on the facts and circumstances, including the

---

[40] *See* 17 C.F.R. § 240.3b-16(a). The Commission adopted Rule 3b-16(b) to exclude explicitly certain systems that the Commission believed did not meet the exchange definition. These systems include systems that merely route orders to other execution facilities and systems that allow persons to enter orders for execution against the bids and offers of a single dealer system. *See* Securities Exchange Act Rel. No. 40760 (Dec. 8, 1998), 63 FR 70844 (Dec. 22, 1998) (Regulation of Exchanges and Alternative Trading Systems) ("Regulation ATS"), 70852.

[41] 15 U.S.C. § 78e. A "national securities exchange" is an exchange registered as such under Section 6 of the Exchange Act. 15 U.S.C. § 78f.

[42] Rule 300(a) of Regulation ATS promulgated under the Exchange Act provides that an ATS is:

> any organization, association, person, group of persons, or system: (1) [t]hat constitutes, maintains, or provides a market place or facilities for bringing together purchasers and sellers of securities or for otherwise performing with respect to securities the functions commonly performed by a stock exchange within the meaning of [Exchange Act Rule 3b-16]; and (2) [t]hat does not: (i) [s]et rules governing the conduct of subscribers other than the conduct of subscribers' trading on such [ATS]; or (ii) [d]iscipline subscribers other than by exclusion from trading.

Regulation ATS, *supra* note 40, Rule 300(a).

[43] *See* 17 C.F.R. § 240.3a1-1(a)(2). Rule 3a1-1 also provides two other exemptions from the definition of "exchange" for any ATS operated by a national securities association, and any ATS not required to comply with Regulation ATS pursuant to Rule 301(a) of Regulation ATS. *See* 17 C.F.R. §§ 240.3a1-1(a)(1) and (3).

economic realities of the transaction. Those who offer and sell securities in the United States must comply with the federal securities laws, including the requirement to register with the Commission or to qualify for an exemption from the registration requirements of the federal securities laws. The registration requirements are designed to provide investors with procedural protections and material information necessary to make informed investment decisions. These requirements apply to those who offer and sell securities in the United States, regardless whether the issuing entity is a traditional company or a decentralized autonomous organization, regardless whether those securities are purchased using U.S. dollars or virtual currencies, and regardless whether they are distributed in certificated form or through distributed ledger technology. In addition, any entity or person engaging in the activities of an exchange, such as bringing together the orders for securities of multiple buyers and sellers using established non-discretionary methods under which such orders interact with each other and buyers and sellers entering such orders agree upon the terms of the trade, must register as a national securities exchange or operate pursuant to an exemption from such registration.

To learn more about registration requirements under the Securities Act, please visit the Commission's website here. To learn more about the Commission's registration requirements for investment companies, please visit the Commission's website here. To learn more about the Commission's registration requirements for national securities exchanges, please visit the Commission's website here. To learn more about alternative trading systems, please see the Regulation ATS adopting release here.

For additional guidance, please see the following Commission enforcement actions involving virtual currencies:

- *SEC v. Trendon T. Shavers and Bitcoin Savings and Trust*, Civil Action No. 4:13-CV-416 (E.D. Tex., complaint filed July 23, 2013)

- *In re Erik T. Voorhees*, Rel. No. 33-9592 (June 3, 2014)

- *In re BTC Trading, Corp. and Ethan Burnside*, Rel. No. 33-9685 (Dec. 8, 2014)

- *SEC v. Homero Joshua Garza, Gaw Miners, LLC, and ZenMiner, LLC (d/b/a Zen Cloud)*, Civil Action No. 3:15-CV-01760 (D. Conn., complaint filed Dec. 1, 2015)

- *In re Bitcoin Investment Trust and SecondMarket, Inc.*, Rel. No. 34-78282 (July 11, 2016)

- *In re Sunshine Capital, Inc.*, File No. 500-1 (Apr. 11, 2017)

And please see the following investor alerts:

- *Bitcoin and Other Virtual Currency-Related Investments* (May 7, 2014)

- *Ponzi Schemes Using Virtual Currencies* (July 2013)

By the Commission.

Cal. Pub. Employees' Ret. Sys. v. ANZ Sec., Inc.

Supreme Court of the United States (2017)

137 S. Ct. 2042, 198 L. Ed. 2d 584, 2017 U.S. LEXIS 4062

■ JUSTICE KENNEDY delivered the opinion of the Court.

The suit giving rise to the case before the Court was filed by a plaintiff who was a member of a putative class in a class action but who later elected to withdraw and proceed in this separate suit, seeking recovery for the same illegalities that were alleged in the class suit. The class-action suit had been filed within the time permitted by statute. Whether the later, separate suit was also timely is the controlling question.

I

A

The Securities Act of 1933 "protects investors by ensuring that companies issuing securities ... make a 'full and fair disclosure of information' relevant to a public offering." *Omnicare, Inc. v. Laborers Dist. Council Constr. Industry Pension Fund,* 575 U.S. ——, ——, 135 S.Ct. 1318 (2015) (quoting *Pinter v. Dahl,* 486 U.S. 622 (1988)); see 48 Stat. 74, as amended, 15 U.S.C. § 77a *et seq.* Companies may offer securities to the public only after filing a registration statement, which must contain information about the company and the security for sale. *Ominicare,* 575 U.S., at ——-——, 135 S. Ct. 1318. Section 11 of the Securities Act "promotes compliance with these disclosure provisions by giving purchasers a right of action against an issuer or designated individuals," including securities underwriters, for any material misstatements or omissions in a registration statement. *Id.,* at ——, 135 S.Ct. 1318, 1323; see 15 U.S.C. § 77k(a).

The Act provides time limits for § 11 suits. These time limits are set forth in a two-sentence section of the Act, § 13. It provides as follows:

"No action shall be maintained to enforce any liability created under [§ 11] unless brought within one year after the discovery of the untrue statement or the omission, or after such discovery should have been made by the exercise of reasonable diligence.... In no event shall any such action be brought to enforce a liability created under [§ 11] more than three years after the security was bona fide offered to the public...." 15 U.S.C. § 77m.

So there are two time bars in the quoted provision; and the second one, the 3–year bar, is central to this case.

B

Lehman Brothers Holdings Inc. formerly was one of the largest investment banks in the United States. In 2007 and 2008, Lehman raised capital through a number of public securities offerings. Petitioner, California Public Employees' Retirement System (sometimes called CalPERS), is the largest public pension fund in the country. Petitioner purchased securities in some of these Lehman offerings; and it is alleged that respondents, various financial firms, are liable under the Act for their participation as underwriters in the transactions. The separate respondents are listed in an appendix to this opinion.

In September 2008, Lehman filed for bankruptcy. Around the same time, a putative class action concerning Lehman securities was filed against respondents in the United States District Court for the Southern District of New York. The operative complaint raised claims under § 11, alleging that the registration statements for certain of Lehman's 2007 and 2008 securities offerings included material misstatements or omissions. The complaint was filed on behalf of all persons who purchased the identified securities, making petitioner a member of the putative class. Petitioner, however, was not one of the named plaintiffs in the suit. The class action was consolidated with other securities suits against Lehman in a single multidistrict litigation.

In February 2011, petitioner filed a separate complaint against respondents in the United States District Court for the Northern District of California. This suit was filed more than three years after the relevant transactions occurred. The complaint alleged identical securities law violations as the class-action complaint, but the claims were on petitioner's own behalf. The suit was transferred and consolidated with the multidistrict litigation in the Southern District of New York. Soon thereafter, a proposed settlement was reached in the putative class action. Petitioner, apparently convinced it could obtain a more favorable recovery in its separate suit, opted out of the class.

Respondents then moved to dismiss petitioner's individual suit alleging § 11 violations as untimely under the 3–year bar in the second sentence of § 13. Petitioner countered that its individual suit was timely because that 3–year period was tolled during the pendency of the class-action filing. The principal authority cited to support petitioner's argument that the 3–year period was tolled was *American Pipe & Constr. Co. v. Utah,* 414 U.S. 538 (1974).

The District Court disagreed with petitioner's argument, holding that the 3–year bar in § 13 is not subject to tolling. The Court of Appeals for the Second Circuit affirmed. In agreement with the District Court, the Court of Appeals held that the tolling principle discussed in *American Pipe* is inapplicable to the 3–year time bar. *In re Lehman Brothers Securities and ERISA Litigation,* 655 Fed.Appx. 13, 15 (2016). As the Court of Appeals noted, there is disagreement about whether the tolling rule of *American Pipe* applies to the 3–year time bar in § 13. Compare *Joseph v. Wiles,* 223 F.3d 1155, 1166–1168 (C.A.10 2000), with *Stein v. Regions Morgan*

Keegan Select High Income Fund, Inc., 821 F.3d 780, 792–795 (C.A.6 2016), and *Dusek v. JPMorgan Chase & Co.,* 832 F.3d 1243, 1246–1249 (C.A.11 2016).

The Court of Appeals also rejected petitioner's alternative argument that its individual claims were "essentially 'filed' in the putative class complaint," so that the filing of the class action within three years made the individual claims timely. 655 Fed. Appx., at 15.

This Court granted certiorari. 580 U.S. ——, 137 S. Ct. 811 (2017).

II

The question then is whether § 13 permits the filing of an individual complaint more than three years after the relevant securities offering, when a class-action complaint was timely filed, and the plaintiff filing the individual complaint would have been a member of the class but for opting out of it. The answer turns on the nature and purpose of the 3–year bar and of the tolling rule that petitioner seeks to invoke. Each will be addressed in turn.

A

As the Court explained in *CTS Corp. v. Waldburger,* 573 U.S. ——, 134 S.Ct. 2175 (2014), statutory time bars can be divided into two categories: statutes of limitations and statutes of repose. Both "are mechanisms used to limit the temporal extent or duration of liability for tortious acts," but "each has a distinct purpose." *Id.,* at —— – ——, 134 S.Ct., at 2182.

Statutes of limitations are designed to encourage plaintiffs "to pursue diligent prosecution of known claims." *Id.,* at ——, 134 S.Ct., at 2182–2183 (internal quotation marks omitted). In accord with that objective, limitations periods begin to run "when the cause of action accrues"—that is, "when the plaintiff can file suit and obtain relief." *Id.,* at ——, 134 S.Ct., at 2182 (internal quotation marks omitted). In a personal-injury or property-damage action, for example, more often than not this will be " 'when the injury occurred or was discovered.' " *Ibid.*

In contrast, statutes of repose are enacted to give more explicit and certain protection to defendants. These statutes "effect a legislative judgment that a defendant should be free from liability after the legislatively determined period of time." *Id.,* at —— – ——, 134 S.Ct., at 2183 (internal quotation marks omitted). For this reason, statutes of repose begin to run on "the date of the last culpable act or omission of the defendant." *Id.,* at ——, 134 S.Ct., at 2182.

The 3–year time bar in § 13 reflects the legislative objective to give a defendant a complete defense to any suit after a certain period. From the structure of § 13, and the language of its second sentence, it is evident that the 3–year bar is a statute of repose. In fact, this Court has already described the provision as establishing "a period of repose," which " 'impose [s] an outside limit' " on temporal liability. *Lampf, Pleva, Lipkind, Prupis & Petigrow v. Gilbertson*, 501 U.S. 350, 363 (1991).

The statute provides in clear terms that "[i]n no event" shall an action be brought more than three years after the securities offering on which it is based. 15 U.S.C. § 77m. This instruction admits of no exception and on its face creates a fixed bar against future liability. See *CTS, supra*, at ——— – ———, 134 S.Ct., at 2182–2183; cf. *United States v. Brockamp*, 519 U.S. 347, 350 (1997) (noting that a statute that "sets forth its time limitations in unusually emphatic form ... cannot easily be read as containing implicit exceptions"). The statute, furthermore, runs from the defendant's last culpable act (the offering of the securities), not from the accrual of the claim (the plaintiff's discovery of the defect in the registration statement). Under *CTS*, this point is close to a dispositive indication that the statute is one of repose.

This view is confirmed by the two-sentence structure of § 13. In addition to the 3–year time bar, § 13 contains a 1–year statute of limitations. The limitations statute runs from the time when the plaintiff discovers (or should have discovered) the securities-law violation. The pairing of a shorter statute of limitations and a longer statute of repose is a common feature of statutory time limits. See, *e.g., Gabelli v. SEC*, 568 U.S. 442, 453 (2013) ("[S]tatutes applying a discovery rule ... often couple that rule with an absolute provision for repose"). The two periods work together: The discovery rule gives leeway to a plaintiff who has not yet learned of a violation, while the rule of repose protects the defendant from an interminable threat of liability. Cf. *Merck & Co. v. Reynolds*, 559 U.S. 633, 650 (2010) (reasoning that 2–year discovery rule would not "subject defendants to liability for acts taken long ago," because the statute also included an "unqualified bar on actions instituted '5 years after such violation' ").

The history of the 3–year provision also supports its classification as a statute of repose. It is instructive to note that the statute was not enacted in its current form. The original version of the 1933 Securities Act featured a 2–year discovery period and a 10–year outside limit, see § 13, 48 Stat. 84, but Congress changed this framework just one year after its enactment. The discovery period was changed to one year and the outside limit to three years. See Securities Exchange Act of 1934, § 207, 48 Stat. 908. The evident design of the shortened statutory period was to protect defendants' financial security in fast-changing markets by reducing the open period for potential liability.

B

The determination that the 3–year period is a statute of repose is critical in this case, for the

28

question whether a tolling rule applies to a given statutory time bar is one "of statutory intent." *Lozano v. Montoya Alvarez,* 572 U.S. 1, ——, 134 S.Ct. 1224, 1232 (2014). The purpose of a statute of repose is to create "an absolute bar on a defendant's temporal liability," *CTS,* 573 U.S., at ——, 134 S.Ct., at 2183 (alteration and internal quotation marks omitted); and that purpose informs the assessment of whether, and when, tolling rules may apply.

In light of the purpose of a statute of repose, the provision is in general not subject to tolling. Tolling is permissible only where there is a particular indication that the legislature did not intend the statute to provide complete repose but instead anticipated the extension of the statutory period under certain circumstances.

For example, if the statute of repose itself contains an express exception, this demonstrates the requisite intent to alter the operation of the statutory period. See 1 C. Corman, Limitation of Actions § 1.1, pp. 4–5 (1991) (Corman); see, *e.g.,* 29 U.S.C. § 1113 (establishing a 6–year statute of repose, but stipulating that, in case of fraud, the 6–year period runs from the plaintiff's discovery of the violation). In contrast, where the legislature enacts a general tolling rule in a different part of the code—*e.g.,* a rule that suspends time limits until the plaintiff reaches the age of majority—courts must analyze the nature and relation of the legislative purpose of each provision to determine which controls. See 2 Corman § 10.2.1, at 108. In keeping with the statute-specific nature of that analysis, courts have reached different conclusions about whether general tolling statutes govern particular periods of repose. *Ibid.,* n. 15.

Of course, not all tolling rules derive from legislative enactments. Some derive from the traditional power of the courts to " 'apply the principles ... of equity jurisprudence.' " *Young v. United States,* 535 U.S. 43, 50 (2002) (alteration omitted). The classic example is the doctrine of equitable tolling, which permits a court to pause a statutory time limit "when a litigant has pursued his rights diligently but some extraordinary circumstance prevents him from bringing a timely action." *Lozano,* 572 U.S., at ——, 134 S.Ct. 1224. Tolling rules of that kind often apply to statutes of limitations based on the presumption that Congress " 'legislate[s] against a background of common-law adjudicatory principles.' " *Id.,* at ——, 134 S.Ct., 1224, 1232.

The purpose and effect of a statute of repose, by contrast, is to override customary tolling rules arising from the equitable powers of courts. By establishing a fixed limit, a statute of repose implements a " 'legislative decisio[n] that as a matter of policy there should be a specific time beyond which a defendant should no longer be subjected to protracted liability.' " *CTS,* 573 U.S., at ——, 134 S.Ct., 2175, 2183. The unqualified nature of that determination supersedes the courts' residual authority and forecloses the extension of the statutory period based on equitable principles. For this reason, the Court repeatedly has stated in broad terms that statutes of repose are not subject to equitable tolling. See, *e.g., id.,* at —— – ——, 134 S.Ct., 2175; *Lampf, Pleva,* 501 U.S., at 363.

C

Petitioner contends that the 3–year provision is subject to tolling based on the rationale and holding in the Court's decision in *American Pipe*. The language of the 3–year statute does not refer to or impliedly authorize any exceptions for tolling. If *American Pipe* had itself been grounded in a legislative enactment, perhaps an argument could be made that the enactment expressed a legislative objective to modify the 3–year period. If, however, the tolling decision in *American Pipe* derived from equity principles, it cannot alter the unconditional language and purpose of the 3–year statute of repose.

In *American Pipe,* a timely class-action complaint was filed asserting violations of federal antitrust law. 414 U.S., at 540, 94 S.Ct. 756. Class certification was denied because the class was not large enough, see Fed. Rule Civ. Proc. 23(a)(1), and individuals who otherwise would have been members of the class then filed motions to intervene as individual plaintiffs. The motions were denied on the grounds that the applicable 4–year time bar had expired. See 15 U.S.C. § 15b. The Court of Appeals reversed, permitting intervention.

This Court affirmed. It held the individual plaintiffs' motions to intervene were timely because "the commencement of a class action suspends the applicable statute of limitations as to all asserted members of the class." *American Pipe,* 414 U.S., at 554. The Court reasoned that this result was consistent "both with the procedures of Rule 23 and with the proper function of the limitations statute" at issue. *Id.,* at 555. First, the tolling furthered "the purposes of litigative efficiency and economy" served by Rule 23. *Id.,* at 556, 94 S.Ct. 756. Without the tolling, "[p]otential class members would be induced to file protective motions to intervene or to join in the event that a class was later found unsuitable," which would "breed needless duplication of motions." *Id.,* at 553–554. Second, the tolling was in accord with "the functional operation of a statute of limitations." *Id.,* at 554. By filing a class complaint within the statutory period, the named plaintiff "notifie[d] the defendants not only of the substantive claims being brought against them, but also of the number and generic identities of the potential plaintiffs who may participate in the judgment." *Id.,* at 555.

As this discussion indicates, the source of the tolling rule applied in *American Pipe* is the judicial power to promote equity, rather than to interpret and enforce statutory provisions. Nothing in the *American Pipe* opinion suggests that the tolling rule it created was mandated by the text of a statute or federal rule. Nor could it have. The central text at issue in *American Pipe* was Rule 23, and Rule 23 does not so much as mention the extension or suspension of statutory time bars.

The Court's holding was instead grounded in the traditional equitable powers of the judiciary. The Court described its rule as authorized by the "judicial power to toll statutes of limitations." *Id.,* at 558; see also *id.,* at 555 ("the tolling rule *we establish here* " (emphasis added)). The

Court also relied on cases that are paradigm applications of equitable tolling principles, explaining with approval that tolling in one such case was based on "considerations 'deeply rooted in our jurisprudence.' " *Id.,* at 559 (quoting *Glus v. Brooklyn Eastern Dist. Terminal,* 359 U.S. 231, 232 (1959); alteration omitted); see also 414 U.S., at 559 (citing *Holmberg v. Armbrecht,* 327 U.S. 392 (1946)). The Court noted too that "bad faith" was not the cause of the District Court's denial of class certification. 414 U.S., at 553 (internal quotation marks omitted).

Perhaps for these reasons, this Court has referred to *American Pipe* as "equitable tolling." See *Irwin v. Department of Veterans Affairs,* 498 U.S. 89, 96 (1990); see also *Young, supra,* at 49, 122 S.Ct. 1036; *Greyhound Corp. v. Mt. Hood Stages, Inc.,* 437 U.S. 322, 338, n. (1978) (Burger, C.J., concurring) (using *American Pipe* as an example of "[t]he authority of a federal court, sitting as a chancellor, to toll a statute of limitations on equitable grounds"). It is true, however, that the *American Pipe* Court did not consider the criteria of the formal doctrine of equitable tolling in any direct manner. It did not analyze, for example, whether the plaintiffs pursued their rights with special care; whether some extraordinary circumstance prevented them from intervening earlier; or whether the defendant engaged in misconduct. See *Holland v. Florida,* 560 U.S. 631, 649 (2010) (identifying these considerations); *Young,* 535 U.S., at 50, 122 S.Ct. 1036 (same). The balance of the Court's reasoning nonetheless reveals a rule based on traditional equitable powers, designed to modify a statutory time bar where its rigid application would create injustice.

D

This analysis shows that the *American Pipe* tolling rule does not apply to the 3–year bar mandated in § 13. As explained above, the 3–year limit is a statute of repose. See *supra,* at 2049 – 2050. And the object of a statute of repose, to grant complete peace to defendants, supersedes the application of a tolling rule based in equity. See *supra,* at 2050 – 2051. No feature of § 13 provides that deviation from its time limit is permissible in a case such as this one. To the contrary, the text, purpose, structure, and history of the statute all disclose the congressional purpose to offer defendants full and final security after three years.

Petitioner raises four counterarguments, but they are not persuasive. First, petitioner contends that this case is indistinguishable from *American Pipe* itself. If the 3–year bar here cannot be tolled, petitioner reasons, then there was no justification for the *American Pipe* Court's contrary decision to suspend the time bar in that case. *American Pipe,* however, is distinguishable. The statute in *American Pipe* was one of limitations, not of repose; it began to run when " 'the cause of action accrued.' " 414 U.S., at 541, n. 2 (quoting 15 U.S.C. § 15b). The statute in the instant case, however, is a statute of repose. Consistent with the different purposes embodied in statutes of limitations and statutes of repose, it is reasonable that the former may be tolled by equitable considerations even though the latter in most circumstances may not. See *supra,* at 7-8.

Second, petitioner argues that the filing of a class-action complaint within three years fulfills the purposes of a statutory time limit with regard to later filed suits by individual members of the class. That is because, according to petitioner, the class complaint puts a defendant on notice as to the content of the claims against it and the set of potential plaintiffs who might assert those claims. It is true that the *American Pipe* Court, in permitting tolling, suggested that generic notice satisfied the purposes of the statute of limitations in that case. See 414 U.S., at 554-555. While this was deemed sufficient in balancing the equities to allow tolling under the antitrust statute, it must be noted that here the analysis differs because the purpose of a statute of repose is to give the defendant full protection after a certain time.

If the number and identity of individual suits, where they may be filed, and the litigation strategies they will use are unknown, a defendant cannot calculate its potential liability or set its own plans for litigation with much precision. The initiation of separate individual suits may thus increase a defendant's practical burdens. See, *e.g.,* Cottreau, Note, The Due Process Right To Opt Out of Class Actions, 73 N.Y.U. L. Rev. 480, 486, and n. 29 (1998) ("A defendant's transaction costs are likely to be reduced by having to defend just one action"). The emergence of individual suits, furthermore, may increase a defendant's financial liability; for plaintiffs who opt out have considerable leverage and, as a result, may obtain outsized recoveries. See, *e.g.,* Coffee, Accountability and Competition in Securities Class Actions: Why "Exit" Works Better Than "Voice," 30 Cardozo L. Rev. 407, 417, 432–433 (2008); Perino, Class Action Chaos? The Theory of the Core and an Analysis of Opt–Out Rights in Mass Tort Class Actions, 46 Emory L.J. 85, 97 (1997). These uncertainties can put defendants at added risk in conducting business going forward, causing destabilization in markets which react with sensitivity to these matters. By permitting a class action to splinter into individual suits, the application of *American Pipe* tolling would threaten to alter and expand a defendant's accountability, contradicting the substance of a statute of repose. All this is not to suggest how best to further equity under these circumstances but simply to support the recognition that a statute of repose supersedes a court's equitable balancing powers by setting a fixed time period for claims to end.

Third, petitioner contends that dismissal of its individual suit as untimely would eviscerate its ability to opt out, an ability this Court has indicated should not be disregarded. See *Wal–Mart Stores, Inc. v. Dukes,* 564 U.S. 338, 363 (2011). It does not follow, however, from any privilege to opt out that an ensuing suit can be filed without regard to mandatory time limits set by statute.

Fourth, petitioner argues that declining to apply *American Pipe* tolling to statutes of repose will create inefficiencies. It contends that nonnamed class members will inundate district courts with protective filings. Even if petitioner were correct, of course, this Court "lack[s] the authority to rewrite" the statute of repose or to ignore its plain import. *Baker Botts L.L.P. v. ASARCO LLX,* 576 U.S. ——, ——, 135 S.Ct. 2158.

And petitioner's concerns likely are overstated. Petitioner has not offered evidence of any recent influx of protective filings in the Second Circuit, where the rule affirmed here has been the law since 2013. This is not surprising. The very premise of class actions is that " 'small recoveries do not provide the incentive for any individual to bring a solo action prosecuting his or her rights.' " *Amchem Products, Inc. v. Windsor,* 521 U.S. 591, 617 (1997). Many individual class members may have no interest in protecting their right to litigate on an individual basis. Even assuming that they do, the process is unlikely to be as onerous as petitioner claims. A simple motion to intervene or request to be included as a named plaintiff in the class-action complaint may well suffice. See, *e.g.,* Brief for Washington Legal Foundation as *Amicus Curiae* 6–11 (describing procedures); Brief for Securities Industry and Financial Markets Association et al. as *Amici Curiae* 16, 19–20 (same). District courts, furthermore, have ample means and methods to administer their dockets and to ensure that any additional filings proceed in an orderly fashion. Cf. *Dietz v. Bouldin,* 579 U.S. ——, ——, 136 S.Ct. 1885. ("[D]istrict courts have the inherent authority to manage their dockets and courtrooms with a view toward the efficient and expedient resolution of cases").

III

Petitioner makes an alternative argument that does not depend on tolling. Petitioner submits its individual suit was timely in any event. Section 13 provides that an "action" must be "brought" within three years of the relevant securities offering. See 15 U.S.C. § 77m. Petitioner argues that requirement is met here because the filing of the class-action complaint "brought" petitioner's individual "action" within the statutory time period.

This argument rests on the premise that an "action" is "brought" when substantive claims are presented to any court, rather than when a particular complaint is filed in a particular court. The term "action," however, refers to a judicial "proceeding," or perhaps to a "suit"—not to the general content of claims. See Black's Law Dictionary 41 (3d ed. 1933) (defining "action" as, *inter alia,* "an ordinary proceeding in a court of justice"); see also *id.,* at 43 ("The terms 'action' and 'suit' are ... nearly, if not entirely, synonymous"). Whether or not petitioner's individual complaint alleged the same securities law violations as the class-action complaint, it defies ordinary understanding to suggest that its filing—in a separate forum, on a separate date, by a separate named party—was the same "action," "proceeding," or "suit."

The limitless nature of petitioner's argument, furthermore, reveals its implausibility. It appears that, in petitioner's view, the bringing of the class action would make any subsequent action raising the same claims timely. Taken to its logical limit, an individual action would be timely even if it were filed decades after the original securities offering—provided a class-action complaint had been filed at some point within the initial 3–year period. Congress would not have intended this result.

Petitioner's argument also fails because it is inconsistent with the reasoning in *American Pipe* itself. If the filing of a class action made all subsequent actions by putative class members timely, there would be no need for tolling at all. Yet this Court has described *American Pipe* as creating a tolling rule, necessary to permit the ensuing individual actions to proceed. See, *e.g., American Pipe,* 414 U.S., at 555; *Irwin,* 498 U.S., at 96, n. 3; *Crown, Cork & Seal Co. v. Parker,* 462 U.S. 345, 350 (1983). Indeed, the *American Pipe* Court reasoned that the class-action complaint "was filed with 11 days yet to run" in the statutory period, so the motions for intervention were timely only if filed within 11 days after the denial of class certification. 414 U.S., at 561. If the filing of the class action "brought" any included individual actions, it would have sufficed for the Court to note the date on which the class action was filed and deem all subsequent individual actions proper, regardless when filed.

* * *

Tolling may be of great value to allow injured persons to recover for injuries that, through no fault of their own, they did not discover because the injury or the perpetrator was not evident until the limitations period otherwise would have expired. This is of obvious utility in the securities market, where complex transactions and events can be obscure and difficult for a market participant to analyze or apprehend. In a similar way, tolling as allowed in *American Pipe* may protect plaintiffs who anticipated their interests would be protected by a class action but later learned that a class suit could not be maintained for reasons outside their control.

The purpose of a statute of repose, on the other hand, is to allow more certainty and reliability. These ends, too, are a necessity in a marketplace where stability and reliance are essential components of valuation and expectation for financial actors. The statute in this case reconciles these different ends by its two-tier structure: a conventional statute of limitations in the first clause and a statute of repose in the second.

The statute of repose transforms the analysis. In a hypothetical case with a different statutory scheme, consisting of a single limitations period without an additional outer limit, a court's equitable power under *American Pipe* in many cases would authorize the relief petitioner seeks. Here, however, the Court need not consider how equitable considerations should be formulated or balanced, for the mandate of the statute of repose takes the case outside the bounds of the *American Pipe* rule.

The final analysis, then, is straightforward. The 3–year time bar in § 13 of the Securities Act is a statute of repose. Its purpose and design are to protect defendants against future liability. The statute displaces the traditional power of courts to modify statutory time limits in the name of equity. Because the *American Pipe* tolling rule is rooted in those equitable powers, it cannot extend the 3–year period. Petitioner's untimely filing of its individual action is ground for dismissal.

The judgment of the Court of Appeals for the Second Circuit is affirmed.

34

It is so ordered.

_____

1. <u>Impact.</u> In her dissent, Justice Ginsburg focused on a number of problems that the majority's decision will likely cause. As she saw it, unless class members file a "protective claim" (i.e., an individual action within the 3-year period), they will likely "forfeit their constitutionally shielded right to opt out of the class." She added that "[t]he majority's ruling will also gum up the works of class litigation because "[d]efendants will have an incentive to slow walk discovery and other pre-certification proceedings so the clock will run on potential opt outs." She also suggested that plaintiff's class counsel will have new responsibilities: "As the repose period nears expiration, it should be incumbent on class counsel, guided by district courts, to notify class members about the consequences of failing to file a protective claim." Such notice by plaintiffs counsel could be costly in the case of a large class.

Cyan, Inc. v. Beaver County Employees Retirement Fund

Supreme Court of the United States (2018)

138 S. Ct. 1061

■ JUSTICE KAGAN delivered the opinion of the Court.

This case presents two questions about the Securities Litigation Uniform Standards Act of 1998 (SLUSA), 112 Stat. 3227. First, did SLUSA strip state courts of jurisdiction over class actions alleging violations of only the Securities Act of 1933 (1933 Act)? And second, even if not, did SLUSA empower defendants to remove such actions from state to federal court? We answer both questions no.

I

A

In the wake of the 1929 stock market crash, Congress enacted two laws, in successive years, to promote honest practices in the securities markets. The 1933 Act required companies offering securities to the public to make "full and fair disclosure" of relevant information. *Pinter v. Dahl,* 486 U.S. 622, 646, 108 S.Ct. 2063, 100 L.Ed.2d 658 (1988). And to aid enforcement of those obligations, the statute created private rights of action. Congress authorized both federal and state courts to exercise jurisdiction over those private suits. See § 22(a), 48 Stat. 86 ("The district courts of the United States ... shall have jurisdiction[,] concurrent with State and Territorial courts, of all suits in equity and actions at law brought to enforce any liability or duty created by this title"). More unusually, Congress also barred the removal of such actions from state to federal court. *Id.,* at 87 ("No case arising under this title and brought in any State court of competent jurisdiction shall be removed to any court of the United States"). So if a plaintiff chose to bring a 1933 Act suit in state court, the defendant could not change the forum.

Congress's next foray, the Securities Exchange Act of 1934 (1934 Act), operated differently...That statute regulated not the original issuance of securities but instead all their subsequent trading, most commonly on national stock exchanges. See *Blue Chip Stamps v. Manor Drug Stores,* 421 U.S. 723, 752 (1975). The 1934 Act, this Court held, could also be enforced through private rights of action. See *id.,* at 730, and n. 4. But Congress determined that all those suits should fall within the "exclusive jurisdiction" of the federal courts. § 27, 48 Stat. 902–903. So a plaintiff could never go to state court to litigate a 1934 Act claim.

In 1995, the Private Securities Litigation Reform Act (Reform Act), amended both the 1933 and the 1934 statutes in mostly identical ways. Congress passed the Reform Act principally to stem "perceived abuses of the class-action vehicle in litigation involving nationally traded securities." *Merrill Lynch, Pierce, Fenner & Smith Inc. v. Dabit,* 547 U.S. 71, 81 (2006). Some of the Reform Act's provisions made substantive changes to the 1933 and 1934 laws, and applied even when a 1933 Act suit was brought in state court. For instance, the statute created a "safe harbor" from federal liability for certain "forward-looking statements" made by company officials. 15 U.S.C. § 77z–2 (1933 Act); § 78u–5 (1934 Act). Other Reform Act provisions modified the procedures used in litigating securities actions, and applied only when such a suit was brought in federal court. To take one example, the statute required a lead plaintiff in any class action brought under the Federal Rules of Civil Procedure to file a sworn certification stating, among other things, that he had not purchased the relevant security "at the direction of plaintiff's counsel." § 77z–1(a)(2)(A)(ii) (1933 Act); § 78u–4(a)(2)(A)(ii) (1934 Act).

But the Reform Act fell prey to the law of "unintended consequence[s]." *Dabit,* 547 U.S., at 82, 126 S.Ct. 1503. As this Court previously described the problem: "Rather than face the obstacles set in their path by the Reform Act, plaintiffs and their representatives began bringing class actions under state law." *Ibid.* That "phenomenon was a novel one"—and an unwelcome one as well. *Ibid.* To prevent plaintiffs from circumventing the Reform Act, Congress again undertook to modify both securities laws.

The result was SLUSA, whose amendments to the 1933 Act are at issue in this case. Those amendments include, as relevant here, two operative provisions, two associated definitions, and two "conforming amendments" to the 1933 law's jurisdictional section. 112 Stat. 3230. (SLUSA's amendments to the 1934 Act include essentially the same operative provisions and definitions. See *Dabit,* 547 U.S., at 82, n. 6. But Congress decided that the 1934 law's exclusive jurisdiction provision needed no conforming amendments.) The added material—now found in §§ 77p and 77v(a) and set out in full in this opinion's appendix—goes as follows.

First, § 77p(b) altogether prohibits certain securities class actions based on state law. That provision—which we sometimes (and somewhat prosaically) refer to as the state-law class-action bar—reads:

"No covered class action based upon the statutory or common law of any State ... may be maintained in any State or Federal court by any private party alleging—

"(1) an untrue statement or omission of a material fact in connection with the purchase or sale of a covered security; or

"(2) that the defendant used or employed any manipulative or deceptive device or contrivance in connection with the purchase or sale of a covered security."

According to SLUSA's definitions, the term "covered class action" means a class action in which "damages are sought on behalf of more than 50 persons." § 77p(f)(2). And the term "covered security" refers to a security listed on a national stock exchange. § 77p(f)(3) (cross-referencing § 77r(b)). So taken all in all, § 77p(b) completely disallows (in both state and federal courts) sizable class actions that are founded on state law and allege dishonest practices respecting a nationally traded security's purchase or sale.

Next, § 77p(c) provides for the removal of certain class actions to federal court, as well as for their subsequent disposition:

> "Any covered class action brought in any State court involving a covered security, as set forth in subsection (b) of this section, shall be removable to the Federal district court for the district in which the action is pending, and shall be subject to subsection (b) of this section."

The first chunk of that provision identifies the removable cases, partly by way of a cross-reference ("as set forth in subsection (b)") to the just-described class-action bar. The final clause of the provision ("and shall be subject to subsection (b)") indicates what should happen to a barred class suit *after* it has been removed: The "proper course is to dismiss" the action. *Kircher v. Putnam Funds Trust,* 547 U.S. 633, 644 (2006). As this Court has explained, § 77p(c) "avails a defendant of a federal forum in contemplation not of further litigation over the merits of a claim brought in state court, but of termination of the proceedings altogether." *Id.,* at 645, n. 12, 126 S.Ct. 2145. The point of providing that option, everyone here agrees, was to ensure the dismissal of a prohibited state-law class action even when a state court "would not adequately enforce" § 77p(b)'s bar. Brief for United States as *Amicus Curiae* 3; see Brief for Petitioners 7; Brief for Respondents 20.

Finally, the 1933 Act's jurisdictional provision, codified at § 77v(a), now includes two new phrases framed as exemptions—SLUSA's self-described "conforming amendments." 112 Stat. 3230; see *supra,* at 1067. The less significant of the pair, for our purposes, reflects the allowance for removing certain class actions described above. Against the backdrop of the 1933 Act's general removal bar, see *supra,* at 1066, that added (italicized) material reads:

> "*Except as provided in section 77p(c) of this title,* no case arising under this subchapter and brought in any State court of competent jurisdiction shall be removed to any court of the United States."

The more important of the conforming amendments in this case expresses a caveat to the general rule, see *supra,* at 1066, that state and federal courts have concurrent jurisdiction over all claims to enforce the 1933 Act. As amended (again, with the new material in italics), the relevant sentence now reads:

> "The district courts of the United States ... shall have jurisdiction [,] concurrent with State and Territorial courts, *except as provided in section 77p of this title with respect to covered class actions,* of all suits in equity and actions at law brought to enforce any liability or duty created by this subchapter."

Throughout this opinion, we refer to the italicized words just above as the "except clause." Its meaning is at the heart of the parties' dispute in this Court.

B

The petitioners in this case are Cyan, a telecommunications company, and its officers and directors (together, Cyan). The respondents are three pension funds and an individual (together, Investors) who purchased shares of Cyan stock in an initial public offering. After the stock declined in value, the Investors brought a damages class action against Cyan in California Superior Court. Their complaint alleges that Cyan's offering documents contained material misstatements, in violation of the 1933 Act. It does not assert any claims based on state law.

Cyan moved to dismiss the Investors' suit for lack of subject matter jurisdiction. It argued that what we have termed SLUSA's "except clause"—*i.e.,* the amendment made to § 77v(a)'s concurrent-jurisdiction grant—stripped state courts of power to adjudicate 1933 Act claims in "covered class actions." The Investors did not dispute that their suit qualifies as such an action under SLUSA's definition, see § 77p(f)(2). But they maintained that SLUSA left intact state courts' jurisdiction over all suits—including "covered class actions"—alleging only 1933 Act claims. The California Superior Court agreed with the Investors and denied Cyan's motion to dismiss. See App. to Pet. for Cert. 6a. The state appellate courts then denied review of that ruling. See *id.,* at 15a–16a.

We granted Cyan's petition for certiorari, 581 U.S. ——, 137 S.Ct. 2325, 198 L.Ed.2d 754 (2017), to resolve a split among state and federal courts about whether SLUSA deprived state courts of jurisdiction over "covered class actions" asserting only 1933 Act claims.

In opposing Cyan's jurisdictional position here, the Federal Government as *amicus curiae* raised another question: whether SLUSA enabled defendants to remove 1933 Act class actions from state to federal court for adjudication. See Brief for United States as *Amicus Curiae* 23–31. That question is not directly presented because Cyan never attempted to remove the Investors' suit. But the removal issue is related to the parties' jurisdictional arguments, and both Cyan and the Investors addressed it in briefing and argument. See Brief for Petitioners 39–40; Brief for Respondents 31–35; Tr. of Arg. 31, 53–56, 74–76, 80. Accordingly, we consider as well the scope of § 77p(c)'s removal authorization.

II

By its terms, § 77v(a)'s "except clause" does nothing to deprive state courts of their jurisdiction to decide class actions brought under the 1933 Act. And Cyan's various appeals to SLUSA's purposes and legislative history fail to overcome the clear statutory language. The statute says what it says—or perhaps better put here, does not say what it does not say.

State-court jurisdiction over 1933 Act claims thus continues undisturbed

A

SLUSA's text, read most straightforwardly, leaves in place state courts' jurisdiction over 1933 Act claims, including when brought in class actions. Recall that the background rule of § 77v(a)—in place since the 1933 Act's passage—gives state courts concurrent jurisdiction over all suits "brought to enforce any liability or duty created by" that statute. See *supra,* at 1066. The except clause—once again, "except as provided in section 77p of this title with respect to covered class actions"—is drafted as a limitation on that rule: It ensures that in any case in which § 77v(a) and § 77p come into conflict, § 77p will control. The critical question for this case is therefore whether § 77p limits state-court jurisdiction over class actions brought under the 1933 Act. It does not. As earlier described, § 77p bars certain securities class actions based on *state* law. See § 77p(b); *supra,* at 1067 - 1068. And as a corollary of that prohibition, it authorizes removal of those suits so that a federal court can dismiss them. See § 77p(c); *supra,* at 1067 - 1068. But the section says nothing, and so does nothing, to deprive state courts of jurisdiction over class actions based on *federal* law. That means the background rule of § 77v(a)—under which a state court may hear the Investors' 1933 Act suit—continues to govern.

Cyan offers an alternative reading, in which one of SLUSA's definitional provisions works to alter state-court jurisdiction. According to Cyan the except clause's reference to "covered class actions" points the reader to, and only to, § 77p(f)(2)'s definition of that term. See Brief for Petitioners 16. And that definition states that a "covered class action" is a suit seeking damages on behalf of more than 50 persons—without mentioning anything about whether the suit is based on state or federal law. Cyan thus concludes that the except clause exempts all sizable class actions—including the Investors' suit—from § 77v(a)'s conferral of jurisdiction on state courts.

But that view cannot be squared with the except clause's wording for two independent reasons. To start with, the except clause points to "section 77p" as a whole—not to paragraph 77p(f)(2). Cyan wants to cherry pick from the material covered by the statutory cross-reference. But if Congress had intended to refer to the definition in § 77p(f)(2) alone, it presumably would have done so—just by adding a letter, a number, and a few parentheticals. As this Court recently explained, "Congress often drafts statutes with hierarchical schemes—section, subsection, paragraph, and on down the line." *NLRB v. SW General, Inc.,* 580 U.S. ——, ——, 137 S.Ct. 929, 938–939 (2017). And "[w]hen Congress want[s] to refer only to a particular subsection or paragraph, it sa[ys] so." *Ibid.* It said no such thing in the except clause.

In any event, the definitional paragraph on which Cyan relies cannot be read to "provide[ ]" an "except[ion]" to the rule of concurrent jurisdiction, in the way SLUSA's except clause requires. A definition does not provide an exception, but instead gives meaning to a term—and Congress well knows the difference between those two functions. Thousands of statutory

40

provisions use the phrase "except as provided in ..." followed by a cross-reference in order to indicate that one rule should prevail over another in any circumstance in which the two conflict; we count more than 30 such constructions in the 1933 and 1934 Acts alone.[3] Not one of those 30–plus provisions cross-references a *definition*; nor has Cyan pointed to a single such example from the whole rest of the U.S. Code. And the Congress enacting SLUSA had no reason to attempt that peculiar maneuver for the first time. If Congress had wanted to deprive state courts of jurisdiction over 1933 Act class actions, it had an easy way to do so: just insert into § 77p an exclusive federal jurisdiction provision (like the 1934 Act's) for such suits. That rule, when combined with the except clause, would have done the trick because it would have "provided" an "except[ion]" to § 77v(a)'s grant of concurrent jurisdiction; by contrast, a mere definition of "covered class action" (as a damages suit on behalf of 50–plus people) does not so provide.

SLUSA's *other* conforming amendment illustrates the two ways in which Cyan's construction of the except clause departs from its language. Recall that § 77v(a) includes a general bar on removal. See *supra,* at 1066. And recall that SLUSA appended to that prohibition the phrase "[e]xcept as provided in section 77p(c)" to reflect the statute's new permission to remove certain class actions. See *supra,* at 1068. In *that* "except as provided" phrase—just four sentences down from the except clause central to this case—Congress pinpointed a subsection of § 77p, rather than citing the entire section for only one of its parts. Still more, that cross-referenced subsection contains an operative provision that could limit a rule, rather than a mere definition of a statutory term. In short, Congress wrote the removal bar's except clause in just the way a reader of legislation would expect—and not in the wholly irregular way Cyan proposes for the except clause at issue here. Especially given the two provisions' "interrelationship and close proximity," *Commissioner v. Lundy,* 516 U.S. 235, 250 (1996), the one conforming amendment highlights how far Cyan seeks to stretch the text of the other.

Cyan's interpretation also fits poorly with the remainder of the statutory scheme. Because Cyan treats the broad definition of "covered class action" as altering § 77v(a)'s jurisdictional grant, its construction would prevent state courts from deciding any 1933 Act class suits seeking damages for more than 50 plaintiffs. That would include suits not involving a "covered security"—*i.e.,* a security traded on a national stock exchange. § 77p(f)(3); Brief for Petitioners 29 (conceding that point). But this Court has emphasized that SLUSA's operative provisions (including its state-law class-action bar, see § 77p(b)) apply to only "transactions in covered securities": The statute "expresses no concern" with "transactions in uncovered securities"—precisely because they are not traded on national markets. *Chadbourne & Parke LLP v. Troice,* 571 U.S. 377 (2014); see Brief for United States as *Amicus Curiae* 16–17 (SLUSA does not regard suits involving uncovered securities as "a matter of distinct federal concern"). Those securities, the Court explained, are "primarily of state concern," and SLUSA "maintains state legal authority" to address them. *Chadbourne,* 571 U.S., at ——, 134 S.Ct., at 1968. Except that under Cyan's view, SLUSA would not. Instead, the law would strip state courts of jurisdiction over suits about securities raising no particular national interest. That result is out of line with SLUSA's overall scope.

And finally, Cyan's take on the except clause reads too much into a mere "conforming amendment." 112 Stat. 3230. The change Cyan claims that clause made to state-court jurisdiction is the very opposite of a minor tweak. When Congress passed SLUSA, state courts had for 65 years adjudicated all manner of 1933 Act cases, including class actions. Indeed, defendants could not even remove those cases to federal court, as schemes of concurrent jurisdiction almost always allow. See *supra,* at 1066. State courts thus had as much or more power over the 1933 Act's enforcement as over any federal statute's. To think Cyan right, we would have to believe that Congress upended that entrenched practice not by any direct means, but instead by way of a conforming amendment to § 77v(a) (linked, in its view, with only a definition). But Congress does not make "radical—but entirely implicit—change[s]" through "technical and conforming amendments." *Director of Revenue of Mo. v. CoBank ACB,* 531 U.S. 316 (2001) (internal quotation marks omitted). Or to use the more general (and snappier) formulation of that rule, relevant to all "ancillary provisions," Congress does not "hide elephants in mouseholes." *Whitman v. American Trucking Assns., Inc.,* 531 U.S. 457, 468 (2001). That is yet one more reason to reject Cyan's view of SLUSA's text.

B

Faced with such recalcitrant statutory language, Cyan stakes much of its case on legislative purpose and history. See Brief for Petitioners 20–33, 36–37; Reply Brief 7–11, 17–21. Its claims come in two forms—one relating to the goals of SLUSA as a whole and the other relating to the aims of the except clause. Even assuming clear text can ever give way to purpose, Cyan would need some monster arguments on this score to create doubts about SLUSA's meaning. The points Cyan raises come nowhere close to that level.

1

According to Cyan's broad purposive argument, Congress could not "make good on the promise of the Reform Act"—which was its principal intention in enacting SLUSA—without divesting state courts of jurisdiction over all sizable 1933 Act class actions. Brief for Petitioners 20. Remember that the Reform Act contained a number of procedural measures (for example, a sworn-certification requirement for lead plaintiffs, see § 77z–1(a)(2)(A)) that apply only in federal court. See *supra,* at 1066 - 1067. Plaintiffs bringing 1933 Act class actions could avoid those provisions simply by filing in state court; after all, those suits were not even removable by defendants. "So," Cyan claims, "Congress enacted SLUSA to finish the job"—by shutting down the state forum and shifting all 1933 Act class actions to the federal one. Brief for Petitioners 21. In support of that view, Cyan cites several statements in SLUSA's legislative reports—in particular, that SLUSA's purpose was "to prevent plaintiffs from seeking to evade the protections that Federal law provides against abusive litigation by filing suit in State, rather than in Federal, court." H.R. Conf. Rep. No. 105–803, p. 13 (1998); see H.R. Rep. No. 105–640, pp. 8–9 (1998); S. Rep. No. 105–182, p. 3 (1998).

But to begin with, Cyan ignores a different way in which SLUSA "serve[d] the [Reform Act's] objectives," Brief for Petitioners 11—which our view of the statute fully effects. Recall that the Reform Act also included substantive sections protecting defendants (like a safe harbor for forward-looking statements) in suits brought under the federal securities laws. See § 77z–2; *supra*, at 1066. Plaintiffs could—and did—avoid those provisions by bringing their complaints of securities misconduct under state law instead. See *supra*, at 1067. Hence emerged SLUSA's bar on state-law class actions (and its removal provision to ensure their dismissal)—which guaranteed that the Reform Act's heightened substantive standards would govern all future securities class litigation. SLUSA itself highlights that aim: Its preamble states that the statute is designed "to limit the conduct of securities class actions under State law, and for other purposes." 112 Stat. 3227. So too, this Court has underscored, over and over, SLUSA's "purpose to preclude certain vexing state-law class actions." *Kircher*, 547 U.S., at 645, n. 12; see *Dabit*, 547 U.S., at 82 (SLUSA stopped plaintiffs from "bringing class actions under state law"); *Amgen Inc. v. Connecticut Retirement Plans and Trust Funds*, 568 U.S. 455, 476 (2013) (SLUSA "curtailed plaintiffs' ability to evade the [Reform Act] by bringing class-action suits under state rather than federal law"). That object—which SLUSA's text actually reflects—does not depend on stripping state courts of jurisdiction over 1933 Act class suits, as Cyan proposes. For wherever those suits go forward, the Reform Act's substantive protections necessarily apply.

Still more, SLUSA ensured that federal courts would play the principal role in adjudicating securities class actions by means of its revisions to the *1934* Act. As explained earlier, SLUSA amended that statute in the same main way it did the 1933 Act—by adding a state-law class-action bar. See § 78bb(f)(1); *supra*, at 1067. But there, the change had a double effect: Because federal courts have exclusive jurisdiction over 1934 Act claims, forcing plaintiffs to bring class actions under the 1934 statute instead of state law also forced them to file in federal court. That meant the bulk of securities class actions would proceed in federal court—because the 1934 Act regulates all trading of securities whereas the 1933 Act addresses only securities offerings. See *Blue Chip Stamps*, 421 U.S., at 752 (characterizing the 1933 Act as "a far narrower statute"). So even without Cyan's contrived reading of the except clause, SLUSA largely accomplished the purpose articulated in its Conference Report: moving securities class actions to federal court.

To be sure, "largely" does not mean "entirely"—but then again, we do not generally expect statutes to fulfill 100% of all of their goals. See, *e.g., Freeman v. Quicken Loans, Inc.,* 566 U.S. 624, 637 (2012) ("No legislation pursues its purposes at all costs" (internal quotation marks and alterations omitted)). Under our reading of SLUSA, all covered securities class actions must proceed under federal law; most (*i.e.,* those alleging 1934 Act claims) must proceed in federal court; some (*i.e.,* those alleging 1933 Act claims) may proceed in state court. We do not know why Congress declined to require as well that 1933 Act class actions be brought in federal court; perhaps it was because of the long and unusually pronounced tradition of according authority to state courts over 1933 Act litigation. See *supra*, at 1071 - 1072. But in any event, we will not revise that legislative choice, by reading a conforming amendment and a definition in a most improbable way, in an effort to make the world of securities litigation more consistent or pure.

43

This Court has long rejected the notion that "*whatever* furthers the statute's primary objective must be the law." *Rodriguez v. United States,* 480 U.S. 522 (1987) (*per curiam*). Even if Congress could or should have done more, still it "wrote the statute it wrote—meaning, a statute going so far and no further." *Michigan v. Bay Mills Indian Community,* 572 U.S. ——, ——, 134 S.Ct. 2024, 2033–2034 (2014) (internal quotation marks omitted).

2

Yet Cyan has a final argument—that the except clause would serve no purpose at all unless it works as Cyan says. See Brief for Petitioners 32–33; Reply Brief 8–11. Here, Cyan relies on an indubitable puzzle. Section 77v(a), as amended by SLUSA, gives state courts jurisdiction over *1933 Act* suits "except as provided in § 77p." But § 77p provides a bar on only certain *state-law* suits. So, Cyan contends, unless we take up its invitation to look to § 77p(f)(2)'s definition of "covered class action," the except clause excepts "exactly nothing." Reply Brief 8. (To use an example of our own, it would be as if a parent told her child "you may have fruit after dinner, except for lollipops.") What on earth, Cyan asks, would be the point of such a provision?

The Investors answer that question with a theory about why Congress enacted the except clause. In their view, the clause was meant to deal with "mixed" securities class actions—containing both claims brought under the 1933 Act and claims arising under state law. See Brief for Respondents 12–13. If not for the except clause, the Investors posit, state courts would have been uncertain about how to handle those suits. Section 77p clearly instructs courts not to adjudicate the state-law claims; but (the Investors continue) § 77v(a) gives state courts jurisdiction over entire "actions" brought to enforce the 1933 Act, even if they include additional state-law claims. What, then, to do? According to the Investors, the except clause's purpose was to resolve that statutory conflict by making clear that § 77p trumps § 77v(a)—in other words, that a state court may not entertain state-law claims precluded by § 77p(b) even when they are conjoined with 1933 Act claims falling within § 77v(a)'s grant of jurisdiction.

Truth be told, we are not sure whether Congress had that issue in mind. On the one hand (and contrary to what the Investors say), we doubt that the except clause was really necessary to address mixed class actions. Even without that clause, a competent state court faced with such a suit would understand that § 77p requires dismissal of the state-law claims—and that § 77v(a)'s jurisdictional grant over 1933 Act suits is not to the contrary. But on the other hand (and now supporting the Investors' principal point), Congress may have thought that class-action lawyers would still try to circumvent SLUSA by tacking a 1933 Act claim onto a forbidden state-law class action, on the off chance of finding an error-prone judge. (After all, the worst that could happen was that the court would throw out the state-law claims, leaving the plaintiff with a permissible 1933 Act suit.) To prevent such gamesmanship—to make clear beyond peradventure that courts could not entertain the state-law half of mixed class actions—Congress might have added the except clause.

But even if Congress never specifically considered mixed suits, it could well have added the except clause in a more general excess of caution—to safeguard § 77p's class-action bar come whatever might. This Court has encountered many examples of Congress legislating in that hyper-vigilant way, to "remov[e] any doubt" as to things not particularly doubtful in the first instance. *Marx v. General Revenue Corp.,* 568 U.S. 371, 383–384 (2013) (citing *Ali v. Federal Bureau of Prisons,* 552 U.S. 214, 226 (2008); *Fort Stewart Schools v. FLRA,* 495 U.S. 641, 646, (1990)). (The idea, to return to our prior example, is to make sure that even if the child thinks orange lollipops count as fruit, she will not act on that view.) And if ever Congress had reason to legislate in that fashion, it was in SLUSA—whose very impetus lay in the success of class-action attorneys in "bypass[ing] ... the Reform Act." *Kircher,* 547 U.S., at 636. Heedful of that history of machinations, Congress may have determined to eliminate any risk—even if unlikely or at the time unknown—that a pre-existing grant of power to state courts could be used to obstruct SLUSA's new limitation on what they could decide. And so (this alternative explanation goes) Congress enacted the except clause—which, in insisting that the limitation prevailed, would function as the ultimate (though with any luck, unneeded) fail-safe device.[4]

But the most important response to this purposive argument echoes what we have said before about the weaknesses of Cyan's own construction of the except clause. In the end, the uncertainty surrounding Congress's reasons for drafting that clause does not matter. Nor does the possibility that the risk Congress addressed (whether specific or inchoate) did not exist. Because irrespective of those points, we have no sound basis for giving the except clause a broader reading than its language can bear. And that is especially true in light of the dramatic change such an interpretation would work in the 1933 Act's jurisdictional framework. Whatever questions remain as to the except clause's precise purpose—and we do not gainsay there are some—they do not give us permission to devise a statute (and at that, a transformative one) of our own.

III

Our last task is to address the Federal Government's proposed halfway-house position. The Government rejects Cyan's view that SLUSA stripped state courts of jurisdiction over 1933 Act class actions, for roughly the same reasons we have given. See Brief for United States as *Amicus Curiae* 11–23. But like Cyan, the Government believes that "Congress would not have been content to leave" such suits "stuck in state court," where the Reform Act's procedural protections do not apply. *Id.,* at 15 (internal quotation marks omitted). So the Government offers a reading of SLUSA—in particular, of § 77p(c)—that would allow defendants to remove 1933 Act class actions to federal court, as long as they allege the kinds of misconduct listed in § 77p(b) (*e.g.,* false statements or deceptive devices in connection with a covered security's purchase or sale). See *id.,* at 24–25.

But most naturally read, § 77p(c)—SLUSA's exception to the 1933 Act's general bar on removal—refutes, not supports, the Government's view. Once again, see *supra,* at 1067 - 1068, §

77p(c) reads as follows:

> "Any covered class action brought in any State court involving a covered security, as set forth in subsection (b) of this section, shall be removable to the Federal district court for the district in which the action is pending, and shall be subject to subsection (b) of this section."

In other words, the covered class actions described in § 77p(b) can be removed to federal court (and, once there, shall be subject to dismissal because precluded, see *supra,* at 1068). And which are the covered class actions described in § 77p(b)? By this point, no one should have to be reminded: They are *state-law* class actions alleging securities misconduct. See § 77p(b) (prohibiting "class action[s] based upon the statutory or common law of any State"). So those state-law suits are removable. But conversely, *federal-law* suits like this one—alleging only 1933 Act claims—are not "class action[s] ... as set forth in subsection (b)." So they remain subject to the 1933 Act's removal ban.

In fact, this Court already held as much, by concluding in *Kircher* that §§ 77p(b) and 77p(c) apply to the exact same universe of class actions. See 547 U.S., at 643-644. *Kircher* involved a securities suit that was unaffected by § 77p(b)'s class-action bar—there, not because it was based on federal law but because it involved a form of conduct falling outside that subsection. The Court of Appeals decided that the suit could be removed under § 77p(c) even though it was not precluded by § 77p(b), thinking (as we later put it) that the removal issue and "the preclusion issue [were] distinct." *Id.,* at 638, 126 S.Ct. 2145. We flatly rejected that understanding of the relationship between § 77p(b) and § 77p(c). The "straightforward reading" of those two provisions, we explained, is that removal is "limited to those [actions] precluded by the terms of subsection (b)." *Id.,* at 643. And if that were not clear enough, we said it again: Removal under § 77p(c) is "restricted to precluded actions defined by subsection (b)." *Id.,* at 643–644, 126 S.Ct. 2145. And just to pound the point home, we said it yet a third time: "A covered [class] action is removable if it is precluded." *Id.,* at 646, 126 S.Ct. 2145. *Kircher* thus forecloses the Government's argument. Section 77p(b) does not preclude federal-law class actions. So under our decision, § 77p(c) does not authorize their removal.

The Government responds with a novel way of understanding § 77p(c), which it thinks would allow us to disregard *Kircher* when a class action like this one is based on federal law. In the Government's view, first presented at oral argument, see Tr. of Oral Arg. 32–33, the words "as set forth in subsection (b)" do not modify the entire preceding phrase (basically, any large class action involving a covered security). Instead, the Government claims, those words modify only the shorter phrase "involving a covered security." To support that view, the Government invokes the "rule of the last antecedent"—under which "the limiting clause is most naturally applied to the thing that comes immediately before it." *Id.,* at 36. The Government then presents a theory of how subsection (b) "set[s] forth" the "involv[ement]" of a covered security. "[T]o figure out what that means," the Government contends, "you look at [§ 77p](b)(1) and (b)(2), which talk about certain types of misconduct"—for example, false statements or deceptive devices in connection with a covered security's sale. *Id.,* at 33–34. As long as conduct of that kind is implicated in a suit, the Government concludes, it can be removed—even if it is based on federal law and thus does not fall within § 77p(b) as a whole. That view is consistent with *Kircher* 's result because the action there did not involve the conduct described in §§ 77p(b)(1) and (2). And as to *Kircher* 's rationale ... well, we should feel free to ignore it.

But even putting aside respect for precedent, that argument is in many ways flawed. To start with, the Government provides no good reason to think that "as set forth in subsection (b)" modifies only the phrase "involving a covered security." As stated above, the most natural way to view the modifier is as applying to the entire preceding clause—again, "[a]ny covered class action brought in any State court involving a covered security." See *supra,* at 1075. That is so because that clause hangs together as a unified whole, referring to a single thing (a type of class action). Consider the following, grammatically identical construction: "The woman dressed to the nines carrying an umbrella, as shown in the picture ..." Would anyone think that "as shown in the picture" referred to anything less than the well-attired and rain-ready *woman* ? No. And so too here, the modifier goes back to the beginning of the preceding clause. The rule of the last antecedent is not to the contrary. We have applied that rule when the alternative reading would "stretch[ ] the modifier too far" by asking it to qualify a remote or otherwise disconnected phrase. *Jama v. Immigration and Customs Enforcement,* 543 U.S. 335, 342 (2005); *Lockhart v. United States,* 577 U.S. ——, ——, 136 S.Ct. 958, 963 (2016) (using the rule "where it takes more than a little mental energy to process" a statute's component parts, "making it a heavy lift to carry the modifier across them all").[6] By contrast, we have not applied the rule when the modifier directly follows a concise and "integrated" clause. *Jama,* 543 U.S., at 344, n. 4. As it does here.

But let us even assume that "as set forth in subsection (b)" modifies "involving a covered security": The language would still fail to explain the Government's position. Remember that the Government reads the resulting phrase (again, "involving a covered security, as set forth in subsection (b)") to point only to the forms of wrongful conduct listed in §§ 77p(b)(1) and (2)—for example, false statements or deceptive devices in securities sales. See *supra,* at 1076 - 1077. The problem is that no one would describe those misdeeds with that phrase. If Congress had meant to refer only to that behavior, rather than to everything in § 77p(b), it would have done two things differently. First, Congress would have written "as set forth in paragraphs (b)(1) and (b)(2)" instead of "as set forth in subsection (b)" as a whole. See *supra,* at 1070 (explaining that when Congress wants to refer only to a particular subsection or paragraph, it says so). And second, Congress would have written something like "involving allegations of misconduct," rather than "involving a covered security"—because the latter phrase does not even passably describe §§ 77(b)(1) and (2)'s catalog of vices. We will not read "involving a covered security, as set forth in subsection (b)" to mean "involving allegations of misconduct, as set forth in paragraphs (b)(1) and (b)(2)" when Congress did not enact that formulation. See *Lozano v. Montoya Alvarez,* 572 U.S. 1, —— (2014) ("Given that the drafters did not adopt that alternative, the natural implication is that they did not intend" to do so).

And (finally, we promise) even if we could put out of mind all these difficulties, the Government's position runs aground on § 77p(c)'s last clause, which states that removed class actions "shall be subject to subsection (b)." That clause, properly understood, points toward dismissal of a removed action. As we earlier explained, and the Government concedes, Congress enacted § 77p(c)'s removal provision out of "concern[ ] that state courts would not adequately enforce" § 77p(b)'s state-law class-action prohibition. Brief for United States as *Amicus Curiae* 3; see *supra,* at 1068. The idea was to allow removal so that a federal court could act as a backstop and order a class action's dismissal—thereby "subject[ing]" it to § 77p(b)'s bar. *Kircher* specifically said as much: Section 77p(c) "avails a defendant of a federal forum in contemplation not of further litigation over the merits of a claim brought in state court, but of termination of the proceedings altogether." 547 U.S., at 645, n. 12; see *supra,* at 1068. But of course, the Government contemplates "further litigation"—*not* "termination"—of a removed 1933 Act class action. See Brief for United States as *Amicus Curiae* 25. That decoupling of § 77p(c)'s linkage between removal and dismissal provides the last reason to reject the Government's argument.

At bottom, the Government makes the same mistake as Cyan: It distorts SLUSA's text because it thinks Congress simply must have wanted 1933 Act class actions to be litigated in federal court. But this Court has no license to "disregard clear language" based on an intuition that "Congress must have intended something broader." *Bay Mills,* 572 U.S., at ——, 134 S.Ct., to 2034 (internal quotation marks omitted). SLUSA did quite a bit to "make good on the promise of the Reform Act" (as Cyan puts it). Brief for Petitioners 20; see *supra,* at 1071 - 1072. If further steps are needed, they are up to Congress.

IV

SLUSA did nothing to strip state courts of their longstanding jurisdiction to adjudicate class actions alleging only 1933 Act violations. Neither did SLUSA authorize removing such suits from state to federal court. We accordingly affirm the judgment below.

It is so ordered.

---

1. Impact. A significant number of securities class actions, generally raising Section 11 claims, are filed in California state court (but very few in other state jurisdictions). Rule 10b-5 claims, however, cannot be filed in state court, because the Securities Exchange

Act of 1934 (unlike the Securities Act of 1933) gives exclusive jurisdiction to federal courts.

In re Petrobras Securities Litig.

United States Court of Appeals, Second Circuit (2017)

862 F.3d 250

■ Before: HALL, LIVINGSTON, CIRCUIT JUDGES, and Opinion by GARAUFIS

This expedited appeal arises out of an order entered in the United States District Court for the Southern District of New Yorki (Rakoff, *J.*) certifying two classes in this securities fraud action against PetróleoBrasileiroS.A.— Petrobras("Petrobras") and various other defendants. *See In re PetrobrasSec. Litig.* (the *"Certification Order"*), 312 F.R.D. 354 (S.D.N.Y. 2016).

Petrobras is a multinational oil and gas company headquartered in Brazil and majority-owned by the Brazilian government. Though Petrobras was once among the largest companies in the world, its value declined precipitously after the exposure of a multi-year, multi-billion-dollar money-laundering and kickback scheme, prompting a class action by holders of Petrobras equity and debt securities ("Plaintiffs") against multiple defendants ("Defendants"): Petrobras and certain wholly owned subsidiaries (the "Subsidiaries"; collectively with Petrobras, the "Petrobras Defendants"); former officers and directors of the Petrobras Defendants; several underwriters of Petrobras debt securities (the "Underwriter Defendants"); and Petrobras's independent auditor.

The district court certified two classes (the "Classes") for money damages under Federal Rule of Civil Procedure 23(b)(3): the first asserts claims under the Securities Exchange Act of 1934 (the "Exchange Act"), 15 U.S.C. §§ 78a *et seq.*; and the second asserts claims under the Securities Act of 1933 (the "Securities Act"), 15 U.S.C. §§ 77a *et seq.* On appeal, the Petrobras Defendants and the Underwriter Defendants (collectively, "Appellants") contest the *Certification Order* on two grounds.

First, Appellants challenge both class definitions insofar as they include all otherwise eligible persons who purchased Petrobras debt securities in "domestic transactions." Because Petrobras's debt securities do not trade on a domestic exchange, the district court must assess each class member's over-the-counter transactions for markers of domesticity under *Morrison v. National Australia Bank Ltd.*, 561 U.S. 247 (2010). Appellants assert that the need for such assessments precludes class certification, particularly in light of concerns over the availability and content of the necessary transaction records. We first address Appellants' arguments regarding the "implied" Rule 23 requirement of "ascertainability," taking this opportunity to clarify the scope of the contested ascertainability doctrine: a class is ascertainable if it is defined using objective criteria that establish a membership with definite boundaries. That threshold requirement is met here. However, we next hold that the district court committed legal error by finding that Rule 23(b)(3)'s predominance requirement was satisfied without considering the need for individual *Morrison* inquiries regarding domestic transactions. We therefore vacate this portion of

Certification Order.

Second, with regard to the Exchange Act Class, the Petrobras Defendants challenge the district court's finding that Plaintiffs were entitled to a presumption of reliance under the "fraud on the market" theory established in *Basic Inc. v. Levinson*, 485 U.S. 224, 108 S.Ct. 978, 99 L.Ed.2d 194 (1988). We find no abuse of discretion in the district court's determination that Plaintiffs met their burden under *Basic* with a combination of direct and indirect evidence of market efficiency. We therefore affirm as to this issue.

For the reasons set forth below, we AFFIRM IN PART and VACATE IN PART the judgment of the district court and REMAND the case for further proceedings consistent with this opinion.

BACKGROUND

We provide here a brief summary of the proceedings below as relevant for the issues on appeal. For additional background on Plaintiffs' allegations and causes of action, see the district court's prior orders. *See In re PetrobrasSec. Litig.* (the "*July 2015 Order*"), 116 F.Supp.3d 368, 373–77 (S.D.N.Y. 2015) (summarizing the original consolidated complaint); *In re PetrobrasSec. Litig.* (the "*December 2015 Order*"), 150 F.Supp.3d 337 (S.D.N.Y. 2015) (discussing new allegations in the amended pleadings).

I. Factual Background

A. Plaintiffs' Allegations of Corruption at Petrobras

Plaintiffs' claims arise out of a conspiracy that began in the first decade of the new millennium, at which time Petrobras was expanding its production capacity. The company used a competitive bidding process for major capital expenditures, including the construction and purchase of oil refineries. Over a period of several years, a cartel of contractors and suppliers coordinated with corrupt Petrobras executives to rig Petrobras's bids at grossly inflated prices. The excess funds were used to pay billions of dollars in bribes and kickbacks to the corrupt executives and to government officials. In addition, the inflated bid prices artificially increased the carrying value of Petrobras's assets. Plaintiffs allege that Petrobras knew about the kickback cartel, and was complicit in concealing information from investors and the public.

Brazil's Federal Police discovered the scheme during a money-laundering investigation, and ultimately arrested a number of the individuals involved. As details of the scandal emerged, Petrobras made corrective disclosures that, according to Plaintiffs, significantly understated the extent of incorrectly capitalized payments and inflated asset values. Even so, the value of Petrobras's securities declined precipitously. Plaintiffs allege that, "[a]t its height in 2009,

Petrobras was the world's fifth-largest company, with a market capitalization of $310 billion"; by early 2015, its worth had allegedly declined to $39 billion. 4th Am. Compl. ¶ 2.

B. Petrobras Securities

Petrobras's common and preferred shares trade on a Brazilian stock exchange, the BM&F BOVESPA. The company sponsors American Depository Shares ("ADS") that represent its common and preferred shares. Those ADS are listed and trade on the New York Stock Exchange ("NYSE").

In addition, Petrobras has issued multiple debt securities (the "Notes"; collectively with ADS, "Petrobras Securities") underwritten by syndicates of domestic and foreign banks. The Notes do not trade on any U.S. exchange. Investors trade Notes in over-the-counter transactions, whether in connection with an initial debt offering or in the global secondary market.

II. Procedural History

In December 2014 and January 2015, Petrobras investors filed five putative class actions asserting substantially similar claims against Petrobras and other defendants. The district court consolidated those actions in February 2015 and certified the Classes in February 2016. The district court also presided over several individual actions involving similar claims.[7]

A. Plaintiffs' Causes of Action

As relevant for this appeal, Plaintiffs assert a cause of action under the Exchange Act against the Petrobras Defendants, and three causes of action under the Securities Act against various Petrobras and Underwriter Defendants.

1. Claims Under the Exchange Act

Plaintiffs' Exchange Act claims are brought against Petrobras and the Subsidiaries on behalf of holders of Petrobras ADS and Notes. Plaintiffs assert that, during the class period of January 22, 2010, to July 28, 2015, the Petrobras Defendants made two types of false and misleading statements in violation of Section 10(b) of the Exchange Act and Rule 10b-5. *See* 15 U.S.C. § 78j(b); 17 C.F.R. § 240.10b–5. First, the Petrobras Defendants produced financial statements with inflated asset values. Second, they assured Petrobras investors that the company adhered to ethical management principles and maintained strict financial controls to prevent fraud and corruption.

2. Claims Under the Securities Act

Plaintiffs rely on similar factual allegations in their claims under the Securities Act, brought on behalf of Petrobras Noteholders. Plaintiffs allege that the Petrobras Defendants and the Underwriter Defendants made materially false representations in registration statements and other documents connected with offerings of Petrobras Notes in May 2013 and March 2014 (the "Offerings"), thereby establishing liability under Sections 11, 12(a)(2), and 15 of the Securities Act. *See* 15 U.S.C. §§ 77k, 77*l*(a)(2), 77*o*.

B. The Certification Order

On February 2, 2016, the district court granted Plaintiffs' motion to certify two classes under Rule 23(b)(3), one asserting claims under the Exchange Act and the other asserting claims under the Securities Act. *Certification Order*, 312 F.R.D. 354.

Because Petrobras Notes do not trade on any U.S.-based exchange, Noteholders in both Classes are only entitled to assert claims under the Exchange Act and the Securities Act if they can show that they acquired their Notes in "domestic transactions." *Morrison*, 561 U.S. at 267. To ensure compliance with *Morrison*, the district court limited both class definitions to "members [who] purchased Notes in domestic transactions." *Certification Order*, 312 F.R.D. at 360.

The Exchange Act Class is defined, in relevant part, as:

> [A]ll purchasers who, between January 22, 2010 and July 28, 2015, ... purchased or otherwise acquired [Petrobras Securities], including debt securities issued by [the Subsidiaries] on the [NYSE] or pursuant to other domestic transactions, and were damaged thereby.

Id. at 372.

The Securities Act Class is defined, in relevant part, as:

> [A]ll purchasers who purchased or otherwise acquired [Notes] in domestic transactions, directly in, pursuant and/or traceable to [U.S.-registered public offerings on May 15, 2013, and March 11, 2014] ..., and were damaged thereby.[9]

Id. The Securities Act Class definition is temporally limited to purchases made "before Petrobras made generally available to its security holders an earnings statement covering a period of at least twelve months beginning after the effective date of the offerings." *Id.* This language conforms to the limitations inherent in Section 11, given the absence of any allegation that Plaintiffs relied on any such earnings statement. *See* 15 U.S.C. § 77k(a).

III. The Instant Appeal

On June 15, 2016, a panel of this Court granted Appellants' timely filed petition for permission to appeal the *Certification Order* under Federal Rule of Civil Procedure 23(f) and Federal Rule of Appellate Procedure 5(a). On August 2, 2016, a separate panel granted Appellants' motion for a stay pending resolution of this expedited interlocutory appeal.

DISCUSSION

A plaintiff seeking certification of a Rule 23(b)(3) class action bears the burden of satisfying the requirements of Rule 23(a)—numerosity, commonality, typicality, and adequacy of representation—as well as Rule 23(b)(3)'s requirements: (1) that "the questions of law or fact common to class members predominate over any questions affecting only individual members" (the "predominance" requirement); and (2) that "a class action is superior to other available methods for fairly and efficiently adjudicating the controversy" (the "superiority" requirement). Fed. R. Civ. P. 23(a), (b)(3); *In re U.S. Foodservice Inc. Pricing Litig.*, 729 F.3d 108, 117 (2d Cir. 2013) ("To certify a class, a district court must ... find that each [Rule 23] requirement is 'established by at least a preponderance of the evidence.' " (quoting *Brown v. Kelly*, 609 F.3d 467, 476 (2d Cir. 2010))). This Court has also "recognized an implied requirement of ascertainability in Rule 23," which demands that a class be "sufficiently definite so that it is administratively feasible for the court to determine whether a particular individual is a member." *Brecher v. Republic of Argentina*, 806 F.3d 22, 24 (2d Cir. 2015) (internal quotation marks and citations omitted).

Appellants do not challenge the district court's findings with regard to the class certification elements under Rule 23(a). Rather, they assert two arguments under Rule 23(b)(3). Appellants first argue that both Classes fail to satisfy ascertainability, predominance, and superiority because putative class members must establish, on an individual basis, that they acquired their securities in "domestic transactions." The Petrobras Defendants assert a second predominance challenge specific to the Exchange Act Class: they argue that the district court erred in finding that Plaintiffs successfully established a class-wide presumption of reliance under the "fraud on the market" theory.

I. Standard of Review

"We review a district court's conclusions as to whether the requirements of Federal Rule of Civil Procedure 23 were met, and in turn whether class certification was appropriate, for abuse

54

of discretion." *In re Vivendi, S.A. Sec. Litig.*, 838 F.3d 223, 263 (2d Cir. 2016) (citations omitted). "While we review the district court's construction of legal standards *de novo,* we review the district court's application of those standards for whether the district court's decision falls within the range of permissible decisions." *Roach v. T.L. Cannon Corp.*, 778 F.3d 401, 405 (2d Cir. 2015) (citing *Myers v. Hertz Corp.*, 624 F.3d 537, 547 (2d Cir. 2010)). "To the extent that the district court's decision as to class certification is premised on a finding of fact, we review that finding for clear error." *UFCW Local 1776 v. Eli Lilly & Co.*, 620 F.3d 121, 130–31 (2d Cir. 2010) (citing *In re Initial Pub. Offerings Sec. Litig.* ("*In re IPO* "), 471 F.3d 24, 40–41 (2d Cir. 2006)); *see also In re Vivendi*, 838 F.3d at 263.

II. "Domestic Transactions" as a Condition for Class Membership

The two certified Classes include all claims arising out of Petrobras Notes purchased in "domestic transactions" during the class period, thereby capturing the broadest membership possible under *Morrison*. Appellants argue that the difficulties inherent in assessing putative class members' transaction records make the Classes uncertifiable for several reasons, the most important of which, for our purposes, are (1) the ascertainability doctrine, which has seen recent developments in this Circuit and others; and (2) predominance. We hold that both class definitions satisfy the ascertainability doctrine as it is defined in this Circuit. We further hold, however, that the district court erred in conducting its predominance analysis without considering the need for individualized *Morrison* inquiries. On that basis, we vacate the district court's certification decision and remand for further proceedings.

A. Extraterritoriality and Federal Securities Law

1. <u>Defining "Domestic Transactions": *Morrison* and *AbsoluteActivist*</u>

"It is a longstanding principle of American law that legislation of Congress, unless a contrary intent appears, is meant to apply only within the territorial jurisdiction of the United States." *Morrison*, 561 U.S. at 255, 130 S.Ct. 2869 (internal quotation marks and citation omitted). Based on that presumption against extraterritoriality, the Supreme Court held in *Morrison* that the reach of U.S. securities law is presumptively limited to (1) "transactions in securities listed on domestic exchanges," and (2) "domestic transactions in other securities." *Id.* at 267, 130 S.Ct. 2869 (discussing Section 10(b) of the Exchange Act); *see also id.* at 268, 130 S.Ct. 2869 (noting that "[t]he same focus on domestic transactions is evident in the Securities Act").

As noted in the margin, we assume that a purchase of Petrobras ADS qualifies under *Morrison*'s first prong as long as the transaction occurs on the NYSE, a "domestic exchange." *See City of Pontiac Policemen's & Firemen's Ret. Sys. v. UBS AG*, 752 F.3d 173, 180–81 (2d Cir. 2014) (holding that mere *listing* on a domestic exchange is not sufficient to establish domesticity if the relevant securities transaction did not *occur* on a domestic exchange). The Notes, however, do not trade on any domestic exchange.[13] Therefore, to assert claims under federal securities laws, Noteholders must show in some other manner that the Notes they hold were acquired in a "domestic transaction."

This Court's decision in *Absolute Activist* elaborated on that standard: for "securities that are not traded on a domestic exchange," a transaction is considered "domestic if [1] irrevocable liability is incurred or [2] title passes within the United States." *Absolute Activist Value Master Fund Ltd. v. Ficeto*, 677 F.3d 60, 67 (2d Cir. 2012). In other words, for a transaction to qualify as domestic, either (1) the purchaser must have "incurred irrevocable liability within the United States to take and pay for a security, or ... the seller [must have] incurred irrevocable liability within the United States to deliver a security," or (2) legal title to the security must have transferred in the United States. *Id.* at 68.

The location or residency of the buyer, seller, or broker will not necessarily establish the situs of the transaction. *Id.* at 68–69. Rather, plaintiffs demonstrate the location where irrevocable liability was incurred or legal title transferred by producing evidence "including, but not limited to, facts concerning the formation of the contracts, the placement of purchase orders, ... or the exchange of money." *Id.* at 70.

2. The District Court's Pre-Certification *Morrison* Inquiries

Before certifying the Classes, the district court twice adjudicated *Morrison-* based challenges to Plaintiffs' claims. When the class action was first consolidated, the court dismissed, without prejudice, all Securities Act claims based on Plaintiffs' failure "to allege that they purchased the relevant securities in domestic transactions." *July 2015 Order*, 116 F.Supp.3d at 386.

Plaintiffs responded with new allegations and documentary evidence regarding Notes transactions for each of the four putative named plaintiffs. Defendants once again moved to dismiss. The district court found that two of the named plaintiffs had adequately pleaded domestic transactions based on their acquisition of Notes directly from U.S. underwriters in the Offerings. *December 2015 Order*, 150 F.Supp.3d at 340. For example, one plaintiff's "traders in Raleigh, North Carolina purchased Notes on May 13, 2013, and March 10, 2014, from underwriters in New York, New York." *Id.* The district court found that this plaintiff had alleged "the kinds of facts required by *Absolute Activist*, including New York area code phone numbers on the confirmations sent by representatives of the underwriters." *Id.* at 340 n.5.

The district court determined that the other two named plaintiffs had failed to satisfy the *Morrison* inquiry and dismissed their Securities Act claims. *Id.* at 340–43. One plaintiff, for example, presented a confirmation slip stating that Petrobras Notes had been purchased "in U.S. dollars and that the Notes were held in '[s]afekeeping of securities abroad, depository country:

U.S.A.' " *Id.* at 341 (quoting the 4th Am. Compl.). According to the district court, this "language suggests that the purchase occurred *outside* the United States because it refers to the United States as 'abroad.' " *Id.* (emphasis added). The district court similarly found insufficient an allegation that an investment manager "located in the United Kingdom[ ] instructed its U.S. affiliate, located in Chicago, Illinois, to transfer Petrobras Notes to [the plaintiff entity,] located in the United Kingdom." *Id.* The court noted that "a 'transfer,' rather than a purchase, [was] all that [was] alleged. Moreover, the allegations suggest that irrevocable liability was incurred in the United Kingdom," where both the plaintiff and the investment manager were located, "rather than in the United States." *Id.*

In an attempt to preserve those claims, Plaintiffs offered two alternative methods for establishing domestic transactions as a matter of law. First, Plaintiffs argued that a securities transaction should qualify as "domestic" if *beneficial* title is transferred when the transaction is settled through a domestic securities depository, such as the Depository Trust Company ("DTC") located in New York City. *Id.* The district court disagreed, finding that "[t]he mechanics of DTC settlement are actions needed to *carry out* transactions, but they involve neither the substantive indicia of a contractual commitment necessary to satisfy *Absolute Activist*'s first prong nor the formal weight of a transfer of [legal] title necessary for its second." *Id.* at 342 (emphasis added); *see also id.* ("[T]he Second Circuit has [ ] indicated that domestic 'actions needed to carry out transactions, and not the transactions themselves,' are insufficient to satisfy *Morrison*." (quoting *Loginovskaya v. Batratchenko*, 764 F.3d 266, 275 (2d Cir. 2014))). The district court also expressed concern that, "assuming the parties are correct that most securities transactions settle through the DTC or similar depository institutions, the entire thrust of *Morrison* and its progeny would be rendered nugatory if all DTC-settled transactions necessarily fell under the reach of the federal securities laws." *Id.*

Finally, Plaintiffs proposed a method for constructively establishing the domesticity of Notes transactions: "allegations that a plaintiff purchased Notes 'on the offering date and at the offering price' [should be] sufficient to demonstrate irrevocable liability because all the underwriters who sold in the initial offerings only did so in the United States." *Id.* at 342 (quoting the 4th Am. Compl.). The district court rejected this theory, noting that certain documents related to the Offerings "imply that some underwriters *did* initially offer the Notes outside the United States." *Id.* (emphasis added).

B. Ascertainability

"Most [ ] circuit courts of appeals have recognized that Rule 23 contains an implicit threshold requirement that the members of a proposed class be readily identifiable," often characterized as "an 'ascertainability' requirement." *Sandusky Wellness Ctr., LLC v. Medtox Sci., Inc.*, 821 F.3d 992, 995 (8th Cir. 2016) (internal quotation marks and citation omitted) (collecting cases). "[C]ourts ascribe widely varied meanings to that term," however. *Briseno v.*

ConAgra Foods, Inc., 844 F.3d 1121, 1124 n.3 (9th Cir. 2017) (describing two versions of the ascertainability requirement); *see generally* Geoffrey C. Shaw, Note, *Class Ascertainability*, 124 Yale L.J. 2354, 2366–88 (2015) (describing different conceptions of ascertainability and critiquing the proffered justifications).

In *Brecher v. Republic of Argentina*, we offered our first and, thus far, only affirmative definition[15] of the implied ascertainability requirement:

> [T]he touchstone of ascertainability is whether the class is sufficiently definite so that it is administratively feasible for the court to determine whether a particular individual is a member. A class is ascertainable when defined by objective criteria that are administratively feasible and when identifying its members would not require a mini-hearing on the merits of each case.

Brecher, 806 F.3d at 24–25 (internal quotation marks and citations omitted). Based on this language, Appellants argue for a "heightened" ascertainability requirement under which any proposed class must be "administratively feasible," over and above the evident requirements that a class be "definite" and "defined by objective criteria," and separate from Rule 23(b)(3)'s requirements of predominance and superiority.

We take this opportunity to clarify the ascertainability doctrine's substance and purpose. We conclude that a freestanding administrative feasibility requirement is neither compelled by precedent nor consistent with Rule 23, joining four of our sister circuits in declining to adopt such a requirement. The ascertainability doctrine that governs in this Circuit requires only that a class be defined using objective criteria that establish a membership with definite boundaries. Applying that doctrine, we determine that ascertainability is not an impediment to certification of the Classes as currently defined.

1. The Proceedings Below and Arguments on Appeal

In its *Certification Order*, the district court rejected Defendants' argument that, "because of the nuances of the 'domestic transaction' standard, determining [class membership] and damages will be an *administratively unfeasible* task for this Court, for putative class members who receive notice of the action, and for future courts facing claims from class members who have not properly opted out." 312 F.R.D. at 363–64 (emphasis added) (footnote omitted).

Appellants renew that argument on appeal, packaged as a challenge to the district court's finding "that the *Morrison* determination is 'administratively feasible.' " *Id.* at 364 (quoting *Brecher*, 806 F.3d at 24). Appellants cite heavily to cases from the Third Circuit, which has formally adopted a "heightened" two-part ascertainability test under which plaintiffs must not only show that "the class is 'defined with reference to objective criteria,' " but also that "there is 'a reliable and administratively feasible mechanism for determining whether putative class members fall within the class definition.' " *Byrd v. Aaron's Inc.*, 784 F.3d 154, 166 (3d Cir. 2015), *as amended* Apr. 28, 2015 (quoting *Hayes v. Wal-Mart Stores, Inc.*, 725 F.3d 349, 355 (3d Cir. 2013)); *see also Carrera v. Bayer Corp.*, 727 F.3d 300, 305 (3d Cir. 2013); *Marcus v. BMW of N. Am., LLC*, 687 F.3d 583, 592-95 (3d Cir. 2012).

With all due respect to our colleagues on the Third Circuit, we decline to adopt a heightened ascertainability theory that requires a showing of administrative feasibility at the class certification stage. The reasoning underlying our decision in *Brecher* does not suggest any such prerequisite, and creating one would upset the careful balance of competing interests codified in the explicit requirements of Rule 23. In declining to adopt an administrative feasibility requirement, we join a growing consensus that now includes the Sixth, Seventh, Eighth, and Ninth Circuits. *See Briseno*, 844 F.3d at 1123; *Sandusky*, 821 F.3d at 995–96; *Rikos v. Procter & Gamble Co.*, 799 F.3d 497, 525 (6th Cir. 2015), *cert. denied*, —— U.S. ——, 136 S.Ct. 1493, 194 L.Ed.2d 597 (2016); *Mullins v. Direct Digital, LLC*, 795 F.3d 654, 657–58 (7th Cir. 2015), *cert. denied*, —— U.S. ——, 136 S.Ct. 1161, 194 L.Ed.2d 175 (2016); *see also Byrd*, 784 F.3d at 177 (Rendell, *J.*, concurring) ("suggest[ing]" that the Third Circuit "retreat from [its] heightened ascertainability requirement" by eliminating the administrative feasibility prong).

2. Our Decision in *Brecher v. Republic of Argentina*

Brecher was one of several opinions in which we assessed a class action initiated by holders of Argentinian bonds "[a]fter Argentina defaulted on between $80 and $100 billion of sovereign debt in 2001." *Brecher*, 806 F.3d at 23 (listing prior decisions). The district court originally "certified a class under a continuous holder requirement, *i.e.*, the class contained only those individuals who [ ] possessed beneficial interests in a particular bond series issued by the Republic of Argentina from the date of the complaint [ ] through the date of final judgment." *Id.*

When the district court granted summary judgment to the plaintiffs, we vacated in part after finding that the district court's method of calculating aggregate damages had likely produced impermissibly inflated awards. *See Seijas v. Republic of Argentina*, 606 F.3d 53, 58–59 (2d Cir. 2010); *Hickory Sec., Ltd. v. Republic of Argentina*, 493 Fed.Appx. 156, 160 (2d Cir. 2012) (summary order). On remand, the district court "modif[ied] the class definition by removing the continuous holder requirement and expanding the class to all holders of beneficial interests in the relevant bond series[,] without limitation as to time held." *Brecher*, 806 F.3d at 24. The defendants appealed once again.

We concluded that, without the continuous holder requirement, the modified class was unascertainable. *Id.* at 26. We first defined the elements of ascertainability, explaining that a proposed class: (1) must be "sufficiently definite so that it is administratively feasible for the

59

court to determine whether a particular individual is a member"; and (2) must be "defined by objective criteria that are administratively feasible," such that "identifying its members would not require a mini-hearing on the merits of each case." *Id*. at 24 (citations omitted). These requirements operate in harmony: "the use of objective criteria cannot alone determine ascertainability when those criteria, taken together, do not establish the definite boundaries of a readily identifiable class." *Id*. at 25 (footnote in original as n.2).

Turning to the facts of the case, we expressed concern that the class was insufficiently bounded:

> The secondary market for Argentine bonds is active and has continued trading after the commencement of this and other lawsuits.... Further, all bonds from the same series have the same trading number identifier (called a CUSIP/ISIN), making it practically impossible to trace purchases and sales of a particular beneficial interest. Thus, when it becomes necessary to determine who holds bonds that fall inside (or outside) of the class, it will be nearly impossible to distinguish between them once traded on the secondary market without a criterion as to time held.

Id. at 25–26 (citations omitted). We concluded that "[t]his case presents [ ] a circumstance where an objective standard—owning a beneficial interest in a bond series without reference to time owned—is insufficiently definite to allow ready identification of the class or the persons who will be bound by the judgment."*Id*. at 25 (footnote omitted).

As this summary clarifies, we reached our decision in *Brecher* by asking whether the class was defined by objective criteria that made the class's membership sufficiently definite, not whether the class was administratively feasible. *See, e.g., id*. at 26 ("The lack of a defined class period ... makes the modified class *insufficiently definite* as a matter of law." (emphasis added)). The opinion's language about "administrative feasibility" and "mini-hearings" was not strictly part of the holding, and was not intended to create an independent element of the ascertainability test; rather, that language conveyed the *purpose* underlying the operative requirements of definiteness and objectivity. That is, a class must be "sufficiently definite *so that* it is administratively feasible for the court to determine whether a particular individual is a member"; a class must be "defined by objective criteria" *so that* it will not be necessary to hold "a mini-hearing on the merits of each case." *Id*. at 24 (emphasis added) (citations omitted).

This interpretation finds further support in the district court cases we cited in *Brecher*'s articulation and application of the ascertainability standard. *Compare Bakalar v. Vavra*, 237 F.R.D. 59, 65 (S.D.N.Y. 2006) (declining to certify a class seeking recovery of artworks traceable to a particular estate—an objective criterion—because the movants were unable to *identify* the specific artworks, and were therefore also unable to identify "the owners, possessors

60

or individuals who participated in transfers of such works"), *with Ebin v. Kangadis Food Inc.*, 297 F.R.D. 561, 567 (S.D.N.Y. 2014) (acknowledging the challenge of identifying individuals who purchased a particular brand of olive oil during the class period, but finding the class ascertainable because "ascertainability ... is designed only to prevent the certification of a class whose membership is *truly indeterminable*" (emphasis added) (internal quotation marks and citations omitted)), *and Charron v. Pinnacle Grp. N.Y. LLC*, 269 F.R.D. 221, 229 (S.D.N.Y. 2010) (finding that ascertainability was satisfied because the proposed class was "defined by objective criteria—namely, whether a given apartment is rent-regulated" and "owned by the [defendant corporation]; and whether the putative Class member is a tenant" on a fixed date—"thus allowing the Court to readily identify Class members without needing to resolve the merits of Plaintiffs' claims").

3. Ascertainability and Rule 23

Having concluded that our decision in *Brecher* did not create an independent administrative feasibility requirement, we now consider whether such a requirement is compulsory under Rule 23, or at least complementary to the requirements enumerated therein. We find that it is neither. In pursuing this analysis, we are mindful that "[c]ourts are not free to amend [the Federal Rules of Civil Procedure] outside the process Congress ordered." *Amchem Prods., Inc. v. Windsor*, 521 U.S. 591, 620, 117 S.Ct. 2231, 138 L.Ed.2d 689 (1997). "The text" of Rule 23 thus "limits judicial inventiveness." *Id.*

The heightened ascertainability test, as articulated by the Third Circuit and endorsed by Appellants, treats administrative feasibility as an absolute standard: plaintiffs must provide adequate "assurance that there can be 'a reliable and administratively feasible mechanism for determining whether putative class members fall within the class definition.'" *Byrd*, 784 F.3d at 164–65 (quoting *Hayes*, 725 F.3d at 355); *cf. Mullins*, 795 F.3d at 663 ("When administrative inconvenience is addressed as a matter of ascertainability, courts tend to look at the problem in a vacuum, considering only the administrative costs and headaches of proceeding as a class action." (citation omitted)).

On its face, this test appears to duplicate Rule 23's requirement that district courts consider "the likely difficulties in managing a class action." Fed. R. Civ. P. 23(b)(3)(D). This apparent redundancy is misleading, however, because of a key difference in analytical orientation. Whereas ascertainability is an absolute standard, manageability is a component of the superiority analysis, which is explicitly comparative in nature: courts must ask whether "a class action is *superior to other available methods* for fairly and efficiently adjudicating the controversy." Fed. R. Civ. P. 23(b)(3) (emphasis added). We share the concern voiced by our sister circuits that heightened ascertainability and superiority could push in opposite directions. Though a court may not ignore concerns about the manageability of a putative class action, it may be that challenges of administrative feasibility are most prevalent in cases "in which there may be no realistic alternative to class treatment," *Briseno*, 844 F.3d at 1128 (agreeing with *Mullins*, 795

F.3d at 663–64), underscoring the importance of a comparative inquiry. This concern is particularly acute in light of our admonition that "failure to certify an action under Rule 23(b)(3) on the sole ground that it would be unmanageable is disfavored and should be the exception rather than the rule." *In re Visa Check/MasterMoney Antitrust Litig.*, 280 F.3d 124, 140 (2d Cir. 2001), *overruled on other grounds by In re IPO*, 471 F.3d at 39–40 (internal quotation marks and citation omitted).

The proposed administrative feasibility test also risks encroaching on territory belonging to the predominance requirement, such as classes that require highly individualized determinations of member eligibility. *See, e.g., Mazzei v. The Money Store*, 829 F.3d 260, 272 (2d Cir. 2016) (internal quotation marks omitted), *cert. denied*, —— U.S. ——, 137 S.Ct. 1332, 197 L.Ed.2d 518 (2017). Like superiority, predominance is a comparative standard: "Rule 23(b)(3) [ ] does *not* require a plaintiff seeking class certification to prove that each element of her claim is susceptible to classwide proof. What the rule does require is that common questions '*predominate* over any questions affecting only individual [class] members.' " *Amgen Inc. v. Conn. Ret. Plans & Tr. Funds*, 568 U.S. 455 (2013) (quoting Fed. R. Civ. P. 23(b)(3); other quotation marks, citations, and alterations omitted).

We conclude that an implied administrative feasibility requirement would be inconsistent with the careful balance struck in Rule 23, which directs courts to weigh the competing interests inherent in any class certification decision. *Accord Briseno*, 844 F.3d at 1128 ("[A] freestanding administrative feasibility requirement" would "have practical consequences inconsistent with the policies embodied in Rule 23."); *Mullins*, 795 F.3d at 658 ("The policy concerns motivating the heightened ascertainability requirement are better addressed by applying carefully the explicit requirements of Rule 23(a) and especially (b)(3)."); *Byrd*, 784 F.3d at 177 (Rendell, *J.*, concurring) (concluding that the Third Circuit's "heightened ascertainability requirement ... contravenes the purpose of Rule 23 and ... disserves the public"); *see also* Shaw, 124 Yale L.J. at 2366 ("Rule 23 already safeguards the interests that the ascertainability requirement supposedly protects and adequately guards against the problems that the requirement supposedly forestalls.").

Our decision in *Brecher* did not create an administrative feasibility requirement, and we decline to adopt one now. The ascertainability requirement, as defined in this Circuit, asks district courts to consider whether a proposed class is defined using objective criteria that establish a membership with definite boundaries. This modest threshold requirement will only preclude certification if a proposed class definition is indeterminate in some fundamental way. If there is no focused target for litigation, the class itself cannot coalesce, rendering the class action an inappropriate mechanism for adjudicating any potential underlying claims. In other words, a class should not be maintained without a clear sense of who is suing about what. Ascertainability does not directly concern itself with the plaintiffs' ability to offer *proof of membership* under a given class definition, an issue that is already accounted for in Rule 23.

4. Application

The district court's analysis in the *Certification Order* is not precisely consistent with the ascertainability standard articulated in this opinion. The district court focused primarily on the types of feasibility concerns that we hold are not controlling of the ascertainability analysis, and effectively addressed ascertainability as a component of superiority. 312 F.R.D. at 363–64. Nonetheless, the district court's findings reflect an understanding that objective criteria would permit the identification of class members. We agree.

The Classes include persons who acquired specific securities during a specific time period, as long as those acquisitions occurred in "domestic transactions." *Id.* at 372. These criteria—securities purchases identified by subject matter, timing, and location—are clearly objective. The definition is also sufficiently definite: there exists a definite subset of Petrobras Securities holders who purchased those Securities in "domestic transactions" during the bounded class period. Appellants vigorously challenge the *practicality* of making the domesticity determination for each putative class member, but as we explain above, the ascertainability analysis is limited to narrower question of whether those determinations are objectively *possible*.

Unlike in *Brecher* or the cases cited therein, neither the parties nor the properties that are the subject of this litigation are fundamentally indeterminate. Finding no error in the district court's conclusion on this point, we reject Appellants' contention that the classes defined by the district court fail on ascertainability grounds.

C. Predominance

1. Legal Standard

A district court may only certify a class under Federal Rule of Civil Procedure 23(b)(3) if "questions of law or fact common to class members predominate over any questions affecting only individual members." This "predominance" requirement is satisfied if: (1) resolution of any material "legal or factual questions ... can be achieved through generalized proof," and (2) "these [common] issues are more substantial than the issues subject only to individualized proof." *Mazzei*, 829 F.3d at 272 (quoting *Myers*, 624 F.3d at 547).

The distinction between "individual" and "common" questions is thus central to the predominance analysis. As the Supreme Court has explained:

An individual question is one where "members of a proposed class will need to present evidence that varies from member to member," while a common question is one where "the same evidence will suffice for each member to make a prima facie showing or the issue is susceptible to generalized class-wide proof."

Tyson Foods, Inc. v. Bouaphakeo, —— U.S. ——, 136 S.Ct. 1036, 1045, 194 L.Ed.2d 124 (2016) (alteration omitted) (quoting 2 William B. Rubenstein, Newberg on Class Actions § 4:50, at 196–97 (5th ed. 2012)).

The predominance inquiry is a core feature of the Rule 23(b)(3) class mechanism, and is not satisfied simply by showing that the class claims are framed by the common harm suffered by potential plaintiffs. *Amchem Prods,*. 521 U.S. at 623–24 (noting that "predominance criterion is far more demanding" than the "commonality" requirement under Rule 23(a)); *see also Johnson v. Nextel Commc'ns Inc.*, 780 F.3d 128, 138 (2d Cir. 2015). Where individualized questions permeate the litigation, those "fatal dissimilarit[ies]" among putative class members "make use of the class-action device inefficient or unfair." *Amgen*, 133 S.Ct. at 1197 (citation omitted); *see also*7AA Charles Alan Wright & Arthur R. Miller, Federal Practice and Procedure § 1778, at 141 (3d ed. 2005). ("[W]hen individual rather than common issues predominate, the economy and efficiency of class-action treatment are lost and... the risk of confusion is magnified." (footnote omitted)).

The predominance inquiry mitigates this risk by "ask[ing] whether the common, aggregation-enabling, issues in the case are *more prevalent or important* than the non-common, aggregation-defeating, individual issues." *Tyson Foods*, 136 S.Ct. at 1045 (emphasis added) (quoting Rubenstein, *supra*, at 195–96); *see also id.* (The "inquiry tests whether proposed classes are sufficiently cohesive to warrant adjudication by representation." (quoting *Amchem Prods.*, 521 U.S. at 623, 117 S.Ct. 2231)). For this reason, the Supreme Court has emphasized district courts' "duty to take a 'close look' at whether common questions predominate over individual ones." *Comcast Corp. v. Behrend*, 569 U.S. 27 (2013) (quoting *Amchem Prods.*, 521 U.S. at 615); *see also Tyson Foods*, 136 S.Ct. at 1045 (2016) (The predominance requirement "calls upon courts to give *careful scrutiny* to the relation between common and individual questions in a case." (emphasis added)). This analysis is "more [ ] qualitative than quantitative," Rubenstein, *supra*, at 197 (footnote omitted), and must account for the nature and significance of the material common and individual issues in the case, *see Roach*, 778 F.3d at 405.

2. Application

A proper assessment of predominance in this action involves two predicate questions about the role of *Morrison* inquiries. First, is the determination of domesticity material to Plaintiffs' class claims? *See* Amchem Prods., 521 U.S. at 623 (explaining that predominance "trains on the legal or factual questions that qualify each class member's case as a genuine controversy"). If so, is that determination "susceptible to generalized class-wide proof" such that it represents a "common" question rather than an "individual" one? *Tyson Foods*, 136 S.Ct. at 1045 (internal quotation marks and citation omitted). We find that the district court failed to meaningfully address the second question. That omission was an error of law, and we vacate the certification decision on that basis. Only by answering *both* predicate questions can the district court properly assess whether, in the case as a whole, common issues are "more prevalent or important" than individual ones. *Id.* (citation omitted).

With regard to the first question, "*Morrison* makes clear that [determining] whether [federal securities law] applies to certain conduct is a 'merits' question." *Absolute Activist*, 677 F.3d at 67 (quoting *Morrison*, 561 U.S. at 254). In other words, a putative class member only has a viable cause of action if the specific Petrobras Securities sued upon were purchased in a qualifying "domestic transaction." *City of Pontiac*, 752 F.3d at 179; *see also Morrison*, 561 U.S. at 273 (holding that securities fraud claims that lack a domestic connection must be dismissed for "fail[ure] to state a claim on which relief can be granted").

The district court clearly recognized *Morrison*'s importance because the class definitions import *Morrison*'s unelaborated legal standard, namely that Petrobras Securities must have been purchased in "domestic transactions." *See Certification Order*, 312 F.R.D. at 372. Indeed, it appears that the district court consciously sought to certify encompassing classes that would extend as far as *Morrison* allows. *See id.* at 364 (rejecting a proposed limitation to the class definition because it "would cut off purchasers who have valid claims under *Morrison*'s second prong"). When it came to predominance, however, the district court did not mention *Morrison* at all. The court found that predominance was satisfied, explaining that, "with the exception of reliance and damages, plaintiffs' claims rest almost exclusively on class-wide questions of law and fact centered around" Petrobras's alleged misconduct "and the effects of these actions and events on the market." *Id.* at 364. The court proceeded to discuss reliance and damages in great detail, *id.* at 364–72, but made no mention of *Morrison*.

The *Certification Order* is susceptible to two possible readings: either the district court implicitly held that *Morrison* inquiries constituted a common issue, or the court simply sidestepped the question. Either way, given the nature of the *Morrison* inquiries at issue, the district court cannot be said to have "give[n] careful scrutiny to the relation between [the] common and individual questions" central to this case. *See Tyson Foods*, 136 S.Ct. at 1045.

On the available record, the investigation of domesticity appears to be an "individual question" requiring putative class members to "present evidence that varies from member to member." *Id.* (citation omitted). As discussed above, a plaintiff may demonstrate the domesticity of a particular transaction by producing evidence "including, but not limited to, facts concerning the formation of the contracts, the placement or purchase orders, the passing of title, or the exchange of money." *Absolute Activist*, 677 F.3d at 70; *see also* Discussion Section II.A, *supra*. These transaction-specific facts are not obviously "susceptible to [ ] class-wide proof," nor did Plaintiffs suggest a form of representative proof that would answer the question of domesticity for individual class members. *See Tyson Foods*, 136 S.Ct. at 1045–46 (explaining that class plaintiffs may rely on representative samples to prove class-wide liability where they can show "that each class member could have relied on that sample to establish liability if he or she had brought an individual action").

In cases that have applied *Morrison* and *Absolute Activist*—including the district court's own experience adjudicating Petrobras-specific inquiries—factfinders have considered various types of evidence offered to prove the domesticity of various types of transactions. *See, e.g.*, *Loginovskaya*, 764 F.3d at 274–75 (finding that domestic wire transfers failed to satisfy *Absolute Activist* because they were "actions needed to carry out the transactions, and not the transactions themselves"); *In re PetrobrasSec. Litig.*, 152 F.Supp.3d 186, 193 (S.D.N.Y. 2016) (explaining that the high-level documentation provided by various plaintiffs was insufficient to plead a domestic transaction); *December 2015 Order*, 150 F.Supp.3d at 340–41 (finding that two proposed class representatives failed to plead domestic transactions in Petrobras Notes).

The district court suggested that the pertinent locational details for each transaction are likely to be found in the "record[s] routinely produced by the modern financial system," and "are highly likely to be documented in a form susceptible to the bureaucratic processes of determining who belongs to a Class." *Certification Order*, 312 F.R.D. at 364. Even if that fact is true, however, it does not obviate the need to consider the plaintiff-specific nature of the *Morrison* inquiry.

The two approved class representatives with Notes-based claims were both located in the United States, placed their Notes purchase orders in the United States, and procured their securities directly from United States underwriters as part of the initial Notes Offerings. *See December 2015 Order*, 150 F.Supp.3d at 340. Appellants argue that those transactions are the easy case. As the Underwriter Defendants observe, the Classes as currently defined potentially "include[ ] numerous foreign and domestic entities that purchased securities from other foreign and domestic entities, possibly through foreign and domestic intermediaries, using different methods, under different circumstances, and reflected in different types of records (assuming any records of the purchases exist at all)." Underwriter Defs.' Br. at 3.

Significantly, the Classes include investors who purchased Notes in the initial Offerings, as well as investors who purchased their Notes on the secondary market. *See Certification Order*, 312 F.R.D. at 372. Aftermarket purchasers asserting claims under Sections 11 and 15 of the Securities Act must not only establish that they acquired their Notes in a domestic secondary transaction, but must also show that the particular Notes they acquired are "traceable to" one of the U.S.-registered Offerings. *See id.* The *Certification Order* offers no indication that the district court considered the ways in which evidence of domesticity might vary in nature or availability across the many permutations of transactions in Petrobras Securities.

The need for *Morrison* inquiries nominally presents a common question because the need to show a "domestic transaction" applies equally to each putative class member. However, Plaintiffs bear the burden of showing that, more often than not, they can provide common *answers*. *Amgen*, 133 S.Ct. at 1196. In this case, the potential for variation across putative class members—who sold them the relevant securities, how those transactions were effectuated, and what forms of documentation might be offered in support of domesticity—appears to generate a set of individualized inquiries that must be considered within the framework of Rule 23(b)(3)'s predominance requirement. *See Tyson Foods*, 136 S.Ct. at 1045–46 (explaining that "[a]n individual question is one where members of a proposed class will need to present evidence that varies from member to member...." (internal quotation marks and citation omitted)).

Consider, for instance, the Supreme Court's recent *Amgen* decision, which similarly involved class claims under Section 10(b) the Exchange Act. 568 U.S. 455, 133 S.Ct. 1184. Such claims require a showing that the defendants made a "*material* misrepresentation or omission." *Id.* at 1195. Materiality—like domesticity—is thus an "essential predicate" of an Exchange Act claim. *Id.* The *Amgen* Court held, however, that *proof* of materiality was not required for the purpose of satisfying predominance at the class certification stage. *Id.* Because materiality is determined objectively from the perspective of the " 'reasonable investor,' materiality can be proved through evidence *common to the class*." *Id.* (emphasis added) (quoting *TSC Industries, Inc. v. Northway, Inc.*, 426 U.S. 438, 445 (1976)). "In no event will the individual circumstances of particular class members bear on the [materiality] inquiry." *Id.* at 1191. "Consequently, materiality is a common question for purposes of Rule 23(b)(3)." *Id.* at 1196 (internal quotation marks, alteration, and citation omitted).

In the present action, by contrast, it cannot be said that the class members' *Morrison* inquiries will "prevail or fail in unison." *Id.* The district court has already adjudicated several individualized *Morrison* inquiries, preserving some plaintiffs' claims and dismissing others. *See* Discussion Section II.A.2, *supra*. "[W]ithout *class-wide* evidence" of domesticity, "the fact-finder would have to look at every class member's [transaction] documents to determine who did and who did not have a valid claim." *Mazzei*, 829 F.3d at 272 (citing *Wal-Mart Stores, Inc. v. Dukes*, 564 U.S. 338, 350, 131 S.Ct. 2541, 180 L.Ed.2d 374 (2011)) (affirming a finding that predominance was not satisfied because the class claims turned on individualized determinations of privity). The predominance analysis must account for such individual questions, particularly when they go to the viability of each class member's claims.

Finally, we emphasize that district courts are authorized to implement management strategies tailored to the particularities of each case. In addition to modifying class definitions and issuing class-wide rulings, district courts can, for example, bifurcate the proceedings to home in on threshold class-wide inquiries; sever claims not properly adjudicated on a class-wide basis to isolate key common issues; or certify subclasses that separate class members into smaller, more homogenous groups defined by common legal or factual questions. *See*Fed. R. Civ. P. 23(c)(4), (c)(5); *see also In re Nassau Cty. Strip Search Cases*, 461 F.3d 219, 227 (2d Cir. 2006); *In re Visa Check*, 280 F.3d at 141 (summarizing various class action "management tools" and collecting cases). While these options need not necessarily be exercised or even planned for prior to class certification, the possibility of post-certification procedural tailoring does not attenuate the obligation to take a "close look" at predominance when assessing the motion for certification itself.

For the foregoing reasons, we vacate the district court's certification of the Classes insofar as they include all otherwise eligible class members who acquired their Securities in "domestic transactions." We take no position as to whether, on remand, the district court might properly certify one or more classes that capture some or all of the Securities holders who fall within the Classes as currently defined. Our purpose is merely to outline the contours of the robust predominance inquiry that Rule 23 demands. We leave the adjudication thereof to the district court in the first instance.

III. "Fraud on the Market" and the Presumption of Reliance

The second issue on appeal concerns the district court's finding that the Exchange Act Class was entitled to a presumption of class-wide reliance on the market price of Petrobras's ADS and Notes. In reaching that conclusion, the district court found that Plaintiffs satisfied their burden of showing that the Petrobras Securities traded in efficient markets, as required under the "fraud on the market" theory established in *Basic Inc. v. Levinson*, 485 U.S. 224 (1988). The Petrobras Defendants challenge that finding, arguing that the district court erred in the relative weight it assigned to the parties' competing evidence. We find no error of law in the district court's blended consideration of direct and indirect evidence of market efficiency, nor do we find any clear error in the district court's factual analysis. We therefore affirm as to this issue.

A. The "Fraud on the Market" Theory

1. Legal Standard

Plaintiffs alleging claims under Section 10(b) of the Exchange Act must prove "(1) a material misrepresentation or omission by the defendant; (2) scienter; (3) a connection between the misrepresentation or omission and the purchase or sale of a security; (4) reliance upon the misrepresentation or omission; (5) economic loss; and (6) loss causation." *Halliburton Co. v. Erica P. John Fund, Inc.* ("*Halliburton II*"), —— U.S. ——, 134 S.Ct. 2398, 2407 (2014) (citation omitted). The key element for the purpose of this appeal is reliance, the element that establishes a sufficient "connection between a defendant's misrepresentation and a plaintiff's injury." *Id.* (citation omitted).

On its face, the reliance element would appear to preclude class certification on predominance grounds: "[e]ach plaintiff would have to prove reliance individually," with the result that "common issues would not 'predominate' over individual ones." *Id.* at 2416 (citation omitted). The Supreme Court resolved that tension almost three decades ago in *Basic Inc. v. Levinson*, reasoning that "[a]n investor who buys or sells stock at the price set by the market does so in reliance on the integrity of that price," and so "an investor's reliance on any public material misrepresentations [ ] may be *presumed* for purposes of a Rule 10b–5 action." 485 U.S. at 247 (emphasis added).

In 2014, the Court affirmed the continued vitality of the "fraud on the market" theory, and clarified that the so-called "*Basic* presumption actually incorporates two constituent presumptions:"

First, if a plaintiff shows that the defendant's misrepresentation was public and material and that the stock traded in a generally efficient market, he is entitled to a presumption that the misrepresentation affected the stock price.

Second, if the plaintiff also shows that he purchased the stock at the market price during the relevant period, he is entitled to a further presumption that he purchased the stock in reliance on the defendant's misrepresentation.

Halliburton II, 134 S.Ct. at 2414. If a putative class successfully establishes the *Basic* presumption, "defendants must be afforded an opportunity ... to defeat the presumption through evidence that [the] alleged misrepresentation [at issue in the plaintiffs' legal claim] did not actually affect the market price of the stock."*Id.* at 2417.

2. Market Efficiency and the *Cammer* Factors

"The fraud-on-the-market theory rests on the premise that certain well developed markets are efficient processors of public information," meaning that "the 'market price of shares' will 'reflect all publicly available information.' " *Amgen*, 133 S.Ct. at 1192 (quoting *Basic*, 485 U.S. at 246, 108 S.Ct. 978 (alteration omitted)).

This Court "has not adopted a test for the market efficiency of stocks or bonds." *Teamsters Local 445 Freight Div. Pension Fund v. Bombardier Inc.*, 546 F.3d 196, 204 n.11 (2d Cir. 2008). A test based on the so-called "*Cammer* factors" has been "routinely applied by district courts considering the efficiency of equity markets," and has also been applied, in modified form, "to bond markets with a recognition of the differences between the manner in which debt bonds and equity securities trade." *Id.*; *see also Cammer v. Bloom*, 711 F.Supp. 1264, 1286–87 (D.N.J. 1989) (articulating five factors); *Krogman v. Sterritt*, 202 F.R.D. 467, 478 (N.D. Tex. 2001) (describing three additional factors that are commonly included in *Cammer* analyses); *In re Enron Corp. Sec.*, 529 F.Supp.2d 644, 747–49 (S.D. Tex. 2006) (applying the *Cammer* factors in modified form to debt securities).

All but one of the *Cammer* factors examine indirect indicia of market efficiency for a particular security, such as high trading volume, extensive analyst coverage, multiple market makers, large market capitalization, and an issuer's eligibility for simplified SEC filings. The fifth *Cammer* factor, however, invites plaintiffs to submit direct evidence, consisting of "empirical facts showing a cause and effect relationship between unexpected corporate events or financial releases and an immediate response in the stock price." *Cammer*, 711 F.Supp. at 1287; *see also Halliburton II*, 134 S.Ct. at 2415 ("[P]laintiffs [ ] can and do introduce evidence of the existence of price impact in connection with 'event studies'—regression analyses that seek to show that the market price of the defendant's stock tends to respond to pertinent publicly reported events." (citation and emphasis omitted)).

B. Application

At the outset, the Petrobras Defendants assert an error of law: they challenge the district court's purported holding that Plaintiffs were entitled to the *Basic* presumption based solely on their *indirect* evidence of market efficiency. This argument mischaracterizes the district court's analysis. True, the court noted that "Petrobras was one of the largest and most-analyzed firms in the world throughout the Class Period," and explained that in instances where "the indirect [*Cammer*] factors overwhelmingly describe a large and well-functioning market for Petrobras securities, common sense suggests that the market would materially react to material disclosures." *Certification Order*, 312 F.R.D. at 367. The opinion did not stop there, however. The court proceeded with an "involved analysis" of Plaintiffs' empirical evidence—which Defendants disputed as to "almost every aspect"—and "ultimately conclude[d] that plaintiffs [had] satisfied the fifth *Cammer* factor." *Id.*; *see also id.* at 367–71. Anything to the contrary was, at most, a holding in the alternative. We therefore decline to reach the Petrobras Defendants' legal question—whether plaintiffs may satisfy the *Basic* presumption without *any* direct evidence of price impact—because the issue is not squarely presented for our review.

Having confirmed the *existence* of Plaintiffs' direct evidence of market efficiency, we turn to the Petrobras Defendants' attack on the *quality* of that evidence. They argue, first, that the district court gave undue weight to Plaintiffs' empirical test, which measured the magnitude of responsive price changes in Petrobras Securities without considering the direction of those changes, and second, that the district court unduly discounted Defendants' rebuttal evidence. We find these arguments unpersuasive.

70

In the class certification proceedings, the parties' "experts [ ] sparred over whether any direct evidence of [*Cammer*'s] fifth factor existed." *Id.* at 367. Plaintiffs' expert ran multiple event studies and reported that "there were more likely to be big price movements on days when important Petrobras events occurred, demonstrating [that] the markets in Petrobras securities were responsive to new information." *Id.* at 367–68. Defendants responded with numerous challenges to "the execution and the sufficiency" of that test. *Id.* at 368. They specifically criticized the test's failure to examine directionality, that is, "whether the price of a security moved up or down as expected based on the precipitating market event." *Id.* at 369; *see also id.* at 370 (describing the defense expert's position that "in an efficient market, the price of a security should *always* move in response to the release of new value-relevant information that is materially different from expectations"). Plaintiffs' expert conducted supplementary analyses of directional price impact, but the district court accorded them "only limited weight" after Defendants highlighted certain methodological flaws. *Id.* at 369–70. As to the non-directional analysis, the court declined to "let the perfect become the enemy of the good":

> In this case, where the indirect *Cammer* factors lay a strong foundation for a finding of efficiency, a statistically significant showing that statistically significant price returns are more likely to occur on event dates is sufficient as direct evidence of market efficiency and thereby to invoke *Basic*'s presumption of reliance at the class certification stage.

Id. at 371.

We find that the district court's conclusion "falls within the range of permissible decisions." *Roach*, 778 F.3d at 405 (citation omitted). The district court properly declined to view direct and indirect evidence as distinct requirements, opting instead for a holistic analysis based on the totality of the evidence presented. *See, e.g., In re JPMorgan Chase & Co. Sec. Litig.*, No. 12 CIV. 03852 (GBD), 2015 WL 10433433, at *7 (S.D.N.Y. Sept. 29, 2015) ("Defendants' criticisms of Plaintiffs' event study distract[ ] from the central question: Does the weight of the evidence tip in favor of the finding that the market for JPMorgan's common stock was efficient during the Class Period?").

The Petrobras Defendants' contentions on appeal amount to an intensified reformulation of the claim we bypassed above: not only should putative class plaintiffs be required to offer direct evidence of market efficiency, they argue, but the evidence must specifically consist of empirical data showing that the price of the relevant securities predictably moved up in response to good news and down in response to bad news. The gravamen of their claim is that plaintiffs would only be entitled to the *Basic* presumption after making a substantial showing of market efficiency based on directional empirical evidence alone, irrespective of any other evidence they may have offered.

We reject this proposition. In short, the Petrobras Defendants are attempting to relabel a *sufficient* condition as a *necessary* one. We noted in *Bombardier* that "[a]n event study that correlates the disclosures of unanticipated, material information about a security with corresponding fluctuations in price has been considered *prima facie* evidence of the existence of such a causal relationship." *Bombardier*, 546 F.3d at 207–08 (citing *In re Xcelera.com Sec. Litig.*, 430 F.3d 503, 512–14, 516 (1st Cir. 2005)). We never suggested, however, that such evidence was the *only* way to prove market efficiency; indeed, we explicitly declined to adopt any particular "test for the market efficiency of stocks or bonds." *Id.* at 204 n.11.

The Supreme Court has similarly declined to define a precise evidentiary standard for market efficiency, but the Court's opinions consistently suggest that the burden is not an onerous one. *See Halliburton II*, 134 S.Ct. at 2410 ("Even the foremost critics of the efficient-capital-markets hypothesis acknowledge that public information generally affects stock prices," and so "[d]ebates about the precise *degree* to which stock prices accurately reflect public information are [ ] largely beside the point."); *id.* at 2417 (Ginsburg, *J.*, concurring) (interpreting the holding in *Halliburton II* as "impos[ing] no heavy toll on securities-fraud plaintiffs with tenable claims"); *Amgen*, 133 S.Ct. at 1192 ("[I]t is reasonable to presume that most investors ... will rely on [a] security's market price as an unbiased assessment of the security's value in light of all public information."); *Basic,* 485 U.S. at 246 n. 24 ("For purposes of accepting the presumption of reliance ..., we need only believe that market professionals generally consider most publicly announced material statements about companies, thereby affecting stock market prices."); *see also id.* at 246 ("The presumption is supported by common sense and probability.").

The Petrobras Defendants' proposed evidentiary hierarchy unreasonably discounts the potential probative value of indirect evidence of market efficiency. As noted above, all but one of the widely used *Cammer* factors focus on elements that would logically appear in, or contribute to, an efficient securities market. Those factors would add little to the *Basic* analysis if courts only ever considered them after finding a strong showing based on direct evidence alone.

Indeed, indirect evidence is particularly valuable in situations where direct evidence does *not* entirely resolve the question. Event studies offer the seductive promise of hard numbers and dispassionate truth, but methodological constraints limit their utility in the context of single-firm analyses. *See generally* Alon Brav & J.B. Heaton, *Event Studies in Securities Litigation: Low Power, Confounding Effects, and Bias*, 93 Wash. U. L. Rev. 583 (2015); *see also id.* at 588 n.11 (collecting academic criticism of single-firm event studies). Notably, small sample sizes may limit statistical power, meaning that only very large-impact events will be detectable. *See id.* at 589–605. In addition, it can be extremely difficult to isolate the price impact of any one piece of information in the presence of confounding factors, such as other simultaneously released news about the company, the industry, or the geographic region. *See id.* at 605–08. These methodological challenges counsel against imposing a blanket rule requiring district courts to, at

72

the class certification stage, rely on directional event studies and directional event studies alone.

In sum, the district court properly considered a combination of direct and indirect evidence in reaching its conclusion that Petrobras ADS and Notes both trade in efficient markets. The court conducted a rigorous analysis of the parties' proffered evidence and objections. We find no abuse of discretion, and therefore affirm the district court's finding that Plaintiffs were entitled to a presumption of reliance on the market price of the Petrobras Securities. We caution that this determination is limited to the district court's class certification order, and is not binding on the ultimate finder of fact.

CONCLUSION

For the foregoing reasons, the district court's *Certification Order* is AFFIRMED IN PART and VACATED IN PART, and the case is REMANDED to the district court for further proceedings consistent with this opinion.

Kokesh v. SEC

Supreme Court of the United States (2017)

137 S.Ct. 1635

■ JUSTICE SOTOMAYOR delivered the opinion of the Court.

A 5-year statute of limitations applies to any "action, suit or proceeding for the enforcement of any civil fine, penalty, or forfeiture, pecuniary or otherwise." 28 U.S.C. § 2462. This case presents the question whether § 2462 applies to claims for disgorgement imposed as a sanction for violating a federal securities law. The Court holds that it does. Disgorgement in the securities-enforcement context is a "penalty" within the meaning of § 2462, and so disgorgement actions must be commenced within five years of the date the claim accrues.

I

A

After rampant abuses in the securities industry led to the 1929 stock market crash and the Great Depression, Congress enacted a series of laws to ensure that "the highest ethical standards prevail in every facet of the securities industry." *SEC v. Capital Gains Research Bureau, Inc.,* 375 U.S. 180, 186–187 (1963) (internal quotation marks omitted). The second in the series—the Securities Exchange Act of 1934—established the Securities and Exchange Commission (SEC or Commission) to enforce federal securities laws. Congress granted the Commission power to prescribe " 'rules and regulations ... as necessary or appropriate in the public interest or for the protection of investors.' " *Blue Chip Stamps v. Manor Drug Stores,* 421 U.S. 723, 728 (1975). In addition to rulemaking, Congress vested the Commission with "broad authority to conduct investigations into possible violations of the federal securities laws." *SEC v. Jerry T. O'Brien, Inc.,* 467 U.S. 735, 741 (1984). If an investigation uncovers evidence of wrongdoing, the Commission may initiate enforcement actions in federal district court.

Initially, the only statutory remedy available to the SEC in an enforcement action was an injunction barring future violations of securities laws. See 1 T. Hazen, Law of Securities Regulation § 1:37 (7th ed., rev. 2016). In the absence of statutory authorization for monetary remedies, the Commission urged courts to order disgorgement as an exercise of their "inherent equity power to grant relief ancillary to an injunction." *SEC v. Texas Gulf Sulphur Co.,* 312 F.Supp. 77, 91 (S.D.N.Y.1970), aff'd in part and rev'd in part, 446 F.2d 1301 (C.A.2 1971). Generally, disgorgement is a form of "[r]estitution measured by the defendant's wrongful gain." Restatement (Third) of Restitution and Unjust Enrichment § 51, Comment *a,* p. 204 (2010) (Restatement (Third)). Disgorgement requires that the defendant give up "those gains ... properly attributable to the defendant's interference with the claimant's legally protected rights." *Ibid.*

Beginning in the 1970's, courts ordered disgorgement in SEC enforcement proceedings in order to "deprive ... defendants of their profits in order to remove any monetary reward for violating" securities laws and to "protect the investing public by providing an effective deterrent to future violations." *Texas Gulf,* 312 F.Supp., at 92.

In 1990, as part of the Securities Enforcement Remedies and Penny Stock Reform Act, Congress authorized the Commission to seek monetary civil penalties. 104 Stat. 932, codified at 15 U.S.C. § 77t(d). The Act left the Commission with a full panoply of enforcement tools: It may promulgate rules, investigate violations of those rules and the securities laws generally, and seek monetary penalties and injunctive relief for those violations. In the years since the Act, however, the Commission has continued its practice of seeking disgorgement in enforcement proceedings.

This Court has already held that the 5–year statute of limitations set forth in 28 U.S.C. § 2462 applies when the Commission seeks statutory monetary penalties. See *Gabelli v. SEC,* 568 U.S. 442, 454 (2013). The question here is whether § 2462, which applies to any "action, suit or proceeding for the enforcement of any civil fine, penalty, or forfeiture, pecuniary or otherwise," also applies when the SEC seeks disgorgement.

B

Charles Kokesh owned two investment-adviser firms that provided investment advice to business-development companies. In late 2009, the Commission commenced an enforcement action in Federal District Court alleging that between 1995 and 2009, Kokesh, through his firms, misappropriated $34.9 million from four of those development companies. The Commission further alleged that, in order to conceal the misappropriation, Kokesh caused the filing of false and misleading SEC reports and proxy statements. The Commission sought civil monetary penalties, disgorgement, and an injunction barring Kokesh from violating securities laws in the future.

After a 5–day trial, a jury found that Kokesh's actions violated the Investment Company Act of 1940, 15 U.S.C. § 80a–36; the Investment Advisers Act of 1940, 15 U.S.C. §§ 80b–5, 80b–6; and the Securities Exchange Act of 1934, 15 U.S.C. §§ 78m, 78n. The District Court then turned to the task of imposing penalties sought by the Commission. As to the civil monetary penalties, the District Court determined that § 2462's 5–year limitations period precluded any penalties for misappropriation occurring prior to October 27, 2004—that is, five years prior to the date the Commission filed the complaint. App. to Pet. for Cert. 26a. The court ordered Kokesh to pay a civil penalty of $2,354,593, which represented "the amount of funds that [Kokesh] himself received during the limitations period." *Id.,* at 31a–32a. Regarding the Commission's request for a $34.9 million disgorgement judgment—$29.9 million of which resulted from violations outside the limitations period—the court agreed with the Commission that because disgorgement is not a "penalty" within the meaning of § 2462, no limitations period applied. The court therefore entered a disgorgement judgment in the amount of $34.9 million and ordered Kokesh to pay an additional $18.1 million in prejudgment interest.

The Court of Appeals for the Tenth Circuit affirmed. 834 F.3d 1158 (2016). It agreed with the District Court that disgorgement is not a penalty, and further found that disgorgement is not a forfeiture. *Id.*, at 1164–1167. The court thus concluded that the statute of limitations in § 2462 does not apply to SEC disgorgement claims.

This Court granted certiorari, 580 U.S. ——, 137 S.Ct. 810 (2017), to resolve disagreement among the Circuits over whether disgorgement claims in SEC proceedings are subject to the 5–year limitations period of § 2462.

II

Statutes of limitations "se[t] a fixed date when exposure to the specified Government enforcement efforts en[d]." *Gabelli,* 568 U.S., at 448. Such limits are " 'vital to the welfare of society' " and rest on the principle that " 'even wrongdoers are entitled to assume that their sins may be forgotten.' " *Id,* at 449. The statute of limitations at issue here—28 U.S.C. § 2462—finds its roots in a law enacted nearly two centuries ago. 568 U.S., at 445. In its current form, § 2462 establishes a 5–year limitations period for "an action, suit or proceeding for the enforcement of any civil fine, penalty, or forfeiture." This limitations period applies here if SEC disgorgement qualifies as either a fine, penalty, or forfeiture. We hold that SEC disgorgement constitutes a penalty. [3]

A

A "penalty" is a "punishment, whether corporal or pecuniary, imposed and enforced by the State, for a crime or offen[s]e against its laws." *Huntington v. Attrill,* 146 U.S. 657, 667 (1892). This definition gives rise to two principles. First, whether a sanction represents a penalty turns in part on "whether the wrong sought to be redressed is a wrong to the public, or a wrong to the individual." *Id.,* at 668. Although statutes creating private causes of action against wrongdoers may appear—or even be labeled—penal, in many cases "neither the liability imposed nor the remedy given is strictly penal." *Id.,* at 667. This is because "[p]enal laws, strictly and properly, are those imposing punishment for an offense committed against the State." *Ibid.* Second, a pecuniary sanction operates as a penalty only if it is sought "for the purpose of punishment, and to deter others from offending in like manner"—as opposed to compensating a victim for his loss.

---

[3] Nothing in this opinion should be interpreted as an opinion on whether courts possess authority to order disgorgement in SEC enforcement proceedings or on whether courts have properly applied disgorgement principles in this context. The sole question presented in this case is whether disgorgement, as applied in SEC enforcement actions, is subject to §2462's limitations period.

Id., at 668.

The Court has applied these principles in construing the term "penalty." In *Brady v. Daly,* 175 U.S. 148 (1899), for example, a playwright sued a defendant in Federal Circuit Court under a statute providing that copyright infringers " 'shall be liable for damages ... not less than one hundred dollars for the first [act of infringement], and fifty dollars for every subsequent performance, as to the court shall appear to be just.' " *Id.,* at 153. The defendant argued that the Circuit Court lacked jurisdiction on the ground that a separate statute vested district courts with exclusive jurisdiction over actions "to recover a penalty." *Id.,* at 152, 20 S.Ct. 62. To determine whether the statutory damages represented a penalty, this Court noted first that the statute provided "for a recovery of damages for an act which violates the rights of the plaintiff, and gives the right of action solely to him" rather than the public generally, and second, that "the whole recovery is given to the proprietor, and the statute does not provide for a recovery by any other person." *Id.,* at 154, 156. By providing a compensatory remedy for a private wrong, the Court held, the statute did not impose a "penalty." *Id.,* at 154.

Similarly, in construing the statutory ancestor of § 2462, the Court utilized the same principles. In *Meeker v. Lehigh Valley R. Co.,* 236 U.S. 412, 421–422 (1915), the Interstate Commerce Commission, a now-defunct federal agency charged with regulating railroads, ordered a railroad company to refund and pay damages to a shipping company for excessive shipping rates. The railroad company argued that the action was barred by Rev. Stat. § 1047, Comp. Stat. 1913, § 1712 (now 28 U.S.C. § 2462), which imposed a 5–year limitations period upon any " 'suit or prosecution for a penalty or forfeiture, pecuniary or otherwise, accruing under the laws of the United States.' " 236 U.S., at 423. The Court rejected that argument, reasoning that "the words 'penalty or forfeiture' in [the statute] refer to something imposed in a punitive way for an infraction of a public law." *Ibid.* A penalty, the Court held, does "not include a liability imposed [solely] for the purpose of redressing a private injury." *Ibid.* Because the liability imposed was compensatory and paid entirely to a private plaintiff, it was not a "penalty" within the meaning of the statute of limitations. *Ibid.;* see also *Gabelli,* 568 U.S., at 451–452, 133 S.Ct. 1216 ("[P]enalties" in the context of §2462 "go beyond compensation, are intended to punish, and label defendants wrongdoers").

B

Application of the foregoing principles readily demonstrates that SEC disgorgement constitutes a penalty within the meaning of § 2462.

First, SEC disgorgement is imposed by the courts as a consequence for violating what we described in *Meeker* as public laws. The violation for which the remedy is sought is committed against the United States rather than an aggrieved individual—this is why, for example, a securities-enforcement action may proceed even if victims do not support or are not parties to the prosecution. As the Government concedes, "[w]hen the SEC seeks disgorgement, it acts in the public interest, to remedy harm to the public at large, rather than standing in the shoes of particular injured parties." Brief for United States 22. Courts agree. See, *e.g., SEC v. Rind,* 991 F.2d 1486, 1491 (C.A.9 1993) ("[D]isgorgement actions further the Commission's public policy mission of protecting investors and safeguarding the integrity of the markets"); *SEC v. Teo,* 746 F.3d 90, 102 (C.A.3 2014) ("[T]he SEC pursues [disgorgement] 'independent of the claims of individual investors' " in order to " 'promot[e] economic and social policies' ").

Second, SEC disgorgement is imposed for punitive purposes. In *Texas Gulf*—one of the first cases requiring disgorgement in SEC proceedings—the court emphasized the need "to deprive the defendants of their profits in order to ... protect the investing public by providing an effective deterrent to future violations." 312 F.Supp., at 92. In the years since, it has become clear that deterrence is not simply an incidental effect of disgorgement. Rather, courts have consistently held that "[t]he primary purpose of disgorgement orders is to deter violations of the securities laws by depriving violators of their ill-gotten gains." *SEC v. Fischbach Corp.,* 133 F.3d 170, 175 (C.A.2 1997); see also *SEC v. First Jersey Securities, Inc.,* 101 F.3d 1450, 1474 (C.A.2 1996) ("The primary purpose of disgorgement as a remedy for violation of the securities laws is to deprive violators of their ill-gotten gains, thereby effectuating the deterrence objectives of those laws"); *Rind,* 991 F.2d, at 1491 (" 'The deterrent effect of [an SEC] enforcement action would be greatly undermined if securities law violators were not required to disgorge illicit profits' "). Sanctions imposed for the purpose of deterring infractions of public laws are inherently punitive because "deterrence [is] not [a] legitimate nonpunitive governmental objectiv[e]." *Bell v. Wolfish,* 441 U.S. 520, 539, n. 20 (1979); see also *United States v. Bajakajian,* 524 U.S. 321, 329 (1998) ("Deterrence ... has traditionally been viewed as a goal of punishment").

Finally, in many cases, SEC disgorgement is not compensatory. As courts and the Government have employed the remedy, disgorged profits are paid to the district court, and it is "within the court's discretion to determine how and to whom the money will be distributed." *Fischbach Corp.,* 133 F.3d, at 175. Courts have required disgorgement "regardless of whether the disgorged funds will be paid to such investors as restitution." *Id.,* at 176; see *id.,* at 175 ("Although disgorged funds may often go to compensate securities fraud victims for their losses, such compensation is a distinctly secondary goal"). Some disgorged funds are paid to victims; other funds are dispersed to the United States Treasury. See, *e.g., id.,* at 171 (affirming distribution of disgorged funds to Treasury where "no party before the court was entitled to the funds and ... the persons who might have equitable claims were too dispersed for feasible identification and payment"); *SEC v. Lund,* 570 F.Supp. 1397, 1404–1405 (C.D.Cal.1983) (ordering disgorgement and directing trustee to disperse funds to victims if "feasible" and to disperse any remaining money to the Treasury). Even though district courts may distribute the funds to the victims, they have not identified any statutory command that they do so. When an individual is made to pay a noncompensatory sanction to the Government as a consequence of a legal violation, the payment operates as a penalty. See *Porter v. Warner Holding Co.,* 328 U.S. 395, 402 (1946) (distinguishing between restitution paid to an aggrieved party and penalties paid to the Government).

SEC disgorgement thus bears all the hallmarks of a penalty: It is imposed as a consequence of violating a public law and it is intended to deter, not to compensate. The 5–year statute of limitations in § 2462 therefore applies when the SEC seeks disgorgement.

C

The Government's primary response to all of this is that SEC disgorgement is not punitive but "remedial" in that it "lessen[s] the effects of a violation" by " 'restor[ing] the status quo.' " Brief for Respondent 17. As an initial matter, it is not clear that disgorgement, as courts have applied it in the SEC enforcement context, simply returns the defendant to the place he would have occupied had he not broken the law. SEC disgorgement sometimes exceeds the profits gained as a result of the violation. Thus, for example, "an insider trader may be ordered to disgorge not only the unlawful gains that accrue to the wrongdoer directly, but also the benefit that accrues to third parties whose gains can be attributed to the wrongdoer's conduct." *SEC v. Contorinis,* 743 F.3d 296, 302 (C.A.2 2014). Individuals who illegally provide confidential trading information have been forced to disgorge profits gained by individuals who received and traded based on that information—even though they never received any profits. *Ibid.*; see also *SEC v. Warde,* 151 F.3d 42, 49 (C.A.2 1998) ("A tippee's gains are attributable to the tipper, regardless whether benefit accrues to the tipper"); *SEC v. Clark,* 915 F.2d 439, 454 (C.A.9 1990) ("[I]t is well settled that a tipper can be required to disgorge his tippees' profits"). And, as demonstrated by this case, SEC disgorgement sometimes is ordered without consideration of a defendant's expenses that reduced the amount of illegal profit. App. to Pet. for Cert. 43a; see Restatement (Third) § 51, Comment *h,* at 216 ("As a general rule, the defendant is entitled to a deduction for all marginal costs incurred in producing the revenues that are subject to disgorgement. Denial of an otherwise appropriate deduction, by making the defendant liable in excess of net gains, results in a punitive sanction that the law of restitution normally attempts to avoid"). In such cases, disgorgement does not simply restore the status quo; it leaves the defendant worse off. The justification for this practice given by the court below demonstrates that disgorgement in this context is a punitive, rather than a remedial, sanction: Disgorgement, that court explained, is intended not only to "prevent the wrongdoer's unjust enrichment" but also "to deter others' violations of the securities laws." App. to Pet. for Cert. 43a.

True, disgorgement serves compensatory goals in some cases; however, we have emphasized "the fact that sanctions frequently serve more than one purpose." *Austin v. United States,* 509 U.S. 602, 610 (1993). " 'A civil sanction that cannot fairly be said *solely* to serve a remedial purpose, but rather can only be explained as also serving either retributive or deterrent purposes, is punishment, as we have come to understand the term.' " *Id.,* at 621; cf. *Bajakajian* 524 U.S., at 331, n. 6 ("[A] modern statutory forfeiture is a 'fine' for Eighth Amendment purposes if it constitutes punishment even in part"). Because disgorgement orders "go beyond compensation, are intended to punish, and label defendants wrongdoers" as a consequence of violating public laws, *Gabelli,* 568 U.S., at 451–452 they represent a penalty and thus fall within the 5–year statute of limitations of § 2462.

III

Disgorgement, as it is applied in SEC enforcement proceedings, operates as a penalty under § 2462. Accordingly, any claim for disgorgement in an SEC enforcement action must be commenced within five years of the date the claim accrued.

The judgment of the Court of Appeals for the Tenth Circuit is reversed.

It is so ordered.

_____

1. Is Another Shoe About to Drop? In footnote 3 of the above decision, the Court hints that at least some of its members may have questions about disgorgement as a remedy or the procedures used to impose it. Was this a deliberate hint or only a modest concession to one or two justices to keep the decision unanimous? More may be learned when the Court decides this term whether SEC Administrative Law Judges have been validly appointed in compliance with the Appointments Clause of the U.S. Constitution. The Court granted certiorari in Raymond J. Lucas v. SEC, 832 F.3d 277 (D.C. Cir. 2016), to resolve this issue, but has not ruled as of the time of this supplement.

S-1/A 1 d553522ds1a.htm S-1/A

Table of Contents

As filed with the Securities and Exchange Commission on March 21, 2018

Registration No. 333-223182

UNITED STATES
SECURITIES AND EXCHANGE COMMISSION
Washington, D.C. 20549

AMENDMENT NO. 2
TO
FORM S-1
REGISTRATION STATEMENT
Under
The Securities Act of 1933

Dropbox, Inc.
(Exact name of Registrant as specified in its charter)

Delaware	7372	26-0138832
(State or other jurisdiction of incorporation or organization)	(Primary Standard Industrial Classification Code Number)	(I.R.S. Employer Identification Number)

Dropbox, Inc.
333 Brannan Street
San Francisco, California 94107
(415) 857-6800
(Address, including zip code, and telephone number, including area code, of Registrant's principal executive offices)

Andrew W. Houston
Chief Executive Officer
Dropbox, Inc.
333 Brannan Street
San Francisco, California 94107
(415) 857-6800
(Name, address, including zip code, and telephone number, including area code, of agent for service)

Copies to:

Tony Jeffries, Esq.	Bart E. Volkmer, Esq.	Kevin P. Kennedy, Esq.
Rezwan D. Pavri, Esq.	Mary Anne Becking, Esq.	Simpson Thacher & Bartlett LLP
Lisa L. Stimmell, Esq.	Cara M. Angelmar, Esq.	2475 Hanover St
Shannon R. Delahaye, Esq.	Dropbox, Inc.	Palo Alto, California 94304
Wilson Sonsini Goodrich & Rosati, P.C.	333 Brannan Street	(650) 251-5000
650 Page Mill Road	San Francisco, California 94107	
Palo Alto, California 94304	(415) 857-6800	
(650) 493-9300		

Approximate date of commencement of proposed sale to the public: As soon as practicable after this registration statement becomes effective.

If any of the securities being registered on this Form are to be offered on a delayed or continuous basis pursuant to Rule 415 under the Securities Act of 1933 check the following box. ☐

If this Form is filed to register additional securities for an offering pursuant to Rule 462(b) under the Securities Act, please check the following box and list the Securities Act registration statement number of the earlier effective registration statement for the same offering. ☐

If this Form is a post-effective amendment filed pursuant to Rule 462(c) under the Securities Act, check the following box and list the Securities Act registration statement number of the earlier effective registration statement for the same offering. ☐

If this Form is a post-effective amendment filed pursuant to Rule 462(d) under the Securities Act, check the following box and list the Securities Act registration statement number of the earlier effective registration statement for the same offering. ☐

Indicate by check mark whether the registrant is a large accelerated filer, an accelerated filer, a non-accelerated filer, a smaller reporting company, or an emerging growth company. See the definitions of "large accelerated filer," "accelerated filer," "smaller reporting company," and "emerging growth company" in Rule 12b-2 of the Exchange Act.

Large accelerated filer	☐	Accelerated filer	☐
Non-accelerated filer	☒ (Do not check if a smaller reporting company)	Smaller reporting company	☐
Emerging growth company	☐		

If an emerging growth company, indicate by check mark if the registrant has elected not to use the extended transition period for complying with any new or revised financial accounting standards provided pursuant to Section 7(a)(2)(B) of the Securities Act. ☐

The Registrant hereby amends this registration statement on such date or dates as may be necessary to delay its effective date until the Registrant will file a further amendment which specifically states that this registration statement will thereafter become effective in accordance with Section 8(a) of the Securities Act of 1933, as amended, or until the registration statement will become effective on such date as the Securities and Exchange Commission, acting pursuant to said Section 8(a), may determine.

The information in this preliminary prospectus is not complete and may be changed. These securities may not be sold until the registration statement filed with the Securities and Exchange Commission is effective. This preliminary prospectus is not an offer to sell nor does it seek an offer to buy these securities in any jurisdiction where the offer or sale is not permitted.

Subject To Completion. Dated March 21, 2018.

36,000,000 Shares

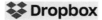

Class A Common Stock

This is an initial public offering of shares of Class A common stock of Dropbox, Inc.

Dropbox, Inc. is offering to sell 26,822,409 shares of Class A common stock in this offering. The selling stockholders identified in this prospectus are offering to sell an additional 9,177,591 shares of Class A common stock. We will not receive any of the proceeds from the sale of the shares being sold by the selling stockholders.

We have three classes of authorized common stock, Class A common stock, Class B common stock, and Class C common stock. The rights of the holders of Class A common stock, Class B common stock, and Class C common stock are identical, except with respect to voting and conversion. Each share of Class A common stock is entitled to one vote per share. Each share of Class B common stock is entitled to ten votes per share and is convertible at any time into one share of Class A common stock. Shares of Class C common stock have no voting rights, except as otherwise required by law, and will convert into Class A common stock, on a share-for-share basis, following the conversion of all outstanding shares of Class B common stock into shares of Class A common stock and upon the date or time specified by the holders of a majority of the outstanding shares of Class A common stock voting as a separate class. Following this offering, outstanding shares of Class B common stock will represent approximately 98.0% of the voting power of our outstanding capital stock.

Prior to this offering, there has been no public market for the Class A common stock. It is currently estimated that the initial public offering price per share will be between $18.00 and $20.00. We have been approved to list the Class A common stock on the Nasdaq Global Select Market under the symbol "DBX".

We will be treated as an "emerging growth company," as defined in the Jumpstart Our Business Startups Act of 2012, for certain purposes until we complete this offering. As such, in this registration statement we have taken advantage of certain reduced disclosure obligations that apply to emerging growth companies regarding selected financial data and executive compensation arrangements.

Salesforce Ventures LLC has entered into an agreement with us pursuant to which it has agreed to purchase $100,000,000 of our Class A common stock in a private placement at a price per share equal to the initial offering price. This transaction is contingent upon, and is scheduled to close immediately subsequent to, the closing of this offering.

See "Risk Factors" beginning on page 16 to read about factors you should consider before buying shares of our Class A common stock.

Neither the Securities and Exchange Commission nor any other regulatory body has approved or disapproved of these securities or passed upon the accuracy or adequacy of this prospectus. Any representation to the contrary is a criminal offense.

	Per share	Total
Initial public offering price	$	$
Underwriting discount(1)	$	$
Proceeds, before expenses, to Dropbox, Inc.	$	$
Proceeds, before expenses, to selling stockholders	$	$

(1) See the section titled "Underwriting (Conflicts of Interest)" for a description of the compensation payable to the underwriters.

To the extent that the underwriters sell more than 36,000,000 shares of Class A common stock, the underwriters have the option to purchase up to an additional 5,400,000 shares from Dropbox, Inc. at the initial public offering price less the underwriting discount.

The underwriters expect to deliver the shares against payment in New York, New York, on or about   , 2018.

Goldman Sachs & Co. LLC	J.P. Morgan	Deutsche Bank Securities	Allen & Company LLC	BofA Merrill Lynch

RBC Capital Markets   Jefferies   Macquarie Capital

Canaccord Genuity   JMP Securities   KeyBanc Capital Markets   Piper Jaffray

Prospectus dated   , 2018

83

Table of Contents

Table of Contents

Photograph by Alexandra Gavillet

Our mission

Unleash the world's creative energy by designing a more enlightened way of working.

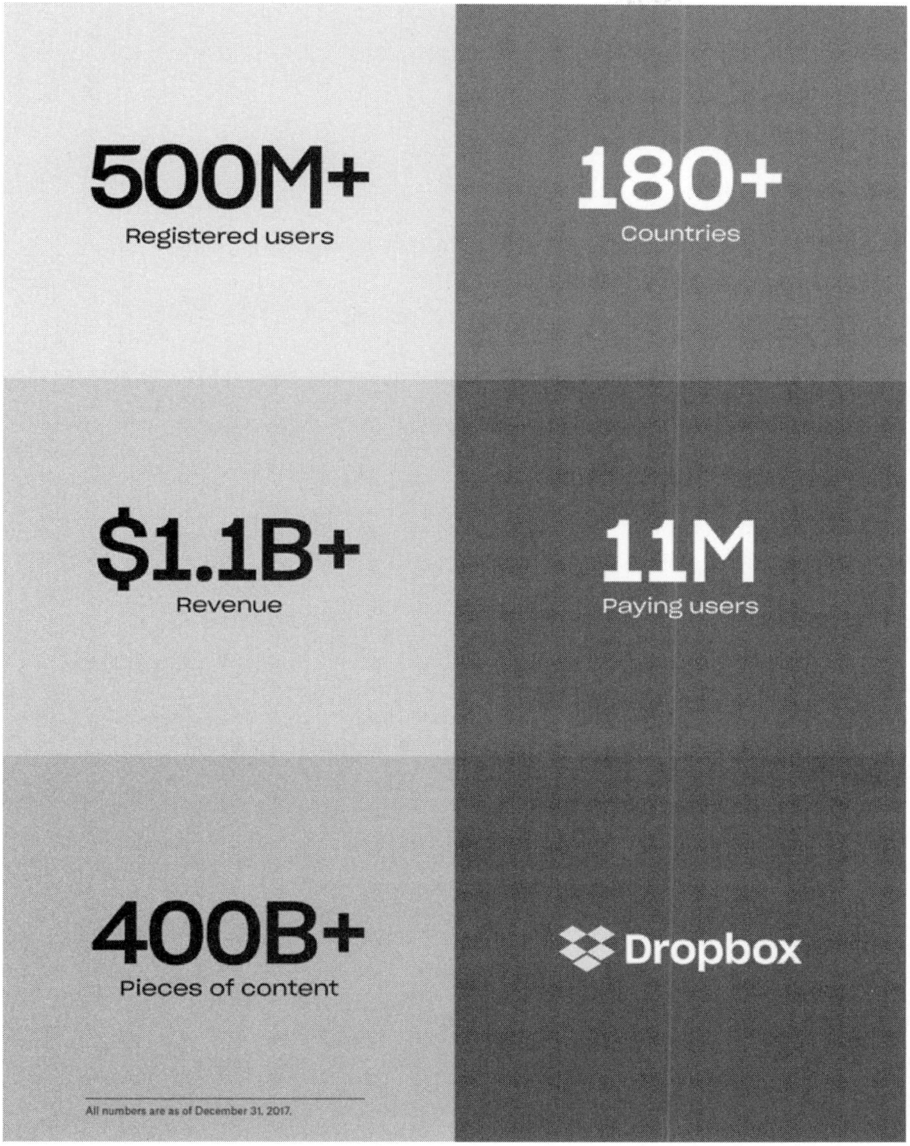
500M+
Registered users
180+
Countries
$1.1B+
Revenue
11M
Paying users
400B+
Pieces of content
Dropbox
All numbers are as of December 31, 2017.

TABLE OF CONTENTS

Prospectus

	Page
Prospectus Summary	1
Risk Factors	16
Special Note Regarding Forward-Looking Statements	46
Industry And Market Data	48
Use of Proceeds	49
Dividend Policy	50
Capitalization	51
Dilution	55
Selected Consolidated Financial and Other Data	59
Management's Discussion and Analysis of Financial Condition and Results of Operations	61
A Letter from Drew & Arash	95
Business	101
Management	137
Executive Compensation	146
Certain Relationships, Related Party Transactions, and Other Transactions	161
Principal and Selling Stockholders	165
Description of Capital Stock	169
Shares Eligible for Future Sale	178
Material U.S. Federal Income Tax Consequences to Non-U.S. Holders of Our Class A Common Stock	181
Underwriting (Conflicts of Interest)	185
Concurrent Private Placement	195
Legal Matters	195
Experts	195
Where You Can Find Additional Information	195
Index to Consolidated Financial Statements	F-1

————————————

Through and including   , 2018 (the 25th day after the date of this prospectus), all dealers effecting transactions in these securities, whether or not participating in this offering, may be required to deliver a prospectus. This is in addition to a dealer's obligation to deliver a prospectus when acting as an underwriter and with respect to an unsold allotment or subscription.

————————————

Neither we, the selling stockholders, nor any of the underwriters have authorized anyone to provide any information or to make any representations other than those contained in this prospectus or in any free writing prospectuses we have prepared. Neither we, the selling stockholders, nor any of the underwriters take responsibility for, and can provide no assurance as to the reliability of, any other information that others may give you. This prospectus is an offer to sell only the shares offered hereby, but only under circumstances and in jurisdictions where it is lawful to do so. The information contained in this prospectus is current only as of its date, regardless of the time of delivery of this prospectus or of any sale of our Class A common stock.

For investors outside the United States: Neither we, the selling stockholders, nor any of the underwriters have done anything that would permit our initial public offering or possession or distribution of this prospectus in any jurisdiction where action for that purpose is required, other than in the United States. Persons outside the United States who come into possession of this prospectus must inform themselves about, and observe any restrictions relating to, the offering of the shares of our Class A common stock and the distribution of this prospectus outside the United States.

PROSPECTUS SUMMARY

This summary highlights selected information that is presented in greater detail elsewhere in this prospectus. This summary does not contain all of the information you should consider before investing in our Class A common stock. You should read this entire prospectus carefully, including the sections titled "Risk Factors" and "Management's Discussion and Analysis of Financial Condition and Results of Operations," and our consolidated financial statements, and the related notes included elsewhere in this prospectus, before making an investment decision. Unless the context otherwise requires, the terms "Dropbox," "the Company," "we," "us," and "our" in this prospectus refer to Dropbox, Inc. and its consolidated subsidiaries, and references to our "common stock" include our Class A common stock, Class B common stock, and Class C common stock.

DROPBOX, INC.

Our Business

Our modern economy runs on knowledge. Today, knowledge lives in the cloud as digital content, and Dropbox is a global collaboration platform where more and more of this content is created, accessed, and shared with the world. We serve more than 500 million registered users across 180 countries.

Dropbox was founded in 2007 with a simple idea: Life would be a lot better if everyone could access their most important information anytime from any device. Over the past decade, we've largely accomplished that mission—but along the way we recognized that for most of our users, sharing and collaborating on Dropbox was even more valuable than storing files.

Our market opportunity has grown as we've expanded from keeping files in sync to keeping teams in sync. Today, Dropbox is well positioned to reimagine the way work gets done. We're focused on reducing the inordinate amount of time and energy the world wastes on "work about work"—tedious tasks like searching for content, switching between applications, and managing workflows.

We want to free up our users to spend more of their time on the work that truly matters. Our mission is to unleash the world's creative energy by designing a more enlightened way of working.

We believe the need for our platform will continue to grow as teams become more fluid and global, and content is increasingly fragmented across incompatible tools and devices. Dropbox breaks down silos by centralizing the flow of information between the products and services our users prefer, even if they're not our own.

By solving these universal problems, we've become invaluable to our users. The popularity of our platform drives viral growth, which has allowed us to scale rapidly and efficiently. We've built a thriving global business with over 11 million paying users.

Our revenue was $603.8 million, $844.8 million, and $1,106.8 million in 2015, 2016, and 2017, respectively, representing an annual growth rate of 40% and 31%, respectively. We generated net losses of $325.9 million, $210.2 million, and $111.7 million in 2015, 2016, and 2017, respectively. We also generated positive free cash flow of $137.4 million and $305.0 million in 2016 and 2017, respectively, compared to negative free cash flow of $63.9 million in 2015.

1

Our Users

We're constantly inspired by the diverse ways people use Dropbox to bring their ideas to life and achieve their missions faster. Here are just a few examples:

- Nobel Prize-winning researchers sync data with collaborators to speed development of new scientific breakthroughs.

- Designers for a sustainable apparel company iterate on new designs and coordinate store openings.

- A commercial construction company shares blueprints with subcontractors on job sites and sends bids to prospective clients.

- A Fortune 500 online travel company keeps its global workforce connected with business partners around the world.

- Pro bono lawyers at a refugee assistance organization collect and share information across continents to save lives.

What Sets Us Apart

Since the beginning, we've focused on simplifying the lives of our users. In a world where business software can be frustrating to use, challenging to integrate, and expensive to sell, we take a different approach.

Simple and intuitive design

While traditional tools developed in the desktop age have struggled to keep up with evolving user demands, Dropbox was designed for the cloud era. We build simple, beautiful products that bring joy to our users and make it easier for them to do their best work. Unencumbered by legacy features, we can perfect the aspects of our platform that matter most today, such as the mobile experience and the ability to work in teams.

Open ecosystem

We know people will continue to use a wide variety of tools and platforms. That's why we've built Dropbox to work seamlessly with other products, integrating with partners from Google and Microsoft to Slack and Autodesk. More than 75% of Dropbox Business teams have linked to one or more third-party applications.

Viral, bottom-up adoption

Our 500 million registered users are our best salespeople. They've spread Dropbox to their friends and brought us into their offices. Every year, millions of individual users sign up for Dropbox at work. Bottom-up adoption within organizations has been critical to our success as users increasingly choose their own tools at work. We generate over 90% of our revenue from self-serve channels—users who purchase a subscription through our app or website.

Performance and security

Our custom-built infrastructure allows us to maintain high standards of performance, availability, and security. Dropbox is built on proprietary, block-level sync technology to achieve industry-leading performance. In 2016, IDC highlighted our sync performance as best-in-class, outperforming competitors on multiple sync tests, including upload and download speeds for large files. We designed our platform with multiple layers of redundancy to guard against data loss and deliver high availability. We also offer numerous layers of protection, from secure file data transfer and encryption to network configuration and application-level controls.

2

Industry Trends in Our Favor

Content is increasingly scattered

The proliferation of devices, operating systems, and applications has dramatically increased the volume and complexity of content in the workplace. Content is now routinely scattered across multiple silos, making it harder to access. According to a 2016 IDC report, more than half of companies ranging from 100 to 5,000+ employees use at least three repositories for accessing documents on a weekly basis.

The tools people use are fragmented

Content created at work tends to follow a predictable pattern: It's authored, sent out for feedback, and shared or published once it's done. At the same time, teams are organizing that content and coordinating tasks around it. But many of the tools people use today don't work well together and support only one or two steps of the content lifecycle. This requires users to constantly switch between these tools and makes it even harder to get work done.

Teams have become more fluid and global

Technology hasn't kept up with a modern workforce that's increasingly fluid and mobile. People work together on teams that span different functions, organizations, and geographies. A 2016 study by Deloitte found that 37% of the global workforce is now mobile, 30% of full-time employees primarily work remotely, and 20% of the workforce is made up of temporary workers, contractors, and freelancers. The ability to swiftly disseminate content and its relevant context is critical to keeping teams in sync.

"Work about work" is wasteful and stifles creativity

The combination of scattered content, fragmented tools, and fluid team structures has led to decreased workplace productivity. According to a report by McKinsey & Company, knowledge workers spend approximately 60% of their time at work on tedious tasks such as searching for content, reviewing email, and re-sharing context to keep team members in the loop—what we call "work about work." This means they spend just 40% of their time doing the jobs they were hired to do.

Individual users are changing the way software is adopted and purchased

Software purchasing decisions have traditionally been made by an organization's IT department, which often deploys products that employees don't like and many refuse to adopt. As individuals increasingly choose their own tools at work, purchasing power has become more decentralized. A 2017 IDC report noted that new devices and software were being adopted at a faster rate by individual users than by IT departments.

Our Solution

Dropbox allows individuals, teams, and organizations to collaborate more effectively. Anyone can sign up for free through our website or app, and upgrade to a paid subscription plan for premium features. Our platform offers an elegant solution to the challenges described above.

Key elements of our platform

- *Unified home for content.* We provide a unified home for the world's content and the relevant context around it. To date, our users have added more than 400 billion pieces of content to Dropbox, totaling over an exabyte (more than 1,000,000,000 gigabytes) of data. When users join Dropbox, they gain

3

access to a digital workspace that supports the full content lifecycle—they can create and organize their content, access it from anywhere, share it with internal and external collaborators, and review feedback and history.

- *Global sharing network.* We've built one of the largest collaboration platforms in the world, with more than 4.5 billion connections to shared content. We cater to the needs of dynamic, dispersed teams. The overwhelming majority of our customers use Dropbox to share and collaborate. As we continue to grow, more users benefit from frictionless sharing, and powerful network effects increase the utility and stickiness of our platform.

- *New product experiences.* The insights we glean from our community of users lead us to develop new product experiences, like Paper, Smart Sync, and Showcase. Machine learning further improves the user experience by enabling more intelligent search and better organization and utility of information. This ongoing innovation broadens the value of our platform and deepens user engagement.

These elements reinforce one another to produce a powerful flywheel effect. As users create and share more content with more people, they expand our global sharing network. This network allows us to gather insights and feedback that help us create new product experiences. And with our scale, we can instantly put these innovations in the hands of millions. This, in turn, helps attract more users and content, which further propels the flywheel.

Our Growth Strategy

Increase adoption and paid conversion

We designed Dropbox to be easy to try, use, and buy. Anyone can create an account and be up and running in minutes. We believe that our current registered user base represents a significant opportunity to increase our revenue. We estimate that approximately 300 million of our registered users have characteristics—including specific email domains, devices, and geographies—that make them more likely than other registered users to pay over time. Substantially all of our paying users share at least one of these characteristics. We reach our users through in-product notifications on our website and across hundreds of millions of actively connected devices without any external marketing spend. We define an actively connected device as a desktop, laptop, phone, or tablet on which our app has been installed, and from which our app has been launched, and made a request to our servers at least once in the most recent quarter.

Upgrade our paying users

We offer a range of paid subscription plans, from Plus and Professional for individuals, to Standard, Advanced, and Enterprise for teams. We analyze usage patterns within our network and run hundreds of targeted marketing campaigns to encourage paying users to upgrade their plans. For example, we prompt individual subscribers who collaborate with others on Dropbox to purchase our Standard or Advanced plans for a better team experience. In 2017, over 40% of new Dropbox Business teams included a member who was previously a subscriber to one of our individual paid plans. We believe that a large majority of individual customers use Dropbox for work, which creates an opportunity to significantly increase conversion to Dropbox Business team offerings over time.

Apply insights to build new product experiences

As our community of users grows, we gain more insight into their needs and pain points. We translate these insights into new product experiences that support the entire content lifecycle. For example, we learned through analytics and research that our users often work with many different types of content. As a result, we added the ability to embed rich media in Paper so they can pull everything together in one place—from InVision graphics and Google slides to Spotify tracks and Vimeo clips.

4

Expand our ecosystem

Our open and thriving ecosystem fosters deeper relationships with our users and makes Dropbox more valuable to them over time. The scale and reach of our platform is enhanced by a number of third-party applications, developers, and technology partners. As of December 31, 2017, Dropbox was receiving over 50 billion API calls per month, and more than 500,000 developers had registered and built applications on our platform.

Our Market Opportunity

Over the past decade, Dropbox has pioneered the worldwide adoption of file sync and share software. We've since expanded our capabilities and introduced new product experiences to help our users get work done. For the second consecutive year, Gartner has named Dropbox a leader in their Magic Quadrant for Content Collaboration Platforms.

Our addressable market includes collaborative applications, content management, project and portfolio management, and public cloud storage. IDC estimates that investment in these categories will total more than $50 billion in 2019.

As one of the few large-scale collaboration platforms that serves customers of all sizes, we also have an opportunity to reach a broad population of independent knowledge and creative workers. We believe that this market hasn't traditionally been included in IT spending estimates.

Risk Factors Summary

Our business is subject to numerous risks and uncertainties, including those highlighted in the section titled "Risk Factors" immediately following this prospectus summary. These risks include, but are not limited to, the following:

- Our business depends on our ability to retain and upgrade paying users, and any decline in renewals or upgrades could adversely affect our future results of operations.

- Our future growth could be harmed if we fail to attract new users or convert registered users to paying users.

- Our revenue growth rate has declined in recent periods and may continue to slow in the future.

- We have a history of net losses, we anticipate increasing expenses in the future, and we may not be able to achieve or maintain profitability.

- Our business could be damaged, and we could be subject to liability if there is any unauthorized access to our data or our users' content, including through privacy and data security breaches.

- Our business could be harmed by any significant disruption of service on our platform or loss of content.

- We generate revenue from sales of subscriptions to our platform, and any decline in demand for our platform or for content collaboration solutions in general could negatively impact our business.

- Our business depends upon the interoperability of our platform across devices, operating systems, and third-party applications that we do not control.

- We operate in competitive markets, and we must continue to compete effectively.

- We may not be able to respond to rapid technological changes, extend our platform, or develop new features.

5

- We may not successfully manage our growth or plan for future growth.

- The multi-class structure of our common stock will have the effect of concentrating voting control with those stockholders who held our capital stock prior to the completion of this offering, and it may depress the trading price of our Class A common stock.

Channels for Disclosure of Information

Investors, the media, and others should note that, following the completion of this offering, we intend to announce material information to the public through filings with the Securities and Exchange Commission, or the SEC, the investor relations page on our website, press releases, public conference calls, webcasts, our company news site at dropbox.com/news, and our corporate blog at blogs.dropbox.com.

The information disclosed by the foregoing channels could be deemed to be material information. As such, we encourage investors, the media, and others to follow the channels listed above and to review the information disclosed through such channels.

Any updates to the list of disclosure channels through which we will announce information will be posted on the investor relations page on our website.

Corporate Information

We were incorporated in May 2007 as Evenflow, Inc., a Delaware corporation, and changed our name to Dropbox, Inc. in October 2009. Our principal executive offices are located at 333 Brannan Street, San Francisco, California, 94107, and our telephone number is (415) 857-6800. Our website address is www.dropbox.com. Information contained on, or that can be accessed through, our website does not constitute part of this prospectus and inclusions of our website address in this prospectus are inactive textual references only.

"Dropbox," "Dropbox Paper," "Dropbox Smart Sync," "Dropbox Showcase," our logo, and our other registered or common law trademarks, service marks, or trade names appearing in this prospectus are the property of Dropbox, Inc. We refer to Dropbox Paper as Paper, Dropbox Smart Sync as Smart Sync, and Dropbox Showcase as Showcase in this prospectus. Other trademarks and trade names referred to in this prospectus are the property of their respective owners.

JOBS Act

We will be treated as an "emerging growth company," as defined in the Jumpstart Our Business Startups Act of 2012, for certain purposes until we complete this offering. As such, in this registration statement we have taken advantage of certain reduced disclosure obligations that apply to emerging growth companies regarding selected financial data and executive compensation arrangements.

6

THE OFFERING

Class A common stock offered by us	26,822,409 shares
Class A common stock offered by the selling stockholders	9,177,591 shares
Class A common stock sold by us in the concurrent private placement	Immediately subsequent to the closing of this offering, Salesforce Ventures LLC will purchase from us in a private placement $100.0 million of our Class A common stock at a price per share equal to the initial public offering price. Based on an assumed initial public offering price of $19.00 per share, which is the midpoint of the estimated offering price range set forth on the cover page of this prospectus, this would be 5,263,158 shares. We will receive the full proceeds and will not pay any underwriting discounts or commissions with respect to the shares that are sold in the private placement. The sale of the shares in the private placement is contingent upon the completion of this offering. The sale of these shares to Salesforce Ventures LLC will not be registered in this offering and will be subject to a market standoff agreement with us and lock-up agreement with the underwriters for a period of up to 180 days after the date of this prospectus. See "Shares Eligible for Future Sale—Lock-Up and Market Standoff Agreements" for additional information regarding such restrictions. We refer to the private placement of these shares of Class A common stock as the concurrent private placement.
Class A common stock to be outstanding after this offering and the concurrent private placement	53,080,406 shares (excluding 14,733,333 shares of our Class A common stock subject to restricted stock awards, or RSAs, that were granted to our co-founders, or collectively, the Co-Founder Grants, and vest upon the satisfaction of a service condition and achievement of certain stock price goals)
Class B common stock to be outstanding after this offering and the concurrent private placement	339,323,858 shares
Class C common stock to be outstanding after this offering and the concurrent private placement	None
Total Class A common stock, Class B common stock, and Class C common stock to be outstanding after this offering and the concurrent private placement	392,404,264 shares
Option to purchase additional shares of Class A common stock from us	5,400,000 shares

7

Use of proceeds	We estimate that the net proceeds to us from the sale of shares of our Class A common stock in this offering and the concurrent private placement will be approximately $579.9 million (or approximately $678.0 million if the underwriters' option to purchase additional shares of our Class A common stock from us and the selling stockholders is exercised in full), based upon the assumed initial public offering price of $19.00 per share, which is the midpoint of the estimated offering price range set forth on the cover page of this prospectus, and after deducting estimated underwriting discounts and commissions and estimated offering expenses payable by us.
	The principal purposes of this offering are to increase our capitalization and financial flexibility, create a public market for our Class A common stock, and enable access to the public equity markets for us and our stockholders. We intend to use a portion of the net proceeds we receive from this offering and the concurrent private placement to repay $193.1 million that is expected to be outstanding immediately prior to the completion of this offering under our revolving credit facility, which we intend to draw down prior to the completion of this offering to satisfy tax withholding and remittance obligations of $193.1 million related to the settlement of certain restricted stock units, or RSUs, for which the service condition was satisfied as of December 31, 2017, and for which we expect the liquidity event-related performance vesting condition, or the Performance Vesting Condition, to be satisfied upon the effectiveness of our registration statement related to this offering. This amount is based upon the assumed initial public offering price of $19.00 per share, which is the midpoint of the estimated offering price range set forth on the cover page of this prospectus. We also intend to use the net proceeds we receive from this offering and the concurrent private placement for general corporate purposes, including working capital, operating expenses, and capital expenditures. Additionally, we may use a portion of the net proceeds we receive from this offering and the concurrent private placement to acquire businesses, products, services, or technologies. However, we do not have agreements or commitments for any material acquisitions at this time. We will not receive any of the proceeds from the sale of Class A common stock in this offering by the selling stockholders. See "Use of Proceeds" for additional information.
Voting rights	Shares of our Class A common stock are entitled to one vote per share.
	Shares of our Class B common stock are entitled to ten votes per share.
	Shares of our Class C common stock have no voting rights, except as otherwise required by law.
	Holders of our Class A common stock and Class B common stock will generally vote together as a single class, unless otherwise

8

required by law or our amended and restated certificate of incorporation. The holders of our outstanding Class B common stock will hold approximately 98.0% of the voting power of our outstanding capital stock following this offering and the concurrent private placement and will have the ability to control the outcome of matters submitted to our stockholders for approval, including the election of our directors and the approval of any change in control transaction. Additionally, our executive officers, directors, and holders of 5% or more of our common stock will hold, in the aggregate, approximately 68.8% of the voting power of our outstanding capital stock following this offering and the concurrent private placement. Prior to the effectiveness of our registration statement related to this offering, our co-founders are expected to enter into voting agreements with certain of our stockholders, which voting agreements will remain in effect after the completion of this offering. These voting agreements may cover an aggregate of up to 7% of the voting power of our outstanding capital stock after our initial public offering and the concurrent private placement. See "Principal and Selling Stockholders" and "Description of Capital Stock" for additional information.

Proposed Nasdaq Global Select Market trading symbol "DBX"

Conflict of interest

Affiliates of Goldman Sachs & Co. LLC, J.P. Morgan Securities LLC, Deutsche Bank Securities Inc., and Merrill Lynch, Pierce, Fenner & Smith Incorporated, underwriters in this offering, will receive at least 5% of the net proceeds of this offering in connection with the repayment of $193.1 million that is expected to be outstanding immediately prior to the completion of this offering under our revolving credit facility. See "Use of Proceeds." Accordingly, this offering is being made in compliance with the requirements of FINRA Rule 5121. This rule requires, among other things, that a "qualified independent underwriter" has participated in the preparation of, and has exercised the usual standards of "due diligence" with respect to, the registration statement. Allen & Company LLC has agreed to act as qualified independent underwriter for this offering and to undertake the legal responsibilities and liabilities of an underwriter under the Securities Act of 1933, as amended, or the Securities Act.

The number of shares of our Class A common stock, Class B common stock, and Class C common stock that will be outstanding after this offering and the concurrent private placement is based on 11,817,248 shares of our Class A common stock, 348,501,449 shares of our Class B common stock, and no shares of our Class C common stock outstanding as of December 31, 2017, and reflects:

- (i) 258,620 shares of preferred stock and 2,609,951 shares of Class B common stock that will convert into Class A common stock immediately prior to the completion of this offering pursuant to the terms of certain transfer agreements, and (ii) 147,310,563 shares of preferred stock that will automatically convert into shares of Class B common stock immediately prior to the completion of this offering

9

pursuant to the terms of our amended and restated certificate of incorporation, which we refer to, collectively, as the Capital Stock Conversions; and

- 15,897,254 shares of our Class B common stock subject to RSUs, for which the service condition was satisfied as of December 31, 2017, and for which we expect the Performance Vesting Condition to be satisfied upon the effectiveness of our registration statement related to this offering (after repurchasing 10,163,817 shares of our Class B common stock subject to RSUs to satisfy tax withholding obligations at an assumed tax rate of 39%, with an equivalent number of shares of our Class A common stock becoming available for issuance under our 2018 Equity Incentive Plan, or our 2018 Plan), or the RSU Settlement.

The shares of our Class A common stock, Class B common stock, and Class C common stock outstanding as of December 31, 2017 excludes the following:

- 14,733,333 shares of our Class A common stock subject to RSAs that were granted pursuant to the Co-Founder Grants, and vest upon the satisfaction of a service condition and achievement of certain stock price goals;

- 4,959,492 shares of our Class B common stock issuable upon the exercise of options to purchase shares of our Class B common stock outstanding as of December 31, 2017, with a weighted-average exercise price of $10.52 per share;

- 16,707,823 shares of our Class A common stock and 12,158,666 shares of our Class B common stock subject to RSUs outstanding, but for which the service condition was not satisfied, as of December 31, 2017;

- 10,921,416 shares of our Class A common stock subject to RSUs granted after December 31, 2017;

- 65,982,109 shares of our Class A common stock reserved for future issuance under our equity compensation plans, consisting of:

  - 51,532,143 shares of our Class A common stock to be reserved for future issuance under our 2018 Plan, which will become effective prior to the completion of this offering (including the shares that will be repurchased by us in connection with the RSU Settlement);

  - 10,313,134 shares of our Class A common stock reserved for future issuance under our 2017 Equity Incentive Plan, or our 2017 Plan, which number of shares includes an additional 1,333,333 shares of our Class A common stock reserved for issuance under our 2017 Plan that was approved by our Board of Directors in February 2018 (and which our stockholders approved in March 2018), and will be added to the shares of our Class A common stock to be reserved for future issuance under our 2018 Plan upon its effectiveness;

  - 4,136,832 shares of our Class A common stock to be reserved for future issuance under our 2018 Employee Stock Purchase Plan, or our ESPP, which will become effective prior to the completion of this offering, but no offering periods under the ESPP will commence unless and until otherwise determined by our Board of Directors; and

- 45,505,158 shares of our Class C common stock reserved for future issuance under certain other equity compensation plans, consisting of:

  - 41,368,326 shares of our Class C common stock to be reserved for future issuance under our 2018 Class C Stock Incentive Plan, or our 2018 Class C Plan, which will become effective prior to the completion of this offering; and

  - 4,136,832 shares of our Class C common stock to be reserved for future issuance under our 2018 Class C Employee Stock Purchase Plan, or our Class C ESPP, which will become effective prior to the completion of this offering, but no offering periods under the Class C ESPP will commence unless and until otherwise determined by our Board of Directors.

The Co-Founder Grants are legally issued and outstanding shares of our Class A common stock and, as a result, the holders have certain stockholder rights, such as the right to vote the shares immediately upon grant and prior to their vesting.

Our 2018 Plan and ESPP each provides for annual automatic increases in the number of shares of our Class A common stock reserved thereunder, and our 2018 Plan also provides for increases to the number of shares of our Class A common stock that may be granted thereunder based on shares under our 2008 Equity Incentive Plan, or our 2008 Plan, and 2017 Plan that expire, are forfeited, or otherwise repurchased by us, as more fully described in the section titled "Executive Compensation—Employee Benefits and Stock Plans." Additionally, if and when our Board of Directors determines to use our 2018 Class C Plan and Class C ESPP, such plans will provide for annual automatic increases in the number of shares of our Class C common stock reserved thereunder.

Except as otherwise indicated, all information in this prospectus assumes:

- a 1-for-1.5 reverse stock split effected on March 7, 2018;

- the Capital Stock Conversions will occur immediately prior to the completion of this offering;

- the issuance of 5,263,158 shares of our Class A common stock to Salesforce Ventures LLC upon the closing of the concurrent private placement immediately subsequent to the closing of this offering, based upon the assumed initial public offering price of $19.00 per share, which is the midpoint of the estimated offering price range set forth on the cover page of this prospectus;

- the filing and effectiveness of our amended and restated certificate of incorporation in Delaware and the effectiveness of our amended and restated bylaws, each of which will occur immediately prior to the completion of this offering;

- the conversion of shares of our Class B common stock held by certain selling stockholders into an equivalent number of shares of our Class A common stock upon the sale by the selling stockholders in this offering;

- no exercise of outstanding stock options or settlement of outstanding RSUs subsequent to December 31, 2017, other than the RSU Settlement; and

- no exercise by the underwriters of their option to purchase up to an additional 5,400,000 shares of our Class A common stock from us.

11

SUMMARY CONSOLIDATED FINANCIAL AND OTHER DATA

The following summary consolidated financial data should be read in conjunction with "Management's Discussion and Analysis of Financial Condition and Results of Operations" and the consolidated financial statements and related notes thereto included elsewhere in this prospectus. The consolidated statements of operations data for each of the years ended December 31, 2015, 2016, and 2017, and the consolidated balance sheet data as of December 31, 2017 are derived from our audited consolidated financial statements that are included elsewhere in this prospectus. Our historical results are not necessarily indicative of our future results. The summary consolidated financial data in this section are not intended to replace the consolidated financial statements and related notes thereto included elsewhere in this prospectus and are qualified in their entirety by the consolidated financial statements and related notes thereto included elsewhere in this prospectus.

Consolidated Statements of Operations Data

	Year ended December 31,		
	2015	2016	2017
	(In millions, except for per share amounts)		
Revenue	$ 603.8	$ 844.8	$ 1,106.8
Cost of revenue(1)	407.4	390.6	368.9
Gross profit	196.4	454.2	737.9
Operating expenses:(1)			
Research and development	201.6	289.7	380.3
Sales and marketing	193.1	250.6	314.0
General and administrative	107.9	107.4	157.3
Total operating expenses	502.6	647.7	851.6
Loss from operations	(306.2)	(193.5)	(113.7)
Interest expense, net	(15.2)	(16.4)	(11.0)
Other income (expense), net	(4.2)	4.9	13.2
Loss before income taxes	(325.6)	(205.0)	(111.5)
Provision for income taxes	(0.3)	(5.2)	(0.2)
Net loss	$ (325.9)	$ (210.2)	$ (111.7)
Net loss per share attributable to common stockholders, basic and diluted(2)	$ (1.77)	$ (1.11)	$ (0.57)
Weighted-average shares used in computing net loss per share attributable to common stockholders, basic and diluted	184.5	189.1	195.9
Pro forma net loss per share attributable to common stockholders, basic and diluted(2)			$ (0.31)
Weighted-average shares used in computing pro forma net loss per share attributable to common stockholders, basic and diluted			358.6

12

(1) Includes stock-based compensation as follows:

	Year ended December 31,		
	2015	2016	2017
	(In millions)		
Cost of revenue	$ 2.6	$ 8.2	$ 12.2
Research and development	36.1	72.7	93.1
Sales and marketing	19.8	44.6	33.7
General and administrative	7.6	22.1	25.6
Total stock-based compensation	$66.1	$147.6	$ 164.6

(2) See Note 12, "Net Loss Per Share" to our consolidated financial statements included elsewhere in this prospectus for an explanation of the method used to calculate basic and diluted net loss per share attributable to common stockholders and Note 13, "Unaudited Pro Forma Net Loss Per Share" for an explanation of the method used to calculate pro forma net loss per share attributable to common stockholders.

Consolidated Balance Sheet Data

	As of December 31, 2017		
	Actual	Pro forma(1)	Pro forma as adjusted(2)(3)
	(In millions)		
Cash and cash equivalents	$ 430.0	$ 430.0	$ 816.6
Working capital	(220.3)	(413.4)	166.3
Property and equipment, net	341.9	341.9	341.9
Total assets	1,019.9	1,019.9	1,406.5
Total deferred revenue	419.2	419.2	419.2
Total capital lease obligations	174.3	174.3	174.3
Revolving credit facility	—	193.1	—
Total stockholders' equity (deficit)	102.9	(90.2)	489.5

(1) The pro forma column in the balance sheet data table above reflects (a) the Capital Stock Conversions, as if such conversions had occurred on December 31, 2017, (b) the filing and effectiveness of our amended and restated certificate of incorporation in Delaware that will become effective immediately prior to the completion of this offering, (c) stock-based compensation expense of $415.6 million associated with the RSU Settlement, (d) the net issuance of 15,897,254 shares of our Class B common stock upon the RSU Settlement, (e) the borrowing of $193.1 million under our revolving credit facility to satisfy our tax withholding and remittance obligations related to the RSU Settlement, and (f) a cash payment of $193.1 million to satisfy our tax withholding and remittance obligations related to the RSU Settlement, which amounts in (e) and (f) are based upon the assumed initial public offering price of $19.00 per share, which is the midpoint of the estimated offering price range set forth on the cover page of this prospectus.

(2) The pro forma as adjusted column in the balance sheet data table above gives effect to (a) the pro forma adjustments set forth above, (b) the sale and issuance by us of 32,085,567 shares of our Class A common stock in this offering and the concurrent private placement, based upon the assumed initial public offering price of $19.00 per share, which is the midpoint of the estimated offering price range set forth on the cover page of this prospectus, and after deducting estimated underwriting discounts and commissions and estimated offering expenses payable by us, and (c) the use of proceeds from the offering to repay $193.1 million drawn down under our revolving credit facility to satisfy our tax withholding and remittance obligations related to the RSU Settlement and pay related net costs of approximately $0.2 million.

(3) Each $1.00 increase or decrease in the assumed initial public offering price of $19.00 per share, which is the midpoint of the estimated offering price range set forth on the cover page of this prospectus, would increase or decrease, as applicable, (a) the amount of our pro forma as adjusted cash and cash equivalents, working capital, total assets, and total stockholders' equity by $25.6 million, assuming that the number of shares offered by us, as set forth on the cover page of

13

this prospectus, remains the same, after deducting estimated underwriting discounts and commissions payable by us, (b) the amount we would be required to draw down under our revolving credit facility to satisfy our tax withholding and remittance obligations related to the RSU Settlement by $10.2 million, and (c) the amount we would be required to pay to satisfy our tax withholding and remittance obligations related to the RSU Settlement by $10.2 million. An increase or decrease of 1.0 million shares in the number of shares offered by us would increase or decrease, as applicable, the amount of our pro forma as adjusted cash and cash equivalents, working capital, total assets, and total stockholders' equity by $18.2 million, assuming the assumed initial public offering price remains the same, and after deducting estimated underwriting discounts and commissions payable by us.

Key Business Metrics

We review a number of operating and financial metrics, including the following key metrics to evaluate our business, measure our performance, identify trends affecting our business, formulate business plans, and make strategic decisions.

Paying users

We define paying users as the number of users who have active paid licenses for access to our platform as of the end of the period. One person would count as multiple paying users if the person had more than one active license. For example, a 50-person Dropbox Business team would count as 50 paying users, and an individual Dropbox Plus user would count as one paying user. If that individual Dropbox Plus user was also part of the 50-person Dropbox Business team, we would count the individual as two paying users.

The below table sets forth the number of paying users as of December 31, 2015, 2016, and 2017:

	As of December 31,		
	2015	2016	2017
	(In millions)		
Paying users	6.5	8.8	11.0

Average revenue per paying user

We define average revenue per paying user, or ARPU, as our revenue for the period presented divided by the average paying users during the same period. For interim periods, we use annualized revenue, which is calculated by dividing the revenue for the particular period by the number of days in that period and multiplying this value by 365 days. Average paying users are calculated based on adding the number of paying users as of the beginning of the period to the number of paying users as of the end of the period, and then dividing by two.

The below table sets forth our ARPU for the years ended December 31, 2015, 2016, and 2017.

	Year ended December 31,		
	2015	2016	2017
ARPU	$113.54	$110.54	$111.91

Free cash flow

We define free cash flow, or FCF, as net cash provided by operating activities less capital expenditures.

14

The following is a reconciliation of FCF to the most comparable GAAP measure, net cash provided by operating activities:

	Year ended December 31,		
	2015	2016	2017
	(In millions)		
Net cash provided by operating activities	$ 14.8	$ 252.6	$330.3
Capital expenditures	(78.7)	(115.2)	(25.3)
Free cash flow	$(63.9)	$ 137.4	$305.0

See the section titled "Management's Discussion and Analysis of Financial Condition and Results of Operations—Non-GAAP Financial Measure" for additional information.

15

RISK FACTORS

Investing in our Class A common stock involves a high degree of risk. You should consider carefully the risks and uncertainties described below, together with all of the other information in this prospectus, including the section titled "Management's Discussion and Analysis of Financial Condition and Results of Operations" and our consolidated financial statements and related notes, before making a decision to invest in our Class A common stock. Our business, results of operations, financial condition, or prospects could also be harmed by risks and uncertainties that are not presently known to us or that we currently believe are not material. If any of the risks actually occur, our business, results of operations, financial condition, and prospects could be materially and adversely affected. In that event, the market price of our Class A common stock could decline, and you could lose all or part of your investment.

Risks Related to Our Business and Our Industry

Our business depends on our ability to retain and upgrade paying users, and any decline in renewals or upgrades could adversely affect our future results of operations.

Our business depends upon our ability to maintain and expand our relationships with our users. Our business is subscription based, and paying users are not obligated to and may not renew their subscriptions after their existing subscriptions expire. As a result, we cannot provide assurance that paying users will renew their subscriptions utilizing the same tier of our products or upgrade to premium offerings. Renewals of subscriptions to our platform may decline or fluctuate because of several factors, such as dissatisfaction with our products and support, a user no longer having a need for our products, or the perception that competitive products provide better or less expensive options. In addition, some paying users downgrade or do not renew their subscriptions.

We encourage paying users to upgrade to our premium offerings by recommending additional features and through in-product prompts and notifications. Additionally, we seek to expand within organizations through viral means by adding new users, having workplaces purchase additional products, or expanding the use of Dropbox into other departments within a workplace. We often see enterprise IT decision-makers deciding to adopt Dropbox after noticing substantial organic adoption by individuals and teams within the organization. If our paying users fail to renew or cancel their subscriptions, or if we fail to upgrade our paying users to premium offerings or expand within organizations, our business, results of operations, and financial condition may be harmed.

Although it is important to our business that our users renew their subscriptions after their existing subscriptions expire and that we expand our commercial relationships with our users, given the volume of our users, we do not track the retention rates of our individual users. As a result, we may be unable to address any retention issues with specific users in a timely manner, which could harm our business.

Our future growth could be harmed if we fail to attract new users or convert registered users to paying users.

We must continually add new users to grow our business beyond our current user base and to replace users who choose not to continue to use our platform. Historically, our revenue has been driven by our self-serve model, and we generate more than 90% of our revenue from self-serve channels. Any decrease in user satisfaction with our products or support could harm our brand, word-of-mouth referrals, and ability to grow.

Additionally, many of our users initially access our platform free of charge. We strive to demonstrate the value of our platform to our registered users, thereby encouraging them to convert to paying users through in-product prompts and notifications, and time-limited trials of paid subscription plans. As of December 31, 2017, we served over 500 million registered users but only 11 million paying users. The actual number of unique users is lower than we report as one person may register more than once for our platform. As a result, we have fewer unique registered users that we may be able to convert to paying users. A majority of our registered users may never convert to a paid subscription to our platform.

16

In addition, our user growth rate may slow in the future as our market penetration rates increase and we turn our focus to converting registered users to paying users rather than growing the total number of registered users. If we are not able to continue to expand our user base or fail to convert our registered users to paying users, demand for our paid services and our revenue may grow more slowly than expected or decline.

Our revenue growth rate has declined in recent periods and may continue to slow in the future.

We have experienced significant revenue growth in prior periods. However, our rates of revenue growth are slowing and may continue to slow in the future. Many factors may contribute to declines in our growth rates, including higher market penetration, increased competition, slowing demand for our platform, a decrease in the growth of the overall content collaboration market, a failure by us to continue capitalizing on growth opportunities, and the maturation of our business, among others. You should not rely on the revenue growth of any prior quarterly or annual period as an indication of our future performance. If our growth rates decline, investors' perceptions of our business and the trading price of our Class A common stock could be adversely affected.

We have a history of net losses, we anticipate increasing expenses in the future, and we may not be able to achieve or maintain profitability.

We have incurred net losses on an annual basis since our inception. We incurred net losses of $325.9 million, $210.2 million, and $111.7 million in 2015, 2016, and 2017, respectively, and we had an accumulated deficit of $1,049.7 million as of December 31, 2017. As we strive to grow our business, we expect expenses to increase in the near term, particularly as we continue to make investments to scale our business. For example, we will need an increasing amount of technical infrastructure to continue to satisfy the needs of our user base. We also expect our research and development expenses to increase as we plan to continue to hire employees for our engineering, product, and design teams to support these efforts. In addition, we will incur additional rent expense in connection with our move to our new corporate headquarters, and additional general and administrative expenses to support both our growth as well as our transition to being a publicly traded company. These investments may not result in increased revenue or growth in our business. We may encounter unforeseen or unpredictable factors, including unforeseen operating expenses, complications, or delays, which may result in increased costs. Furthermore, it is difficult to predict the size and growth rate of our market, user demand for our platform, user adoption and renewal of our platform, the entry of competitive products and services, or the success of existing competitive products and services. As a result, we may not achieve or maintain profitability in future periods. If we fail to grow our revenue sufficiently to keep pace with our investments and other expenses, our results of operations and financial condition would be adversely affected.

Our business could be damaged, and we could be subject to liability if there is any unauthorized access to our data or our users' content, including through privacy and data security breaches.

The use of our platform involves the transmission, storage, and processing of user content, some of which may be considered personally identifiable, confidential, or sensitive. We face security threats from malicious third parties that could obtain unauthorized access to our systems and networks. We anticipate that these threats will continue to grow in scope and complexity over time. For example, in 2016, we learned that an old set of Dropbox user credentials for approximately 68 million accounts was released. These credentials consisted of email addresses and passwords protected by cryptographic techniques known as hashing and salting. Hashing and salting can make it more difficult to obtain the original password, but may not fully protect the original password from being obtained. We believe these Dropbox user credentials were obtained in 2012 and related to a security incident we disclosed to users. In response, we notified all existing users we believed to be affected and completed a password reset for anyone who had not updated their password since mid-2012. We have responded to this event by expanding our security team and data monitoring capabilities and continuing to work on features such as two-factor authentication to increase protection of user information. While we believe our corrective actions will reduce the likelihood of similar incidents occurring in the future, third parties might use techniques

17

that we are unable to defend against to compromise and infiltrate our systems and networks. We may fail to detect the existence of a breach of user content and be unable to prevent unauthorized access to user and company content. The techniques used to obtain unauthorized access, disable or degrade service, or sabotage systems change frequently and are often not recognized until launched against a target. They may originate from less regulated or remote areas around the world, or from state-sponsored actors. If our security measures are breached, or our users' content is otherwise accessed through unauthorized means, or if any such actions are believed to occur, our platform may be perceived as insecure, and we may lose existing users or fail to attract and retain new users.

We may rely on third parties when deploying our infrastructure, and in doing so, expose it to security risks outside of our direct control. We rely on outside vendors and contractors to perform services necessary for the operation of the business, and they may fail to adequately secure our user and company content.

Third parties may attempt to compromise our employees and their privileged access into internal systems to gain access to accounts, our information, our networks, or our systems. Employee error, malfeasance, or other errors in the storage, use, or transmission of personal information could result in an actual or perceived breach of user privacy. Our users may also disclose or lose control of their passwords, or use the same or similar passwords on third parties' systems, which could lead to unauthorized access to their accounts on our platform.

Any unauthorized or inadvertent access to, or an actual or perceived security breach of, our systems or networks could result in an actual or perceived loss of, or unauthorized access to, our data or our users' content, regulatory investigations and orders, litigation, indemnity obligations, damages, penalties, fines, and other costs in connection with actual and alleged contractual breaches, violations of applicable laws and regulations, and other liabilities. Any such incident could also materially damage our reputation and harm our business, results of operations, and financial condition, including reducing our revenue, causing us to issue credits to users, negatively impacting our ability to accept and process user payment information, eroding our users' trust in our services and payment solutions, subjecting us to costly user notification or remediation, harming our ability to retain users, harming our brand, or increasing our cost of acquiring new users. We maintain errors, omissions, and cyber liability insurance policies covering certain security and privacy damages. However, we cannot be certain that our coverage will be adequate for liabilities actually incurred or that insurance will continue to be available to us on economically reasonable terms, or at all. Further, if a high profile security breach occurs with respect to another content collaboration solutions provider, our users and potential users could lose trust in the security of content collaboration solutions providers generally, which could adversely impact our ability to retain users or attract new ones.

Our business could be harmed by any significant disruption of service on our platform or loss of content.

Our brand, reputation, and ability to attract, retain, and serve our users are dependent upon the reliable performance of our platform, including our underlying technical infrastructure. Our users rely on our platform to store digital copies of their valuable content, including financial records, business information, documents, photos, and other important content. Our technical infrastructure may not be adequately designed with sufficient reliability and redundancy to avoid performance delays or outages that could be harmful to our business. If our platform is unavailable when users attempt to access it, or if it does not load as quickly as they expect, users may not use our platform as often in the future, or at all.

As our user base and the amount and types of information stored, synced, and shared on our platform continues to grow, we will need an increasing amount of technical infrastructure, including network capacity and computing power, to continue to satisfy the needs of our users. During 2015 and 2016, we migrated the vast majority of user content to our own custom-built infrastructure in co-location facilities that we directly lease and operate. As we add to our infrastructure, we may move or transfer additional content.

Further, as we continue to grow and scale our business to meet the needs of our users, we may overestimate or underestimate our infrastructure capacity requirements, which could adversely affect our results of operations.

18

The costs associated with leasing and maintaining our custom-built infrastructure in co-location facilities and third-party datacenters already constitute a significant portion of our capital and operating expenses. We continuously evaluate our short- and long-term infrastructure capacity requirements to ensure adequate capacity for new and existing users while minimizing unnecessary excess capacity costs. If we overestimate the demand for our platform and therefore secure excess infrastructure capacity, our operating margins could be reduced. If we underestimate our infrastructure capacity requirements, we may not be able to service the expanding needs of new and existing users, and our hosting facilities, network, or systems may fail.

In addition, the datacenters that we use are vulnerable to damage or interruption from human error, intentional bad acts, earthquakes, floods, fires, war, terrorist attacks, power losses, hardware failures, systems failures, telecommunications failures, and similar events, any of which could disrupt our service, destroy user content, or prevent us from being able to continuously back up or record changes in our users' content. In the event of significant physical damage to one of these datacenters, it may take a significant period of time to achieve full resumption of our services, and our disaster recovery planning may not account for all eventualities. Damage or interruptions to these datacenters could harm our platform and business.

We generate revenue from sales of subscriptions to our platform, and any decline in demand for our platform or for content collaboration solutions in general could negatively impact our business.

We generate, and expect to continue to generate, revenue from the sale of subscriptions to our platform. As a result, widespread acceptance and use of content collaboration solutions in general, and our platform in particular, is critical to our future growth and success. If the content collaboration market fails to grow or grows more slowly than we currently anticipate, demand for our platform could be negatively affected.

Changes in user preferences for content collaboration may have a disproportionately greater impact on us than if we offered multiple platforms or disparate products. Demand for content collaboration solutions in general, and our platform in particular, is affected by a number of factors, many of which are beyond our control. Some of these potential factors include:

- awareness of the content collaboration category generally;
- availability of products and services that compete with ours;
- ease of adoption and use;
- features and platform experience;
- performance;
- brand;
- security and privacy;
- customer support; and
- pricing.

The content collaboration market is subject to rapidly changing user demand and trends in preferences. If we fail to successfully predict and address these changes and trends, meet user demands, or achieve more widespread market acceptance of our platform, our business, results of operations, and financial condition could be harmed.

Our business depends upon the interoperability of our platform across devices, operating systems, and third-party applications that we do not control.

One of the most important features of our platform is its broad interoperability with a range of diverse devices, operating systems, and third-party applications. Our platform is accessible from the web and from

19

107

devices running Windows, Mac OS, iOS, Android, WindowsMobile, and Linux. We also have integrations with Microsoft, Adobe, Apple, Salesforce, Atlassian, Slack, IBM, Cisco, VMware, Okta, Symantec, Palo Alto Networks, and a variety of other productivity, collaboration, data management, and security vendors. We are dependent on the accessibility of our platform across these third-party operating systems and applications that we do not control. Several of our competitors own, develop, operate, or distribute operating systems, app stores, third-party datacenter services, and other software, and also have material business relationships with companies that own, develop, operate, or distribute operating systems, applications markets, third-party datacenter services, and other software that our platform requires in order to operate. Moreover, some of these competitors have inherent advantages developing products and services that more tightly integrate with their software and hardware platforms or those of their business partners.

Third-party services and products are constantly evolving, and we may not be able to modify our platform to assure its compatibility with that of other third parties following development changes. In addition, some of our competitors may be able to disrupt the operations or compatibility of our platform with their products or services, or exert strong business influence on our ability to, and terms on which we, operate and distribute our platform. For example, we currently offer products that directly compete with several large technology companies that we rely on to ensure the interoperability of our platform with their products or services. As our respective products evolve, we expect this level of competition to increase. Should any of our competitors modify their products or standards in a manner that degrades the functionality of our platform or gives preferential treatment to competitive products or services, whether to enhance their competitive position or for any other reason, the interoperability of our platform with these products could decrease and our business, results of operations, and financial condition could be harmed.

We operate in competitive markets, and we must continue to compete effectively.

The market for content collaboration platforms is competitive and rapidly changing. Certain features of our platform compete in the cloud storage market with products offered by Amazon, Apple, Google, and Microsoft, and in the content collaboration market with products offered by Atlassian, Google, and Microsoft. We compete with Box on a more limited basis in the cloud storage market for deployments by large enterprises. We also compete with smaller private companies that offer point solutions in the cloud storage market or the content collaboration market. We believe the principal competitive factors in our markets include the following:

- user-centric design;

- ease of adoption and use;

- scale of user network;

- features and platform experience;

- performance;

- brand;

- security and privacy;

- accessibility across several devices, operating systems, and applications;

- third-party integration;

- customer support;

- continued innovation; and

- pricing.

With the introduction of new technologies and market entrants, we expect competition to intensify in the future. Many of our actual and potential competitors benefit from competitive advantages over us, such as greater

20

108

name recognition, longer operating histories, more varied products and services, larger marketing budgets, more established marketing relationships, access to larger user bases, major distribution agreements with hardware manufacturers and resellers, and greater financial, technical, and other resources. Some of our competitors may make acquisitions or enter into strategic relationships to offer a broader range of products and services than we do. These combinations may make it more difficult for us to compete effectively. We expect these trends to continue as competitors attempt to strengthen or maintain their market positions.

Demand for our platform is also sensitive to price. Many factors, including our marketing, user acquisition and technology costs, and our current and future competitors' pricing and marketing strategies, can significantly affect our pricing strategies. Certain of our competitors offer, or may in the future offer, lower-priced or free products or services that compete with our platform or may bundle and offer a broader range of products and services. Similarly, certain competitors may use marketing strategies that enable them to acquire users at a lower cost than us. There can be no assurance that we will not be forced to engage in price-cutting initiatives or to increase our marketing and other expenses to attract and retain users in response to competitive pressures, either of which could materially and adversely affect our business, results of operations, and financial condition.

We may not be able to respond to rapid technological changes, extend our platform, or develop new features.

The content collaboration market is characterized by rapid technological change and frequent new product and service introductions. Our ability to grow our user base and increase revenue from existing users will depend heavily on our ability to enhance and improve our platform, introduce new features and products, and interoperate across an increasing range of devices, operating systems, and third-party applications. Users may require features and capabilities that our current platform does not have. We invest significantly in research and development, and our goal is to focus our spending on measures that improve quality and ease of adoption and create organic user demand for our platform. For example, we recently introduced Paper, a new collaborative product experience, and Smart Sync, a new advanced productivity feature, to add additional functionality to our platform. There is no assurance that our enhancements to our platform or our new product experiences, features, or capabilities will be compelling to our users or gain market acceptance. If our research and development investments do not accurately anticipate user demand, or if we fail to develop our platform in a manner that satisfies user preferences in a timely and cost-effective manner, we may fail to retain our existing users or increase demand for our platform.

The introduction of new products and services by competitors or the development of entirely new technologies to replace existing offerings could make our platform obsolete or adversely affect our business, results of operations, and financial condition. We may experience difficulties with software development, design, or marketing that could delay or prevent our development, introduction, or implementation of new product experiences, features, or capabilities. We have in the past experienced delays in our internally planned release dates of new features and capabilities, and there can be no assurance that new product experiences, features, or capabilities will be released according to schedule. Any delays could result in adverse publicity, loss of revenue or market acceptance, or claims by users brought against us, all of which could have a material and adverse effect on our reputation, business, results of operations, and financial condition. Moreover, new productivity features to our platform, such as Smart Sync, may require substantial investment, and we have no assurance that such investments will be successful. If users do not widely adopt our new product experiences, features, and capabilities, we may not be able to realize a return on our investment. If we are unable to develop, license, or acquire new features and capabilities to our platform on a timely and cost-effective basis, or if such enhancements do not achieve market acceptance, our business, results of operations, and financial condition could be adversely affected.

We may not successfully manage our growth or plan for future growth.

Since our founding in 2007, we have experienced rapid growth. For example, our headcount has grown from 1,446 employees as of December 31, 2015, to 1,858 employees as of December 31, 2017, with employees

21

located both in the United States and internationally. The growth and expansion of our business places a continuous significant strain on our management, operational, and financial resources. Further growth of our operations to support our user base or our expanding third-party relationships, our information technology systems, and our internal controls and procedures may not be adequate to support our operations. In addition, as we continue to grow, we face challenges of integrating, developing, and motivating a rapidly growing employee base in various countries around the world. Certain members of our management have not previously worked together for an extended period of time and some do not have experience managing a public company, which may affect how they manage our growth. Managing our growth will also require significant expenditures and allocation of valuable management resources.

In addition, our rapid growth may make it difficult to evaluate our future prospects. Our ability to forecast our future results of operations is subject to a number of uncertainties, including our ability to effectively plan for and model future growth. We have encountered in the past, and may encounter in the future, risks and uncertainties frequently experienced by growing companies in rapidly changing industries. If we fail to achieve the necessary level of efficiency in our organization as it grows, or if we are not able to accurately forecast future growth, our business, results of operations, and financial condition could be harmed.

Our lack of a significant outbound sales force may limit the potential growth of our business.

Historically, our business model has been driven by organic adoption and viral growth, with more than 90% of our revenue generated from self-serve channels. As a result, we do not have a significant outbound sales force, which has enabled us to be more efficient with our sales and marketing spend. Although we believe our business model can continue to scale without a large outbound sales force, our word-of-mouth and user referral marketing model may not continue to be as successful as we anticipate, and our limited experience selling directly to large organizations through our outbound sales force may impede our future growth. As we continue to scale our business, an enhanced sales infrastructure could assist in reaching larger organizations and growing our revenue. Identifying and recruiting additional qualified sales personnel and training them would require significant time, expense, and attention, and would significantly impact our business model. Further, adding more sales personnel would change our cost structure and results of operations, and we may have to reduce other expenses in order to accommodate a corresponding increase in sales and marketing expenses. If our limited experience selling and marketing to large organizations prevents us from reaching larger organizations and growing our revenue, and if we are unable to hire, develop, and retain talented sales personnel in the future, our business, results of operations, and financial condition could be adversely affected.

We may expand sales to large organizations, which could lengthen sales cycles and result in greater deployment challenges.

As our business evolves, we may need to invest more resources into sales to large organizations. Large organizations may undertake a significant evaluation and negotiation process, which can lengthen our sales cycle. We may also face unexpected deployment challenges with large organizations or more complicated deployment of our platform. Large organizations may demand more configuration and integration of our platform or require additional security management or control features. We may spend substantial time, effort, and money on sales efforts to large organizations without any assurance that our efforts will produce any sales. As a result, sales to large organizations may lead to greater unpredictability in our business, results of operations, and financial condition.

Any failure to offer high-quality customer support may harm our relationships with our users and our financial results.

We have designed our platform to be easy to adopt and use with minimal to no support necessary. Any increased user demand for customer support could increase costs and harm our results of operations. In addition, as we continue to grow our operations and support our global user base, we need to be able to continue to provide

22

efficient customer support that meets our customers' needs globally at scale. Paying users receive additional customer support features and the number of our paying users has grown significantly, which will put additional pressure on our support organization. For example, the number of paying users has grown from 6.5 million as of December 31, 2015, to 11 million as of December 31, 2017. If we are unable to provide efficient customer support globally at scale, our ability to grow our operations may be harmed and we may need to hire additional support personnel, which could harm our results of operations. Our new user signups are highly dependent on our business reputation and on positive recommendations from our existing users. Any failure to maintain high-quality customer support, or a market perception that we do not maintain high-quality customer support, could harm our reputation, business, results of operations, and financial condition.

Our quarterly results may fluctuate significantly and may not fully reflect the underlying performance of our business.

Our quarterly results of operations, including our revenue, gross margin, operating margin, profitability, cash flow from operations, and deferred revenue, may vary significantly in the future and period-to-period comparisons of our results of operations may not be meaningful. Accordingly, the results of any one quarter should not be relied upon as an indication of future performance. Our quarterly results of operations may fluctuate as a result of a variety of factors, many of which are outside of our control, and as a result, may not fully reflect the underlying performance of our business. Fluctuation in quarterly results may negatively impact the value of our securities. Factors that may cause fluctuations in our quarterly results of operations include, without limitation, those listed below:

- our ability to retain and upgrade paying users;

- our ability to attract new paying users and convert registered to paying users;

- the timing of expenses and recognition of revenue;

- the amount and timing of operating expenses related to the maintenance and expansion of our business, operations, and infrastructure, as well as entry into operating and capital leases;

- the timing of expenses related to acquisitions;

- any large indemnification payments to our users or other third parties;

- changes in our pricing policies or those of our competitors;

- the timing and success of new product feature and service introductions by us or our competitors;

- network outages or actual or perceived security breaches;

- changes in the competitive dynamics of our industry, including consolidation among competitors;

- changes in laws and regulations that impact our business; and

- general economic and market conditions.

Our results of operations may not immediately reflect downturns or upturns in sales because we recognize revenue from our users over the term of their subscriptions with us.

We recognize revenue from subscriptions to our platform over the terms of these subscriptions. Our subscription arrangements generally have monthly or annual contractual terms, and we also have a small percentage of multi-year contractual terms. Amounts that have been billed are initially recorded as deferred revenue until the revenue is recognized. As a result, a large portion of our revenue for each quarter reflects deferred revenue from subscriptions entered into during previous quarters, and downturns or upturns in subscription sales, or renewals and potential changes in our pricing policies may not be reflected in our results of operations until later periods. Our subscription model also makes it difficult for us to rapidly increase our revenue through additional sales in any period, as subscription revenue from new users is recognized over the

23

applicable subscription term. By contrast, a significant majority of our costs are expensed as incurred, which occurs as soon as a user starts using our platform. As a result, an increase in users could result in our recognition of more costs than revenue in the earlier portion of the subscription term. We may not attain sufficient revenue to maintain positive cash flow from operations or achieve profitability in any given period.

We depend on our key personnel and other highly qualified personnel, and if we fail to attract, integrate, and retain our personnel, and maintain our unique corporate culture, our business could be harmed.

We depend on the continued service and performance of our key personnel. In particular, Andrew W. Houston, our President and Chief Executive Officer and one of our co-founders, is critical to our vision, strategic direction, culture, and offerings. Some of our other key personnel have recently joined us and are still being integrated into our company. We may continue to make changes to our management team, which could make it difficult to execute on our business plans and strategies. New hires also require significant training and, in most cases, take significant time before they achieve full productivity. Our failure to successfully integrate these key personnel into our business could adversely affect our business.

We do not have long-term employment agreements with any of our officers or key personnel. In addition, many of our key technologies and systems are custom-made for our business by our key personnel. The loss of key personnel, including key members of our management team, as well as certain of our key marketing, sales, product development, or technology personnel, could disrupt our operations and have an adverse effect on our ability to grow our business.

To execute our growth plan, we must attract and retain highly qualified personnel. Competition for these employees is intense, particularly in the San Francisco Bay Area where our headquarters are located, and we may not be successful in attracting and retaining qualified personnel. We have from time to time in the past experienced, and we expect to continue to experience, difficulty in hiring and retaining highly skilled employees with appropriate qualifications. Our recent hires and planned hires may not become as productive as we expect, and we may be unable to hire, integrate, or retain sufficient numbers of qualified individuals. Many of the companies with which we compete for experienced personnel have greater resources than we have. In addition, in making employment decisions, particularly in the internet and high-technology industries, job candidates often consider the value of the equity they are to receive in connection with their employment. Employees may be more likely to leave us if the shares they own or the shares underlying their equity incentive awards have significantly appreciated or significantly reduced in value. Many of our employees may receive significant proceeds from sales of our equity in the public markets after this offering, which may reduce their motivation to continue to work for us. If we fail to attract new personnel, or fail to retain and motivate our current personnel, our business and growth prospects could be harmed.

Additionally, if we do not maintain and continue to develop our corporate culture as we grow and evolve, it could harm our ability to foster the innovation, creativity, and teamwork we believe that we need to support our growth. Additions of executive-level management and large numbers of employees could significantly and adversely impact our culture.

Our business depends on a strong brand, and if we are not able to maintain and enhance our brand, our ability to expand our base of users will be impaired and our business, results of operations, and financial condition will be harmed.

We believe that our brand identity and awareness have contributed to our success and have helped fuel our efficient go-to-market strategy. We also believe that maintaining and enhancing the Dropbox brand is critical to expanding our base of users. We anticipate that, as our market becomes increasingly competitive, maintaining and enhancing our brand may become increasingly difficult and expensive. Any unfavorable publicity or consumer perception of our platform or the providers of content collaboration solutions generally could adversely affect our reputation and our ability to attract and retain users. Additionally, if we fail to promote and maintain

24

the Dropbox brand, or if we incur excessive expenses in this effort, our business, results of operations, and financial condition will be materially and adversely affected.

We are continuing to expand our operations outside the United States, where we may be subject to increased business and economic risks that could impact our results of operations.

We have paying users across 180 countries and approximately half of our revenue in the year ended December 31, 2017 was generated from paying users outside the United States. We expect to continue to expand our international operations, which may include opening offices in new jurisdictions and providing our platform in additional languages. Any new markets or countries into which we attempt to sell subscriptions to our platform may not be receptive. For example, we may not be able to expand further in some markets if we are not able to satisfy certain government- and industry-specific requirements. In addition, our ability to manage our business and conduct our operations internationally requires considerable management attention and resources and is subject to the particular challenges of supporting a rapidly growing business in an environment of multiple languages, cultures, customs, legal and regulatory systems, alternative dispute systems, and commercial markets. International expansion has required, and will continue to require, investment of significant funds and other resources. Operating internationally subjects us to new risks and may increase risks that we currently face, including risks associated with:

- recruiting and retaining talented and capable employees outside the United States, and maintaining our company culture across all of our offices;

- providing our platform and operating our business across a significant distance, in different languages and among different cultures, including the potential need to modify our platform and features to ensure that they are culturally appropriate and relevant in different countries;

- compliance with applicable international laws and regulations, including laws and regulations with respect to privacy, data protection, consumer protection, and unsolicited email, and the risk of penalties to our users and individual members of management or employees if our practices are deemed to be out of compliance;

- management of an employee base in jurisdictions that may not give us the same employment and retention flexibility as does the United States;

- operating in jurisdictions that do not protect intellectual property rights to the same extent as does the United States;

- compliance by us and our business partners with anti-corruption laws, import and export control laws, tariffs, trade barriers, economic sanctions, and other regulatory limitations on our ability to provide our platform in certain international markets;

- foreign exchange controls that might require significant lead time in setting up operations in certain geographic territories and might prevent us from repatriating cash earned outside the United States;

- political and economic instability;

- double taxation of our international earnings and potentially adverse tax consequences due to changes in the income and other tax laws of the United States or the international jurisdictions in which we operate; and

- higher costs of doing business internationally, including increased accounting, travel, infrastructure, and legal compliance costs.

Compliance with laws and regulations applicable to our global operations substantially increases our cost of doing business in international jurisdictions. We may be unable to keep current with changes in laws and regulations as they change. Although we have implemented policies and procedures designed to support compliance with these laws and regulations, there can be no assurance that we will always maintain compliance

25

or that all of our employees, contractors, partners, and agents will comply. Any violations could result in enforcement actions, fines, civil and criminal penalties, damages, injunctions, or reputational harm. If we are unable comply with these laws and regulations or manage the complexity of our global operations successfully, our business, results of operations, and financial condition could be adversely affected.

Our results of operations, which are reported in U.S. dollars, could be adversely affected if currency exchange rates fluctuate substantially in the future.

We conduct our business across 180 countries around the world. As we continue to expand our international operations, we will become more exposed to the effects of fluctuations in currency exchange rates. This exposure is the result of selling in multiple currencies and operating in foreign countries where the functional currency is the local currency. In 2017, 29% of our sales were denominated in currencies other than U.S. dollars. Our expenses, by contrast, are primarily denominated in U.S. dollars. As a result, any increase in the value of the U.S. dollar against these foreign currencies could cause our revenue to decline relative to our costs, thereby decreasing our gross margins. Our results of operations are primarily subject to fluctuations in the euro and British pound sterling. Because we conduct business in currencies other than U.S. dollars, but report our results of operations in U.S. dollars, we also face remeasurement exposure to fluctuations in currency exchange rates, which could hinder our ability to predict our future results and earnings and could materially impact our results of operations. We do not currently maintain a program to hedge exposures to non-U.S. dollar currencies.

We depend on our infrastructure and third-party datacenters, and any disruption in the operation of these facilities or failure to renew the services could adversely affect our business.

We host our services and serve all of our users using a combination of our own custom-built infrastructure that we lease and operate in co-location facilities and third-party datacenter services such as Amazon Web Services. While we typically control and have access to the servers we operate in co-location facilities and the components of our custom-built infrastructure that are located in those co-location facilities, we control neither the operation of these facilities nor our third-party service providers. Furthermore, we have no physical access or control over the services provided by Amazon Web Services.

Datacenter leases and agreements with the providers of datacenter services expire at various times. The owners of these datacenters and providers of these datacenter services may have no obligation to renew their agreements with us on commercially reasonable terms, or at all. Problems faced by datacenters, with our third-party datacenter service providers, with the telecommunications network providers with whom we or they contract, or with the systems by which our telecommunications providers allocate capacity among their users, including us, could adversely affect the experience of our users. Our third-party datacenter operators could decide to close their facilities or cease providing services without adequate notice. In addition, any financial difficulties, such as bankruptcy, faced by our third-party datacenters operators or any of the service providers with whom we or they contract may have negative effects on our business, the nature and extent of which are difficult to predict.

If the datacenters and service providers that we use are unable to keep up with our growing needs for capacity, or if we are unable to renew our agreements with datacenters, and service providers on commercially reasonable terms, we may be required to transfer servers or content to new datacenters or engage new service providers, and we may incur significant costs, and possible service interruption in connection with doing so. Any changes in third-party service levels at datacenters or any real or perceived errors, defects, disruptions, or other performance problems with our platform could harm our reputation and may result in damage to, or loss or compromise of, our users' content. Interruptions in our platform might, among other things, reduce our revenue, cause us to issue refunds to users, subject us to potential liability, harm our reputation, or decrease our renewal rates.

26

We have relationships with third parties to provide, develop, and create applications that integrate with our platform, and our business could be harmed if we are not able to continue these relationships.

We use software and services licensed and procured from third parties to develop and offer our platform. We may need to obtain future licenses and services from third parties to use intellectual property and technology associated with the development of our platform, which might not be available to us on acceptable terms, or at all. Any loss of the right to use any software or services required for the development and maintenance of our platform could result in delays in the provision of our platform until equivalent technology is either developed by us, or, if available from others, is identified, obtained, and integrated, which could harm our platform and business. Any errors or defects in third-party software or services could result in errors or a failure of our platform, which could harm our business, results of operations, and financial condition.

We also depend on our ecosystem of developers to create applications that will integrate with our platform. As of December 31, 2017, Dropbox was receiving over 50 billion API calls per month, and more than 500,000 developers had registered and built applications on our platform. Our reliance on this ecosystem of developers creates certain business risks relating to the quality of the applications built using our APIs, service interruptions of our platform from these applications, lack of service support for these applications, and possession of intellectual property rights associated with these applications. We may not have the ability to control or prevent these risks. As a result, issues relating to these applications could adversely affect our business, brand, and reputation.

We are subject to a variety of U.S. and international laws that could subject us to claims, increase the cost of operations, or otherwise harm our business due to changes in the laws, changes in the interpretations of the laws, greater enforcement of the laws, or investigations into compliance with the laws.

We are subject to compliance with various laws, including those covering copyright, indecent content, child protection, consumer protection, and similar matters. There have been instances where improper or illegal content has been stored on our platform without our knowledge. As a service provider, we do not regularly monitor our platform to evaluate the legality of content stored on it. While to date we have not been subject to material legal or administrative actions as result of this content, the laws in this area are currently in a state of flux and vary widely between jurisdictions. Accordingly, it may be possible that in the future we and our competitors may be subject to legal actions, along with the users who uploaded such content. In addition, regardless of any legal liability we may face, our reputation could be harmed should there be an incident generating extensive negative publicity about the content stored on our platform. Such publicity could harm our business and results of operations.

We are also subject to consumer protection laws that may impact our sales and marketing efforts, including laws related to subscriptions, billing, and auto-renewal. These laws, as well as any changes in these laws, could adversely affect our self-serve model and make it more difficult for us to retain and upgrade paying users and attract new ones. Additionally, we have in the past, are currently, and may from time to time in the future become the subject of inquiries and other actions by regulatory authorities as a result of our business practices, including our subscription, billing, and auto-renewal policies. Consumer protection laws may be interpreted or applied by regulatory authorities in a manner that could require us to make changes to our operations or incur fines, penalties or settlement expenses, which may result in harm to our business, results of operations, and brand.

Our platform depends on the ability of our users to access the internet and our platform has been blocked or restricted in some countries for various reasons. For example, our platform is blocked in the People's Republic of China. If we fail to anticipate developments in the law, or fail for any reason to comply with relevant law, our platform could be further blocked or restricted and we could be exposed to significant liability that could harm our business.

We are also subject to various U.S. and international anti-corruption laws, such as the U.S. Foreign Corrupt Practices Act and the U.K. Bribery Act, as well as other similar anti-bribery and anti-kickback laws and

27

115

regulations. These laws and regulations generally prohibit companies and their employees and intermediaries from authorizing, offering, or providing improper payments or benefits to officials and other recipients for improper purposes. Although we take precautions to prevent violations of these laws, our exposure for violating these laws increases as we continue to expand our international presence and any failure to comply with such laws could harm our reputation and our business.

We are subject to export and import control laws and regulations that could impair our ability to compete in international markets or subject us to liability if we violate such laws and regulations.

We are subject to U.S. export controls and sanctions regulations that prohibit the shipment or provision of certain products and services to certain countries, governments, and persons targeted by U.S. sanctions. While we take precautions to prevent our products and services from being exported in violation of these laws, including implementing IP address blocking, we cannot guarantee that the precautions we take will prevent violations of export control and sanctions laws. For example, in 2011, we provided certain downloadable portions of our software to international users that, prior to export, required either a one-time product review or application for an encryption registration number in lieu of such product review. These exports were likely made in violation of U.S. export control and sanction laws. In March 2011, we filed a Final Voluntary Self Disclosure with the U.S. Department of Commerce's Bureau of Industry and Security, or BIS, concerning these potential violations. In June 2012, BIS notified us that it had completed its review of these matters and closed its review with the issuance of a Warning Letter. No monetary penalties were assessed against us by BIS with respect to the 2011 filing. In addition, in 2017, we discovered that our platform has been accessed by certain users in apparent violation of United States sanctions regulations. We filed an Initial Voluntary Self Disclosure in October 2017 with the Office of Foreign Assets Control, or OFAC, and a Final Voluntary Self Disclosure with OFAC in February 2018. If we are found to be in violation of U.S. sanctions or export control laws, it could result in substantial fines and penalties for us and for the individuals working for us.

In addition, various countries regulate the import and export of certain encryption and other technology, including import and export permitting and licensing requirements, and have enacted laws that could limit our ability to distribute our products or could limit our users' ability to access our platform in those countries. Changes in our platform or client-side software, or future changes in export and import regulations may prevent our users with international operations from deploying our platform globally or, in some cases, prevent the export or import of our platform to certain countries, governments, or persons altogether. Any change in export or import regulations, economic sanctions or related legislation, or change in the countries, governments, persons or technologies targeted by such regulations, could result in decreased use of our platform by, or in our decreased ability to export or sell subscriptions to our platform to, existing or potential users with international operations. Any decreased use of our platform or limitation on our ability to export or sell our products would likely adversely affect our business, results of operations, and financial results.

Our actual or perceived failure to comply with privacy, data protection, and information security laws, regulations, and obligations could harm our business.

We receive, store, process, and use personal information and other user content. There are numerous federal, state, local, and international laws and regulations regarding privacy, data protection, information security, and the storing, sharing, use, processing, transfer, disclosure, and protection of personal information and other content, the scope of which are changing, subject to differing interpretations, and may be inconsistent among countries, or conflict with other rules. We are also subject to the terms of our privacy policies and obligations to third parties related to privacy, data protection, and information security. We strive to comply with applicable laws, regulations, policies, and other legal obligations relating to privacy, data protection, and information security to the extent possible. However, the regulatory framework for privacy and data protection worldwide is, and is likely to remain, uncertain for the foreseeable future, and it is possible that these or other actual or alleged obligations may be interpreted and applied in a manner that is inconsistent from one jurisdiction to another and may conflict with other rules or our practices.

28

We also expect that there will continue to be new laws, regulations, and industry standards concerning privacy, data protection, and information security proposed and enacted in various jurisdictions. For example, European legislators have adopted a General Data Protection Regulation, or GDPR, that will, when effective in May 2018, supersede current European Union, or EU, data protection legislation, impose more stringent EU data protection requirements, and provide for greater penalties for noncompliance. Further, following a referendum in June 2016 in which voters in the United Kingdom approved an exit from the EU, the United Kingdom government has initiated a process to leave the EU, or Brexit. Brexit has created uncertainty with regard to the regulation of data protection in the United Kingdom. In particular, it is unclear whether the United Kingdom will enact data protection laws or regulations designed to be consistent with the pending EU General Data Protection Regulation and how data transfers to and from the United Kingdom will be regulated. Additionally, although we have self-certified under the U.S.-EU and U.S.-Swiss Privacy Shield Frameworks with regard to our transfer of certain personal data from the EU and Switzerland to the United States, some regulatory uncertainty remains surrounding the future of data transfers from the EU and Switzerland to the United States, and we are closely monitoring regulatory developments in this area.

Any failure or perceived failure by us to comply with our privacy policies, our privacy-related obligations to users or other third parties, or any of our other legal obligations relating to privacy, data protection, or information security may result in governmental investigations or enforcement actions, litigation, claims, or public statements against us by consumer advocacy groups or others and could result in significant liability or cause our users to lose trust in us, which could have an adverse effect on our reputation and business. Furthermore, the costs of compliance with, and other burdens imposed by, the laws, regulations, and policies that are applicable to the businesses of our users may limit the adoption and use of, and reduce the overall demand for, our services.

Additionally, if third parties we work with, such as vendors or developers, violate applicable laws or regulations or our policies, such violations may also put our users' content at risk and could in turn have an adverse effect on our business. Any significant change to applicable laws, regulations, or industry practices regarding the collection, use, retention, security, or disclosure of our users' content, or regarding the manner in which the express or implied consent of users for the collection, use, retention, or disclosure of such content is obtained, could increase our costs and require us to modify our services and features, possibly in a material manner, which we may be unable to complete, and may limit our ability to store and process user data or develop new services and features.

Our business could be adversely impacted by changes in internet access for our users or laws specifically governing the internet.

Our platform depends on the quality of our users' access to the internet. Certain features of our platform require significant bandwidth and fidelity to work effectively. Internet access is frequently provided by companies that have significant market power that could take actions that degrade, disrupt or increase the cost of user access to our platform, which would negatively impact our business. We could incur greater operating expenses and our user acquisition and retention could be negatively impacted if network operators:

- implement usage-based pricing;
- discount pricing for competitive products;
- otherwise materially change their pricing rates or schemes;
- charge us to deliver our traffic at certain levels or at all;
- throttle traffic based on its source or type;
- implement bandwidth caps or other usage restrictions; or
- otherwise try to monetize or control access to their networks.

29

On December 14, 2017, the Federal Communications Commission voted to repeal the "net neutrality" rules and return to a "light-touch" regulatory framework. However, the repeal has not yet taken effect and a number of parties have already stated their intent to appeal this order; thus, the future impact of such repeal and any challenge thereto remains uncertain. The rules were designed to ensure that all online content is treated the same by internet service providers and other companies that provide broadband services. Should the repeal of net neutrality rules take effect, we could incur greater operating expenses, which could harm our results of operations.

As the internet continues to experience growth in the number of users, frequency of use, and amount of data transmitted, the internet infrastructure that we and our users rely on may be unable to support the demands placed upon it. The failure of the internet infrastructure that we or our users rely on, even for a short period of time, could undermine our operations and harm our results of operations.

In addition, there are various laws and regulations that could impede the growth of the internet or other online services, and new laws and regulations may be adopted in the future. These laws and regulations could, in addition to limiting internet neutrality, involve taxation, tariffs, privacy, data protection, content, copyrights, distribution, electronic contracts and other communications, consumer protection, and the characteristics and quality of services, any of which could decrease the demand for, or the usage of, our platform. Legislators and regulators may make legal and regulatory changes, or interpret and apply existing laws, in ways that require us to incur substantial costs, expose us to unanticipated civil or criminal liability, or cause us to change our business practices. These changes or increased costs could materially harm our business, results of operations, and financial condition.

We are currently, and may be in the future, party to intellectual property rights claims and other litigation matters and, if resolved adversely, they could have a significant impact on our business, results of operations, or financial condition.

We own a large number of patents, copyrights, trademarks, domain names, and trade secrets and, from time to time, are subject to litigation based on allegations of infringement, misappropriation or other violations of intellectual property, or other rights. As we face increasing competition and gain an increasingly high profile, the possibility of intellectual property rights claims, commercial claims, and other assertions against us grows. We have in the past been, are currently, and may from time to time in the future become, a party to litigation and disputes related to our intellectual property, our business practices, and our platform. The costs of supporting litigation and dispute resolution proceedings are considerable, and there can be no assurances that a favorable outcome will be obtained. We may need to settle litigation and disputes on terms that are unfavorable to us, or we may be subject to an unfavorable judgment that may not be reversible upon appeal. The terms of any settlement or judgment may require us to cease some or all of our operations or pay substantial amounts to the other party. With respect to any intellectual property rights claim, we may have to seek a license to continue practices found to be in violation of third-party rights, which may not be available on reasonable terms and may significantly increase our operating expenses. A license to continue such practices may not be available to us at all, and we may be required to develop alternative non-infringing technology or practices or discontinue the practices. The development of alternative, non-infringing technology or practices could require significant effort and expense. Our business, results of operations, and financial condition could be materially and adversely affected as a result.

Our failure to protect our intellectual property rights and proprietary information could diminish our brand and other intangible assets.

We rely and expect to continue to rely on a combination of patent, patent licenses, trade secret, and domain name protection, trademark, and copyright laws, as well as confidentiality and license agreements with our employees, consultants, and third parties, to protect our intellectual property and proprietary rights. In the United States and abroad, we have over 600 issued patents and more than 600 pending patent applications. However, third parties may knowingly or unknowingly infringe our proprietary rights, third parties may challenge our

30

118

proprietary rights, pending and future patent, trademark, and copyright applications may not be approved, and we may not be able to prevent infringement without incurring substantial expense. We have also devoted substantial resources to the development of our proprietary technologies and related processes. In order to protect our proprietary technologies and processes, we rely in part on trade secret laws and confidentiality agreements with our employees, consultants, and third parties. These agreements may not effectively prevent disclosure of confidential information and may not provide an adequate remedy in the event of unauthorized disclosure of confidential information. In addition, others may independently discover our trade secrets, in which case we would not be able to assert trade secret rights, or develop similar technologies and processes. Further, laws in certain jurisdictions may afford little or no trade secret protection, and any changes in, or unexpected interpretations of, the intellectual property laws in any country in which we operate may compromise our ability to enforce our intellectual property rights. Costly and time-consuming litigation could be necessary to enforce and determine the scope of our proprietary rights. If the protection of our proprietary rights is inadequate to prevent use or appropriation by third parties, the value of our platform, brand, and other intangible assets may be diminished and competitors may be able to more effectively replicate our platform and its features. Any of these events could materially and adversely affect our business, results of operations, and financial condition.

Our use of open source software could negatively affect our ability to offer and sell subscriptions to our platform and subject us to possible litigation.

A portion of the technologies we use incorporates open source software, and we may incorporate open source software in the future. Open source software is generally licensed by its authors or other third parties under open source licenses. These licenses may subject us to certain unfavorable conditions, including requirements that we offer our platform that incorporates the open source software for no cost, that we make publicly available source code for modifications or derivative works we create based upon, incorporating or using the open source software, and/or that we license such modifications or derivative works under the terms of the particular open source license. Additionally, if a third-party software provider has incorporated open source software into software that we license from such provider, we could be required to disclose any of our source code that incorporates or is a modification of our licensed software. If an author or other third party that distributes open source software that we use or license were to allege that we had not complied with the conditions of the applicable license, we could be required to incur significant legal expenses defending against those allegations and could be subject to significant damages, enjoined from offering or selling our solutions that contained the open source software, and required to comply with the foregoing conditions. Any of the foregoing could disrupt and harm our business, results of operations, and financial condition.

Our ability to sell subscriptions to our platform could be harmed by real or perceived material defects or errors in our platform.

The software technology underlying our platform is inherently complex and may contain material defects or errors, particularly when first introduced or when new features or capabilities are released. We have from time to time found defects or errors in our platform, and new defects or errors in our existing platform or new software may be detected in the future by us or our users. There can be no assurance that our existing platform and new software will not contain defects. Any real or perceived errors, failures, vulnerabilities, or bugs in our platform could result in negative publicity or lead to data security, access, retention, or other performance issues, all of which could harm our business. The costs incurred in correcting such defects or errors may be substantial and could harm our results of operations and financial condition. Moreover, the harm to our reputation and legal liability related to such defects or errors may be substantial and could harm our business, results of operations, and financial condition.

We also utilize hardware purchased or leased and software and services licensed from third parties to offer our platform. Any defects in, or unavailability of, our or third-party software, services, or hardware that cause interruptions to the availability of our services, loss of data, or performance issues could, among other things:

- cause a reduction in revenue or delay in market acceptance of our platform;

31

119

- require us to issue refunds to our users or expose us to claims for damages;

- cause us to lose existing users and make it more difficult to attract new users;

- divert our development resources or require us to make extensive changes to our platform, which would increase our expenses;

- increase our technical support costs; and

- harm our reputation and brand.

We may acquire other businesses or receive offers to be acquired, which could require significant management attention, disrupt our business, or dilute stockholder value.

Part of our business strategy is to make acquisitions of other companies, products, and technologies. We have limited experience in acquisitions. We may not be able to find suitable acquisition candidates and we may not be able to complete acquisitions on favorable terms, if at all. If we do complete acquisitions, we may not ultimately strengthen our competitive position or achieve our goals, and any acquisitions we complete could be viewed negatively by users, developers, or investors. In addition, we may not be able to integrate acquired businesses successfully or effectively manage the combined company following an acquisition. If we fail to successfully integrate our acquisitions, or the people or technologies associated with those acquisitions, into our company, the results of operations of the combined company could be adversely affected. Any integration process will require significant time and resources, require significant attention from management, and disrupt the ordinary functioning of our business, and we may not be able to manage the process successfully, which could adversely affect our business, results of operations, and financial condition. In addition, we may not successfully evaluate or utilize the acquired technology and accurately forecast the financial impact of an acquisition transaction, including accounting charges.

We may have to pay cash, incur debt, or issue equity securities to pay for any such acquisition, each of which could affect our financial condition or the value of our capital stock. The sale of equity to finance any such acquisitions could result in dilution to our stockholders. If we incur more debt, it would result in increased fixed obligations and could also subject us to covenants or other restrictions that would impede our ability to flexibly operate our business.

Our business may be significantly impacted by a change in the economy, including any resulting effect on consumer or business spending.

Our business may be affected by changes in the economy generally, including any resulting effect on spending by our business and consumer users. Some of our users may view a subscription to our platform as a discretionary purchase, and our paying users may reduce their discretionary spending on our platform during an economic downturn. If an economic downturn were to occur, we may experience such a reduction in the future, especially in the event of a prolonged recessionary period. As a result, our business, results of operations, and financial condition may be significantly affected by changes in the economy generally.

Our business could be disrupted by catastrophic events.

Occurrence of any catastrophic event, including earthquake, fire, flood, tsunami, or other weather event, power loss, telecommunications failure, software or hardware malfunctions, cyber-attack, war, or terrorist attack, could result in lengthy interruptions in our service. In particular, our U.S. headquarters and some of the datacenters we utilize are located in the San Francisco Bay Area, a region known for seismic activity, and our insurance coverage may not compensate us for losses that may occur in the event of an earthquake or other significant natural disaster. In addition, acts of terrorism could cause disruptions to the internet or the economy as a whole. Even with our disaster recovery arrangements, our service could be interrupted. If our systems were to fail or be negatively impacted as a result of a natural disaster or other event, our ability to deliver products to our

32

120

users would be impaired or we could lose critical data. If we are unable to develop adequate plans to ensure that our business functions continue to operate during and after a disaster, and successfully execute on those plans in the event of a disaster or emergency, our business, results of operations, financial condition, and reputation would be harmed.

We may have exposure to greater than anticipated tax liabilities, which could adversely impact our results of operations.

While to date we have not incurred significant income taxes in operating our business, we are subject to income taxes in the United States and various jurisdictions outside of the United States. Our effective tax rate could fluctuate due to changes in the mix of earnings and losses in countries with differing statutory tax rates. Our tax expense could also be impacted by changes in non-deductible expenses, changes in excess tax benefits of stock-based compensation, changes in the valuation of deferred tax assets and liabilities and our ability to utilize them, the applicability of withholding taxes and effects from acquisitions.

Our tax provision could also be impacted by changes in accounting principles, changes in U.S. federal, state, or international tax laws applicable to corporate multinationals such as the recent legislation enacted in the United States, United Kingdom and Australia, other fundamental law changes currently being considered by many countries, and changes in taxing jurisdictions' administrative interpretations, decisions, policies, and positions. Additionally, in October 2015, the Organization for Economic Co-Operation and Development released final guidance covering various topics, including transfer pricing, country-by-country reporting, and definitional changes to permanent establishment that could ultimately impact our tax liabilities.

We are subject to review and audit by U.S. federal, state, local, and foreign tax authorities. Such tax authorities may disagree with tax positions we take and if any such tax authority were to successfully challenge any such position, our financial results and operations could be materially and adversely affected. We may also be subject to additional tax liabilities due to changes in non-income based taxes resulting from changes in federal, state, or international tax laws, changes in taxing jurisdictions' administrative interpretations, decisions, policies, and positions, results of tax examinations, settlements or judicial decisions, changes in accounting principles, changes to the business operations, including acquisitions, as well as the evaluation of new information that results in a change to a tax position taken in a prior period.

Our ability to use our net operating loss carryforwards and certain other tax attributes may be limited.

As of December 31, 2017, we had $312.2 million of federal and $143.0 million of state net operating loss carryforwards available to reduce future taxable income, which will begin to expire in 2031 for federal and 2030 for state tax purposes. As of December 31, 2017, we also had $289.3 million of foreign net operating loss carryforwards available to reduce future taxable income, which will carryforward indefinitely. In addition, we had $22.9 million of foreign acquired net operating losses, which will carryforward indefinitely. It is possible that we will not generate taxable income in time to use these net operating loss carryforwards before their expiration or at all. Under Sections 382 and 383 of the Internal Revenue Code of 1986, as amended, or the Code, if a corporation undergoes an "ownership change," the corporation's ability to use its pre-change net operating loss carryforwards and other pre-change attributes, such as research tax credits, to offset its post-change income may be limited. In general, an "ownership change" will occur if there is a cumulative change in our ownership by "5-percent shareholders" that exceeds 50 percentage points over a rolling three-year period. Similar rules may apply under state tax laws. We performed a study for the period through December 31, 2017, and determined that no ownership changes exceeding 50 percentage points had occurred. Our ability to use net operating loss and tax credit carryforwards to reduce future taxable income and liabilities may be subject to annual limitations as a result of ownership changes from January 1, 2018, and subsequent years or as a result of this offering.

Our operating results may be harmed if we are required to collect sales or other related taxes for our subscription services in jurisdictions where we have not historically done so.

We collect sales and value-added tax as part of our subscription agreements in a number of jurisdictions. One or more states or countries may seek to impose incremental or new sales, use, or other tax collection obligations on us, including for past sales by us or our resellers and other partners. A successful assertion by a state, country, or other jurisdiction that we should have been or should be collecting additional sales, use, or other taxes on our services could, among other things, result in substantial tax liabilities for past sales, create significant administrative burdens for us, discourage users from purchasing our platform, or otherwise harm our business, results of operations, and financial condition.

Our results of operations and financial condition could be materially affected by the enactment of legislation implementing changes in the U.S. or foreign taxation of international business activities or the adoption of other tax reform policies.

On December 22, 2017, the legislation commonly referred to as the Tax Cuts and Jobs Act, or the Tax Reform Act, was enacted, which contains significant changes to U.S. tax law, including, but not limited to, a reduction in the corporate tax rate and a transition to a new territorial system of taxation. The primary impact of the new legislation on our provision for income taxes was a reduction of the future tax benefits of our deferred tax assets as a result of the reduction in the corporate tax rate. However, since we have recorded a full valuation allowance against our deferred tax assets, we do not currently anticipate that these changes will have a material impact on our consolidated financial statements. The impact of the Tax Reform Act will likely be subject to ongoing technical guidance and accounting interpretation, which we will continue to monitor and assess. Provisional accounting impacts may change in future reporting periods until the accounting analysis is finalized, which will occur no later than one year from the date the Tax Reform Act was enacted. As we expand the scale of our international business activities, any changes in the U.S. or foreign taxation of such activities may increase our worldwide effective tax rate and harm our business, results of operations, and financial condition.

If we fail to maintain an effective system of disclosure controls and internal control over financial reporting, our ability to produce timely and accurate financial statements or comply with applicable regulations could be impaired.

As a public company, we will be subject to the reporting requirements of the Securities Exchange Act of 1934, as amended, or the Exchange Act, the Sarbanes-Oxley Act of 2002, or the Sarbanes-Oxley Act, and the rules and regulations of the applicable listing standards of the Nasdaq Global Select Market, or Nasdaq. We expect that the requirements of these rules and regulations will continue to increase our legal, accounting, and financial compliance costs, make some activities more difficult, time-consuming and costly, and place significant strain on our personnel, systems, and resources.

The Sarbanes-Oxley Act requires, among other things, that we maintain effective disclosure controls and procedures and internal control over financial reporting. We are continuing to develop and refine our disclosure controls and other procedures that are designed to ensure that information required to be disclosed by us in the reports that we will file with the SEC is recorded, processed, summarized, and reported within the time periods specified in SEC rules and forms and that information required to be disclosed in reports under the Exchange Act is accumulated and communicated to our principal executive and financial officers. We are also continuing to improve our internal control over financial reporting. In order to maintain and improve the effectiveness of our disclosure controls and procedures and internal control over financial reporting, we have expended, and anticipate that we will continue to expend, significant resources, including accounting-related costs and significant management oversight.

Our current controls and any new controls that we develop may become inadequate because of changes in conditions in our business. Further, weaknesses in our disclosure controls and internal control over financial

34

reporting may be discovered in the future. Any failure to develop or maintain effective controls or any difficulties encountered in their implementation or improvement could harm our results of operations or cause us to fail to meet our reporting obligations and may result in a restatement of our financial statements for prior periods. Any failure to implement and maintain effective internal control over financial reporting also could adversely affect the results of periodic management evaluations and annual independent registered public accounting firm attestation reports regarding the effectiveness of our internal control over financial reporting that we will eventually be required to include in our periodic reports that will be filed with the SEC. Ineffective disclosure controls and procedures and internal control over financial reporting could also cause investors to lose confidence in our reported financial and other information, which would likely have a negative effect on the trading price of our Class A common stock. In addition, if we are unable to continue to meet these requirements, we may not be able to remain listed on Nasdaq. We are not currently required to comply with the SEC rules that implement Section 404 of the Sarbanes-Oxley Act and are therefore not required to make a formal assessment of the effectiveness of our internal control over financial reporting for that purpose. As a public company, we will be required to provide an annual management report on the effectiveness of our internal control over financial reporting commencing with our second annual report on Form 10-K.

Our independent registered public accounting firm is not required to formally attest to the effectiveness of our internal control over financial reporting until our first annual report filed with the SEC where we are an "accelerated filer" or a "large accelerated filer". At such time, our independent registered public accounting firm may issue a report that is adverse in the event it is not satisfied with the level at which our internal control over financial reporting is documented, designed, or operating. Any failure to maintain effective disclosure controls and internal control over financial reporting could materially and adversely affect our business, results of operations, and financial condition and could cause a decline in the trading price of our Class A common stock.

Although we ceased to be an "emerging growth company," we can continue to take advantage of certain reduced disclosure requirements in this registration statement, which may make our Class A common stock less attractive to investors.

We ceased to be an "emerging growth company," as defined in the Jumpstart Our Business Startups Act of 2012, or the JOBS Act, on December 31, 2017. However, because we ceased to be an "emerging growth company" after we confidentially submitted our registration statement related to this offering to the SEC, we will continue to be treated as an "emerging growth company" for certain purposes until the earlier of the date on which we complete this offering or December 31, 2018. As such, we have taken advantage of certain reduced disclosure obligations regarding selected financial data and executive compensation arrangements in our registration statement related to this offering that are not available to non-emerging growth companies. We cannot predict if investors will find our Class A common stock less attractive because we have relied on these exemptions. If some investors find our Class A common stock less attractive as a result, there may be less demand for our Class A common stock and the price that some investors are willing to pay for our Class A common stock may decrease.

Our reported results of operations may be adversely affected by changes in accounting principles generally accepted in the United States.

Generally accepted accounting principles in the United States are subject to interpretation by the Financial Accounting Standards Board, or FASB, the SEC, and various bodies formed to promulgate and interpret appropriate accounting principles. A change in these principles or interpretations could have a significant effect on our reported results of operations, and may even affect the reporting of transactions completed before the announcement or effectiveness of a change. For example, in May 2014, the FASB issued Accounting Standards Update, or ASU, No. 2014-09, *Revenue from Contracts with Customers (Topic 606)*, or Topic 606, which superseded nearly all existing revenue recognition guidance. We adopted the requirements of Topic 606 as of January 1, 2017, utilizing the full retrospective method of transition. As such, Topic 606 is reflected in our financial results for all periods presented in this prospectus. The adoption of Topic 606 primarily resulted in

35

changes to our accounting policies for revenue recognition and deferred commissions, which we believe to be critical accounting policies. While the impact of adopting Topic 606 on our revenue was not material, it is difficult to predict the impact of future changes to accounting principles or our accounting policies, any of which could negatively affect our results of operations.

We recently implemented a new enterprise resource planning system, and if this new system proves ineffective or if we experience issues with the transition, we may be unable to timely or accurately prepare financial reports, make payments to our suppliers and employees, or invoice and collect from our users.

In 2017, we implemented a new enterprise resource planning, or ERP, system, including our systems for tracking revenue recognition. Our ERP system is critical to our ability to accurately maintain books and records and to prepare our financial statements. The transition to our new ERP system may be disruptive to our business if the ERP system does not work as planned or if we experience issues relating to the implementation. Such disruptions could impact our ability to timely or accurately make payments to our suppliers and employees, and could also inhibit our ability to invoice, and collect from our users. Data integrity problems or other issues may be discovered which, if not corrected, could impact our business or financial results. In addition, we may experience periodic or prolonged disruption of our financial functions arising out of this conversion, general use of such system, other periodic upgrades or updates, or other external factors that are outside of our control. If we encounter unforeseen problems with our ERP system or other related systems and infrastructure, our business, results of operations, and financial condition could be adversely affected.

Certain of our market opportunity estimates, growth forecasts, and key metrics included in this prospectus could prove to be inaccurate, and any real or perceived inaccuracies may harm our reputation and negatively affect our business.

Market opportunity estimates and growth forecasts are subject to significant uncertainty and are based on assumptions and estimates that may not prove to be accurate. The estimates and forecasts in this prospectus relating to the size and expected growth of our target market may prove to be inaccurate. Even if the markets in which we compete meet the size estimates and growth forecasted in this prospectus, our business could fail to grow at similar rates, if at all. We also rely on assumptions and estimates to calculate certain of our key metrics, such as paying users, average revenue per paying user, and free cash flow. We regularly review and may adjust our processes for calculating our key metrics to improve their accuracy. Our key metrics may differ from estimates published by third parties or from similarly titled metrics of our competitors due to differences in methodology. We have found that aggregate user activity metrics are not leading indicators of revenue or conversion. For that reason, we do not comprehensively track user activity across the Dropbox platform for financial planning and forecasting purposes. If investors or analysts do not perceive our metrics to be accurate representations of our business, or if we discover material inaccuracies in our metrics, our reputation, business, results of operations, and financial condition would be harmed.

Our revolving credit facility provides our lenders with a first-priority lien against substantially all of our intellectual property and certain other assets, and contains financial covenants and other restrictions on our actions that may limit our operational flexibility or otherwise adversely affect our results of operations.

We are party to a revolving credit and guarantee agreement, as amended, which contains a number of covenants that limit our ability and our subsidiaries' ability to, among other things, incur additional indebtedness, pay dividends, make redemptions and repurchases of stock, make investments, loans and acquisitions, create liens, engage in transactions with affiliates, merge or consolidate with other companies, or sell substantially all of our assets. We are also required to maintain certain financial covenants, including a maximum consolidated leverage ratio and a minimum liquidity balance. The terms of our revolving credit facility may restrict our current and future operations and could adversely affect our ability to finance our future operations or capital needs or to execute preferred business strategies. In addition, complying with these covenants may make it more difficult for us to successfully execute our business strategy and compete against companies who are not subject to such restrictions.

36

A failure by us to comply with the covenants or payment requirements specified in our credit agreement, as amended, could result in an event of default under the agreement, which would give the lenders the right to terminate their commitments to provide additional loans under our revolving credit facility and to declare all borrowings outstanding, together with accrued and unpaid interest and fees, to be immediately due and payable. In addition, the lenders would have the right to proceed against the collateral we granted to them, which consists of substantially all our intellectual property and certain other assets. If the debt under our revolving credit facility were to be accelerated, we may not have sufficient cash or be able to borrow sufficient funds to refinance the debt or sell sufficient assets to repay the debt, which could immediately materially and adversely affect our business, cash flows, results of operations, and financial condition. Even if we were able to obtain new financing, it may not be on commercially reasonable terms or on terms that are acceptable to us.

Our operations may be interrupted and our business, results of operations, and financial condition could be adversely affected if we default on our leasing or credit obligations.

We finance a significant portion of our expenditures through leasing arrangements, some of which are not required to be reflected on our balance sheet, and we may enter into additional similar arrangements in the future. As of December 31, 2017, we had an aggregate of $1,687.0 million of commitments to settle contractual obligations. In particular, we have used these types of arrangements to finance some of our equipment and datacenters. In addition, we may draw upon our revolving credit facility to finance our operations or for other corporate purposes, such as funding our tax withholding and remittance obligations in connection with the settlement of restricted stock units, or RSUs. If we default on these leasing or credit obligations, our leasing partners and lenders may, among other things:

- require repayment of any outstanding lease obligations;

- terminate our leasing arrangements;

- terminate our access to the leased datacenters we utilize;

- stop delivery of ordered equipment;

- sell or require us to return our leased equipment;

- require repayment of any outstanding amounts drawn on our revolving credit facility;

- terminate our revolving credit facility; or

- require us to pay significant fees, penalties, or damages.

In October 2017, we entered into a new lease agreement to rent office space in San Francisco, California, to serve as our new corporate headquarters. The total minimum obligations under this lease agreement are expected to be approximately $827.0 million. Before moving to our new corporate headquarters, we will continue to operate in our current corporate headquarters, during which time we will be incurring rent expense on both our current and new corporate headquarters. After moving to our new corporate headquarters, we plan to vacate our current corporate headquarters with the intention of subleasing the space to a third-party for the remainder of the lease term, which terminates in the third quarter of 2027. If we are unable to find sublessors for all or a portion of our current corporate headquarters, our results of operations will be adversely impacted as a result of this additional rent expense through 2027.

If some or all of these events were to occur, our operations may be interrupted and our ability to fund our operations or obligations, as well as our business, results of operations, and financial condition, could be adversely affected.

We may need additional capital, and we cannot be certain that additional financing will be available on favorable terms, or at all.

Historically, we have funded our operations and capital expenditures primarily through equity issuances, cash generated from our operations, and debt financing for capital purchases. Although we currently anticipate

37

that our existing cash and cash equivalents, amounts available under our existing credit facilities, and cash flow from operations will be sufficient to meet our cash needs for the foreseeable future, we may require additional financing. We evaluate financing opportunities from time to time, and our ability to obtain financing will depend, among other things, on our development efforts, business plans, operating performance, and condition of the capital markets at the time we seek financing. We cannot assure you that additional financing will be available to us on favorable terms when required, or at all. If we raise additional funds through the issuance of equity or equity-linked or debt securities, those securities may have rights, preferences or privileges senior to the rights of our Class A common stock, and our stockholders may experience dilution.

Risks Related to Ownership of Our Class A Common Stock

An active trading market for our Class A common stock may never develop or be sustained.

We have been approved to list our Class A common stock on Nasdaq under the symbol "DBX". However, we cannot assure you that an active trading market for our Class A common stock will develop on that exchange or elsewhere or, if developed, that any market will be sustained. Accordingly, we cannot assure you of the likelihood that an active trading market for our Class A common stock will develop or be maintained, the liquidity of any trading market, your ability to sell your shares of our Class A common stock when desired or the prices that you may obtain for your shares.

The trading price of our Class A common stock may be volatile, and you could lose all or part of your investment.

Prior to this offering, there has been no public market for shares of our Class A common stock. The initial public offering price of our Class A common stock was determined through negotiation among us, the selling stockholders, and the underwriters. This price does not necessarily reflect the price at which investors in the market will be willing to buy and sell shares of our Class A common stock following this offering. In addition, the trading price of our Class A common stock following this offering is likely to be volatile and could be subject to fluctuations in response to various factors, some of which are beyond our control. These fluctuations could cause you to lose all or part of your investment in our Class A common stock since you might be unable to sell your shares at or above the price you paid in this offering. Factors that could cause fluctuations in the trading price of our Class A common stock include the following:

- price and volume fluctuations in the overall stock market from time to time;

- volatility in the trading prices and trading volumes of technology stocks;

- changes in operating performance and stock market valuations of other technology companies generally, or those in our industry in particular;

- sales of shares of our Class A common stock by us or our stockholders;

- failure of securities analysts to maintain coverage of us, changes in financial estimates by securities analysts who follow our company, or our failure to meet these estimates or the expectations of investors;

- the financial projections we may provide to the public, any changes in those projections, or our failure to meet those projections;

- announcements by us or our competitors of new products, features, or services;

- the public's reaction to our press releases, other public announcements, and filings with the SEC;

- rumors and market speculation involving us or other companies in our industry;

- actual or anticipated changes in our results of operations or fluctuations in our results of operations;

38

- actual or anticipated developments in our business, our competitors' businesses or the competitive landscape generally;

- litigation involving us, our industry, or both, or investigations by regulators into our operations or those of our competitors;

- developments or disputes concerning our intellectual property or other proprietary rights;

- announced or completed acquisitions of businesses, products, services, or technologies by us or our competitors;

- new laws or regulations or new interpretations of existing laws or regulations applicable to our business;

- changes in accounting standards, policies, guidelines, interpretations, or principles;

- any significant change in our management; and

- general economic conditions and slow or negative growth of our markets.

In addition, in the past, following periods of volatility in the overall market and the market price of a particular company's securities, securities class action litigation has often been instituted against these companies. This litigation, if instituted against us, could result in substantial costs and a diversion of our management's attention and resources.

The multi-class structure of our common stock will have the effect of concentrating voting control with those stockholders who held our capital stock prior to the completion of this offering and the concurrent private placement, and it may depress the trading price of our Class A common stock.

Our Class A common stock, which is the stock we are offering in this offering and the concurrent private placement, has one vote per share, our Class B common stock has ten votes per share, and our Class C common stock has no voting rights, except as otherwise required by law. Following this offering and the concurrent private placement, our directors, executive officers and holders of more than 5% of our common stock, and their respective affiliates, will hold in the aggregate 68.8% of the voting power of our capital stock (including the Co-Founder Grants). We are including the Co-Founder Grants in this calculation since they are legally issued and outstanding shares of our Class A common stock and our co-founders are able to vote these shares immediately upon grant and prior to their vesting. Because of the ten-to-one voting ratio between our Class B and Class A common stock, the holders of our Class B common stock collectively will continue to control a majority of the combined voting power of our common stock and therefore be able to control all matters submitted to our stockholders for approval so long as the shares of Class B common stock represent at least 9.1% of all outstanding shares of our Class A and Class B common stock. This concentrated control will limit or preclude your ability to influence corporate matters for the foreseeable future, including the election of directors, amendments of our organizational documents and any merger, consolidation, sale of all or substantially all of our assets, or other major corporate transaction requiring stockholder approval. In addition, this may prevent or discourage unsolicited acquisition proposals or offers for our capital stock that you may feel are in your best interest as one of our stockholders.

Future transfers or sales by holders of Class B common stock will generally result in those shares converting to Class A common stock, except for certain transfers described in our amended and restated certificate of incorporation, including transfers effected for estate planning purposes where sole dispositive power and exclusive voting control with respect to the shares of Class B common stock is retained by the transferring holder and transfers between our co-founders. In addition, each outstanding share of Class B common stock held by a stockholder who is a natural person, or held by the permitted entities or permitted transferees of such stockholder (as described in our amended and restated certificate of incorporation), will convert automatically into one share of Class A common stock upon the death of such natural person. In the event of the death or permanent and total

39

disability of a co-founder, shares of Class B common stock held by such co-founder, his permitted entities or permitted transferees will convert to Class A common stock, provided that the conversion will be deferred for nine months, or up to 18 months if approved by a majority of our independent directors, following his death or permanent and total disability. Transfers between our co-founders are permitted transfers and will not result in conversion of the shares of Class B common stock that are transferred; however, upon the death or total and permanent disability of the transferring co-founder, the transferred shares would convert to Class A common stock following the deferral period of nine months, or up to 18 months if approved by a majority of our independent directors. See the section titled "Description of Capital Stock – Conversion of Class B Common Stock" for additional information about conversions. The conversion of Class B common stock to Class A common stock will have the effect, over time, of increasing the relative voting power of those individual holders of Class B common stock who retain their shares in the long term.

In addition, because our Class C common stock carries no voting rights (except as otherwise required by law), if we issue Class C common stock in the future, the holders of Class B common stock may be able to elect all of our directors and to determine the outcome of most matters submitted to a vote of our stockholders for a longer period of time than would be the case if we issued Class A common stock rather than Class C common stock in such transactions. See the section titled "Description of Capital Stock—Anti-Takeover Provisions" for additional information.

In addition, in July 2017, FTSE Russell and Standard & Poor's announced that they would cease to allow most newly public companies utilizing dual or multi-class capital structures to be included in their indices. Affected indices include the Russell 2000 and the S&P 500, S&P MidCap 400, and S&P SmallCap 600, which together make up the S&P Composite 1500. Under the announced policies, our multi-class capital structure would make us ineligible for inclusion in any of these indices, and as a result, mutual funds, exchange-traded funds, and other investment vehicles that attempt to passively track these indices will not be investing in our stock. These policies are very new and it is as of yet unclear what effect, if any, they will have on the valuations of publicly traded companies excluded from the indices, but it is possible that they may depress these valuations compared to those of other similar companies that are included.

Because of the relatively small number of shares of our Class A common stock outstanding immediately after this offering and the number of shares of Class A common stock held by our founders as a result of their RSAs, which shares have full voting rights, our co-founders will have significant influence over any vote of the Class A common stock voting as a separate class.

Based on 26,550,581 shares of Class A common stock (including the Capital Stock Conversions) outstanding as of December 31, 2017, inclusive of 14,733,333 shares of Class A common stock subject to RSAs that were granted pursuant to our Co-Founder Grants, following this offering, we will have 67,813,739 shares of Class A common stock legally issued and outstanding. As a result, until the public float of our Class A common stock increases, which is expected to occur primarily as a result of conversion of shares of Class B common stock into shares of Class A common stock upon transfer, our co-founders will hold a significant percentage of the outstanding Class A common stock. Although the terms of our amended and restated certificate of incorporation only provide for a separate vote of the holders of the Class A common stock as a class, under Delaware law, certain actions may require the approval of the holders of the Class A common stock voting as a separate class. For example, if we amend our amended and restated certificate of incorporation to adversely affect our Class A common stock, Delaware law could require approval of the holders of our Class A common stock voting separately as a single class. For any vote of the Class A common stock voting as a separate class, our co-founders will heavily influence such vote until the number of outstanding shares of Class A common stock significantly increases. Further, our co-founders will have the right to vote those shares until the termination of the award even if the performance targets have not been met or are not expected to be met. To the extent that the RSAs vest, our co-founders will have the ability to gain liquidity by selling shares of our Class A common stock without reducing their voting power by converting their Class B common stock.

40

A substantial portion of the outstanding shares of our Class A common stock and Class B common stock after this offering and the concurrent private placement will be restricted from immediate resale, but may be sold on a stock exchange in the near future. The large number of shares of our capital stock eligible for public sale or subject to rights requiring us to register them for public sale could depress the market price of our Class A common stock.

The market price of our Class A common stock could decline as a result of sales of a large number of shares of our Class A common stock in the market after this offering and the concurrent private placement, and the perception that these sales could occur may also depress the market price of our Class A common stock. Based on 11,817,248 shares of our Class A common stock (including the Capital Stock Conversions) and 348,501,449 shares of our Class B common stock (including the Capital Stock Conversions and the RSU Settlement) outstanding as of December 31, 2017, we will have 53,080,406 shares of our Class A common stock and 339,323,858 shares Class B common stock outstanding after this offering and the concurrent private placement. Our executive officers, directors, and the holders of substantially all of our capital stock and securities convertible into or exchangeable for our capital stock have entered into market standoff agreements with us or have entered into lock-up agreements with the underwriters under which they have agreed, subject to specific exceptions, not to sell any of our stock for 180 days following the date of this prospectus. We refer to such period as the lock-up period. Pursuant to the lock-up agreements with the underwriters, if (i) at least 120 days have elapsed since the date of this prospectus, (ii) we have publicly released our earnings results for the quarterly period during which this offering occurred, and (iii) such lock-up period is scheduled to end during or within five trading days prior to a broadly applicable period during which trading in our securities would not be permitted under our insider trading policy, or a blackout period, such lock-up period will end ten trading days prior to the commencement of such blackout period. We and the underwriters may release certain stockholders from the market standoff agreements or lock-up agreements prior to the end of the lock-up period.

As a result of these agreements and the provisions of our investors' rights agreement described further in the section titled "Description of Capital Stock—Registration Rights," and subject to the provisions of Rule 144 or Rule 701, shares of our Class A common stock and Class B common stock will be available for sale in the public market as follows:

- beginning on the date of this prospectus, all shares of our Class A common stock sold in this offering will be immediately available for sale in the public market; and

- beginning 181 days after the date of this prospectus (subject to the terms of the lock-up agreements and market standoff agreements described above), the remainder of the shares of our Class A common stock and Class B common stock will be eligible for sale in the public market from time to time thereafter, subject in some cases to the volume and other restrictions of Rule 144, as described below.

Upon completion of this offering and the concurrent private placement, stockholders owning an aggregate of up to 144,907,822 shares of our Class B common stock and 5,521,778 shares of our Class A common stock will be entitled, under our investors' rights agreement, to require us to register shares owned by them for public sale in the United States. In addition, we intend to file a registration statement to register shares reserved for future issuance under our equity compensation plans. Upon effectiveness of that registration statement, subject to the satisfaction of applicable exercise periods and the expiration or waiver of the market standoff agreements and lock-up agreements referred to above, the shares issued upon exercise of outstanding stock options or upon settlement of outstanding RSU awards will be available for immediate resale in the United States in the open market.

Sales of our shares as restrictions end or pursuant to registration rights may make it more difficult for us to sell equity securities in the future at a time and at a price that we deem appropriate. These sales also could cause the trading price of our Class A common stock to fall and make it more difficult for you to sell shares of our Class A common stock.

If you purchase our Class A common stock in this offering, you will incur immediate and substantial dilution.

The initial public offering price is substantially higher than the pro forma as adjusted net tangible book value per share of our outstanding common stock of $0.95 per share as of December 31, 2017. Investors purchasing shares of our Class A common stock in this offering will pay a price per share that substantially exceeds the book value of our tangible assets after subtracting our liabilities. As a result, investors purchasing Class A common stock in this offering will incur immediate dilution of $18.05 per share, based on the assumed initial public offering price of $19.00 per share, which is the midpoint of the estimated offering price range set forth on the cover page of this prospectus.

This dilution is due to the substantially lower price paid by our investors who purchased shares prior to this offering as compared to the price offered to the public in this offering, and any previous exercise of stock options granted to our service providers. In addition, as of December 31, 2017, options to purchase 4,959,492 shares of our Class B common stock with a weighted-average exercise price of approximately $10.52 per share were outstanding as well as 16,707,823 shares of our Class A common stock and 38,219,737 shares of our Class B common stock subject to RSUs. The exercise of any of these options and settlement of any of these RSUs would result in additional dilution. Our Board of Directors has approved the acceleration of the Performance Vesting Condition for 26,061,071 RSUs (which are included in the 38,219,737 shares of our Class B common stock subject to RSUs referenced above) for which the service condition was satisfied as of December 31, 2017, to occur upon the effectiveness of our registration statement related to this offering, which will result in the net issuance of 15,897,254 shares of our Class B common stock upon the RSU Settlement. As a result of the dilution to investors purchasing shares in this offering, investors may receive less than the purchase price paid in this offering, if anything, in the event of our liquidation.

We have broad discretion over the use of the net proceeds from this offering and the concurrent private placement and we may not use them effectively.

We cannot specify with any certainty the particular uses of the net proceeds that we will receive from this offering and the concurrent private placement. Our management will have broad discretion in the application of the net proceeds from this offering and the concurrent private placement, including for any of the purposes described in "Use of Proceeds," and you will not have the opportunity as part of your investment decision to assess whether the net proceeds are being used appropriately. Because of the number and variability of factors that will determine our use of the net proceeds from this offering and the concurrent private placement, their ultimate use may vary substantially from their currently intended use. The failure by our management to apply these proceeds effectively could adversely affect our business, results of operations, and financial condition. Pending their use, we may invest our proceeds in a manner that does not produce income or that loses value. Our investments may not yield a favorable return to our investors and may negatively impact the price of our Class A common stock.

Delaware law and provisions in our restated certificate of incorporation and restated bylaws could make a merger, tender offer, or proxy contest difficult, thereby depressing the market price of our Class A common stock.

Our status as a Delaware corporation and the anti-takeover provisions of the Delaware General Corporation Law may discourage, delay, or prevent a change in control by prohibiting us from engaging in a business combination with an interested stockholder for a period of three years after the person becomes an interested stockholder, even if a change of control would be beneficial to our existing stockholders. In addition, our restated certificate of incorporation and restated bylaws contain provisions that may make the acquisition of our company more difficult, including the following:

- any transaction that would result in a change in control of our company requires the approval of a majority of our outstanding Class B common stock voting as a separate class;

42

- our multi-class common stock structure, which provides our holders of Class B common stock with the ability to significantly influence the outcome of matters requiring stockholder approval, even if they own significantly less than a majority of the shares of our outstanding Class A common stock, Class B common stock, and Class C common stock;

- when the outstanding shares of Class B common stock represent less than a majority of the total combined voting power of our Class A and Class B common stock, or the Voting Threshold Date, our Board of Directors will be classified into three classes of directors with staggered three-year terms, and directors will only be able to be removed from office for cause;

- until the Class B common stock, as a class, converts to Class A common stock, any amendments to our restated certificate of incorporation will require the approval of two-thirds of the combined vote of our then-outstanding shares of Class A common stock and Class B common stock; and following the conversion of our Class B common stock, as a class, to Class A common stock, certain amendments to our amended and restated certificate of incorporation will require the approval of two-thirds of our then outstanding voting power;

- our amended and restated bylaws will provide that approval of stockholders holding two-thirds of our outstanding voting power voting as a single class is required for stockholders to amend or adopt any provision of our bylaws;

- after the Voting Threshold Date our stockholders will only be able to take action at a meeting of stockholders, and will not be able to take action by written consent for any matter;

- until the Voting Threshold Date, our stockholders will be able to act by written consent only if the action is first recommended or approved by the Board of Directors;

- vacancies on our Board of Directors will be able to be filled only by our Board of Directors and not by stockholders;

- only our chairman of the Board of Directors, chief executive officer, a majority of Board of Directors or until the Class B common stock, as a class, converts to Class A common stock, a stockholder holding thirty percent of the combined voting power of our Class A and Class B common stock are authorized to call a special meeting of stockholders;

- certain litigation against us can only be brought in Delaware;

- our restated certificate of incorporation authorizes undesignated preferred stock, the terms of which may be established and shares of which may be issued, without the approval of the holders of Class A common stock; and

- advance notice procedures apply for stockholders to nominate candidates for election as directors or to bring matters before an annual meeting of stockholders.

These anti-takeover defenses could discourage, delay, or prevent a transaction involving a change in control of our company. These provisions could also discourage proxy contests and make it more difficult for stockholders to elect directors of their choosing and to cause us to take other corporate actions they desire, any of which, under certain circumstances, could limit the opportunity for our stockholders to receive a premium for their shares of our capital stock, and could also affect the price that some investors are willing to pay for our Class A common stock.

Our amended and restated bylaws will designate a state or federal court located within the State of Delaware as the exclusive forum for substantially all disputes between us and our stockholders, and also provide that the federal district courts will be the exclusive forum for resolving any complaint asserting a cause of action arising under the Securities Act, each of which could limit our stockholders' ability to choose the judicial forum for disputes with us or our directors, officers, or employees.

Our amended and restated bylaws, which will become effective immediately prior to the completion of this offering, will provide that, unless we consent in writing to the selection of an alternative forum, the sole and

43

exclusive forum for (1) any derivative action or proceeding brought on our behalf, (2) any action asserting a claim of breach of a fiduciary duty owed by any of our directors, officers, or other employees to us or our stockholders, (3) any action arising pursuant to any provision of the Delaware General Corporation Law, or the certificate of incorporation or the amended and restated bylaws or (4) any other action asserting a claim that is governed by the internal affairs doctrine shall be the Court of Chancery of the State of Delaware (or, if the Court of Chancery does not have jurisdiction, the federal district court for the District of Delaware), in all cases subject to the court having jurisdiction over indispensable parties named as defendants.

Our amended and restated bylaws will also provide that the federal district courts of the United States of America will be the exclusive forum for resolving any complaint asserting a cause of action arising under the Securities Act.

Any person or entity purchasing or otherwise acquiring any interest in any of our securities shall be deemed to have notice of and consented to this provision. These exclusive-forum provisions may limit a stockholder's ability to bring a claim in a judicial forum of its choosing for disputes with us or our directors, officers, or other employees, which may discourage lawsuits against us and our directors, officers, and other employees. If a court were to find either exclusive-forum provision in our amended and restated bylaws to be inapplicable or unenforceable in an action, we may incur additional costs associated with resolving the dispute in other jurisdictions, which could harm our results of operations.

Affiliates of several of the underwriters in this offering may receive at least 5% of the net proceeds of this offering and may have an interest in this offering beyond customary underwriting discounts and commissions.

Goldman Sachs & Co. LLC, J.P. Morgan Securities LLC, Deutsche Bank Securities Inc., and Merrill Lynch, Pierce, Fenner & Smith Incorporated are underwriters in this offering and their affiliates will receive at least 5% of the net proceeds of this offering in connection with the repayment of $193.1 million that is expected to be outstanding under our revolving credit facility immediately prior to the completion of this offering. As such, Goldman Sachs & Co. LLC, J.P. Morgan Securities LLC, Deutsche Bank Securities Inc., and Merrill Lynch, Pierce, Fenner & Smith Incorporated are each deemed to have a "conflict of interest" under Rule 5121 of the Financial Industry Regulatory Authority Inc., or Rule 5121. Accordingly, this offering will be made in compliance with the applicable provisions of Rule 5121. This rule requires, among other things, that a "qualified independent underwriter" has participated in the preparation of, and has exercised the usual standards of "due diligence" with respect to, the registration statement. Allen & Company LLC has agreed to act as qualified independent underwriter for this offering and to undertake the legal responsibilities and liabilities of an underwriter under the Securities Act. Allen & Company LLC will not receive any additional fees for serving as qualified independent underwriter in connection with this offering. Although Allen & Company LLC has, in its capacity as qualified independent underwriter, participated in due diligence and the preparation of this prospectus and the registration statement of which this prospectus forms a part, we cannot assure you that this will adequately address all potential conflicts of interest. We have agreed to indemnify Allen & Company LLC against liabilities incurred in connection with acting as qualified independent underwriter, including liabilities under the Securities Act. Pursuant to FINRA Rule 5121, Goldman Sachs & Co. LLC, J.P. Morgan Securities LLC, Deutsche Bank Securities Inc., and Merrill Lynch, Pierce, Fenner & Smith Incorporated will not confirm sales of securities to any account over which it exercises discretionary authority without the prior written approval of the customer. See "Underwriting (Conflicts of Interest)" for additional information.

Our Class A common stock market price and trading volume could decline if securities or industry analysts do not publish research or publish inaccurate or unfavorable research about our business.

The trading market for our Class A common stock will depend in part on the research and reports that securities or industry analysts publish about us or our business. The analysts' estimates are based upon their own opinions and are often different from our estimates or expectations. If one or more of the analysts who cover us downgrade our Class A common stock or publish inaccurate or unfavorable research about our business, the price

44

of our securities would likely decline. If few securities analysts commence coverage of us, or if one or more of these analysts cease coverage of us or fail to publish reports on us regularly, demand for our securities could decrease, which might cause the price and trading volume of our Class A common stock to decline.

We do not intend to pay dividends for the foreseeable future.

We have never declared nor paid cash dividends on our capital stock. We currently intend to retain any future earnings to finance the operation and expansion of our business, and we do not expect to declare or pay any dividends in the foreseeable future. As a result, stockholders must rely on sales of their Class A common stock after price appreciation as the only way to realize any future gains on their investment. In addition, our revolving credit facility contains restrictions on our ability to pay dividends.

45

SPECIAL NOTE REGARDING FORWARD-LOOKING STATEMENTS

This prospectus contains forward-looking statements within the meaning of the federal securities laws, which statements involve substantial risks and uncertainties. Forward-looking statements generally relate to future events or our future financial or operating performance. In some cases, you can identify forward-looking statements because they contain words such as "may," "will," "should," "expects," "plans," "anticipates," "could," "intends," "target," "projects," "contemplates," "believes," "estimates," "predicts," "potential," or "continue" or the negative of these words or other similar terms or expressions that concern our expectations, strategy, plans, or intentions. Forward-looking statements contained in this prospectus include, but are not limited to, statements about:

- our ability to retain and upgrade paying users;

- our ability to attract new users or convert registered users to paying users;

- our future financial performance, including trends in revenue, costs of revenue, gross profit or gross margin, operating expenses, paying users, and free cash flow;

- our ability to achieve or maintain profitability;

- the demand for our platform or for content collaboration solutions in general;

- possible harm caused by significant disruption of service or loss or unauthorized access to users' content;

- our ability to effectively integrate our platform with others;

- our ability to compete successfully in competitive markets;

- our ability to respond to rapid technological changes;

- our expectations and management of future growth;

- our ability to grow due to our lack of a significant outbound sales force;

- our ability to attract large organizations as users;

- our ability to offer high-quality customer support;

- our ability to manage our international expansion;

- our ability to attract and retain key personnel and highly qualified personnel;

- our ability to protect our brand;

- our ability to prevent serious errors or defects in our platform;

- our ability to maintain, protect, and enhance our intellectual property;

- our ability to successfully identify, acquire, and integrate companies and assets;

- the increased expenses associated with being a public company; and

- our anticipated uses of net proceeds from this offering and the concurrent private placement.

We caution you that the foregoing list may not contain all of the forward-looking statements made in this prospectus.

You should not rely upon forward-looking statements as predictions of future events. We have based the forward-looking statements contained in this prospectus primarily on our current expectations and projections about future events and trends that we believe may affect our business, financial condition, results of operations, and prospects. The outcome of the events described in these forward-looking statements is subject to risks,

46

uncertainties and other factors described in the section titled "Risk Factors" and elsewhere in this prospectus. Moreover, we operate in a very competitive and rapidly changing environment. New risks and uncertainties emerge from time to time, and it is not possible for us to predict all risks and uncertainties that could have an impact on the forward-looking statements contained in this prospectus. We cannot assure you that the results, events, and circumstances reflected in the forward-looking statements will be achieved or occur, and actual results, events, or circumstances could differ materially from those described in the forward-looking statements.

The forward-looking statements made in this prospectus relate only to events as of the date on which the statements are made. We undertake no obligation to update any forward-looking statements made in this prospectus to reflect events or circumstances after the date of this prospectus or to reflect new information or the occurrence of unanticipated events, except as required by law. We may not actually achieve the plans, intentions, or expectations disclosed in our forward-looking statements, and you should not place undue reliance on our forward-looking statements. Our forward-looking statements do not reflect the potential impact of any future acquisitions, mergers, dispositions, joint ventures, or investments we may make.

In addition, statements that "we believe" and similar statements reflect our beliefs and opinions on the relevant subject. These statements are based upon information available to us as of the date of this prospectus, and while we believe such information forms a reasonable basis for such statements, such information may be limited or incomplete, and our statements should not be read to indicate that we have conducted an exhaustive inquiry into, or review of, all potentially available relevant information. These statements are inherently uncertain and investors are cautioned not to unduly rely upon these statements.

47

INDUSTRY AND MARKET DATA

This prospectus contains estimates and information concerning our industry, including market size of the markets in which we participate, that are based on industry publications and reports. This information involves a number of assumptions and limitations, and you are cautioned not to give undue weight to these estimates. We have not independently verified the accuracy or completeness of the data contained in these industry publications and reports. The markets in which we operate are subject to a high degree of uncertainty and risk due to a variety of factors, including those described in the section titled "Risk Factors." These and other factors could cause results to differ materially from those expressed in these publications and reports.

The source of certain statistical data, estimates and forecasts contained in this prospectus are the following independent industry publications or reports:

- Gartner, Inc., Magic Quadrant for Content Collaboration Platforms, July 2017.*

- International Data Corporation, Inc., Market Forecast: Worldwide Collaborative Applications Forecast, 2017-2021: Creating Productivity Growth with Customer Experience, July 2017.

- International Data Corporation, Inc., Market Forecast: Worldwide Project and Portfolio Management Forecast, 2017-2021: Agile Governance in the Cloud Drives Market, June 2017.

- International Data Corporation, Inc., Market Forecast: Worldwide Enterprise Content Management Software Forecast, 2017-2021, May 2017.

- International Data Corporation, Inc., IDC's Forecast Scenario Assumptions for the ICT Markets and Historical Market Values and Exchange Rates, Version 1, March 2017.

- International Data Corporation, Inc., Market Forecast: Worldwide Storage for Public and Private Cloud Forecast 2016-2020, December 2016.

- International Data Corporation, Inc., EFSS Evaluation Guide: Dropbox Sync Performance, July 2016.

- International Data Corporation, Inc., Knowledge Worker Outlook on Content Managed Systems, June 2016.

- McKinsey Global Institute, The Social Economy: Unlocking Value and Productivity Through Social Technologies, July 2012.

- Deloitte Consulting LLP, Transitioning to the Future of Work and the Workplace: Embracing Digital Culture, Tools and Approaches, A White Paper on the Future of Work Research Study, 2016.

---

* The Gartner Report described herein, or the Gartner Report, represents research opinion or viewpoints published, as part of a syndicated subscription service, by Gartner, Inc., or Gartner, and are not representations of fact. The Gartner Report speaks as of its original publication date (and not as of the date of this prospectus), and the opinions expressed in the Gartner Report are subject to change without notice. Gartner has advised us that it does not endorse any vendor, product, or service depicted in its research publications, and does not advise technology users to select only those vendors with the highest ratings or other designation. Gartner research publications consist of the opinions of Gartner's research organization and should not be construed as statements of fact. Gartner has advised us that it disclaims all warranties, expressed or implied, with respect to this research, including any warranties of merchantability or fitness for a particular purpose.

48

USE OF PROCEEDS

We estimate that the net proceeds to us from the sale of shares of our Class A common stock in this offering and the concurrent private placement will be approximately $579.9 million, based upon the assumed initial public offering price of $19.00 per share, which is the midpoint of the estimated offering price range set forth on the cover page of this prospectus, and after deducting estimated underwriting discounts and commissions and estimated offering expenses payable by us. If the underwriters' option to purchase additional shares of our Class A common stock from us is exercised in full, we estimate that the net proceeds to us would be approximately $678.0 million, after deducting estimated underwriting discounts and commissions and estimated offering expenses payable by us. We will not receive any of the proceeds from the sale of Class A common stock in this offering by the selling stockholders.

Each $1.00 increase or decrease in the assumed initial public offering price of $19.00 per share, which is the midpoint of the estimated offering price range set forth on the cover page of this prospectus, would increase or decrease the net proceeds that we receive from this offering and the concurrent private placement by approximately $25.6 million, assuming that the number of shares offered by us, as set forth on the cover page of this prospectus, remains the same and after deducting the estimated underwriting discounts and commissions payable by us. Similarly, each increase or decrease of 1.0 million in the number of shares of our Class A common stock offered by us would increase or decrease the net proceeds that we receive from this offering and the concurrent private placement by approximately $18.2 million, assuming the assumed initial public offering price remains the same and after deducting the estimated underwriting discounts and commissions payable by us.

The principal purposes of this offering are to increase our capitalization and financial flexibility, create a public market for our Class A common stock, and enable access to the public equity markets for us and our stockholders.

We intend to use a portion of the net proceeds we receive from this offering and the concurrent private placement to repay $193.1 million that is expected to be outstanding immediately prior to the completion of this offering under our revolving credit facility, which we intend to draw down prior to the completion of this offering to satisfy tax withholding and remittance obligations of $193.1 million related to the RSU Settlement. This amount is based upon the assumed initial public offering price of $19.00 per share, which is the midpoint of the estimated offering price range set forth on the cover page of this prospectus. See the section titled "Management's Discussion and Analysis of Financial Condition and Results of Operations— Liquidity and Capital Resources" for additional information regarding our revolving credit facility.

We also intend to use the net proceeds we receive from this offering and the concurrent private placement for general corporate purposes, including working capital, operating expenses, and capital expenditures. Additionally, we may use a portion of the net proceeds we receive from this offering and the concurrent private placement to acquire businesses, products, services, or technologies. However, we do not have agreements or commitments for any material acquisitions at this time. We cannot specify with certainty the particular uses of the net proceeds that we will receive from this offering and the concurrent private placement. Accordingly, we will have broad discretion in using these proceeds. Pending the use of proceeds from this offering as described above, we may invest the net proceeds that we receive in this offering and the concurrent private placement in short-term, investment grade, interest-bearing instruments.

DIVIDEND POLICY

We have never declared or paid any cash dividends on our capital stock. We currently intend to retain any future earnings and do not expect to pay any dividends in the foreseeable future. Any future determination to declare cash dividends will be made at the discretion of our Board of Directors, subject to applicable laws, and will depend on a number of factors, including our financial condition, results of operations, capital requirements, contractual restrictions, general business conditions, and other factors that our Board of Directors may deem relevant. In addition, the terms of our revolving credit facility place certain limitations on the amount of cash dividends we can pay, even if no amounts are currently outstanding.

CAPITALIZATION

The following table sets forth cash and cash equivalents, as well as our capitalization, as of December 31, 2017, as follows:

- on an actual basis;

- on a pro forma basis, giving effect to (i) the Capital Stock Conversions, as if such conversions had occurred on December 31, 2017, (ii) the filing and effectiveness of our amended and restated certificate of incorporation in Delaware that will become effective immediately prior to the completion of this offering, (iii) stock-based compensation expense of $415.6 million associated with the RSU Settlement, (iv) the net issuance of 15,897,254 shares of our Class B common stock upon the RSU Settlement, (v) the borrowing of $193.1 million under our revolving credit facility to satisfy our tax withholding and remittance obligations related to the RSU Settlement, and (vi) a cash payment of $193.1 million to satisfy our tax withholding and remittance obligations related to the RSU Settlement, which amounts in (v) and (vi) are based upon the assumed initial public offering price of $19.00 per share, which is the midpoint of the estimated offering price range set forth on the cover page of this prospectus; and

- on a pro forma as adjusted basis, giving effect to (i) the pro forma adjustments set forth above, (ii) the sale and issuance by us of 32,085,567 shares of our Class A common stock in this offering and the concurrent private placement, based upon the assumed initial public offering price of $19.00 per share, which is the midpoint of the estimated offering price range set forth on the cover page of this prospectus, and after deducting estimated underwriting discounts and commissions and estimated offering expenses payable by us, (iii) the conversion of 9,177,591 shares of our Class B common stock held by certain selling stockholders into an equivalent number of shares of our Class A common stock upon the sale by the selling stockholders in this offering, and (iv) the use of proceeds from the offering to repay $193.1 million drawn down under our revolving credit facility to satisfy our tax withholding and remittance obligations related to the RSU Settlement and pay related net costs of approximately $0.2 million.

51

The pro forma as adjusted information set forth in the table below is illustrative only and will be adjusted based on the actual initial public offering price and other terms of this offering determined at pricing. You should read this table together with our consolidated financial statements and related notes, and the sections titled "Selected Consolidated Financial and Other Data" and "Management's Discussion and Analysis of Financial Condition and Results of Operations" that are included elsewhere in this prospectus.

	Actual	Pro forma(1)	Pro forma as adjusted(2)
	\multicolumn{3}{c}{As of December 31, 2017}		
	\multicolumn{3}{c}{(In millions, except share and per share data)}		
Cash and cash equivalents	$ 430.0	$ 430.0	$ 816.6
Revolving credit facility	$ —	$ 193.1	$ —
Stockholders' equity (deficit):			
Convertible preferred stock, par value $0.00001 per share: 151,212,292 shares authorized, 147,569,183 issued and outstanding, actual; no shares authorized, issued and outstanding, pro forma, and pro forma as adjusted	615.3	—	—
Preferred stock, par value $0.00001 per share: no shares authorized, issued and outstanding, actual; 240,000,000 shares authorized, no shares issued and outstanding, pro forma, and pro forma as adjusted	—	—	—
Class A common stock, par value $0.00001 per share: 533,333,333 shares authorized, 8,948,677 shares issued and outstanding, actual; 2,400,000,000 shares authorized, 11,817,248 shares issued and outstanding, pro forma, and 2,400,000,000 shares authorized, 53,080,406 shares issued and outstanding, pro forma as adjusted	—	—	—
Class B common stock, par value $0.00001 per share: 466,666,666 shares authorized, 187,903,583 shares issued and outstanding, actual; 475,000,000 shares authorized, 348,501,449 shares issued and outstanding, pro forma, and 475,000,000 shares authorized, 339,323,858 shares issued and outstanding, pro forma as adjusted	—	—	—
Class C common stock, par value $0.00001 per share: no shares authorized, issued and outstanding, actual; 800,000,000 shares authorized, no shares issued and outstanding, pro forma, and 800,000,000 shares authorized, no shares issued and outstanding, pro forma as adjusted	—	—	—
Additional paid-in capital	533.1	1,370.9	1,950.8
Accumulated deficit	(1,049.7)	(1,465.3)	(1,465.5)
Accumulated other comprehensive income	4.2	4.2	4.2
Total stockholders' equity (deficit)	102.9	(90.2)	489.5
Total capitalization	$ 102.9	$ 102.9	$ 489.5

(1) The pro forma data as of December 31, 2017, gives effect to stock-based compensation expense of $415.6 million associated with the RSU Settlement. The pro forma adjustment related to stock-based compensation expense of $415.6 million has been reflected as an increase to additional paid-in capital and accumulated deficit.

(2) Each $1.00 increase or decrease in the assumed initial public offering price of $19.00 per share, which is the midpoint of the estimated offering price range set forth on the cover page of this prospectus, would increase or decrease, as applicable, (i) the amount of our pro forma as adjusted cash and cash equivalents, additional paid-in capital, total stockholders' equity, and total capitalization by approximately $25.6 million, assuming that the number of shares offered by us, as set forth on the cover page of this prospectus, remains the same and after deducting estimated underwriting discounts and commissions payable by us, (ii) the amount we would be required to draw down under our revolving credit facility to satisfy our tax withholding and remittance obligations related to the RSU Settlement by $10.2 million, and

(iii) the amount we would be required to pay to satisfy our tax withholding and remittance obligations related to the RSU Settlement by $10.2 million. An increase or decrease of 1.0 million shares in the number of shares offered by us would increase or decrease, as applicable, the amount of our pro forma as adjusted cash, and cash equivalents, additional paid-in capital, total stockholders' equity, and total capitalization by approximately $18.2 million, assuming the assumed initial public offering price remains the same, and after deducting estimated underwriting discounts and commissions payable by us.

If the underwriters' option to purchase additional shares of our Class A common stock from us were exercised in full, pro forma as adjusted cash and cash equivalents, additional paid-in capital, total stockholders' equity, total capitalization, and Class A shares outstanding as of December 31, 2017, would be $914.7 million, $2,048.9 million, $587.6 million, $587.6 million, and 58,480,406 shares, respectively.

The number of shares of our Class A common stock, Class B common stock, and Class C common stock that will be outstanding after this offering and the concurrent private placement is based on 11,817,248 shares of our Class A common stock (including the Capital Stock Conversions), 348,501,449 shares of our Class B common stock (including the Capital Stock Conversions and the RSU Settlement), and no shares of our Class C common stock outstanding as of December 31, 2017, and excludes the following:

- 14,733,333 shares of our Class A common stock subject to RSAs that were granted pursuant to the Co-Founder Grants, and vest upon the satisfaction of a service condition and achievement of certain stock price goals;

- 4,959,492 shares of our Class B common stock issuable upon the exercise of options to purchase shares of our Class B common stock outstanding as of December 31, 2017, with a weighted-average exercise price of $10.52 per share;

- 16,707,823 shares of our Class A common stock and 12,158,666 shares of our Class B common stock subject to RSUs outstanding, but for which the service condition was not satisfied as of December 31, 2017;

- 10,921,416 shares of our Class A common stock subject to RSUs granted after December 31, 2017;

- 65,982,109 shares of our Class A common stock reserved for future issuance under our equity compensation plans, consisting of:

  - 51,532,143 shares of our Class A common stock to be reserved for future issuance under our 2018 Plan, which will become effective prior to the completion of this offering (including the shares that will be repurchased by us in connection with the RSU Settlement);

  - 10,313,134 shares of our Class A common stock reserved for future issuance under our 2017 Plan, which number of shares includes an additional 1,333,333 shares of our Class A common stock reserved for issuance under our 2017 Plan that was approved by our Board of Directors in February 2018 (and which our stockholders approved in March 2018), and will be added to the shares of our Class A common stock to be reserved for future issuance under our 2018 Plan upon its effectiveness;

  - 4,136,832 shares of our Class A common stock to be reserved for future issuance under our ESPP, which will become effective prior to the completion of this offering, but no offering periods under the ESPP will commence unless and until otherwise determined by our Board of Directors; and

- 45,505,158 shares of our Class C common stock reserved for future issuance under certain other equity compensation plans, consisting of:

  - 41,368,326 shares of our Class C common stock to be reserved for future issuance under our 2018 Class C Equity Incentive Plan, or our 2018 Class C Plan, which will become effective prior to the completion of this offering; and

  - 4,136,832 shares of our Class C common stock to be reserved for future issuance under our 2018 Class C Employee Stock Purchase Plan, or our Class C ESPP, which will become effective prior

53

to the completion of this offering, but no offering periods under the Class C ESPP will commence unless and until otherwise determined by our Board of Directors.

Our 2018 Plan and ESPP each provides for annual automatic increases in the number of shares of our Class A common stock reserved thereunder, and our 2018 Plan also provides for increases to the number of shares of our Class A common stock that may be granted thereunder based on shares under our 2008 Equity Incentive Plan, or our 2008 Plan, and 2017 Plan that expire, are forfeited, or otherwise repurchased by us, as more fully described in the section titled "Executive Compensation—Employee Benefits and Stock Plans." Additionally, if and when our Board of Directors determines to use our 2018 Class C Plan and Class C ESPP, such plans will provide for annual automatic increases in the number of shares of our Class C common stock reserved thereunder.

DILUTION

If you invest in our Class A common stock in this offering, your ownership interest will be diluted to the extent of the difference between the initial public offering price per share of our Class A common stock and the pro forma as adjusted net tangible book value per share of our common stock immediately after this offering and the concurrent private placement. Net tangible book value dilution per share to new investors represents the difference between the amount per share paid by purchasers of shares of our Class A common stock in this offering and the pro forma as adjusted net tangible book value per share of our common stock immediately after completion of this offering and the concurrent private placement.

Net tangible book value per share is determined by dividing our total tangible assets less our total liabilities by the number of shares of our common stock outstanding. Our historical net tangible book value as of December 31, 2017, was $(13.0) million, or $(0.04) per share. Our pro forma net tangible book value as of December 31, 2017, was $(206.2) million, or $(0.57) per share, based on the total number of shares of our Class A common stock and Class B common stock outstanding as of December 31, 2017, after giving effect to the Capital Stock Conversions and the RSU Settlement.

After giving effect to the sale by us of 32,085,567 shares of our Class A common stock in this offering and the concurrent private placement at the assumed initial public offering price of $19.00 per share, which is the midpoint of the estimated offering price range set forth on the cover page of this prospectus, and after deducting estimated underwriting discounts and commissions and estimated offering expenses payable by us, our pro forma as adjusted net tangible book value as of December 31, 2017, would have been $373.8 million, or $0.95 per share. This represents an immediate increase in pro forma net tangible book value of $1.52 per share to our existing stockholders and an immediate dilution in pro forma net tangible book value of $18.05 per share to investors purchasing shares of our Class A common stock in this offering at the assumed initial public offering price. The following table illustrates this dilution:

Assumed initial public offering price per share		$19.00
Pro forma net tangible book value per share as of December 31, 2017	$(0.57)	
Increase in pro forma net tangible book value per share attributable to new investors purchasing shares of Class A common stock in this offering and the concurrent private placement	1.52	
Pro forma as adjusted net tangible book value per share after this offering and the concurrent private placement		0.95
Dilution in pro forma net tangible book value per share to new investors in this offering and the concurrent private placement		$18.05

Each $1.00 increase or decrease in the assumed initial public offering price of $19.00 per share, which is the midpoint of the estimated offering price range set forth on the cover page of this prospectus, would increase or decrease, as applicable, our pro forma as adjusted net tangible book value per share to new investors by $0.07, and would increase or decrease, as applicable, dilution per share to new investors purchasing shares of our Class A common stock in this offering by $0.93, assuming that the number of shares offered by us, as set forth on the cover page of this prospectus, remains the same and after deducting estimated underwriting discounts and commissions and estimated offering expenses payable by us. Similarly, each increase or decrease of 1.0 million shares in the number of shares of our Class A common stock offered by us would increase or decrease, as applicable, our pro forma as adjusted net tangible book value by approximately $0.04 per share and increase or decrease, as applicable, the dilution to new investors purchasing shares of our Class A common stock in this offering by $0.04 per share, assuming the assumed initial public offering price remains the same, and after deducting underwriting discounts and commissions and estimated offering expenses payable by us.

55

If the underwriters' option to purchase additional shares of our Class A common stock from us is exercised in full, the pro forma as adjusted net tangible book value per share of our common stock, as adjusted to give effect to this offering and the concurrent private placement, would be $1.19 per share, and the dilution in pro forma net tangible book value per share to new investors purchasing shares of our Class A common stock in this offering would be $17.81 per share.

The following table presents, as of December 31, 2017, after giving effect to the Capital Stock Conversions and the RSU Settlement, the differences between the existing stockholders and the new investors purchasing shares of our Class A common stock in this offering and the concurrent private placement with respect to the number of shares purchased from us, the total consideration paid or to be paid to us, which includes net proceeds received from the issuance of our Class A common stock and the average price per share paid or to be paid to us at the assumed initial public offering price of $19.00 per share, which is the midpoint of the estimated offering price range set forth on the cover page of this prospectus, before deducting estimated underwriting discounts and commissions and estimated offering expenses payable by us:

	Shares purchased		Total consideration		Average price per share
	Number	Percent	Amount	Percentage	
Existing stockholders	360,318,697	91.8%	$ 639,593,106	51.2%	$ 1.78
New investors	26,822,409	6.8%	$ 509,625,771	40.8%	$19.00
Concurrent private placement investor	5,263,158	1.4%	$ 100,000,002	8.0%	$19.00
Totals	392,404,264	100.0%	$1,249,218,879	100%	

Each $1.00 increase or decrease in the assumed initial public offering price of $19.00 per share, which is the midpoint of the estimated offering price range set forth on the cover page of this prospectus, would increase or decrease, as applicable, the total consideration paid by new investors and total consideration paid by all stockholders by approximately $25.6 million, assuming that the number of shares of our Class A common stock offered by us, as set forth on the cover page of this prospectus, remains the same and after deducting estimated underwriting discounts and commissions and estimated offering expenses payable by us. Similarly, each increase or decrease of 1.0 million in the number of shares of our Class A common stock offered by us would increase or decrease the total consideration paid by new investors and total consideration paid by all stockholders by approximately $18.2 million, assuming the assumed initial public offering price remains the same and after deducting the estimated underwriting discounts and commissions payable by us.

Except as otherwise indicated, the above discussion and tables assume no exercise of the underwriters' option to purchase additional shares of our Class A common stock from us. If the underwriters' option to purchase additional shares of our Class A common stock were exercised in full, our existing stockholders would own 90.6% and our new investors would own 9.4% of the total number of shares of our common stock outstanding upon completion of this offering and the concurrent private placement.

Sales by the selling stockholders in this offering will cause the number of shares held by existing stockholders to be reduced to 351,141,106 shares, or 89.5% of the total number of shares of our common stock outstanding following the completion of this offering and the concurrent private placement, and will increase the number of shares held by new investors to 41,263,158 shares, or 10.5% of the total number of shares outstanding following the completion of this offering and the concurrent private placement.

56

The number of shares of our Class A common stock, Class B common stock, and Class C common stock that will be outstanding after this offering and the concurrent private placement is based on 11,817,248 shares of our Class A common stock (including the Capital Stock Conversions), 348,501,449 shares of our Class B common stock (including the Capital Stock Conversions and the RSU Settlement) and no shares of our Class C common stock outstanding as of December 31, 2017, and excludes the following:

- 14,733,333 shares of our Class A common stock subject to RSAs that were granted pursuant to the Co-Founder Grants, and vest upon the satisfaction of a service condition and achievement of certain stock price goals;

- 4,959,492 shares of our Class B common stock issuable upon the exercise of options to purchase shares of our Class B common stock outstanding as of December 31, 2017, with a weighted-average exercise price of $10.52 per share;

- 16,707,823 shares of our Class A common stock and 12,158,666 shares of our Class B common stock subject to RSUs outstanding, but for which the service condition was not satisfied, as of December 31, 2017;

- 10,921,416 shares of our Class A common stock subject to RSUs granted after December 31, 2017;

- 65,982,109 shares of our Class A common stock reserved for future issuance under our equity compensation plans, consisting of:

  - 51,532,143 shares of our Class A common stock to be reserved for future issuance under our 2018 Equity Incentive Plan, or our 2018 Plan, which will become effective prior to the completion of this offering (including the shares that will be repurchased by us in connection with the RSU Settlement);

  - 10,313,134 shares of our Class A common stock reserved for future issuance under our 2017 Equity Incentive Plan, or our 2017 Plan, which number of shares includes an additional 1,333,333 shares of our Class A common stock reserved for issuance under our 2017 Plan that was approved by our Board of Directors in February 2018 (and which our stockholders approved in March 2018), and will be added to the shares of our Class A common stock to be reserved for future issuance under our 2018 Plan upon its effectiveness;

  - 4,136,832 shares of our Class A common stock to be reserved for future issuance under our ESPP, which will become effective prior to the completion of this offering, but no offering periods under the ESPP will commence unless and until otherwise determined by our Board of Directors; and

- 45,505,158 shares of our Class C common stock reserved for future issuance under certain other equity compensation plans, consisting of:

  - 41,368,326 shares of our Class C common stock to be reserved for future issuance under our 2018 Class C Stock Incentive Plan, or our 2018 Class C Plan, which will become effective prior to the completion of this offering; and

  - 4,136,832 shares of our Class C common stock to be reserved for future issuance under our 2018 Class C Employee Stock Purchase Plan, or our Class C ESPP, which will become effective prior to the completion of this offering, but no offering periods under the Class C ESPP will commence unless and until otherwise determined by our Board of Directors.

Our 2018 Plan and ESPP each provides for annual automatic increases in the number of shares of our Class A common stock reserved thereunder, and our 2018 Plan also provides for increases to the number of shares of our Class A common stock that may be granted thereunder based on shares under our 2008 Equity Incentive Plan, or our 2008 Plan, and 2017 Plan that expire, are forfeited, or otherwise repurchased by us, as more fully described in the section titled "Executive Compensation—Employee Benefits and Stock Plans." Additionally, if and when our Board of Directors determines to use our 2018 Class C Plan and Class C ESPP,

57

145

such plans will provide for annual automatic increases in the number of shares of our Class C common stock reserved thereunder.

To the extent that any outstanding options to purchase our common stock are exercised, RSUs are settled or new awards are granted under our equity compensation plans, there will be further dilution to investors participating in this offering.

58

146

SELECTED CONSOLIDATED FINANCIAL AND OTHER DATA

The following selected consolidated financial data should be read in conjunction with "Management's Discussion and Analysis of Financial Condition and Results of Operations" and the consolidated financial statements and related notes thereto included elsewhere in this prospectus. The consolidated statements of operations data for each of the years ended December 31, 2015, 2016, and 2017 and the consolidated balance sheet data as of December 31, 2016 and 2017, are derived from our audited consolidated financial statements that are included elsewhere in this prospectus. Our historical results are not necessarily indicative of our future results. The selected consolidated financial data in this section are not intended to replace the consolidated financial statements and related notes thereto included elsewhere in this prospectus and are qualified in their entirety by the consolidated financial statements and related notes thereto included elsewhere in this prospectus.

Consolidated Statements of Operations Data

| | Year ended December 31, | | |
	2015	2016	2017
	(In millions except for per share amounts)		
Revenue	$ 603.8	$ 844.8	$1,106.8
Cost of revenue(1)	407.4	390.6	368.9
Gross profit	196.4	454.2	737.9
Operating expenses:(1)			
Research and development	201.6	289.7	380.3
Sales and marketing	193.1	250.6	314.0
General and administrative	107.9	107.4	157.3
Total operating expenses	502.6	647.7	851.6
Loss from operations	(306.2)	(193.5)	(113.7)
Interest expense, net	(15.2)	(16.4)	(11.0)
Other income (expense), net	(4.2)	4.9	13.2
Loss before income taxes	(325.6)	(205.0)	(111.5)
Provision for income taxes	(0.3)	(5.2)	(0.2)
Net loss	$(325.9)	$(210.2)	$ (111.7)
Net loss per share attributable to common stockholders, basic and diluted(2)	$ (1.77)	$ (1.11)	$ (0.57)
Weighted-average shares used in computing net loss per share attributable to common stockholders, basic and diluted	184.5	189.1	195.9
Pro forma net loss per share attributable to common stockholders, basic and diluted(2)			$ (0.31)
Weighted-average shares used in computing pro forma net loss per share attributable to common stockholders, basic and diluted			358.6

59

(1) Includes stock-based compensation as follows:

	Year ended December 31,		
	2015	2016	2017
	(In millions)		
Cost of revenue	$ 2.6	$ 8.2	$ 12.2
Research and development	36.1	72.7	93.1
Sales and marketing	19.8	44.6	33.7
General and administrative	7.6	22.1	25.6
Total stock-based compensation	$66.1	$147.6	$164.6

(2) See Note 12, "Net Loss Per Share" to our consolidated financial statements included elsewhere in this prospectus for an explanation of the method used to calculate basic and diluted net loss per share attributable to common stockholders and Note 13, "Unaudited Pro Forma Net Loss Per Share" for an explanation of the method used to calculate pro forma net loss per share attributable to common stockholders.

Consolidated Balance Sheet Data

	As of December 31,	
	2016	2017
	(In millions)	
Cash and cash equivalents	$ 352.7	$ 430.0
Working capital	(221.9)	(220.3)
Property and equipment, net	444.0	341.9
Total assets	1,004.2	1,019.9
Total deferred revenue	354.9	419.2
Total capital lease obligations	257.2	174.3
Total stockholders' equity	122.8	102.9

60

MANAGEMENT'S DISCUSSION AND ANALYSIS OF FINANCIAL CONDITION AND RESULTS OF OPERATIONS

The following discussion and analysis of our financial condition and results of operations should be read in conjunction with the section titled "Selected Consolidated Financial and Other Data" and the consolidated financial statements and related notes thereto included elsewhere in this prospectus. This discussion contains forward-looking statements that involve risks and uncertainties. Our actual results could differ materially from those discussed below. Factors that could cause or contribute to such differences include, but are not limited to, those identified below and those discussed in the section titled "Risk Factors" included elsewhere in this prospectus.

Our Business

Our modern economy runs on knowledge. Today, knowledge lives in the cloud as digital content, and Dropbox is a global collaboration platform where more and more of this content is created, accessed, and shared with the world. We serve more than 500 million registered users across 180 countries.

Dropbox was founded in 2007 with a simple idea: Life would be a lot better if everyone could access their most important information anytime from any device. Over the past decade, we've largely accomplished that mission—but along the way we recognized that for most of our users, sharing and collaborating on Dropbox was even more valuable than storing files.

Our market opportunity has grown as we've expanded from keeping files in sync to keeping teams in sync. Today, Dropbox is well positioned to reimagine the way work gets done. We're focused on reducing the inordinate amount of time and energy the world wastes on "work about work"—tedious tasks like searching for content, switching between applications, and managing workflows.

We've built a thriving global business with 11 million paying users. Our revenue was $603.8 million, $844.8 million, and $1,106.8 million in 2015, 2016, and 2017, respectively, representing an annual growth rate of 40% and 31%, respectively. We generated net losses of $325.9 million, $210.2 million, and $111.7 million in 2015, 2016, and 2017, respectively. We also generated positive free cash flow of $137.4 million and $305.0 million in 2016 and 2017, respectively, compared to negative free cash flow of $63.9 million in 2015.

61

149

Our History

Since our founding, we've built one of the largest collaboration platforms in the world.

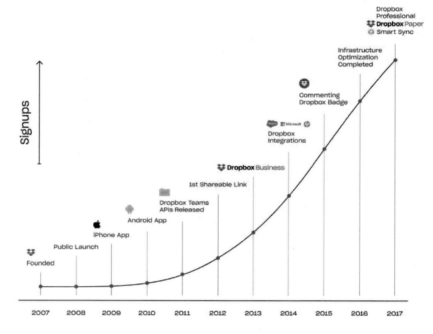

Where we are now

500M+ Registered users
180+ Countries
$1.1B+ GAAP revenue
11M+ Total paying users
400B+ Pieces of content added to Dropbox

Our Subscription Plans

We generate revenue from individuals, teams, and organizations by selling subscriptions to our platform, which serve the varying needs of our diverse customer base. Of our 11 million paying users, approximately 30% use Dropbox for work on a Dropbox Business team plan, and we estimate that an additional 50% use Dropbox for work on an individual plan, collectively totaling approximately 80% of paying users. As of December 31,

2017, approximately 92% of Fortune 500 companies had paying Dropbox users within their organization, and approximately 56% had at least one paying Dropbox Business team. We had more than 300,000 paying Dropbox Business teams as of December 31, 2017. Each Dropbox Business team represents a separately billed deployment that is managed through a single administrative dashboard. Each team must have a minimum of three users, but we also serve teams that can have more than tens of thousands of users. Customers can choose between an annual or monthly plan, with a small number of large organizations on multi-year plans. A majority of our customers opt for our annual plans. We typically bill our customers at the beginning of their respective terms and recognize revenue ratably over the term of the subscription period. International customers can pay in U.S. dollars or a select number of foreign currencies.

	Individuals			Teams (Branded as Dropbox Business)		
	Basic	Plus	Professional	Standard	Advanced	Enterprise
First launched	2008	2008	2017	2011	2017	2015
Number of users	1 user	1 user	1 user	3+ users	3+ users	Large deployments
Base price ($USD) per user	Free	$9.99/month $99/year	$19.99/month $199/year	$15.00/month $150/year	$25.00/month $240/year	Negotiated pricing
Advanced sharing permissions			✔	✔	✔	✔
Version history	30 days	30 days	120 days	120 days	120 days	120 days
Smart Sync			✔	✔	✔	✔
Showcase			✔		✔	✔
Team folders				✔	✔	✔
Unlimited API access*				✔	✔	✔
Paper	✔	✔	✔	✔	✔	✔
Storage	2GB	1TB	1TB	2TB	As much as needed	As much as needed
Support	Basic email support	Priority email support	Priority chat support	Live chat support	Business hours phone support	24/7 phone support Assigned account success manager
Advanced admin & security features		Remote device wipe	Remote device wipe	Admin console Managed groups Access permissions Account transfer tool HIPAA support	*Everything in Standard* Device approval Audit log Tiered admin roles SSO integration	*Everything in Advanced* EMM Network control Domain insights Integration support

*Teams have unlimited API access to productivity and security partners but may be subject to a cap on API calls to data transport partners.

63

151

Our premium subscription plans, such as Professional and Advanced, provide more functionality than other subscription plans and are offered at higher prices per user. Our Standard and Advanced subscription plans offer robust capabilities for businesses, and the vast majority of Dropbox Business teams, including those at Fortune 500 companies, purchase our Standard or Advanced subscription plans. While our Enterprise subscription plan offers more opportunities for customization, companies can subscribe to any of these team plans for their business needs.

Our Business Model

Drive new signups

We acquire users efficiently and at relatively low costs through word-of-mouth referrals, direct in-product referrals, and sharing of content.

Anyone can create a Dropbox account for free through our website or app and be up and running in minutes. These users often share and collaborate with other non-registered users, attracting new signups into our network. For example, many people use Dropbox for work and spread our platform by collaborating on projects or sharing content externally. We also acquire a small proportion of our registered users through paid marketing and distribution partnerships in which hardware manufacturers pre-install our software on their devices.

We have over 500 million registered users on our platform, of which over 100 million signed up since the beginning of 2017.

Increase conversion of registered users to our paid subscription plans

Dropbox Basic, the free version of our product, serves as a major funnel for conversions to our paid subscription plans. It fosters brand awareness, product familiarity, and organic adoption of Dropbox. When they purchase a subscription, our users gain access to premium features such as richer collaboration tools, administrative controls, and advanced security features, as well as larger storage capacity. We believe that our current registered user base represents a significant opportunity to increase our revenue. We estimate that approximately 300 million of our registered users have at least one characteristic that we believe makes them more likely than other registered users to pay over time. These characteristics include: (i) having signed up for Dropbox with a business domain email; (ii) having used specific types of computers or mobile devices to access our platform; or (iii) having signed up from certain countries in more developed markets in North America, Europe, and Asia Pacific, and having linked a desktop or laptop to our platform. Substantially all of our paying users share at least one of these characteristics. We've found that aggregate user activity metrics aren't leading indicators of revenue or conversion. For that reason, we don't comprehensively track user activity across the Dropbox platform for financial planning and forecasting purposes.

We generate over 90% of our revenue from self-serve channels—users who purchase a subscription through our app or website. We actively encourage our registered users to become paying users through in-product prompts and notifications, time-limited free trials of paid subscription plans, email campaigns, and lifecycle marketing.

During the fourth quarter of 2017, hundreds of millions of devices—including computers, phones, and tablets—were actively connected to the Dropbox platform. Because our users have installed Dropbox on many devices, we have multiple opportunities to inform them about new product experiences and premium subscription plans via in-product notifications, without any external marketing spend.

Our scale enables us to experiment and optimize the conversion marketing process. We run hundreds of product tests and targeted marketing campaigns simultaneously, and analyze usage patterns within our network to continually improve our user targeting and marketing messaging.

64

Upgrade and expand existing customers

We offer a range of paid subscription plans, from Plus and Professional for individuals to Standard, Advanced, and Enterprise for teams. We analyze usage patterns within our network and run hundreds of targeted marketing campaigns to encourage paying users to upgrade their plans. For example, we prompt individual subscribers who collaborate with others on Dropbox to purchase our Standard or Advanced plans for a better team experience. They can do this by either joining an existing Dropbox Business team or by creating a new Dropbox Business team and inviting others to join. In 2017, over 40% of new Dropbox Business teams included a member who was previously a subscriber to one of our individual paid plans.

We believe that a large majority of individual customers use Dropbox for work, which creates an opportunity to significantly increase conversion to Dropbox Business team offerings over time. We also encourage existing Dropbox Business teams to purchase additional licenses or to upgrade to premium subscription plans.

Within an organization, Dropbox usage may be spread between a mix of Basic users, Plus and Professional subscribers, and one or more Dropbox Business teams. Our outbound sales team focuses on converting and consolidating these separate pockets of usage into a centralized deployment. Nearly all of our largest outbound deals originated as smaller self-serve deployments.

Our Attractive Cohort Economics

We define a cohort as all registered users who signed up for Dropbox in a given period of time. We track the total monthly subscription amount of all paying users in each cohort as of the end of the month, or the monthly subscription amount. For paying users who opt for our monthly plans, the monthly subscription amount is equal to the price of the monthly plan. For paying users who opt for our annual plans, which a majority of our users do, the monthly subscription amount is equal to the price of the annual plan divided by twelve. These amounts increase as more registered users in each cohort convert to paying users, paying users upgrade to premium subscription offerings, and team administrators purchase additional licenses. These amounts decrease when paying users terminate their subscriptions, downgrade their subscriptions to a lower tier, or team administrators reduce the number of licenses on their subscription plans. We continuously focus on adding new users and increasing the value we offer to them. As a result, each cohort of new users typically generates higher subscription amounts over time.

65

153

The chart below reflects the monthly subscription amount from January 2013 to December 2017 of all paying users in each quarterly cohort, including those who signed up for our platform prior to 2013.

Monthly subscription amount
By quarterly cohort

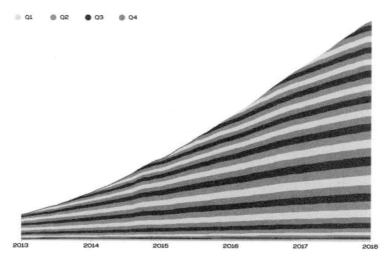

We continuously focus on adding new users and increasing the value we offer to them. As a result, each cohort of new users typically generates higher subscription amounts over time. For example, the monthly subscription amount generated by the January 2015 cohort doubled in less than three years after signup. We believe this cohort is representative of a typical cohort in recent periods.

66

154

Moreover, as we continue to innovate and optimize our go-to-market strategy, we have successfully increased monetization for subsequent cohorts. Comparing January cohorts from the last three years, at virtually every point in time after signup, the January 2017 cohort generated a higher monthly subscription amount than the January 2016 cohort, which in turn generated a higher monthly subscription amount than the January 2015 cohort.

Monthly subscription amount
Indexed to month 1 of January 2015 cohort

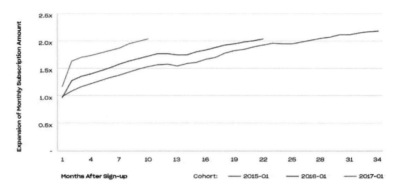

Our Global, Diversified Customer Base

The growing need for a unified home for content and the viral nature of our business have allowed us to scale globally. We have paying users across 180 countries, and we generated approximately half of our revenue in 2017 from customers outside the United States.

Our customer base is highly diversified, and in the periods presented, no customer accounted for more than 1% of our revenue. Our customers include individuals, teams, and organizations of all sizes, from freelancers and small businesses to Fortune 100 companies. They work across a wide range of industries, including professional services, technology, media, education, industrials, consumer and retail, and financial services. Within companies, our platform is used by all types of teams and functions, including sales, marketing, product, design, engineering, finance, legal, and human resources.

67

Our Predictable Subscription Revenue

Taken together, our subscription revenue model, consistent cohort trends, self-serve monetization engine, and large and diversified global customer base resulted in linear and predictable revenue generation over the duration of the quarters presented in the chart below.

Quarterly revenue generation

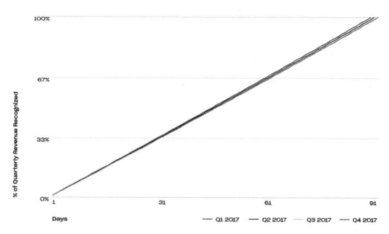

As of December 31, 2017, more than 80% of our annualized revenue came from existing individual users and Dropbox Business teams who were on our platform as of December 31, 2016.

As of December 31, 2017, our Annualized Net Revenue Retention for paying Dropbox Business customers was approximately 100%. Annualized Net Revenue Retention is the percentage of annualized revenue retained over a 365-day period, inclusive of changes in price, changes in number of licenses, upgrades and downgrades to different subscription plans, and churn. We calculate Annualized Net Revenue Retention by aggregating the annualized revenue from all paying Dropbox Business customers subscribing to a Dropbox Business plan at the beginning of the period, then aggregating the annualized revenue from those same Dropbox Business customers at the end of the period. For customers whose renewal is pending at the end of the period, we include their annualized revenue in the ending total if they resume payment within 30 days from the end of that period. Annualized Net Revenue Retention is equal to ending annualized revenue divided by beginning annualized revenue.

As of December 31, 2017, our blended Annualized Net Revenue Retention across the entire business, including individuals and Dropbox Business customers, was over 90%.

Key Factors Affecting Our Performance

We believe that the growth and future success of our business depends on many factors. While each of these factors presents significant opportunities for our business, they also pose important challenges that we must successfully address in order to sustain our growth and improve our results of operations.

Attract Users and Expand Relationships with Them. Our business model is based on attracting new users to our platform, converting registered users to paying users, and retaining and expanding paying users' subscriptions over time. Our continued success depends in part on our ability to offer compelling subscription plans with valuable capabilities, and to market these plans effectively to users. In addition, we must continue to provide a quality user experience to retain paying customers and encourage existing Dropbox Business teams to purchase additional licenses for their organizations over time. We intend to continue driving organic adoption by individual users and Dropbox Business teams through our self-serve model, and supplement this with our outbound sales force.

Continued Investment in Growth. We intend to continue to make focused investments to increase revenue and scale operations to support the growth of our business, and therefore expect expenses to increase. We plan to further invest in research and development as we hire employees in engineering, product, and design to enhance our platform and support the needs of our growing user base. We also plan to invest in sales and marketing activities to drive our self-serve business model and increase our brand awareness. We expect to incur additional general and administrative expenses to support our growth and our transition to being a publicly traded company. Further, we continue to make investments in our technical infrastructure to support user growth, and in our office locations to support employee growth, which will increase expenses and capital expenditures. As cost of revenue, operating expenses, and capital expenditures fluctuate over time, we may experience short-term, negative impacts to our results of operations and cash flows, but we are undertaking such investments in the belief that they will contribute to long-term growth.

Ongoing Innovation in a Rapidly Changing Environment. The market for content collaboration platforms is characterized by rapid technological change and frequent new product and service introductions. Our ability to acquire, retain, and upgrade paying users will depend in part on our ability to enhance our platform, introduce new features, and interoperate across an increasing range of devices, operating systems, and third-party applications. Certain features of our platform compete directly with products offered by Amazon, Apple, Atlassian, Box, Google, and Microsoft. We will need to continue to innovate in the face of this rapidly changing landscape to remain competitive.

Key Business Metrics

We review a number of operating and financial metrics, including the following key metrics to evaluate our business, measure our performance, identify trends affecting our business, formulate business plans, and make strategic decisions.

Paying users

We define paying users as the number of users who have active paid licenses for access to our platform as of the end of the period. One person would count as multiple paying users if the person had more than one active license. For example, a 50-person Dropbox Business team would count as 50 paying users, and an individual Dropbox Plus user would count as one paying user. If that individual Dropbox Plus user was also part of the 50-person Dropbox Business team, we would count the individual as two paying users.

We have experienced growth in the number of paying users across our products, with the vast majority of paying users for the periods presented coming from our self-serve channels.

The below table sets forth the number of paying users as of December 31, 2015, 2016, and 2017:

	As of December 31,		
	2015	2016	2017
	(In millions)		
Paying users	6.5	8.8	11.0

69

157

Average revenue per paying user

We define average revenue per paying user, or ARPU, as our revenue for the period presented divided by the average paying users during the same period. For interim periods, we use annualized revenue, which is calculated by dividing the revenue for the particular period by the number of days in that period and multiplying this value by 365 days. Average paying users are calculated based on adding the number of paying users as of the beginning of the period to the number of paying users as of the end of the period, and then dividing by two.

Our ARPU declined for the year ended December 31, 2016, compared to the year ended December 31, 2015, primarily due to foreign currency fluctuations related to our sales that are denominated in foreign currencies. Our ARPU increased for the year ended December 31, 2017, compared to the year ended December 31, 2016, primarily due to an increased mix of sales towards our higher priced subscription plans, including our new Dropbox Business Advanced plan.

The below table sets forth our ARPU for the years ended December 31, 2015, 2016, and 2017.

| | Year ended December 31, | | |
	2015	2016	2017
ARPU	$113.54	$110.54	$111.91

Non-GAAP Financial Measure

In addition to our results determined in accordance with U.S. generally accepted accounting principles, or GAAP, we believe that free cash flow, or FCF, a non-GAAP financial measure, is useful in evaluating our liquidity.

Free cash flow

We define FCF as GAAP net cash provided by operating activities less capital expenditures. We believe that FCF is a liquidity measure and that it provides useful information regarding cash provided by operating activities and cash used for investments in property and equipment required to maintain and grow our business. FCF is presented for supplemental informational purposes only and should not be considered a substitute for financial information presented in accordance with GAAP. FCF has limitations as an analytical tool, and it should not be considered in isolation or as a substitute for analysis of other GAAP financial measures, such as net cash provided by operating activities. Some of the limitations of FCF are that FCF does not reflect our future contractual commitments, excludes investments made to acquire assets under capital leases, and may be calculated differently by other companies in our industry, limiting its usefulness as a comparative measure.

We have experienced an increase in our FCF as a result of an increase in net cash provided by operating activities, primarily due to our Infrastructure Optimization discussed below in " —Recent Initiative," increased sales in the periods presented, and a decrease in capital expenditures relating to infrastructure equipment and leasehold improvements for our office spaces. We expect our FCF to fluctuate in future periods as we purchase infrastructure equipment to support our user base and invest in our new and existing office spaces, including our new corporate headquarters, to support our plans for growth. These activities, along with certain increased operating expenses as described below, may result in a decrease in FCF as a percentage of revenue in future periods.

70

The following is a reconciliation of FCF to the most comparable GAAP measure, net cash provided by operating activities:

	Year ended December 31,		
	2015	2016	2017
	(In millions)		
Net cash provided by operating activities	$ 14.8	$ 252.6	$330.3
Capital expenditures	(78.7)	(115.2)	(25.3)
Free cash flow	$(63.9)	$ 137.4	$305.0

Recent Initiative

Infrastructure Optimization

In recent years, we have taken several steps to improve the efficiency of the infrastructure that supports our platform. These efforts include an initiative that focused on migrating the vast majority of user data stored on the infrastructure of third-party service providers to our own lower cost, custom-built infrastructure in co-location facilities that we directly lease and operate. In order to host user data on our own infrastructure, we leased or purchased infrastructure that is depreciated within our cost of revenue. During the migration to our internal infrastructure, we duplicated our users' data between our internal infrastructure and that of our third-party service providers, resulting in higher storage costs. We reduced this practice over time until we completed the migration in the fourth quarter of 2016. Related to this initiative, we no longer duplicate data between our internal infrastructure and that of any third-party service providers. We expect to continue to realize benefits from expanding our internal infrastructure due to our operating scale and lower unit costs.

Starting in 2016, we also took measures to manage the storage footprint of certain long-inactive Basic users, freeing up additional storage capacity. Specifically, we closed the accounts of certain Basic users who had not engaged in any activity on the Dropbox platform in the last year and did not respond to multiple e-mail inquiries from us regarding their inactivity. We continue to regularly take similar measures to manage long-inactive and non-responsive Basic user accounts, and our total registered user numbers do not include accounts that have been closed. This effort, along with additional usage optimizations in 2017, enabled us to continue operating our business within our existing infrastructure base without a need for extensive incremental capital expenditures and leasing activity.

These efforts are collectively referred to as our Infrastructure Optimization, and some are ongoing.

Our Infrastructure Optimization reduced unit costs and helped limit capital expenditures and associated depreciation. Combined with the concurrent increase in our base of paying users, we experienced a reduction in our cost of revenue, an increase in our gross margins, and an improvement in our free cash flow in the periods presented.

Components of Our Results of Operations

Revenue

We generate revenue from sales of subscriptions to our platform.

Revenue is recognized ratably over the related contractual term generally beginning on the date that our platform is made available to a customer. Our subscription agreements typically have monthly or annual contractual terms, although a small percentage have multi-year contractual terms. Our agreements are generally non-cancelable. We typically bill in advance for monthly contracts and annually in advance for contracts with terms of one year or longer. Amounts that have been billed are initially recorded as deferred revenue until the revenue is recognized.

Our revenue is driven primarily by the number of paying users and the price we charge for access to our platform, which varies based on the type of plan to which a customer subscribes. We generate over 90% of our revenue from self-serve channels. No customer represented more than 1% of our revenue in the periods presented.

Cost of revenue and gross margin

Cost of revenue. Our cost of revenue consists primarily of expenses associated with the storage, delivery, and distribution of our platform for both paying users and Basic users. These costs, which we refer to as infrastructure costs, include depreciation of our servers located in co-location facilities that we lease and operate, rent and facilities expense for those datacenters, network and bandwidth costs, support and maintenance costs for our infrastructure equipment, and payments to third-party datacenter service providers. Cost of revenue also includes costs, such as salaries, bonuses, benefits, travel-related expenses, and stock-based compensation, which we refer to as employee-related costs, for employees whose primary responsibilities relate to supporting our infrastructure and delivering user support. Other non-employee costs included in cost of revenue include credit card fees related to processing customer transactions, and allocated overhead, such as facilities, including rent, utilities, depreciation on leasehold improvements and other equipment shared by all departments, and shared information technology costs. In addition, cost of revenue includes amortization of developed technologies, professional fees related to user support initiatives, and property taxes related to the datacenters.

We plan to continue increasing the capacity and enhancing the capability and reliability of our infrastructure to support user growth and increased use of our platform. We expect that cost of revenue, excluding the impact of certain stock-based compensation charges described in "—Significant Impacts of Stock-Based Compensation", will increase in absolute dollars in future periods. In addition, as a result of certain stock-based compensation charges described in "—Significant Impacts of Stock-Based Compensation," we expect our cost of revenue to increase significantly in absolute dollars in the quarter during which we complete this offering.

Gross margin. Gross margin is gross profit expressed as a percentage of revenue. Our gross margin may fluctuate from period to period based on the timing of additional capital expenditures and the related depreciation expense, or other increases in our infrastructure costs, as well as revenue fluctuations. As we continue to increase the utilization of our internal infrastructure, we generally expect our gross margin, excluding the impact of certain stock-based compensation charges described in "—Significant Impacts of Stock-Based Compensation", to remain relatively constant in the near term and to increase modestly in the long term. Taking into account these charges, we expect our gross margin to decrease significantly in the quarter during which we complete this offering.

Operating expenses

Research and development. Our research and development expenses consist primarily of employee-related costs for our engineering, product, and design teams, and allocated overhead. Additionally, research and development expenses include internal development-related third-party hosting fees. We have expensed almost all of our research and development costs as they were incurred.

We plan to continue to hire employees for our engineering, product, and design teams to support our research and development efforts. We expect that research and development costs will increase in absolute dollars in future periods and, excluding the impact of certain stock-based compensation charges described in "—Significant Impacts of Stock-Based Compensation", vary from period to period as a percentage of revenue.

Sales and marketing. Our sales and marketing expenses relate to both self-serve and outbound sales activities, and consist primarily of employee-related costs, brand campaign fees, lead generation fees, and allocated overhead. Sales commissions earned by our outbound sales team and the related payroll taxes, as well as commissions earned by third-party resellers that we consider to be incremental and recoverable costs of obtaining a contract with a user, are deferred and amortized over an estimated period of benefit of five years. Additionally, sales and marketing expenses include non-employee costs related to app store fees and fees payable to third-party sales representatives.

We plan to continue to invest in sales and marketing to grow our user base and increase our brand awareness, including marketing efforts to continue to drive our self-serve business model. The trend and timing of sales and marketing expenses will depend in part on the timing of marketing campaigns. We expect that sales and marketing expenses will increase in absolute dollars in future periods and, excluding the impact of certain stock-based compensation charges described in "—Significant Impacts of Stock-Based Compensation", vary from period to period as a percentage of revenue.

General and administrative. Our general and administrative expenses consist primarily of employee-related costs for our legal, finance, human resources, and other administrative teams, as well as certain executives. In addition, general and administrative expenses include allocated overhead, outside legal, accounting and other professional fees, and non-income based taxes.

We expect to incur additional general and administrative expenses to support the growth of the Company as well as our transition to being a publicly traded company, which includes the recognition of stock-based compensation expense related to grants of restricted stock made to our co-founders. We expect that general and administrative expenses will increase in absolute dollars in future periods and, excluding the impact of certain stock-based compensation charges described in "—Significant Impacts of Stock-Based Compensation", vary from period to period as a percentage of revenue.

As a result of certain stock-based compensation charges described in "—Significant Impacts of Stock-Based Compensation," we expect our research and development, sales and marketing, and general and administrative expenses to increase significantly in absolute dollars and as a percentage of revenue in the quarter during which we complete this offering.

Interest expense, net

Interest expense, net consists primarily of interest expense related to our capital lease obligations for infrastructure and our imputed financing obligation for our obligation to the legal owner of our previous corporate headquarters, partially offset by interest income earned on our money market funds classified as cash and cash equivalents.

Other income (expense), net

Other income (expense), net consists of other non-operating gains or losses, including those related to ongoing subleases and foreign currency transaction gains and losses.

Provision for income taxes

Provision for income taxes consists primarily of U.S. federal and state income taxes and income taxes in certain foreign jurisdictions in which we conduct business. For the periods presented, the difference between the U.S. statutory rate and our effective tax rate is primarily due to the valuation allowance on deferred tax assets. Our effective tax rate is also impacted by earnings realized in foreign jurisdictions with statutory tax rates lower than the federal statutory tax rate. We maintain a full valuation allowance on our net deferred tax assets for federal, state, and certain foreign jurisdictions as we have concluded that it is not more likely than not that the deferred assets will be realized.

As of December 31, 2017, we had $312.2 million of federal and $143.0 million of state net operating loss carryforwards available to reduce future taxable income, which will begin to expire in 2031 for federal and 2030

73

161

for state tax purposes. As of December 31, 2017, we also had $289.3 million of foreign net operating loss carryforwards available to reduce future taxable income, which will carryforward indefinitely. In addition, we had $22.9 million of foreign acquired net operating losses, which will carryforward indefinitely. It is possible that we will not generate taxable income in time to use these net operating loss carryforwards before their expiration. In addition, under Section 382 and 383 of the Internal Revenue Code of 1986, as amended, or the Code, if a corporation undergoes an "ownership change," the corporation's ability to use its pre-change net operating loss carryforwards and other pre-change attributes, such as research tax credits, to offset its post-change income may be limited. In general, an "ownership change" will occur if there is a cumulative change in our ownership by "5-percent shareholders" that exceeds 50 percentage points over a rolling three-year period. Similar rules may apply under state tax laws. We performed a study for the period through December 31, 2017, and determined that no ownership changes exceeding 50 percentage points have occurred. Our ability to use net operating loss and tax credit carryforwards to reduce future taxable income and liabilities may be subject to annual limitations as a result of ownership changes from January 1, 2018, and subsequent years, or as a result of this offering.

The Tax Cuts and Jobs Act, or the Tax Reform Act, was enacted on December 22, 2017 and provides for significant changes to U.S. tax law. Among other provisions, the Tax Reform Act reduces the U.S. corporate income tax rate to 21% effective in 2018. The Tax Reform Act also contains a number of provisions that may impact us in future years. Since the Tax Reform Act was recently finalized and ongoing guidance and accounting interpretation is expected over the next twelve months, we have made certain provisional accounting estimates, as permitted under Staff Accounting Bulletin No. 118, and continue to analyze our accounting policies in this area. The U.S. Treasury Department, the IRS, and other standard-setting bodies could interpret or issue guidance on how provisions of the Tax Reform Act will be applied or otherwise administered that is different from our interpretation. As we complete our analysis of the Tax Reform Act, collect and prepare necessary data, and interpret any additional guidance, the we may make adjustments to provisional amounts that we have recorded that may be material in the period in which the adjustments are made. The final accounting analysis will occur no later than one year from the date the Tax Reform Act was enacted.

As a result of the reduction in the corporate rate, we have remeasured our U.S. deferred tax assets and liabilities as of December 31, 2017 to reflect the lower rate expected to apply when these temporary differences reverse. We provisionally estimate that the remeasurement resulted in a reduction in deferred tax assets of $63.1 million, which was fully offset by a corresponding change to our valuation allowance. Although the tax rate reduction is known, we have not collected all of the necessary data to complete our analysis of the effect of the Tax Reform Act on the underlying deferred taxes and as such, the amounts recorded as of December 31, 2017 are provisional. However, we anticipate that any adjustment to provisional amounts recorded would be fully offset by a corresponding change to our valuation allowance.

The Tax Reform Act repeals the corporate alternative minimum tax, or AMT, effective beginning in 2018 and permits AMT credit carryforwards to be refunded to the extent unused through 2021. Since we do not anticipate the use of these credits to reduce future federal taxes, we recognized an income tax benefit and established an income tax receivable to reflect anticipated refunds of $1.4 million for our 2016 AMT credit carryforward during the year ended December 31, 2017. We have not collected all of the necessary data to complete our analysis of the classification of the AMT tax credit as a receivable and as such, the amounts recorded as an income tax receivable as of December 31, 2017 are provisional.

The Tax Reform Act also provides for a transition to a new territorial system of taxation and generally requires companies to include certain untaxed foreign earnings of non-U.S. subsidiaries into taxable income in 2017, or the Transition Tax. As a result of the cumulative deficits in our foreign subsidiaries, we estimate that we will have no Transition Tax inclusion.

We continue to evaluate our accounting policy for recording deferred taxes, if any, that would arise as a result of other new provisions including the global intangible low-taxed income tax and the base erosion tax

74

regimes established under the Tax Reform Act. This evaluation will be completed no later than one year from the date the Tax Reform Act was enacted.

Results of Operations

The following tables set forth our results of operations for the periods presented and as a percentage of our total revenue for those periods:

	Year ended December 31,		
	2015	2016	2017
		(In millions)	
Revenue	$ 603.8	$ 844.8	$1,106.8
Cost of revenue[1]	407.4	390.6	368.9
Gross profit	196.4	454.2	737.9
Operating expenses:[1]			
Research and development	201.6	289.7	380.3
Sales and marketing	193.1	250.6	314.0
General and administrative	107.9	107.4	157.3
Total operating expenses	502.6	647.7	851.6
Loss from operations	(306.2)	(193.5)	(113.7)
Interest expense, net	(15.2)	(16.4)	(11.0)
Other income (expense), net	(4.2)	4.9	13.2
Loss before income taxes	(325.6)	(205.0)	(111.5)
Provision for income taxes	(0.3)	(5.2)	(0.2)
Net loss	$(325.9)	$(210.2)	$ (111.7)

75

(1) Includes stock-based compensation as follows:

	Year ended December 31,		
	2015	2016	2017
		(In millions)	
Cost of revenue	$ 2.6	$ 8.2	$ 12.2
Research and development	36.1	72.7	93.1
Sales and marketing	19.8	44.6	33.7
General and administrative	7.6	22.1	25.6
Total stock-based compensation	$ 66.1	$ 147.6	$ 164.6

	Year ended December 31,		
	2015	2016	2017
		(As a % of revenue)	
Revenue	100%	100%	100%
Cost of revenue	67	46	33
Gross profit	33	54	67
Operating expenses:			
Research and development	33	34	34
Sales and marketing	32	30	28
General and administrative	18	13	14
Total operating expenses	83	77	77
Loss from operations	(51)	(23)	(10)
Interest expense, net	(3)	(2)	(1)
Other income (expense), net	(1)	1	1
Loss before income taxes	(54)	(24)	(10)
Provision for income taxes	—	(1)	—
Net loss	(54)%	(25)%	(10)%

Comparison of the year ended December 31, 2016 and 2017

Revenue

	Year Ended December 31,		$ Change	% Change
	2016	2017		
	(In millions)			
Revenue	$844.8	$1,106.8	$ 262.0	31%

Revenue increased $262.0 million or 31% during 2017, as compared to 2016. This increase was primarily due to a 25% increase in the number of paying users between periods. The average revenue per paying user also increased slightly between periods primarily due to an increased mix of sales towards our higher priced subscription plans, including our new Dropbox Business Advanced plan.

Cost of revenue, gross profit, and gross margin

	Year Ended December 31,		$ Change	% Change
	2016	2017		
	(In millions)			
Cost of revenue	$390.6	$368.9	$ (21.7)	(6)%
Gross profit	454.2	737.9	283.7	62%
Gross margin	54%	67%		

76

Cost of revenue decreased $21.7 million or 6% during 2017, as compared to 2016, primarily due to a $35.1 million decrease in our infrastructure costs due to our Infrastructure Optimization. Further, the decrease in cost of revenue was due to a $5.9 million decrease in amortization of developed technologies, as certain intangible assets became fully amortized during 2016. These decreases were partially offset by an increase of $11.0 million in employee-related expenses, which was due to headcount growth, an increase of $5.3 million in credit card transaction fees due to higher sales and an increase of $3.0 million in professional fees for user support.

Our gross margin increased from 54% during 2016 to 67% during 2017, primarily due to a 31% increase in our revenue during the period and our Infrastructure Optimization.

Research and development

	Year Ended December 31,		$ Change	% Change
	2016	2017		
	(In millions)			
Research and development	$289.7	$380.3	$ 90.6	31%

Research and development expenses increased $90.6 million or 31% during 2017, as compared to 2016, primarily due to an increase of $64.7 million in employee-related expenses, which was due to headcount growth. Further, the increase in research and development expense was due to an increase of $14.1 million in overhead-related costs and an increase of $4.5 million in internal development-related third-party hosting fees.

Sales and marketing

	Year Ended December 31,		$ Change	% Change
	2016	2017		
	(In millions)			
Sales and marketing	$250.6	$314.0	$ 63.4	25%

Sales and marketing expenses increased $63.4 million or 25% during 2017, as compared to 2016, primarily due to an increase of $40.9 million in variable spend related to brand campaign fees, lead generation fees, and third-party sales representative fees. In addition, sales and marketing expenses increased due to $17.8 million in employee-related expenses excluding stock-based compensation, which was due to headcount growth. Stock-based compensation decreased $10.9 million due to the modification of an executive stock grant during 2016, that resulted in a charge of $18.8 million in that prior period. Sales and marketing expenses also increased $8.4 million due to app store fees as a result of increased sales and $7.6 million due to overhead-related costs.

General and administrative

	Year Ended December 31,		$ Change	% Change
	2016	2017		
	(In millions)			
General and administrative	$107.4	$157.3	$ 49.9	46%

General and administrative expenses increased $49.9 million or 46% during 2017, as compared to 2016, primarily due to an increase of $17.3 million in non-income based taxes as a result of the growth in our business. General and administrative expenses during 2016 included a $12.4 million benefit relating to a non-income based tax ruling. In addition, employee-related expenses increased $13.3 million during 2017, as compared to 2016,

77

due to headcount growth, and other general and administrative expenses increased $11.3 million related to the funding of the Dropbox Charitable Foundation. Included in this amount was an equity-based charitable contribution of $9.4 million and cash contributions of $1.9 million. Further, general and administrative expenses increased $4.3 million due to legal-related expenses and accounting services.

Interest expense, net

Interest expense, net decreased $5.4 million during 2017, as compared to 2016, primarily due to a decrease in interest expense of $3.3 million due to fewer assets acquired under capital leases. In addition, interest income from our money market funds increased by $2.1 million.

Other income (expense), net

Other income (expense), net increased $8.3 million during 2017, as compared to 2016, primarily due to an increase of $8.6 million in foreign currency gains related to monetary assets and liabilities denominated in euros and British pound sterling.

Provision for income taxes

Provision for income taxes decreased by $5.0 million during 2017 as compared to 2016, primarily as a result of a change in our U.S. AMT position. We were subject to U.S. AMT during 2016, and we do not expect to be subject to U.S. AMT during 2017. In addition, as a result of the repeal of AMT as part of the Tax Reform Act, we recognized a benefit and established a receivable in 2017 to reflect anticipated refunds of our 2016 AMT credit carryforward.

Comparison of the year ended December 31, 2015 and 2016

Revenue

	Year ended December 31,		$ Change	% Change
	2015	2016		
	(In millions)			
Revenue	$603.8	$844.8	$ 241.0	40%

Revenue increased $241.0 million or 40% during 2016 as compared to 2015. This increase was primarily due to a 35% increase in the number of paying users between periods. The average revenue per paying user also decreased slightly between periods.

Cost of revenue, gross profit, and gross margin

	Year ended December 31,		$ Change	% Change
	2015	2016		
	(In millions)			
Cost of revenue	$407.4	$390.6	$ (16.8)	(4)%
Gross profit	196.4	454.2	257.8	131%
Gross margin	33%	54%		

Cost of revenue decreased $16.8 million or 4% during 2016, as compared to 2015, primarily due to a net decrease of $39.5 million in our infrastructure costs due to our Infrastructure Optimization. The net decrease of $39.5 million included a $92.5 million decrease in expense related to our third-party datacenter service provider, offset by a $53.0 million increase in depreciation, facilities, and support expense related to our infrastructure

78

equipment in co-location facilities that we directly lease and operate. Further, the decrease in cost of revenue was due to a $5.2 million decrease in amortization of developed technologies, as certain intangible assets became fully amortized during 2016. These decreases in cost of revenue were also partially offset by an increase of $13.8 million in employee-related expenses due to headcount growth, an increase of $5.5 million in credit card transaction fees due to higher sales, an increase of $9.9 million related to property taxes for our co-location facilities, professional fees for user support, and overhead-related costs primarily due to the completion of construction on our new corporate headquarters.

Our gross margin increased from 33% during 2015 to 54% during 2016 primarily due to our Infrastructure Optimization and a 40% increase in our revenue during the period.

Research and development

	Year ended December 31,		$ Change	% Change
	2015	2016		
	(In millions)			
Research and development	$201.6	$289.7	$ 88.1	44%

Research and development expenses increased $88.1 million or 44% during 2016, as compared to 2015, primarily due to an increase of $66.9 million in employee-related expenses due to headcount growth. Further, the increase in research and development expense was due to an increase of $17.7 million in overhead-related costs primarily due to the completion of construction on our new corporate headquarters, and an increase of $5.3 million in internal development-related third-party hosting fees.

Sales and marketing

	Year ended December 31,		$ Change	% Change
	2015	2016		
	(In millions)			
Sales and marketing	$193.1	$250.6	$ 57.5	30%

Sales and marketing expenses increased $57.5 million or 30% during 2016, as compared to 2015, primarily due to an increase of $53.4 million in employee-related expenses. This increase in employee-related expenses was primarily due to an increase in stock-based compensation of $24.8 million, which included a charge of $18.8 million due to the modification of an executive stock grant, headcount growth, and an increase in commission and bonus expense. In addition, the increase in sales and marketing expense was due to an increase of $10.1 million in overhead-related costs primarily due to the completion of construction on our new corporate headquarters. The increase in sales and marketing expense was partially offset by a decrease of $11.8 million in marketing expenses primarily due to a reduction in brand campaign fees.

General and administrative

	Year ended December 31,		$ Change	% Change
	2015	2016		
	(In millions)			
General and administrative	$107.9	$107.4	$ (0.5)	— %

General and administrative expenses decreased $0.5 million during 2016, as compared to 2015, primarily due to a decrease of $12.4 million resulting from a non-income based tax ruling and a decrease of $7.3 million in

79

other non-income based taxes in 2016. These decreases were offset by an increase of $7.3 million in employee-related expenses, which was due to headcount growth. Further, the decrease in general and administrative expense was offset by an increase of $8.0 million in overhead-related costs primarily due to the completion of construction on our new corporate headquarters, and an increase of $3.4 million in professional fees for increased legal and accounting services.

Interest expense, net

Interest expense, net increased $1.2 million during 2016, as compared to 2015, primarily due to an increase of $1.9 million in interest expense primarily due to assets acquired under capital leases, offset by $0.7 million of interest income from our money market funds.

Other income (expense), net

Other income (expense), net increased $9.1 million during 2016, as compared to 2015, primarily due to the commencement of sublease income of $7.0 million and a net gain of $1.6 million related to fixed asset disposals.

Provision for income taxes

Provision for income taxes increased by $4.9 million during 2016, as compared to 2015, primarily due to an increase in taxes as a result of being subject to the U.S. alternative minimum tax and foreign taxes related to our foreign operations.

Quarterly Results of Operations

The following table sets forth our unaudited quarterly statements of operations data for each of the last eight quarters ended December 31, 2017. The information for each of these quarters has been prepared on the same basis as the audited annual financial statements included elsewhere in this prospectus and, in the opinion of management, includes all adjustments, which includes only normal recurring adjustments, necessary for the fair statement of the results of operations for these periods. This data should be read in conjunction with our audited consolidated financial statements and related notes thereto included elsewhere in this prospectus. These quarterly results of operations are not necessarily indicative of our future results of operations that may be expected for any future period.

	Three months ended							
	March 31, 2016	June 30, 2016	September 30, 2016	December 31, 2016	March 31, 2017	June 30, 2017	September 30, 2017	December 31, 2017
				(In millions)				
Revenue	$ 185.0	$200.8	$ 221.0	$ 238.0	$ 247.9	$266.7	$ 286.7	$ 305.5
Cost of revenue(1)	99.8	102.7	98.8	89.3	93.5	92.2	91.5	91.7
Gross profit	85.2	98.1	122.2	148.7	154.4	174.5	195.2	213.8
Operating expenses:(1)								
Research and development	67.9	72.6	75.1	74.1	89.3	89.8	97.2	104.0
Sales and marketing	73.8	57.5	55.4	63.9	67.2	69.2	74.7	102.9
General and administrative	25.3	18.4	32.8	30.9	31.3	42.2	39.6	44.2
Total operating expenses	167.0	148.5	163.3	168.9	187.8	201.2	211.5	251.1
Loss from operations	$ (81.8)	$ (50.4)	$ (41.1)	$ (20.2)	$ (33.4)	$ (26.7)	$ (16.3)	$ (37.3)

(1) Includes stock-based compensation as follows:

	Three months ended							
	March 31, 2016	June 30, 2016	September 30, 2016	December 31, 2016	March 31, 2017	June 30, 2017	September 30, 2017	December 31, 2017
	(In millions)							
Cost of revenue	$ 1.5	$ 2.1	$ 2.3	$ 2.3	$ 3.1	$ 3.3	$ 2.9	$ 2.9
Research and development	14.5	19.0	19.3	19.9	21.8	21.7	22.9	26.7
Sales and marketing(a)	24.4	6.6	6.7	6.9	7.7	7.7	7.5	10.8
General and administrative	3.5	4.7	9.0	4.9	6.2	6.0	6.4	7.0
Total stock-based compensation	$ 43.9	$ 32.4	$ 37.3	$ 34.0	$ 38.8	$ 38.7	$ 39.7	$ 47.4

(a) Stock-based compensation included in sales and marketing expenses for the three months ended March 31, 2016 includes $18.8 million related to a stock option modification for an executive officer.

	Three months ended							
	March 31, 2016	June 30, 2016	September 30, 2016	December 31, 2016	March 31, 2017	June 30, 2017	September 30, 2017	December 31, 2017
	(As a % of revenue)							
Revenue	100%	100%	100%	100%	100%	100%	100%	100%
Cost of revenue	54	51	45	38	38	35	32	30
Gross profit	46	49	55	62	62	65	68	70
Operating expenses:								
Research and development	37	36	34	31	36	34	34	34
Sales and marketing	40	29	25	27	27	26	26	34
General and administrative	14	9	15	13	13	16	14	14
Total operating expenses	90	74	74	71	76	75	74	82
Loss from operations	(44)%	(25)%	(19)%	(8)%	(13)%	(10)%	(6)%	(12)%

Quarterly revenue trends

Our revenue increased sequentially in each of the quarters presented primarily due to increases in the number of paying users. Seasonality in our revenue is not material.

Quarterly cost of revenue and gross margin trends

Our cost of revenue fluctuated in each of the quarters presented primarily due to the timing of our Infrastructure Optimization, which combined with increases in our revenue caused our gross margins to increase or remain constant.

Quarterly operating expense trends

Except for the three months ended June 30, 2016, our total quarterly operating expenses increased sequentially in the quarters presented primarily due to headcount growth in connection with the expansion of our business and other events that are discussed herein.

81

Research and development

Our research and development expenses increased at a faster rate during the three months ended March 31, 2017, comparatively to other quarters, primarily due to headcount growth and employee-related costs.

Sales and marketing

Our sales and marketing expenses generally increased in the quarters presented primarily due to employee-related expenses and brand advertising campaigns. The timing of brand advertising campaigns can impact the trends in sales and marketing expenses. The sequential decline in our sales and marketing expenses during the three months ended June 30, 2016 was due to a stock-based compensation charge of $18.8 million related to the modification of an executive stock grant recorded in the three months ended March 31, 2016. Our sales and marketing expenses increased at a faster rate during the three months ended December 31, 2017, as we accelerated our investment in our global brand advertising campaign.

General and administrative

Our general and administrative expenses fluctuated in the quarters presented, primarily due to increases in employee-related expenses and legal, accounting, and other professional fees. Our general and administrative expenses for certain quarters included certain charges and benefits as follows: the three months ended June 30, 2016 included a benefit of $12.4 million resulting from a non-income based tax ruling, and the three months ended June 30, 2017 included expense of $9.4 million for a non-cash charitable donation of shares of our common stock as initial funding for the Dropbox Charitable Foundation.

Liquidity and Capital Resources

As of December 31, 2017, we had cash and cash equivalents of $430.0 million. Our cash and cash equivalents consist primarily of cash and money market funds. As of December 31, 2017, we had $86.3 million of our cash and cash equivalents held by our foreign subsidiaries. We do not expect to incur material taxes in the event we repatriate any of these amounts.

Since our inception, we have financed our operations primarily through equity issuances, cash generated from our operations, and capital leases to finance infrastructure-related assets in co-location facilities that we directly lease and operate. We enter into capital leases in part to better match the timing of payments for infrastructure-related assets with that of cash received from our paying users. In our business model, some of our registered users convert to paying users over time, and consequently there is a lag between initial investment in infrastructure assets and cash received from some of our users. We expect to increase our use of capital leases to finance infrastructure equipment as certain assets reach the end of their useful lives in future periods.

Our principal uses of cash in recent periods have been funding our operations, making principal payments on our capital lease obligations, the satisfaction of tax withholdings in connection with the settlement of restricted stock units, and making capital expenditures.

In April 2017, we entered into a $600.0 million credit facility with a syndicate of financial institutions. The revolving credit facility has an accordion option, which, if exercised, would allow us to increase the aggregate commitments by up to $150.0 million, subject to obtaining additional lender commitments and satisfying certain conditions. Pursuant to the terms of the revolving credit facility, we may issue letters of credit under the revolving credit facility, which reduce the total amount available for borrowing under such facility. The revolving credit facility terminates on April 4, 2022.

Interest on borrowings under the revolving credit facility accrues at a variable rate tied to the prime rate or the LIBOR rate, at our election. Interest is payable quarterly in arrears. Pursuant to the terms of the revolving credit facility, we are required to pay an annual commitment fee that accrues at a rate of 0.20% per annum on the

82

170

unused portion of the borrowing commitments under the revolving credit facility. In addition, we are required to pay a fee in connection with letters of credit issued under the revolving credit facility that accrues at a rate of 1.5% per annum on the amount to be drawn under such letters of credit outstanding. There is an additional fronting fee of 0.125% per annum multiplied by the average aggregate daily maximum amount available to be drawn under all letters of credit.

The revolving credit facility contains customary conditions to borrowing, events of default, and covenants, including covenants that restrict our ability to incur indebtedness, grant liens, make distributions to our holders or our subsidiaries' equity interests, make investments, or engage in transactions with our affiliates. In addition, the revolving credit facility contains financial covenants, including a consolidated leverage ratio covenant and a minimum liquidity balance. We were in compliance with all covenants under the revolving credit facility as of December 31, 2017.

As of December 31, 2017, we had no amounts outstanding under the revolving credit facility and an aggregate of $82.6 million in letters of credit outstanding under the revolving credit facility. Our total available borrowing capacity under the revolving credit facility was $517.4 million as of December 31, 2017.

In February 2018, we amended our revolving credit facility to, among other things, permit us to make certain investments, enter into an unsecured standby letter of credit facility, and increase our standby letter of credit sublimit to $187.5 million. We also increased our borrowing capacity under the revolving credit facility from $600.0 million to $725.0 million. We may from time to time request increases in our borrowing capacity under our revolving credit facility of up to $275.0 million, provided no event of default has occurred or is continuing or would result from such increase.

We believe our existing cash and cash equivalents, together with cash provided by operations and amounts available under the revolving credit facility, will be sufficient to meet our needs for the foreseeable future. Our future capital requirements will depend on many factors including our revenue growth rate, subscription renewal activity, billing frequency, the timing and extent of spending to support further infrastructure development and research and development efforts, the timing and extent of additional capital expenditures to invest in existing and new office spaces, such as our new corporate headquarters, the satisfaction of tax withholding obligations for the release of restricted stock units, the expansion of sales and marketing and international operation activities, the introduction of new product capabilities and enhancement of our platform, and the continuing market acceptance of our platform. We may in the future enter into arrangements to acquire or invest in complementary businesses, services, and technologies, including intellectual property rights. We may be required to seek additional equity or debt financing. In the event that additional financing is required from outside sources, we may not be able to raise it on terms acceptable to us or at all. If we are unable to raise additional capital when desired, our business, results of operations, and financial condition would be materially and adversely affected.

Our cash flow activities were as follows for the periods presented:

| | Year ended December 31, | | |
| | 2015 | 2016 | 2017 |
	(In millions)		
Net cash provided by operating activities	$ 14.8	$ 252.6	$ 330.3
Net cash used in investing activities	(85.6)	(118.0)	(23.9)
Net cash used in financing activities	(89.6)	(134.5)	(231.7)
Effect of exchange rate changes on cash and cash equivalents	(0.9)	(4.3)	2.6
Net increase (decrease) in cash and cash equivalents	$(161.3)	$ (4.2)	$ 77.3

Operating activities

Our largest source of operating cash is cash collections from our paying users for subscriptions to our platform. Our primary uses of cash from operating activities are for employee-related expenditures,

83

infrastructure-related costs, and marketing expenses. Net cash provided by operating activities is impacted by our net loss adjusted for certain non-cash items, including depreciation and amortization expenses and stock-based compensation, as well as the effect of changes in operating assets and liabilities.

For the year ended December 31, 2017, net cash provided by operating activities was $330.3 million, which mostly consisted of our net loss of $111.7 million, adjusted for depreciation and amortization expenses of $181.8 million and stock-based compensation expense of $164.6 million, and net cash inflow of $81.3 million from operating assets and liabilities. The inflow from operating assets and liabilities was primarily due to an increase of $64.3 million in deferred revenue from increased subscription sales, as a majority of our paying users are invoiced in advance. The increase in net cash provided by operating activities during the year ended December 31, 2017, compared to the year ended December 31, 2016, was primarily due to a reduction of our net loss, as adjusted for stock-based compensation and depreciation and amortization expenses, as well as cash inflow from changes in operating assets and liabilities.

For the year ended December 31, 2016, net cash provided by operating activities was $252.6 million, which primarily consisted of our net loss of $210.2 million, adjusted for depreciation and amortization expenses of $191.6 million and stock-based compensation expense of $147.6 million, as well as a net cash inflow of $118.8 million from operating assets and liabilities. The inflow from operating assets and liabilities was primarily due to an increase of $87.6 million in deferred revenue from increased subscription sales, as a majority of our paying users are invoiced in advance, and an increase of $35.6 million in accrued compensation and benefits due to the introduction of our annual bonus plan. The increase in net cash from operating activities during 2016 compared to 2015 was primarily due to a reduction of our net loss, as adjusted for stock-based compensation and depreciation and amortization expenses, as well as cash inflow from changes in operating assets and liabilities.

For the year ended December 31, 2015, net cash provided by operating activities was $14.8 million, which mostly consisted of our net loss of $325.9 million, adjusted for depreciation and amortization expenses of $149.6 million and stock-based compensation expense of $66.1 million, as well as a net cash inflow of $123.6 million from operating assets and liabilities. The inflow from operating assets and liabilities was primarily due to an increase of $82.0 million in deferred revenue from increased subscription sales, as a majority of our paying users are invoiced in advance, and an increase of $50.6 million in current and non-current liabilities.

Investing activities

Net cash used in investing activities is primarily impacted by purchases of property and equipment, particularly for purchasing infrastructure equipment in co-location facilities that we directly lease and operate, and for making improvements to existing and new office spaces.

For the year ended December 31, 2017, net cash used in investing activities was $23.9 million, which mostly consisted of capital expenditures related to our infrastructure equipment and office build-outs. The decrease in cash used in investing activities during the year ended December 31, 2017, compared to the year ended December 31, 2016, was primarily due to decreases in capital expenditures for infrastructure equipment and leasehold improvements related to our current corporate headquarters.

For the year ended December 31, 2016, net cash used in investing activities was $118.0 million, which mostly consisted of capital expenditures related to our infrastructure and office build-outs. The increase in cash used in investing activities during 2016 compared to 2015 was primarily due to increases in capital expenditures and patent purchases.

For the year ended December 31, 2015, net cash used in investing activities was $85.6 million, which mostly consisted of capital expenditures related to our infrastructure equipment and office build-outs.

84

Financing activities

Net cash used in financing activities is primarily impacted by capital lease obligations for our infrastructure equipment and repurchases of common stock to satisfy the tax withholding obligation for the release of restricted stock units ("RSUs"). In 2017, we began releasing shares of common stock underlying vested one-tier RSUs, which generally have a service-based vesting condition over a four-year period and resulted in cash outflows to satisfy the employee tax withholding obligation for those employees who elected to net share settle their awards. See "—Significant Impacts of Stock-Based Compensation" for additional information.

For the year ended December 31, 2017, net cash used in financing activities was $231.7 million, which primarily consisted of $133.0 million in principal payments against capital lease obligations and $87.9 million for the satisfaction of tax withholding obligations for the release of restricted stock units. The increase in cash used by financing activities during the year ended December 31, 2017, compared to the year ended December 31, 2016, was primarily due to the increase of $87.9 million related to the satisfaction of tax withholding obligations for the release of restricted stock units.

For the year ended December 31, 2016, net cash used in financing activities was $134.5 million, which primarily consisted of $137.9 million in principal payments against capital lease obligations and $3.8 million in principal payments against the note payable issued in 2015 as described below, offset by $8.8 million in proceeds received for a sale-leaseback agreement. The increase in cash used in financing activities during 2016 compared to 2015 was primarily due to an increase of $36.7 million in principal payments on capital leases for our infrastructure, a decrease of $11.9 million in cash received through the issuance of a note payable issued in 2015, as well as an increase of $3.8 million in payments against the note payable in 2016, partially offset by $8.8 million in cash received in a sale lease-back agreement.

For the year ended December 31, 2015, net cash used in financing activities was $89.6 million, which primarily consisted of $101.2 million in principal payments against capital lease obligations, offset by $11.9 million in cash received through the issuance of a note payable to finance our infrastructure.

Contractual Obligations

Our principal commitments consist of obligations under operating leases for office space and datacenter operations, and capital leases for datacenter equipment. The following table summarizes our commitments to settle contractual obligations in cash as of December 31, 2017, for the periods presented below:

	Total	Less than 1 year	1 - 3 years	3 - 5 years	More than 5 years
			(In millions)		
Operating lease commitments(1)	$1,349.9	$ 91.5	$ 336.8	$ 201.8	$ 719.8
Capital lease commitments(2)	182.0	108.3	73.7	—	—
Other commitments(3)	155.1	64.0	86.3	0.6	4.2
Total contractual obligations	$1,687.0	$ 263.8	$ 496.8	$ 202.4	$ 724.0

(1) Consists of future non-cancelable minimum rental payments under operating leases for our offices and datacenters, excluding rent payments from our sub-tenants and variable operating expenses. Non-cancelable rent payments from our sub-tenants as of December 31, 2017, for the next six years are expected to be $72.1 million.

(2) Consists of future non-cancelable minimum rental payments under capital leases primarily for our infrastructure.

(3) Consists of commitments to third-party vendors for services related to our infrastructure, infrastructure warranty contracts, payments related to the imputed financing obligation for our previous headquarters, asset retirement obligations for office modifications, and a note payable related to financing of our infrastructure.

In addition to the contractual obligations set forth above, as of December 31, 2017, we had an aggregate of $82.6 million in letters of credit outstanding under our revolving credit facility.

85

In October 2017, we entered into a new lease agreement for office space in San Francisco, California, to serve as our new corporate headquarters. We expect to start making recurring rental payments under the lease in the third quarter of 2019. Included in the operating lease commitments above are our total expected minimum obligations under the lease agreement of $827.0 million, which exclude expected tenant improvement reimbursements from the landlord of approximately $73.6 million and variable operating expenses. Our obligations under the lease are supported by a $34.2 million letter of credit, which reduced the borrowing capacity under our revolving credit facility.

We plan to take possession of our new corporate headquarters over several phases. We expect to take initial possession in mid-2018, after which time we plan to incur capital expenditures on leasehold improvements and to begin recording rent expense for the portion of the new corporate headquarters that we have the right to use. Capital expenditures will continue to increase as we take possession of the remaining space over the next few years. We will continue to operate in our current corporate headquarters until the new corporate headquarters is ready for occupancy, which is expected to be in 2019. We intend to sublease our current corporate headquarters once we occupy the new corporate headquarters. However, unless we transfer our contractual obligation, we will continue to include the committed lease payments for our current corporate headquarters in the table above.

Off-Balance Sheet Arrangements

As of December 31, 2017, we did not have any relationships with unconsolidated entities or financial partnerships, such as entities often referred to as structured finance or variable interest entities, which would have been established for the purpose of facilitating off balance sheet arrangements or other contractually narrow or limited purposes.

Significant Impacts of Stock-Based Compensation

Restricted Stock Units

We have granted restricted stock units, or RSUs, to our employees and members of our Board of Directors under our 2008 Equity Incentive Plan, or 2008 Plan, and our 2017 Equity Incentive Plan, or 2017 Plan. We have two types of RSUs outstanding as of December 31, 2017:

- One-tier RSUs, which have a service-based vesting condition over a four-year period. These awards typically have a cliff vesting period of one year and continue to vest quarterly thereafter. We recognize compensation expense associated with one-tier RSUs ratably on a straight-line basis over the requisite service period.

- Two-tier RSUs, which have both a service-based vesting condition and a liquidity event-related performance vesting condition. These awards typically have a service-based vesting period of four years with a cliff vesting period of one year and continue to vest monthly thereafter. Upon satisfaction of the Performance Vesting Condition, these awards will vest quarterly. The Performance Vesting Condition is satisfied on the earlier of (i) an acquisition or change in control of the Company or (ii) the earlier of (a) six months after our initial public offering or (b) March 15 of the year following our initial public offering. Our Board of Directors has approved the acceleration of the Performance Vesting Condition for two-tier RSUs for which the service condition was satisfied as of December 31, 2017, to occur upon the effectiveness of our registration statement related to this offering. Our last grant date for two-tier RSUs was May 2015.

As of December 31, 2017, all compensation expense related to two-tier RSUs remained unrecognized because the Performance Vesting Condition was not satisfied. At the time the Performance Vesting Condition becomes probable, we will recognize the cumulative stock-based compensation expense for the two-tier RSUs that have met their service-based vesting condition using the accelerated attribution method. If the Performance Vesting Condition had occurred on December 31, 2017, we would have recorded $415.6 million of stock-based compensation expense. As of December 31, 2017, 28.2 million two-tier RSUs were outstanding, of which 26.1 million had met their service condition. If the Performance Vesting Condition had been satisfied on these two-tier RSUs as of December 31, 2017, we would recognize unamortized stock-based compensation expense of $5.6 million over a weighted-average period of approximately one year if the requisite service is provided.

Co-Founder Grants

In December 2017, the Board of Directors approved a grant to our co-founders of restricted stock awards, or RSAs, with respect to 14.7 million shares of Class A Common Stock in the aggregate, or collectively, the Co-Founder Grants, of which 10.3 million RSAs were granted to Mr. Houston, the Company's co-founder and Chief Executive Officer, and 4.4 million RSAs were granted to Mr. Ferdowsi, the Company's co-founder and Director. These Co-Founder Grants have service-based, market-based, and performance-based vesting conditions. These Co-Founder Grants have certain stockholder rights, such as the right to vote the shares immediately upon grant and prior to their vesting.

The Co-Founder Grants are eligible to vest over the ten-year period following the closing of this offering. The Co-Founder Grants comprise nine tranches that are eligible to vest based on the achievement of stock price goals, or, each, a Stock Price Target, measured over a consecutive thirty-day trading period during the Performance Period, as follows:

Company Stock Price Target	Shares Eligible to Vest for Mr. Houston	Shares Eligible to Vest for Mr. Ferdowsi
$30.00	2,066,667	880,000
$37.50	1,033,334	440,000
$45.00	1,033,334	440,000
$52.50	1,033,333	440,000
$60.00	1,033,333	440,000
$67.50	1,033,333	440,000
$75.00	1,033,333	440,000
$82.50	1,033,333	440,000
$90.00	1,033,333	440,000

The Performance Period begins on the first trading day following the later of (a) the expiration of the lock-up period following the first date the Company's shares are traded on an established national securities exchange or automated quotation system, or the IPO Date, and (b) January 1, 2019, and ends on the earliest to occur of: (i) the date on which all shares subject to the Co-Founder Grants vest, (ii) the date the applicable co-founder ceases to satisfy the service-based vesting condition, (iii) the tenth anniversary of the IPO Date, and (iv) the occurrence of an acquisition of the Company prior to the IPO Date.

During the first four years of the Performance Period, no more than 20% of the shares subject to each Co-Founder Grant would be eligible to vest in any calendar year. After the first four years, all shares are eligible to vest based on the achievement of the Company Stock Price Targets.

The Co-Founder Grants contain an implied performance-based vesting condition satisfied upon the IPO Date, because no shares subject to the Co-Founder Grants will vest unless the IPO Date occurs. Accordingly, as of December 31, 2017, all compensation expense related to the Co-Founder Grants remained unrecognized because the performance-based vesting condition was not deemed probable of being achieved.

We estimated the grant date fair value of the Co-Founder Grants using a model based on multiple stock price paths developed through the use of a Monte Carlo simulation that incorporates into the valuation the possibility that the Stock Price Targets may not be satisfied. The average grant date fair value of each Co-Founder Grant was estimated to be $10.60 per share, and we will recognize total stock-based compensation expense of $156.2 million over the requisite service period of each tranche, which ranged from 2.9 to 6.9 years,

87

using the accelerated attribution method. If the Stock Price Targets are met sooner than the derived service period, we will adjust our stock-based compensation to reflect the cumulative expense associated with the vested awards. We will recognize stock-based compensation expense if the requisite service period is provided, regardless of whether the market conditions are achieved.

In the period the relevant performance vesting condition becomes probable, we will recognize the cumulative unrecognized expense of our two-tier RSUs and Co-Founder Grants, which will increase our cost of revenue and operating expenses with respect to our two-tier RSUs, and will increase our general and administrative expenses with respect to our Co-Founder Grants, for the quarter and year of our initial public offering. We expect that our research and development expenses will be the line item most significantly impacted by the cumulative expense to be recognized.

See Note 1, "Description of the Business and Summary of Significant Accounting Policies" and Note 11, "Stockholders' Equity" to our consolidated financial statements included elsewhere in this prospectus for more information.

Critical Accounting Policies and Judgments

Our consolidated financial statements and the related notes thereto included elsewhere in this prospectus are prepared in accordance with generally accepted accounting principles, or GAAP, in the United States. The preparation of consolidated financial statements also requires us to make estimates and assumptions that affect the reported amounts of assets, liabilities, revenue, costs and expenses, and related disclosures. We base our estimates on historical experience and on various other assumptions that we believe to be reasonable under the circumstances. Actual results could differ significantly from the estimates made by management. To the extent that there are differences between our estimates and actual results, our future financial statement presentation, financial condition, results of operations, and cash flows will be affected.

We believe that the accounting policies described below involve a greater degree of judgment and complexity. Accordingly, these are the policies we believe are the most critical to aid in fully understanding and evaluating our consolidated financial condition and results of operations.

In May 2014, the Financial Accounting Standards Board, or FASB, issued Accounting Standards Update, or ASU, No. 2014-09 *Revenue from Contracts with Customers (Topic 606)*, or Topic 606. Topic 606 supersedes the revenue recognition requirements in Accounting Standards Codification, *Revenue Recognition*, or Topic 605, and requires the recognition of revenue when promised goods or services are transferred to customers in an amount that reflects the consideration to which the entity expects to be entitled to in exchange for those goods or services. Topic 606 also includes Subtopic 340-40, *Other Assets and Deferred Costs—Contracts with Customers*, which requires the deferral of incremental costs of obtaining a contract with a customer.

We adopted the requirements of Topic 606 as of January 1, 2017, utilizing the full retrospective method of transition. As such, Topic 606 is reflected in our financial results for all periods presented in this prospectus. The adoption of Topic 606 resulted in changes to our accounting policies for revenue recognition and deferred commissions.

The impact of adopting Topic 606 on our revenue was not material to any of the periods presented. The primary impact of adopting Topic 606 relates to the deferral of incremental costs of obtaining customer contracts and the amortization of those costs over a longer period of benefit.

Revenue recognition

We generate revenue from sales of subscriptions to our platform. Subscription fees exclude sales and other indirect taxes. We determine revenue recognition through the following steps:

- Identification of the contract, or contracts, with a customer

88

- Identification of the performance obligations in the contract
- Determination of the transaction price
- Allocation of the transaction price to the performance obligations in the contract
- Recognition of revenue when, or as, we satisfy a performance obligation

Our subscription agreements typically have monthly or annual contractual terms, and a small percentage have multi-year contractual terms. Revenue is recognized ratably over the related contractual term generally beginning on the date that our platform is made available to a customer. Our agreements are generally non-cancelable. We typically bill in advance for monthly contracts and annually in advance for contracts with terms of one year or longer.

Deferred commissions

Sales commissions and the related payroll taxes earned by our outbound sales team, as well as commissions earned by third-party resellers, are considered to be incremental and recoverable costs of obtaining a contract with a customer. These costs are deferred and then amortized over a period of benefit that we have determined to be five years. We determined the period of benefit by taking into consideration our historical customer attrition rates, the useful life of our technology, and the impact of competition in our industry. Changing the period of benefit by one year would result in a change to expense of approximately $1.0 million or less in each of the periods presented. Amortization of deferred commissions is included in sales and marketing expenses.

Common stock valuations

Since August 2015, we have granted RSUs as the only stock-based payment awards to our employees, excluding the Co-Founder Grants. While we stopped granting stock options in August 2015, we currently have stock options outstanding that will continue to vest through 2019 if the requisite service is provided.

The fair values of the common stock underlying the RSUs were determined by our Board of Directors, with input from management and contemporaneous third-party valuations, which were performed at least quarterly. If RSUs were granted a short period of time prior to the date of a valuation report, we retrospectively assessed the fair value used for financial reporting purposes after considering the fair value reflected in the subsequent valuation report and other facts and circumstances on the date of grant as discussed below.

Given the absence of a public trading market for our common stock, and in accordance with the American Institute of Certified Public Accountants Practice Guide, *Valuation of Privately-Held-Company Equity Securities Issued as Compensation,* or AICPA Guide, our Board of Directors exercised reasonable judgment and considered numerous objective and subjective factors to determine the best estimate of the fair value of our common stock including:

- The results of contemporaneous valuations of our common stock by unrelated third parties;
- The rights, preferences, and privileges of our convertible preferred stock relative to those of our common stock;
- Market multiples of comparable public companies in our industry as indicated by their market capitalization and guideline merger and acquisition transactions;
- Our performance and market position relative to our competitors, who may change from time to time;
- Our historical financial results and estimated trends and prospects for our future performance;
- Valuations published by institutional investors that hold investments in our capital stock;
- The economic and competitive environment;

89

- The likelihood and timeline of achieving a liquidity event, such as an initial public offering or sale, given prevailing market conditions;

- Any adjustments necessary to recognize a lack of marketability for our common stock; and

- Precedent sales of or offers to purchase our capital stock.

In valuing our common stock, our Board of Directors determined the fair value of our common stock using both the income and market approach valuation methods. The income approach estimates value based on the expectation of future cash flows that a company will generate. These future cash flows are discounted to their present values using a discount rate based on our weighted-average cost of capital, and is adjusted to reflect the risks inherent in our cash flows. The market approach estimates value based on a comparison of the subject company to comparable public companies in a similar line of business. From the comparable companies, a representative market value multiple is determined and then applied to the subject company's financial forecasts to estimate the value of the subject company.

For valuations prior to August 31, 2017, the equity valuation was based on both the income and the market approach valuation methods, in addition to giving consideration to recent secondary sales of our common stock. The Option Pricing Method was selected as the principal equity allocation method. These methods were consistent with prior valuations.

For valuations as of and subsequent to August 31, 2017, we have used a hybrid method to determine the fair value of our common stock, in addition to giving consideration to recent secondary sales of our common stock. Under the hybrid method, multiple valuation approaches were used and then combined into a single probability weighted valuation. Our approach included the use of initial public offering scenarios, a scenario assuming continued operation as a private entity, and a scenario assuming an acquisition of the company.

Application of these approaches involves the use of estimates, judgment, and assumptions that are highly complex and subjective, such as those regarding our expected future revenue, expenses, and cash flows, discount rates, market multiples, the selection of comparable companies, and the probability of future events. Changes in any or all of these estimates and assumptions, or the relationships between those assumptions, impact our valuations as of each valuation date and may have a material impact on the valuation of common stock.

For valuations after the completion of this initial public offering, our Board of Directors will determine the fair value of each share of underlying common stock based on the closing price of our Class A common stock as reported on the date of the grant.

Fair value of market condition awards

The Co-Founder Grants contain market-based vesting conditions. The market-based vesting condition is considered when calculating the grant date fair value of these awards, which requires the use of various estimates and assumptions. The grant date fair value of the Co-Founder Grants was estimated using a model based on multiple stock price paths developed through the use of a Monte Carlo simulation that incorporates into the valuation the possibility that the market condition may not be satisfied. A Monte Carlo simulation requires the use of various assumptions, including our underlying stock price, volatility, and the risk-free interest rate as of the valuation date, corresponding to the length of time remaining in the performance period, and expected dividend yield. A Monte Carlo simulation also calculates a derived service period for each of the nine vesting tranches, which is the measure of the expected time to achieve the market conditions. Expense associated with market-based awards is recognized over the requisite service period of each tranche using the accelerated attribution method, regardless of whether the market conditions are achieved.

Business combinations and valuation of goodwill and other acquired intangible assets

When we acquire a business, we allocate the purchase price to the net tangible and identifiable intangible assets acquired based on their fair values. Any residual purchase price is recorded as goodwill. The estimation of

90

the fair value of acquired assets and assumed liabilities requires management to apply significant judgment, especially with respect to intangible assets, which consist primarily of developed technologies.

These estimates are based upon a number of factors, including historical experience, market conditions, and information obtained from the management of acquired companies. To determine the fair value of acquired intangible assets, we make estimates that can include, but are not limited to, the cash flows that an asset is expected to generate in the future, the appropriate weighted-average cost of capital to utilize, the cost savings expected to be derived from acquiring an asset, and the expected use of the asset. These same factors are also considered in determining the useful life of acquired intangible assets, which impacts the timing of future amortization expense.

Recent Accounting Pronouncements

In February 2016, the FASB issued ASU No. 2016-02, *Leases (Topic 842)*. Most prominent among the changes in the standard is the recognition of right of use assets and lease liabilities by lessees for those leases classified as operating leases under current GAAP. Under the standard, disclosures are required to meet the objective of enabling users of financial statements to assess the amount, timing, and uncertainty of cash flows arising from leases. We will be required to recognize and measure leases existing at, or entered into after, the beginning of the earliest comparative period presented using a modified retrospective approach, with certain practical expedients available. The new standard is effective for fiscal years beginning after December 15, 2018. Early adoption by public entities is permitted. We are in the initial stage of our assessment of the new standard and are currently evaluating the timing of adoption, the quantitative impact of adoption, and the related disclosure requirements. We anticipate the adoption of this standard will result in a substantial increase in our non-current assets and liabilities recorded on the consolidated balance sheets. The adoption of the standard is not expected to have a material impact on the consolidated statement of operations. While we are assessing all potential impacts of the adoption of the standard, we currently expect the most significant impact to be the capitalization of right-to-use assets and lease liabilities for our office space and datacenter operating leases. We expect our accounting for capital leases related to infrastructure equipment to remain substantially unchanged under the new standard.

See Note 1, "Description of the Business and Summary of Significant Accounting Policies" to our consolidated financial statements included elsewhere in this prospectus for more information about other recent accounting pronouncements.

Quantitative and Qualitative Disclosures about Market Risk

We are exposed to market risks in the ordinary course of our business, including interest rate, foreign currency exchange, and inflation risks.

Interest rate risk

We had cash and cash equivalents of $430.0 million as of December 31, 2017. We hold our cash and cash equivalents for working capital purposes. Our cash and cash equivalents are held in cash deposits and money market funds. The primary objectives of our investment activities are the preservation of capital, the fulfillment of liquidity needs, and the control of cash and investments. We do not enter into investments for trading or speculative purposes. Due to the short-term nature of these instruments, we believe that we do not have any material exposure to changes in the fair value of our investment portfolio as a result of changes in interest rates. Decreases in interest rates, however, would reduce future interest income.

Any borrowings under the revolving credit facility bear interest at a variable rate tied to the prime rate or the LIBOR rate. As of December 31, 2017, we had no amounts outstanding under the revolving credit facility. We do not have any other long-term debt or financial liabilities with floating interest rates that would subject us to interest rate fluctuations.

A hypothetical 10% change in interest rates during any of the periods presented would not have had a material impact on our financial statements.

Foreign currency exchange risk

Our results of operations and cash flows are subject to fluctuations due to changes in foreign currency exchange rates relative to U.S. dollars, our reporting currency. Our revenue is generated in U.S. dollars, euros, British pounds sterling, Australian dollars, Canadian dollars, and Japanese yen. Our expenses are generally denominated in the currencies in which our operations are located, which are primarily the United States and, to a lesser extent, Europe and Asia. The functional currency of Dropbox International Unlimited, our international headquarters and largest international entity, is denominated in U.S. dollars. Our results of operations and cash flows are, therefore, subject to fluctuations due to changes in foreign currency exchange rates in ways that are unrelated to our operating performance. As exchange rates may fluctuate significantly between periods, revenue and operating expenses, when converted into U.S. dollars, may also experience significant fluctuations between periods. Historically, a majority of our revenue and operating expenses have been denominated in U.S. dollars, euros, and British pounds sterling. Although we are impacted by the exchange rate movements from a number of currencies relative to the U.S. dollar, our results of operations are particularly impacted by fluctuations in the U.S. dollar-euro and U.S. dollar-British pounds sterling exchange rate. In 2017, 29% of our sales were denominated in currencies other than U.S. dollars. Our expenses, by contrast, are primarily denominated in U.S. dollars. As a result, any increase in the value of the U.S. dollar against these foreign currencies could cause our revenue to decline relative to our costs, thereby decreasing our gross margins.

We recorded $4.6 million and $3.6 million in net foreign currency transaction losses in the years ended December 31, 2015 and 2016, respectively, and $5.0 million in net foreign currency transaction gains in the year ended December 31, 2017. A hypothetical 10% change in foreign currency rates would not have resulted in material gains or losses for the years ended December 31, 2015, 2016, and 2017.

To date, we have not engaged in any hedging activities. As our international operations grow, we will continue to reassess our approach to managing risks relating to fluctuations in currency rates.

Inflation risk

We do not believe that inflation has had a material effect on our business, results of operations, or financial condition. Nonetheless, if our costs were to become subject to significant inflationary pressures, we may not be able to fully offset such higher costs. Our inability or failure to do so could harm our business, results of operations, or financial condition.

[THIS PAGE INTENTIONALLY LEFT BLANK]

[THIS PAGE INTENTIONALLY LEFT BLANK]

Table of Contents

From the founders

A letter from Drew & Arash

The early days

Arash and I started Dropbox with the idea that life would be better if our most important information lived in the cloud.

Seemingly overnight, millions of people around the world were using Dropbox to sync their photos and documents. Many of them would write in saying how much they loved the product, and their stories were fascinating.

We heard from scientists researching Alzheimer's, filmmakers at Sundance, and disaster relief workers rescuing earthquake victims. We even got fan mail from an inventive group of farmers who were using Dropbox to coordinate tractors via satellite (we never really figured out how that worked).

These people had something in common. For them, Dropbox wasn't just about keeping files in sync. It was about keeping people in sync—connecting people and their most important information.

We were intrigued. Helping teams work better wasn't the problem we set out to solve, but following our users would take us on a much bigger journey.

How teams work today

As we observed teams more closely, it became clear to us that while technology had made working life better in many ways, there was also a dark side.

We were shocked by how much time our users were spending on things like searching for information, keeping teammates in the loop, and dealing with email. In fact, many employees spent more time on these tasks—all the "work about work"—than on the jobs they were hired to do. This overhead only increased as teams grew larger.

To make matters worse, newer collaboration tools were turning the workday into a blizzard of interruptions. Notifications pinged at all hours, demanding immediate responses. Work was spilling over into every waking moment, contributing to deeper problems like anxiety and burnout.

Modern technology is clearly making us busier. But is it making us more productive? It feels like our "productivity tools" are robbing us of the time and space to think. You'd think they'd be working for us, but somehow we've ended up working for them.

Why this matters

"Work about work" and constant distractions aren't just exhausting us, they're also wasting our potential.

Think about it: if Einstein were alive today, he'd start his day by clearing Groupons and LinkedIn invitations out of his inbox. Then he'd get down to work—and right before his Eureka moment, his phone would buzz with a Slack message. Would we still understand relativity?

As a species, over and over we've used our ingenuity to profoundly improve our lives. This is the engine of human progress: our time and creativity go in, and solutions to our biggest problems come out.

So we need to start treating our collective creative energy like the incredibly precious resource it is—the fuel for human progress. We can't make more of this fuel. But we can get better mileage.

We can fix this

In the last decade, psychology and neuroscience have shed light on what we need to be productive and feel fulfilled. Research shows that we perform at our best when we can focus, when we're well rested, and when we have a sense of purpose.

Wouldn't it be great if our working environment—and the tools we use—were designed with these needs in mind? Imagine if we finished work every day knowing what we did really mattered.

This is possible, and Dropbox is connecting the dots. Last year, we unveiled a new mission: Unleash the world's creative energy by designing a more enlightened way of working. That might sound a little out there, but our first mission did, too.

How we'll get there

The path to enlightened work starts with creating a better environment. More and more, the work we do every day happens on screens. We believe that these virtual spaces should be as thoughtfully designed as our most inspiring physical spaces.

How will Dropbox make this happen?

To start, teams need to have all their information in one place. It's crazy that in 2018, it's easier to search all of human knowledge than a company's knowledge—at home we have one search box, but at work we have ten. We see a big opportunity to solve this problem by continuing to tie the world's different tools and ecosystems together.

We also need to design a calm environment that fosters flow. Our workspace should feel organized and surface only what's relevant. It should tune out the chatter—more communication isn't always better. The experience should be seamless. You shouldn't have to use one app to write a doc and another to talk about it. Our newer products like Dropbox Paper are designed with these principles in mind.

And over time, machine intelligence will allow Dropbox to better understand both you and your team. Imagine getting to work in the morning to find your calendar reorganized so you have a three-hour block of time to actually focus. Imagine starting your day and seeing the perfect to-do list—one based on a deep understanding of your priorities and your team's priorities.

We're on our way

For millions of people and businesses, Dropbox is already a living workspace—the place where people come together and their ideas come to life. These users entrust us with their most valuable information. We think this is a huge advantage that will serve as the foundation of our reimagined work experience.

Dropbox is also operating at a scale that few companies have achieved. We have over 500 million registered users who collectively store a billion gigabytes of data on our platform. And we've made this cost-effective by building one of the largest, most efficient cloud infrastructures in the world.

Along the way, we've written a new playbook for business software. Our millions of users are our best salespeople and have helped us acquire customers with incredible efficiency. As a result, we reached a billion dollar revenue run rate faster than any software-as-a-service company in history.

And while we're at scale, we can still move quickly. We have a lot less baggage than the incumbents. The legacy office suites have had a good run, but they were designed for a world where the most important thing you did was print something out. There's a reason why BlackBerry didn't come up with the iPhone. Sometimes it's better to start fresh.

But what gives Arash and me the most confidence is our team of nearly 2,000 Dropboxers around the world. We're a little biased, but we think we have one of the most talented teams ever assembled, and we grow stronger every year.

Join us

We all deserve a fulfilling work life.

Imagine if every minute at work were well spent—if we could focus and spend our time on the things that matter. Imagine how much more inspired we'd be. Imagine how much better equipped we'd be to tackle humanity's biggest challenges.

This is the world we want to live in. We hope you'll join us.

.

Drew & Arash

Table of Contents

188

BUSINESS

Our Business

Our modern economy runs on knowledge. Today, knowledge lives in the cloud as digital content, and Dropbox is a global collaboration platform where more and more of this content is created, accessed, and shared with the world. We serve more than 500 million registered users across 180 countries.

Dropbox was founded in 2007 with a simple idea: Life would be a lot better if everyone could access their most important information anytime from any device. Over the past decade, we've largely accomplished that mission—but along the way we recognized that for most of our users, sharing and collaborating on Dropbox was even more valuable than storing files.

Our market opportunity has grown as we've expanded from keeping files in sync to keeping teams in sync. Today, Dropbox is well positioned to reimagine the way work gets done. We're focused on reducing the inordinate amount of time and energy the world wastes on "work about work"—tedious tasks like searching for content, switching between applications, and managing workflows.

We want to free up our users to spend more of their time on the work that truly matters. Our mission is to unleash the world's creative energy by designing a more enlightened way of working.

We believe the need for our platform will continue to grow as teams become more fluid and global, and content is increasingly fragmented across incompatible tools and devices. Dropbox breaks down silos by centralizing the flow of information between the products and services our users prefer, even if they're not our own.

By solving these universal problems, we've become invaluable to our users. The popularity of our platform drives viral growth, which has allowed us to scale rapidly and efficiently. We've built a thriving global business with over 11 million paying users.

Our revenue was $603.8 million, $844.8 million, and $1,106.8 million in 2015, 2016, and 2017, respectively, representing an annual growth rate of 40% and 31%, respectively. We generated net losses of $325.9 million, $210.2 million, and $111.7 million in 2015, 2016, and 2017, respectively. We also generated positive free cash flow of $137.4 million and $305.0 million in 2016 and 2017, respectively, compared to negative free cash flow of $63.9 million in 2015.

Our Users

We're constantly inspired by the diverse ways people use Dropbox to bring their ideas to life and achieve their missions faster. Here are just a few examples:

- Nobel Prize-winning researchers sync data with collaborators to speed development of new scientific breakthroughs.

- Designers for a sustainable apparel company iterate on new designs and coordinate store openings.

- A commercial construction company shares blueprints with subcontractors on job sites and sends bids to prospective clients.

- A Fortune 500 online travel company keeps its global workforce connected with business partners around the world.

- Pro bono lawyers at a refugee assistance organization collect and share information across continents to save lives.

101

What Sets Us Apart

Since the beginning, we've focused on simplifying the lives of our users. In a world where business software can be frustrating to use, challenging to integrate, and expensive to sell, we take a different approach.

Simple and intuitive design

While traditional tools developed in the desktop age have struggled to keep up with evolving user demands, Dropbox was designed for the cloud era. We build simple, beautiful products that bring joy to our users and make it easier for them to do their best work. Unencumbered by legacy features, we can perfect the aspects of our platform that matter most today, such as the mobile experience and the ability to work in teams.

Open ecosystem

We know people will continue to use a wide variety of tools and platforms. That's why we've built Dropbox to work seamlessly with other products, integrating with partners from Google and Microsoft to Slack and Autodesk. More than 75% of Dropbox Business teams have linked to one or more third-party applications.

Viral, bottom-up adoption

Our 500 million registered users are our best salespeople. They've spread Dropbox to their friends and brought us into their offices. Every year, millions of individual users sign up for Dropbox at work. Bottom-up adoption within organizations has been critical to our success as users increasingly choose their own tools at work. We generate over 90% of our revenue from self-serve channels—users who purchase a subscription through our app or website.

Performance and security

Our custom-built infrastructure allows us to maintain high standards of performance, availability, and security. Dropbox is built on proprietary, block-level sync technology to achieve industry-leading performance. In 2016, IDC highlighted our sync performance as best-in-class, outperforming competitors on multiple sync tests, including upload and download speeds for large files. We designed our platform with multiple layers of redundancy to guard against data loss and deliver high availability. We also offer numerous layers of protection, from secure file data transfer and encryption to network configuration and application-level controls.

Industry Trends in Our Favor

Content is increasingly scattered

The proliferation of devices, operating systems, and applications has dramatically increased the volume and complexity of content in the workplace. Content is now routinely scattered across multiple silos, making it harder to access. According to a 2016 IDC report, more than half of companies ranging from 100 to 5,000+ employees use at least three repositories for accessing documents on a weekly basis.

The tools people use are fragmented

Content created at work tends to follow a predictable pattern: It's authored, sent out for feedback, and shared or published once it's done. At the same time, teams are organizing that content and coordinating tasks around it. But many of the tools people use today don't work well together and support only one or two steps of the content lifecycle. This requires users to constantly switch between these tools and makes it even harder to get work done.

102

Teams have become more fluid and global

Technology hasn't kept up with a modern workforce that's increasingly fluid and mobile. People work together on teams that span different functions, organizations, and geographies. A 2016 study by Deloitte found that 37% of the global workforce is now mobile, 30% of full-time employees primarily work remotely, and 20% of the workforce is made up of temporary workers, contractors, and freelancers. The ability to swiftly disseminate content and its relevant context is critical to keeping teams in sync.

"Work about work" is wasteful and stifles creativity

The combination of scattered content, fragmented tools, and fluid team structures has led to decreased workplace productivity. According to a report by McKinsey & Company, knowledge workers spend approximately 60% of their time at work on tedious tasks such as searching for content, reviewing email, and re-sharing context to keep team members in the loop—what we call "work about work." This means they spend just 40% of their time doing the jobs they were hired to do.

Individual users are changing the way software is adopted and purchased

Software purchasing decisions have traditionally been made by an organization's IT department, which often deploys products that employees don't like and many refuse to adopt. As individuals increasingly choose their own tools at work, purchasing power has become more decentralized. A 2017 IDC report noted that new devices and software were being adopted at a faster rate by individual users than by IT departments.

Our Solution

Dropbox allows individuals, teams, and organizations to collaborate more effectively. Anyone can sign up for free through our website or app, and upgrade to a paid subscription plan for premium features. Our platform offers an elegant solution to the challenges described above.

Key elements of our platform

- *Unified home for content.* We provide a unified home for the world's content and the relevant context around it. To date, our users have added more than 400 billion pieces of content to Dropbox, totaling over an exabyte (more than 1,000,000,000 gigabytes) of data. When users join Dropbox, they gain access to a digital workspace that supports the full content lifecycle—they can create and organize their content, access it from anywhere, share it with internal and external collaborators, and review feedback and history.

- *Global sharing network.* We've built one of the largest collaboration platforms in the world, with more than 4.5 billion connections to shared content. We cater to the needs of dynamic, dispersed teams. The overwhelming majority of our customers use Dropbox to share and collaborate. As we continue to grow, more users benefit from frictionless sharing, and powerful network effects increase the utility and stickiness of our platform.

- *New product experiences.* The insights we glean from our community of users lead us to develop new product experiences, like Paper, Smart Sync, and Showcase. Machine learning further improves the user experience by enabling more intelligent search and better organization and utility of information. This ongoing innovation broadens the value of our platform and deepens user engagement.

These elements reinforce one another to produce a powerful flywheel effect. As users create and share more content with more people, they expand our global sharing network. This network allows us to gather insights and feedback that help us create new product experiences. And with our scale, we can instantly put these innovations in the hands of millions. This, in turn, helps attract more users and content, which further propels the flywheel.

103

Our Growth Strategy

Increase adoption and paid conversion

We designed Dropbox to be easy to try, use, and buy. Anyone can create an account and be up and running in minutes. We believe that our current registered user base represents a significant opportunity to increase our revenue. We estimate that approximately 300 million of our registered users have characteristics—including specific email domains, devices, and geographies—that make them more likely than other registered users to pay over time. Substantially all of our paying users share at least one of these characteristics. We reach our users through in-product notifications on our website and across hundreds of millions of actively connected devices, without any external marketing spend. We define an actively connected device as a desktop, laptop, phone, or tablet on which our app has been installed, and from which our app has been launched, and made a request to our servers at least once in the most recent quarter.

Upgrade our paying users

We offer a range of paid subscription plans, from Plus and Professional for individuals to Standard, Advanced, and Enterprise for teams. We analyze usage patterns within our network and run hundreds of targeted marketing campaigns to encourage paying users to upgrade their plans. For example, we prompt individual subscribers who collaborate with others on Dropbox to purchase our Standard or Advanced plans for a better team experience. In 2017, over 40% of new Dropbox Business teams included a member who was previously a subscriber to one of our individual paid plans. We believe that a large majority of individual customers use Dropbox for work, which creates an opportunity to significantly increase conversion to Dropbox Business team offerings over time.

Apply insights to build new product experiences

As our community of users grows, we gain more insight into their needs and pain points. We translate these insights into new product experiences that support the entire content lifecycle. For example, we learned through analytics and research that our users often work with many different types of content. As a result, we added the ability to embed rich media in Paper so they can pull everything together in one place—from InVision graphics and Google slides to Spotify tracks and Vimeo clips.

Expand our ecosystem

Our open and thriving ecosystem fosters deeper relationships with our users and makes Dropbox more valuable to them over time. The scale and reach of our platform is enhanced by a number of third-party applications, developers, and technology partners. As of December 31, 2017, Dropbox was receiving over 50 billion API calls per month, and more than 500,000 developers had registered and built applications on our platform.

Our Market Opportunity

Over the past decade, Dropbox has pioneered the worldwide adoption of file sync and share software. We've since expanded our capabilities and introduced new product experiences to help our users get work done. For the second consecutive year, Gartner has named Dropbox a leader in their Magic Quadrant for Content Collaboration Platforms.

Our addressable market includes collaborative applications, content management, project and portfolio management, and public cloud storage. IDC estimates that investment in these categories will total more than $50 billion in 2019.

As one of the few large-scale collaboration platforms that serves customers of all sizes, we also have an opportunity to reach a broad population of independent knowledge and creative workers. We believe that this market hasn't traditionally been included in IT spending estimates.

Our Capabilities

Dropbox is a digital workspace where individuals and teams can create content, access it from anywhere, and share it with collaborators. The power of our platform lies in the breadth of our capabilities and the diverse ways our users make Dropbox work for them. We monetize through a range of subscription plans. Our platform capabilities are described below:

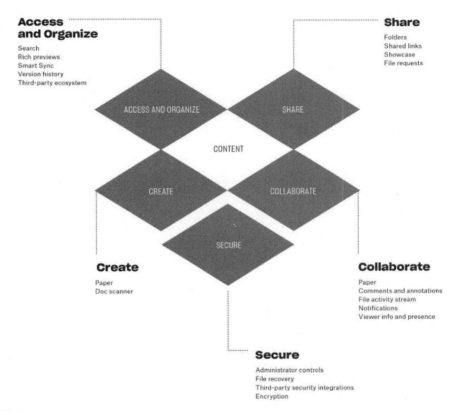

The Dropbox collaboration platform

Access and Organize

Search
Rich previews
Smart Sync
Version history
Third-party ecosystem

Share

Folders
Shared links
Showcase
File requests

ACCESS AND ORGANIZE

SHARE

CONTENT

CREATE

COLLABORATE

SECURE

Create

Paper
Doc scanner

Collaborate

Paper
Comments and annotations
File activity stream
Notifications
Viewer info and presence

Secure

Administrator controls
File recovery
Third-party security integrations
Encryption

105

Table of Contents

Create

Paper. We introduced Paper in January 2017 as a collaborative surface to bring people and ideas together. With Paper, users can co-author content, tag others, assign tasks with due dates, embed and comment on files, tables, checklists, code snippets, and rich media—all in real-time. We designed Paper to be simple and beautiful so users can focus on the most important ideas and tasks at hand.

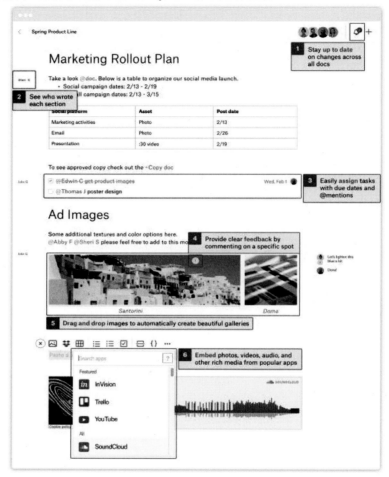

Table of Contents

Doc scanner. The doc scanner in our mobile app lets users create content in Dropbox from hard copies. This includes transforming everything from printed materials to whiteboard brainstorming sessions into digital documents that users can edit and share. We apply proprietary machine learning techniques to automatically detect the document being scanned, extract it from the background, fit it to a rectangular shape, remove shadows, adjust the contrast, and save it as a PDF or image file. For Dropbox Business teams, scanned content is analyzed using Optical Character Recognition so text within these scans is searchable in Dropbox.

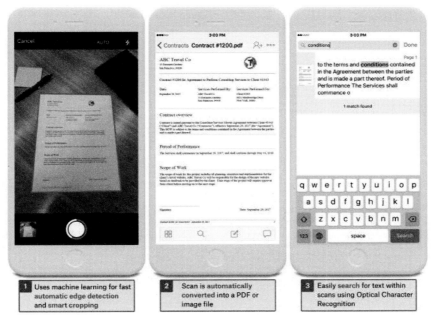

1 Uses machine learning for fast automatic edge detection and smart cropping

2 Scan is automatically converted into a PDF or image file

3 Easily search for text within scans using Optical Character Recognition

107

Table of Contents

Access and organize

Search. Dropbox has powerful search capabilities that allow users to quickly find the files and folders they need. Our autocomplete technology surfaces and prioritizes content based on users' previous activity. For Dropbox Professional subscribers and Dropbox Business teams, full text search allows users to scan the entire content of their files.

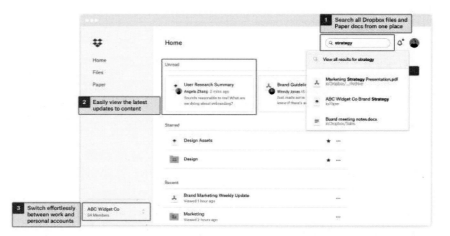

Rich previews. Rich previews allow users to easily interact with files across any device without having to open different applications. Users can comment on, annotate, review, and present files, and see who viewed and edited them. We support previews of over 280 file types, and Dropbox users currently preview files tens of millions of times every day.

108

Table of Contents

Smart Sync. With Smart Sync, users can access all of their content natively on their computers without taking up storage space on their local hard drives. We intelligently sync files to a user's computer as they need them, and users can control which files or folders are always synced locally. With Smart Sync, files that are only stored in the cloud appear in the local file system and can be opened directly from Windows File Explorer or Mac Finder, instead of having to navigate to our web interface. Smart Sync is available to Dropbox Professional subscribers and Dropbox Business teams.

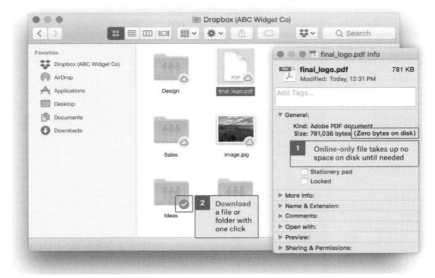

Version history. As paying users work on files, our servers keep snapshots of all their changes. Users can see a file's complete version history so they can reference and retrieve older versions if needed. Version histories are kept between 30 to 120 days for paying users, depending on subscription plan.

Third-party ecosystem. Our open and thriving ecosystem fosters deeper relationships with our users and developers. Developers can build applications that connect to Dropbox through our DBX Developer Platform. For example, email apps can plug into Dropbox to send attachments or shared links, and note-taking apps can allow users to save to Dropbox so they can open their notes on another device. As of December 31, 2017, Dropbox was receiving over 50 billion API calls per month and over 500,000 developers had registered and built applications on our platform. In addition, more than 75% of Dropbox Business teams have linked to one or more third-party applications.

Share

Folders. There are three types of folders in Dropbox: private, shared, and team folders. A private folder allows an individual to sync files between devices. A shared folder allows users to quickly and easily start a project space for group collaboration. A team folder, which is only available for Dropbox Business teams, is a central, administrator-managed hub where they can store and collaborate on content.

109

Table of Contents

Shared links. Users can share files and folders with anyone, including non-Dropbox users, by creating a Dropbox link. Once created, the link can be sent through email, text, Facebook, Twitter, instant message, or other channels. The recipient can view the file with a rich preview or see all the files in a shared folder. Dropbox Professional subscribers and Dropbox Business teams can set passwords and expiration dates and specify whether recipients can comment on or download the files.

Showcase. Showcase gives users a way to present their work to clients and business partners through a customizable, professionally branded webpage. Users can display visual previews of multiple files on the same page and add relevant context with introductory text and captions and an introduction. Showcase also lets users track how recipients engage with their content, including analytics on who has viewed, commented, or downloaded content on a per-person and per-file basis.

110

Table of Contents

File requests. With file requests, users can invite anyone to submit files into a specified Dropbox folder through a simple link—regardless of whether the recipient has a Dropbox account. File requests are ideal for tasks such as collecting bids from contractors or requesting submissions from coworkers and clients. All submitted files are organized into a Dropbox folder that's private to the requesting user.

111

Table of Contents

Collaborate

Comments and annotations. Dropbox comments and annotations marry content with the conversations and relevant context around it. Instead of being scattered across separate silos, such as email and chat, the editing and development of content are tied to a file. Users can give feedback on specific parts of files through a rich, innovative overlay on our web and mobile platforms.

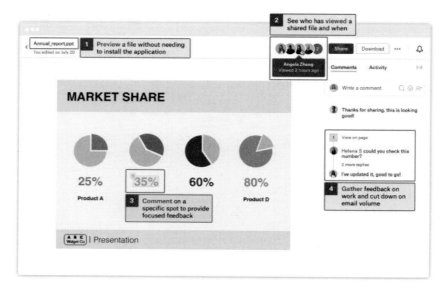

File activity stream. An activity feed lives next to every file preview on our web interface, telling users what's happening with a file. The feed shows when someone opens a file, edits a file, or shares a file.

Notifications. We use real-time notifications across all our channels—web, desktop, email, and mobile—to keep users up-to-date on what's happening with their work. Users can choose to be notified when someone opens, edits, shares, or comments on a file, or adds a file to their shared folders. These notifications keep collaborators in sync without having to open the file or doc.

Viewer information and presence. On both file previews and Paper docs, Dropbox shows users in real-time who's viewing a doc and when a doc was last viewed by other users. On desktop, the Dropbox badge is a subtle overlay to Microsoft Word, Excel, and PowerPoint that lets users know if someone opens or edits the file they're working in. The Dropbox badge gives users real-time insight into how others are interacting with their content, bringing modern collaboration features often found only in web-based documents to desktop files.

Secure

Security protections. We employ strong protections for all of the data on our platform.

- *Encryption.* Dropbox file data at rest is encrypted using 256-bit Advanced Encryption Standard, or AES. To protect data in transit between Dropbox apps such as desktop, mobile, API, or web and our

112

servers, Dropbox uses Secure Sockets Layer, or SSL, and Transport Layer Security, or TLS, for data transfer, creating a secure tunnel protected by 128-bit or higher AES encryption.

- *File recovery*. Every deletion event in Dropbox is recorded, including when groups of files are deleted. Users can easily recover files through our web interface. Dropbox Plus subscribers may recover prior versions for up to 30 days after deletion, and Dropbox Professional and Dropbox Business subscribers may recover prior versions for up to 120 days after deletion.

Administrator controls. Dropbox Business team administrators have many ways to customize security settings in both global and granular ways.

- *Sharing permissions*: Team administrators can set up and monitor how their members share team folders, and can set sharing permissions on all folders, sub-folders, and links through the sharing tab.

- *Remote device wipe*: Team administrators can delete their organization's Dropbox content from a member's linked devices, which is especially useful should someone lose a device or leave the team.

- *Audit log*: Team administrators can monitor which members are sharing files and logging into Dropbox, among other events. They can review activity logs, create full reports for specific time ranges, and pull activity reports on specific members. Advanced and Enterprise team administrators have access to audit logs with file-event tracking.

- *Device approvals*: Advanced and Enterprise team administrators can manage how members access Dropbox on their devices.

- *Tiered administrator roles*: Advanced and Enterprise teams have the ability to set multiple administrator roles, each with a different set of permissions.

- *Network control*: Enterprise team administrators can restrict personal Dropbox usage on their organization's network.

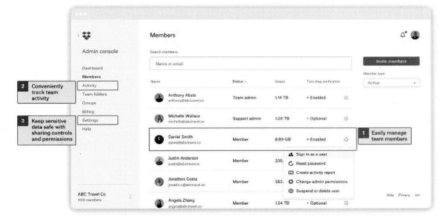

Third-party security integrations. We've partnered with industry-leading third parties to enable us to provide a wide range of IT processes and satisfy industry compliance standards, including:

- *Security information and event management*: Allows Dropbox Business administrators to oversee and manage employee activity, and access sensitive data through the administrator page.

113

- *Data loss prevention*: Protects sensitive data like personally identifiable information and payment card industry data stored in Dropbox Business accounts.

- *eDiscovery and legal hold*: Enables secure search and the ability to collect and preserve electronically stored information in Dropbox Business accounts.

- *Digital rights management*: Provides third-party encryption for company data stored in Dropbox Business accounts.

- *Data migration and on-premises backup*: Assists in transferring large amounts of data between locations and securing sensitive information with on-site data backup.

- *Identity management*: Allows companies to keep their Dropbox Business team authenticated with an external identity provider like Active Directory.

114

Our Subscription Plans

We offer subscription plans to serve the varying needs of our diverse customer base, which includes individuals, teams, and organizations of all sizes.

	Individuals			Teams (Branded as Dropbox Business)		
	Basic	Plus	Professional	Standard	Advanced	Enterprise
First launched	2008	2008	2017	2011	2017	2015
Number of users	1 user	1 user	1 user	3+ users	3+ users	Large deployments
Base price ($USD) per user	Free	$9.99/month $99/year	$19.99/month $199/year	$15.00/month $150/year	$25.00/month $240/year	Negotiated pricing
Advanced sharing permissions			✓	✓	✓	✓
Version history	30 days	30 days	120 days	120 days	120 days	120 days
Smart Sync			✓	✓	✓	✓
Showcase			✓		✓	✓
Team folders				✓	✓	✓
Unlimited API access*				✓	✓	✓
Paper	✓	✓	✓	✓	✓	✓
Storage	2GB	1TB	1TB	2TB	As much as needed	As much as needed
Support	Basic email support	Priority email support	Priority chat support	Live chat support	Business hours phone support	24/7 phone support Assigned account success manager
Advanced admin & security features		Remote device wipe	Remote device wipe	Admin console Managed groups Access permissions Account transfer tool HIPAA support	*Everything in Standard* Device approval Audit log Tiered admin roles SSO integration	*Everything in Advanced* EMM Network control Domain insights Integration support

*Teams have unlimited API access to productivity and security partners but may be subject to a cap on API calls to data transport partners.

Our Customers

We've built a thriving global business with over 11 million paying users. Of these subscribers, approximately 30% use Dropbox for work on a Dropbox Business team plan, and we estimate that an additional

115

50% use Dropbox for work on an individual plan, collectively totaling approximately 80% of paying subscribers. As of December 31, 2017, we had more than 300,000 paying Dropbox Business teams, and approximately 56% of Fortune 500 companies had at least one Dropbox Business team within their organization. Our customer base is highly diversified, and in 2015, 2016, and 2017, no customer accounted for more than 1% of our revenue. Our customers include individuals, teams, and organizations of all sizes, from freelancers and small businesses to Fortune 100 companies. They work across a wide range of industries, including professional services, technology, media, education, industrials, consumer and retail, and financial services. Within companies, our platform is used by all types of teams and functions, including sales, marketing, product, design, engineering, finance, legal, and human resources.

How we support our customers

All of our users can access support through the following resources:

- *Help center*: Provides an online repository of helpful information about our platform, responses to frequently asked questions, and best practices for use.

- *Community support*: Facilitates collaboration between users on answers, solutions, and ideas about our platform in an online community.

- *Twitter support*: Provides users real-time product and service updates, and offers tips and troubleshooting information.

- *Guided troubleshooting*: Offers step-by-step instructions to resolve common questions and provides a portal to submit help requests for questions that aren't otherwise available.

We also offer additional support for our paying users as described above in "Our Subscription Plans."

Case Studies

The customer examples below illustrate how businesses from different industries benefit from our platform.

116

Table of Contents

Customer stories

Expedia

Expedia offers online travel booking for flights, hotels, car rentals, and more through its portfolio of over 200 web properties. The company encourages its more than 20,000 employees in 72 offices worldwide to use technology they know and love. This presents a unique business challenge: how does a global team work well together when their tools do not? After learning that many employees already relied on Dropbox to coordinate on projects, Expedia purchased 10,000 Dropbox Business licenses in 2015.

It was an easy transition: the platform required little or no training, and Dropbox integrated seamlessly with the wide array of platforms and apps the business ran on—a key reason why so many Expedians had already adopted Dropbox. After just one month of deployment, the number of shared Dropbox folders increased six-fold and the number of mobile devices connected to Dropbox doubled, supporting greater productivity for employees as they traveled. Expedia also saved on IT costs as their workflows moved to the cloud.

———

"A lot of times when we deploy software, we first hear about the challenges. But during our phased deployment of Dropbox Business, we mostly just heard employees saying, 'Can I get that now?'"

Chris Burgess
Vice President of Information Technology
Expedia Group

Table of Contents

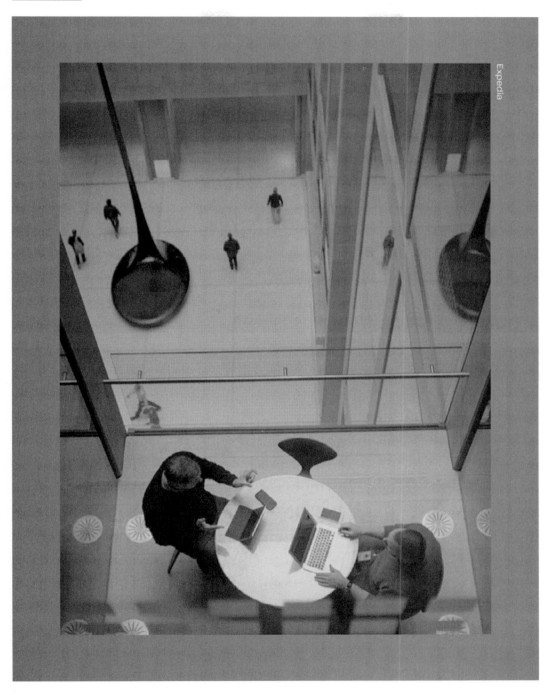

207

Golden State Warriors

The defending NBA champions are known for their innovative thinking and teamwork on and off the court. Part of the Warriors' organizational philosophy is to break down communication barriers, but their existing tools weren't maximizing efficiency. Ease of use, security, and seamless on-boarding were among the deciding factors in adopting Dropbox. The IT team also loves that Smart Sync frees up hard drive space, allowing for leaner hardware choices. After starting with 15 Dropbox Business licenses in 2013, today the Warriors have requested 450 Business licenses to keep up with user demand.

The Warriors use Dropbox across the organization. Basketball operations and analytics departments share scouting videos, "heat maps" that show where a player is most successful on the court, and complex models in Excel to ensure they're keeping their competitive edge. As the Warriors prepare for their move to Chase Center in 2019, designers, architects, and engineers collaborate on CAD file schematics in Dropbox. The Warriors say that using Dropbox helps keep them ahead of the curve in their industry.

—

"The beauty of Dropbox is that it lets us collaborate across any team, from any location. We owe a lot of our success to how well our organization works together, and Dropbox is right there at the top of the list of reasons why."

Chip Bowers
Chief Marketing Officer
Golden State Warriors

Table of Contents

Golden State Warriors

209

Les Lunes

Les Lunes is a fashion and apparel company. Designers in Paris and Los Angeles, manufacturers in Shanghai, and business teams in San Francisco and New York collaborate to make clothing out of sustainable bamboo fabrics. As the company grew from three employees to 20, Les Lunes adopted Dropbox Business in 2013 to centralize their workflow.

Les Lunes' entire product development process now happens in Dropbox Paper. Designers use it to iterate on sketches in real time, while store managers comment in the same document to relay customer feedback. Employees track everything from vendor deliveries to logo approvals with Paper's task management and deadline features. To date, Les Lunes has used Paper to design 10 clothing lines and plan six new store and showroom openings. Since adopting Dropbox, Les Lunes has also saved around $200,000 a year on infrastructure, including costs associated with laptops, on-premise storage systems, security software, file servers, IT personnel, and competing SaaS solutions.

—

"Dropbox Paper is our new best friend. It has eliminated long email chains and really enabled us to communicate better as a team—it saves us hours of work on every project."

Tobe Sheldon
Regional Manager
Les Lunes

Table of Contents

Table of Contents

Brandt

Brandt is a large mechanical, electrical, and plumbing contractor that services facilities like schools and hospitals across Texas. Before adopting Dropbox, Brandt's field technicians relied on paperwork, scanners, printers, and fax machines to communicate with their company headquarters and customers. In 2014, Brandt purchased 120 Dropbox Business licenses and deployed them on tablets for technicians on job sites to update forms and work orders in shared Dropbox folders. Brandt also integrated its own digital signature app with Dropbox to make the process even easier. Signed forms save automatically to the appropriate Dropbox shared folder, which notifies the approving supervisor.

Brandt has since expanded its deployment to 250 Dropbox Business licenses, and estimates that each field technician saves up to one hour per service call on document processing. With 120 technicians each completing two service calls per day on average, Brandt calculates savings of $400,000 per year—or more than three times the annual cost of the company's Dropbox Business subscription.

—

"Our technicians are more efficient, our customers are getting what they need more quickly, and we are delivering to the bottom line in ways that were unforeseeable when we began this process."

Jim Stagg
Vice President of Service
Brandt

Table of Contents

Brandt

Maple Hill Creamery

Maple Hill Creamery is the pioneer in organic 100% grass-fed dairy products with top-selling items in stores across the U.S. As the company grew to include 150 organic dairy farms across the state of New York, and remote teams across the country, they needed a more sustainable and centralized way to share information than email and personal Dropbox accounts. In 2015, Maple Hill upgraded to Dropbox Business—a decision they now describe as "priceless."

By creating shared folders with each of their team members and departments, Maple Hill manages contracts, organic certificates, and other key documents without having to track down email attachments. Salespeople use shared folders to access product summaries, distributor profiles, and other marketing assets. With the Dropbox badge, employees keep tabs on milk flow as production from 150 farms is updated to reflect expected volumes in Excel spreadsheets. By making it easy to coordinate with distributors and eliminating the need to maintain file servers, Dropbox has helped Maple Hill keep IT costs low as they've expanded into the dairy aisles of more than 6,000 stores.

——

"We're able to do things you could do in the past only with a full-fledged IT department. So Dropbox keeps us very small and nimble."

Tim Joseph
Founder
Maple Hill Creamery

Table of Contents

215

World Bicycle Relief

World Bicycle Relief (WBR) was founded in the aftermath of the December 2004 Indian Ocean tsunami. Co-founders F.K. Day and Leah Missbach Day saw how bicycles helped the people who had been relocated from their homes, schools, and places of work to get moving again. The nonprofit designs, manufactures, and delivers durable bicycles to developing countries where typically available, low-quality bikes often fall apart in these rugged, rural conditions. Operating on a limited budget, WBR needed a better way to centralize collaboration among employees on four continents who often needed to share large files.

In 2015, WBR decided to buy 50 Dropbox Business licenses because many of its employees were already familiar with the product. Employees in Chicago and Europe use Dropbox to share design files with manufacturers in Taiwan and distribute product manuals with field teams in Africa, who then assemble the bicycles. The platform's reliable performance in low-bandwidth environments has allowed WBR to effectively manage its supply chain communications and product orders, enabling the nonprofit to put more bicycles in the hands of people who need them. To date, WBR has delivered over 350,000 Buffalo Bicycles in 19 countries.

"Our investments in technology are a key reason we've been able to scale our efforts, and Dropbox is right at the top of the list of tools we use every day."

Ruth-Anne Renaud
Director of Global Marketing
World Bicycle Relief

Table of Contents

World Bicycle Relief

Table of Contents

Our Sales and Marketing Approach

As users share content and collaborate on our platform, they introduce and invite new users, driving viral growth. We generate 90% of our revenue from self-serve channels, which reduces customer acquisition costs.

We've developed an efficient marketing function that's focused on building brand awareness and reinforcing our self-serve model. Our goal is to rapidly demonstrate the value of our platform to our users in order to convert them to paying users and upgrade them to our premium offerings. We reach them through in-product prompts and notifications, time-limited trials of paid subscription plans, email, and lifecycle marketing. During the fourth quarter of 2017, hundreds of millions of devices—including computers, phones, and tablets—were actively connected to the Dropbox platform, representing a large number of touchpoints to communicate with our users.

We complement our self-serve strategy with a focused outbound sales effort targeted at organizations with existing organic adoption of Dropbox. Once prospects are identified, our sales team works to broaden adoption of our platform into wider-scale deployments. We also acquire some users through paid marketing and distribution partnerships in which hardware manufacturers pre-install our software on their devices.

Our Technology Infrastructure and Operations

Our users trust us with their most important content, and we focus on providing them with a secure and easy-to-use platform. More than 90% of our users' data is stored on our own custom-built infrastructure, which has been designed from the ground up to be reliable and secure, and to provide annual data durability of at least 99.999999999%. We have datacenter co-location facilities in California, Texas, and Virginia.

We also utilize Amazon Web Services, or AWS, for the remainder of our users' storage needs and to help deliver our services. These AWS datacenters are located in the United States and Europe, which allows us to localize where content is stored. Our technology infrastructure, combined with select use of AWS resources, provides us with a distributed and scalable architecture on a global scale.

We designed our platform with multiple layers of redundancy to guard against data loss and deliver high availability. Incremental backups are performed hourly and full backups are performed daily. In addition, as a default, redundant copies of content are stored independently in at least two separate geographic regions and replicated reliably within each region.

Our Research and Development Approach

We invest substantial resources in research and development to enhance our platform, develop new products and features, and improve our infrastructure.

Our research and development organization consists of world-class engineering, product, and design teams. As of December 31, 2017, we had more than 870 professionals across these teams, representing approximately 47% of our full-time employees. They have a diverse set of skills and industry experience, including expertise in massively distributed systems and user-centric application engineering.

Our engineering, product, and design teams work together to bring our products to life, from conception and validation to implementation. We continually improve our existing products, update them to work with the latest platforms and technologies, and launch new and innovative products and features.

131

Our Values

Since our founding, we've focused on building a culture of innovation and teamwork. As our company grew, we developed five core values that are critical to our success. Our values are a compass and part of everyday life for Dropboxers. Each one guides how we treat each other and our users.

- ### Be worthy of trust

  Take care of each other and our users, and keep their best interests at heart. Millions of people and businesses trust us to safeguard their most important information. We strive to be as transparent as possible with them and each other.

- ### Sweat the details

  Obsess over quality and strive to master your craft. We believe that truly insightful solutions emerge from a deep understanding of problems and a dedication to iteration. We push ourselves (and each other) to get to the root of problems, and we don't accept sloppy solutions or band-aids.

- ### Aim higher

  Set audacious goals. We believe in taking risks and being willing to disrupt ourselves, so we don't squander an opportunity to build something much bigger. With the density of incredible talent at Dropbox and the size of the opportunity in front of us, we owe it to each other to push limits.

- ### We, not I

  We're a village, and as members, we each need to do our part for the village to thrive. We tackle a never-ending stream of people, product, and business challenges, many of which are far too hard to be solved by a single person or team. We believe in people really knowing each other and in putting the welfare of the company and our users before ourselves.

-

  Surprise and delight each other and our users. Cupcake is about adding an authentic, human touch to everything we do. But more than that, it's about finding creative ways to make our users (and each other) smile—whether it's our quirky illustrations, or bringing a roving ice cream cart to the office to celebrate a product launch. We believe that the magic we create together as Dropboxers translates into magic for our users.

Our Employees

As of December 31, 2017, we had 1,858 full-time employees. We also engage contractors and consultants. None of our employees are represented by a labor union. We have not experienced any work stoppages, and we believe that our employee relations are strong.

Our Commitment to Security and Privacy

Trust is the foundation of our relationship with our users, and we take significant measures every day to protect their privacy and security.

Security

Our sophisticated infrastructure is designed to protect our users' content while it is transferred, stored, and processed. We offer multiple layers of protection, including secure file data transfer, encryption, network configuration, and application-level controls. For Dropbox Business teams, our tools also empower

132

administrators with control and visibility features that allow them to customize our platform to their organizations' needs. Our information security policies and management framework are designed to build a culture of security, and we continually assess risks and improve the security, confidentiality, integrity, and availability of our systems.

We voluntarily engage third-party security auditors to test our systems and controls at least annually against the most widely recognized security standards and regulations. Our Dropbox Trust Program consists of key infrastructure processes such as change management, access control, security management, and human resource management. Our program also serves as an Information Security Management System, or ISMS, as prescribed by the International Organization for Standardization, or ISO, and the International Electrotechnical Commission 27001:2013 international information security standard. It also qualifies as a Business Continuity Management System, or BCMS, as prescribed by the ISO 22301:2012 international business continuity standard.

The ISO has developed a series of standards for information security and related areas. We've received the following ISO certifications:

- ISO 27001 (Information Security Management)
- ISO 27017 (Cloud Security)
- ISO 27018 (Cloud Privacy and Data Protection)
- ISO 22301 (Business Continuity Management)

We've also completed a SOC 1, SOC 2, and SOC 3 examination. Service Organization Controls, or SOC, are standards established by the American Institute of Certified Public Accountants for reporting on internal control environments implemented within an organization. Our datacenter facilities and services providers also regularly undergo ISO 27001, SOC 1, and/or SOC 2 audits to verify their security practices. The ISO 27001 security standard specifies the requirements for establishing, implementing, operating, monitoring, reviewing, maintaining, and improving a documented Information Security Management System within the context of the organization's overall business risks. This standard addresses confidentiality, access control, vulnerability, and risk assessment.

In addition, we have CSA STAR Level 1 and Level 2 certifications from the Cloud Security Alliance, or CSA, a security assurance program for cloud services. CSA Security, Trust & Assurance Registry, or STAR, is a free, publicly-accessible registry that offers a security assurance program for cloud services, helping users assess the security posture of cloud providers they currently use or are considering contracting with. CSA STAR Level 2 Certification requires a third-party independent assessment of our security controls based on the requirements of ISO 27001 and the CSA Cloud Controls Matrix, or CCM, v.3.0.1, a set of criteria that measures the capability levels of cloud services. The CSA STAR Level 1 Self-Assessment is a rigorous survey based on CSA's Consensus Assessments Initiative Questionnaire, which aligns with the CCM, and provides answers to almost 300 questions a cloud customer or a cloud security auditor may ask. We're also listed in the UK Digital Marketplace for government cloud services procurement under the current framework, known as G-Cloud 9.

Dropbox supports HIPAA and HITECH compliance. We sign business associate agreements with our customers who require them in order to comply with the Health Insurance Portability and Accountability Act, or HIPAA, and the Health Information Technology for Economic and Clinical Health Act, or HITECH. We also offer a HIPAA assessment report performed by an independent third party.

Privacy

We're committed to keeping user data private. Our privacy policy details how users' information is protected and the steps we take to protect it. Dropbox also has terms and guidelines for third-party developers to create applications that connect to Dropbox while respecting user privacy. Dropbox is certified under the EU-U.S. and Swiss-U.S. Privacy Shield and is working towards compliance with the EU General Data Protection Regulation, or GDPR, framework.

133

We believe in transparency with our users and have adopted guiding principles regarding how we handle requests from government and law enforcement agencies seeking information about our users and their content. These guiding principles are:

- *Be transparent*

    - We believe that online services should be allowed to publish the number and types of government requests they receive, and to notify individuals when information about them has been requested. We'll continue to publish detailed information about these requests and advocate for the right to provide more information.

- *Fight overly broad requests*

    - We believe that government data requests should be limited in the information they seek and narrowly tailored to specific people and legitimate investigations. We'll resist blanket and overly broad requests.

- *Provide trusted services*

    - We believe that governments should never install backdoors into online services or compromise infrastructure to obtain user data. We'll continue to work to protect our systems and to change laws to make it clear that this type of activity is illegal.

- *Protect all users*

    - We believe that laws that give people different protections based on where they live or their citizenship are antiquated and don't reflect the global nature of online services. We're committed to providing the same level of protection to all of our users. That means that we use our guiding principles to scrutinize all the requests we receive, regardless of the origin of the request or user.

Our Competition

The market for content collaboration platforms is competitive and rapidly changing. Certain features of our platform compete in the cloud storage market with products offered by Amazon, Apple, Google, and Microsoft, and in the content collaboration market with products offered by Atlassian, Google, and Microsoft. We compete with Box on a more limited basis in the cloud storage market for deployments by large enterprises. We also compete with smaller private companies that offer point solutions in the cloud storage market or the content collaboration market.

We believe that the principal competitive factors in our markets include the following:

- user-centric design;

- ease of adoption and use;

- scale of user network;

- features and platform experience;

- performance;

- brand;

- security and privacy;

- accessibility across several devices, operating systems, and applications;

- third-party integration;

- customer support;

134

222

- continued innovation; and

- pricing.

We believe we compete favorably across these factors and are largely unhindered by legacy constraints. However, some of our competitors may have greater name recognition, longer operating histories, more varied services, the ability to bundle a broader range of products and services, larger marketing budgets, established marketing relationships, access to larger user bases, major distribution agreements with hardware manufacturers and resellers, and greater financial, technical, and other resources.

Intellectual Property

We believe that our intellectual property rights are valuable and important to our business. We rely on patents, patent applications, trademarks, copyrights, trade secrets, know-how license agreements, confidentiality procedures, non-disclosure agreements, employee disclosure and invention assignment agreements, and other contractual rights to establish and protect our proprietary rights. In addition, from time to time we've purchased patents, inbound licenses, trademarks, domain names, and patent applications from third parties.

We have over 600 issued patents and more than 600 pending patent applications in the United States and abroad. These patents and patent applications seek to protect our proprietary inventions relevant to our business. In addition, we have a large number of inbound licenses to key patents in the file collaboration, storage, syncing, and sharing markets.

We have trademark rights in our name, our logo, and other brand indicia, and have trademark registrations for select marks in the United States and many other jurisdictions around the world. We also have registered domain names for websites that we use in our business, such as www.dropbox.com, and similar variations.

We intend to pursue additional intellectual property protection to the extent we believe it would be beneficial and cost effective. Despite our efforts to protect our intellectual property rights, they may not be respected in the future or may be invalidated, circumvented, or challenged. In addition, the laws of various foreign countries where our products are distributed may not protect our intellectual property rights to the same extent as laws in the United States.

Legal Proceedings

We are currently involved in, and may in the future be involved in, legal proceedings, claims, and government investigations in the ordinary course of business, including legal proceedings with third parties asserting infringement of their intellectual property rights. For example, in April 2015, Synchronoss Technologies, Inc., a public company that provides cloud-based products, filed a patent infringement lawsuit against us in the United States District Court for the District of New Jersey, claiming three counts of patent infringement and seeking injunctive relief. The case was subsequently transferred to the United States District Court for the Northern District of California. We do not currently believe that this matter is likely to have a material adverse impact on our consolidated results of operations, cash flows, or our financial position, and we intend to vigorously defend this lawsuit, and believe we have valid defenses to the claims. However, any litigation is inherently uncertain, and any judgment or injunctive relief entered against us or any adverse settlement could materially and adversely impact our business, results of operations, financial condition, and prospects.

Future litigation may be necessary, among other things, to defend ourselves or our users by determining the scope, enforceability, and validity of third-party proprietary rights or to establish our proprietary rights. The results of any current or future litigation cannot be predicted with certainty, and regardless of the outcome, litigation can have an adverse impact on us because of defense and settlement costs, diversion of management resources, and other factors.

135

Our Facilities

Our corporate headquarters is located in San Francisco, California, pursuant to operating leases that expire in 2033. We lease additional offices in San Francisco and around the world, including in Austin, Texas; Seattle, Washington; New York, New York; Dublin, Ireland; London, United Kingdom; Tel Aviv, Israel; Sydney, Australia; and Tokyo, Japan. We have datacenter co-location facilities in California, Texas, and Virginia. We believe that these facilities are generally suitable to meet our needs.

136

MANAGEMENT

Executive Officers and Directors

The following table provides information regarding our executive officers and directors as of March 8, 2018:

Name	Age	Position
Executive officers:		
Andrew W. Houston	35	Chief Executive Officer, Co-Founder, and Chairman
Arash Ferdowsi	32	Co-Founder and Director
Quentin J. Clark	46	Senior Vice President of Engineering, Product, and Design
Ajay V. Vashee	34	Chief Financial Officer
Bart E. Volkmer	43	General Counsel
Dennis M. Woodside	49	Chief Operating Officer
Non-executive directors:		
Donald W. Blair	59	Director
Paul E. Jacobs	55	Director
Robert J. Mylod, Jr.	51	Director
Condoleezza Rice	63	Director
R. Bryan Schreier	39	Director
Margaret C. Whitman	61	Director

Executive officers

Andrew W. Houston. Mr. Houston is one of our co-founders and has served as a member of our Board of Directors and our Chief Executive Officer since June 2007. Mr. Houston holds a B.S. in Computer Science from the Massachusetts Institute of Technology.

Mr. Houston was selected to serve on our Board of Directors because of the perspective and experience he brings as our Chief Executive Officer and as one of our co-founders.

Arash Ferdowsi. Mr. Ferdowsi is one of our co-founders and has served as a member of our Board of Directors since June 2007. From June 2007 to October 2016, Mr. Ferdowsi served as our Chief Technology Officer. Mr. Ferdowsi attended the Massachusetts Institute of Technology.

Mr. Ferdowsi was selected to serve on our Board of Directors because of the perspective and experience he brings as one of our co-founders.

Quentin J. Clark. Mr. Clark has served as our Senior Vice President of Engineering, Product, and Design since September 2017. From November 2014 to September 2016, Mr. Clark served as Executive Vice President for SAP America, Inc., a developer of business software solutions, as its Chief Business Officer from October 2015 to September 2016, and as its Chief Technology Officer from November 2014 to October 2015. Prior to joining SAP, Mr. Clark served at Microsoft Corporation, a global technology company, and as a Corporate Vice President of enterprise business units since 2011, and held various engineering and product leadership roles at Microsoft since 1994. Mr. Clark holds a B.S. in Physics from the University of Massachusetts Amherst.

Ajay V. Vashee. Mr. Vashee has served as our Chief Financial Officer since September 2016. From February 2015 to September 2016, Mr. Vashee served as our Head of Corporate Development. From April 2012 to February 2015, Mr. Vashee served as our Head of Finance. Mr. Vashee holds a B.A. in Economics-Political Science from Columbia University.

137

Bart E. Volkmer. Mr. Volkmer has served as our General Counsel since June 2016. From August 2011 to June 2016, Mr. Volkmer served as our Head of Litigation & Regulatory. Mr. Volkmer holds a J.D. from Santa Clara University School of Law and a B.A. in English from Creighton University.

Dennis M. Woodside. Mr. Woodside has served as our Chief Operating Officer since April 2014. From May 2012 to April 2014, Mr. Woodside served as Chief Executive Officer for Motorola Mobility LLC, a consumer electronics and telecommunications company now owned by Lenovo Group Ltd. From March 2009 to September 2011, Mr. Woodside served as President, Americas & Senior Vice President for Google Inc., a global technology company. Mr. Woodside holds a J.D. from Stanford Law School and a B.S. in Industrial Relations from Cornell University.

Non-executive directors

Donald W. Blair. Mr. Blair has served as a member of our Board of Directors since December 2017. From November 1999 to October 2015, Mr. Blair served as Executive Vice President and Chief Financial Officer for NIKE, Inc., or NIKE, a global footwear and apparel company. Prior to joining NIKE, for fifteen years, Mr. Blair served in a number of senior executive-level corporate and operating unit financial assignments for PepsiCo, Inc., or PepsiCo, a food and beverage company, including Chief Financial Officer for PepsiCo Japan (based in Tokyo) and Pepsi-Cola International's Asia Division (based in Hong Kong). Mr. Blair currently serves as a member of the board of directors for Corning Incorporated, a global manufacturing company. Mr. Blair holds an M.B.A. and a B.S. in Economics from the University of Pennsylvania.

Mr. Blair was selected to serve on our Board of Directors because of his extensive financial expertise, and business management and governance experience.

Paul E. Jacobs, Ph.D. Dr. Jacobs has served as a member of our Board of Directors since April 2016. From March 2014 to March 2018, Dr. Jacobs served as Executive Chairman for Qualcomm, a semiconductor and telecommunications equipment company. From March 2009 to March 2014, Dr. Jacobs served as Chairman of the board of directors for Qualcomm. From July 2005 to March 2017, Dr. Jacobs served as Chief Executive Officer for Qualcomm Inc. Dr. Jacobs also currently serves as a member of the board of directors for a number of private companies. Dr. Jacobs holds a Ph.D. in Electrical Engineering and Computer Science, a M.S. in Electrical Engineering, and a B.S. in Electrical Engineering and Computer Science from the University of California, Berkeley.

Dr. Jacobs was selected to serve on our Board of Directors because of his extensive business, operations, and management experience.

Robert J. Mylod Jr. Mr. Mylod has served as a member of our Board of Directors since September 2014. Mr. Mylod has served as Managing Partner for Annox Capital Management, a venture capital firm that he founded, since January 2013. Mr. Mylod served as Head of Worldwide Strategy & Planning and Vice Chairman for The Priceline Group Inc., an online travel services provider, from January 2009 to March 2011 and as its Chief Financial Officer and Vice Chairman from November 2000 to January 2009. Mr. Mylod currently serves as the Chairman of the board of directors for Redfin Corporation, a real estate company that provides web-based real estate database and brokerage services, and as a member of the board of directors for The Priceline Group, Inc. and a number of private companies. Mr. Mylod holds an M.B.A. from the University of Chicago Booth School of Business and an A.B. in English from the University of Michigan.

Mr. Mylod was selected to serve on our Board of Directors because of his financial expertise and extensive business, operations, and management experience.

Condoleezza Rice, Ph.D. Dr. Rice has served as a member of our Board of Directors since April 2014. Since September 2010, Dr. Rice has served as the Denning Professor of Global Business and the Economy for the Stanford Graduate School of Business. Since March 2009, Dr. Rice has served as a Senior Fellow of Public

138

Policy for the Hoover Institution, Stanford University, as a Senior Fellow for the Freeman Spogli Institute for International Studies, Stanford University, and as a Professor of Political Science for Stanford University. Dr. Rice has served as a partner at RiceHadleyGates LLC, an international strategic consulting firm that Dr. Rice founded, since November 2009. From January 2005 to January 2009, Dr. Rice served as the Secretary of State of the United States of America. From January 2001 to January 2005, Dr. Rice served as Chief National Security Advisor to President George W. Bush. Beginning in 1981, she served in various roles at Stanford University, including serving as Provost from 1993-1999. Dr. Rice previously served as a member of the board of directors of Charles Schwab Corporation, a bank and brokerage firm, Chevron Corporation, a multinational energy corporation, Transamerica Corporation, a life insurance and investment company, and KiOR, Inc., a renewable fuels company. Dr. Rice currently serves as an advisor for a number of other public companies, and as a member of the board directors for a number of private companies, including C3IoT and Makena Capital Management, LLC. Dr. Rice holds a Ph.D. in Political Science from the University of Denver, an M.A. in Political Science from the University of Notre Dame and a B.A in Political Science from the University of Denver.

Dr. Rice was selected to serve on our Board of Directors because of her deep global expertise and business experience from her prior roles as a director of multiple public companies and her background in policymaking, education, and innovation.

R. Bryan Schreier. Mr. Schreier has served as a member of our Board of Directors since July 2009. Since March 2008, Mr. Schreier has served as a partner at Sequoia Capital, a venture capital firm. Mr. Schreier currently serves as a member of the board of directors for a number of private companies. Mr. Schreier holds a B.A. in Computer Science from Princeton University.

Mr. Schreier was selected to serve on our Board of Directors because of his financial and managerial experience and because he represents our largest stockholder.

Margaret C. Whitman. Ms. Whitman has served as a member of our Board of Directors since September 2017. Since February 2018, Ms. Whitman has served as Chief Executive Officer for NewTV, a mobile media company. From June 2017 to January 2018, Ms. Whitman served as Chief Executive Officer for Hewlett Packard Enterprise Company, or HPE, a multinational enterprise information technology company, and as its President and Chief Executive Officer from November 2015 to June 2017. From July 2014 to November 2015, Ms. Whitman served as President, Chief Executive Officer, and Chairman for Hewlett-Packard Company (now known as HP Inc.), the former parent of Hewlett Packard Enterprise Company, and as its President and Chief Executive Officer from September 2011 to November 2015. Prior to joining HP Inc., Ms. Whitman was the Republican Party's nominee for the 2010 gubernatorial race in California. From March 2011 to September 2011, Ms. Whitman served as a part-time strategic advisor to Kleiner Perkins Caufield & Byers, a private equity firm. From 1998 to 2008, Ms. Whitman served as President and Chief Executive Officer of eBay Inc., an online marketplace and payments company. Ms. Whitman also currently serves as a member of the board of directors for The Procter & Gamble Company, a consumer goods company, Hewlett Packard Enterprise Company, and DXC Technology Company, an information technology and consulting services company. Ms. Whitman previously served as a member of the board of directors for HP Inc. and for a number of private companies. Ms. Whitman holds an M.B.A from Harvard Business School and an A.B. in Economics from Princeton University.

Ms. Whitman was selected to serve on our Board of Directors because of her extensive leadership, strategy, risk management, and consumer industry experience.

Code of Business Conduct and Ethics

Our Board of Directors has adopted a code of business conduct and ethics that applies to all of our employees, officers, and directors, including our Chief Executive Officer, Chief Financial Officer, and other executive and senior financial officers. The full text of our code of business conduct and ethics will be posted on the investor relations page on our website. We intend to disclose any amendments to our code of business conduct and ethics, or waivers of its requirements, on our website or in filings under the Exchange Act.

Board of Directors

Our business and affairs are managed under the direction of our Board of Directors. Our Board of Directors consists of eight directors, six of whom qualify as "independent" under the listing standards of Nasdaq. Pursuant to our current certificate of incorporation and amended and restated voting agreement, our current directors were elected as follows:

- Messrs. Ferdowsi, Houston, Blair, Jacobs, and Mylod, and Mmes. Rice and Whitman were elected as the designees nominated by holders of our common stock, excluding the common stock issued upon conversion of our convertible preferred stock; and

- Mr. Schreier was elected as the preferred stock designee nominated by entities affiliated with Sequoia Capital.

Our amended and restated voting agreement will terminate and the provisions of our current certificate of incorporation by which our directors were elected will be amended and restated in connection with this offering. After this offering, the number of directors will be fixed by our Board of Directors, subject to the terms of our amended and restated certificate of incorporation and amended and restated bylaws that will become effective immediately prior to the completion of this offering. Each of our current directors will continue to serve as a director until the election and qualification of his or her successor, or until his or her earlier death, resignation, or removal.

Classified Board of Directors

Until the outstanding shares of our Class B common stock represent less than a majority of the combined voting power of common stock, we will have a single class of directors who are each elected for one-year terms and until their successors are duly elected and qualified. When the outstanding shares of our Class B common stock represent less than a majority of the combined voting power of common stock, we will have a classified Board of Directors consisting of three classes of approximately equal size, each serving staggered three-year terms. Our directors will be assigned by the then-current Board of Directors to a class.

At such times as we have a classified Board of Directors, upon expiration of the term of a class of directors, directors for that class will be elected for three-year terms at the annual meeting of stockholders in the year in which that term expires. As a result, only one class of directors will be elected at each annual meeting of our stockholders, with the other classes continuing for the remainder of their respective three-year terms. Each director's term continues until the election and qualification of his or her successor, or his or her earlier death, resignation, or removal.

Only our Board of Directors may fill vacancies on our board. At such times as our Board of Directors is classified, any additional directorships resulting from an increase in the number of directors will be distributed among the three classes so that, as nearly as possible, each class will consist of one-third of the total number of directors.

The classification of our Board of Directors may have the effect of delaying or preventing changes in our control or management. See "Description of Capital Stock—Anti-Takeover Provisions—Restated Certificate of Incorporation and Bylaw Provisions."

Director Independence

Our Board of Directors has undertaken a review of the independence of each director. Based on information provided by each director concerning his or her background, employment and affiliations, our Board of Directors

140

has determined that Mmes. Rice and Whitman and Messrs. Blair, Jacobs, Mylod, and Schreier do not have a relationship that would interfere with the exercise of independent judgment in carrying out the responsibilities of a director and that each of these directors is "independent" as that term is defined under the listing standards of Nasdaq. In making these determinations, our Board of Directors considered the current and prior relationships that each non-employee director has with our company and all other facts and circumstances our Board of Directors deemed relevant in determining their independence, including the beneficial ownership of our capital stock by each non-employee director, and the transactions involving them described in the section titled "Certain Relationships and Related Party Transactions."

Committees of the Board of Directors

Our Board of Directors has established an audit committee, a compensation committee, and a nominating and corporate governance committee. The composition and responsibilities of each of the committees of our Board of Directors is described below. Members will serve on these committees until their resignation or until as otherwise determined by our Board of Directors.

Audit committee

Following the completion of this offering, our audit committee will consist of Ms. Whitman and Messrs. Blair and Mylod, with Mr. Mylod serving as Chairperson, each of whom will meet the requirements for independence under the listing standards of Nasdaq and SEC rules and regulations. Each member of our audit committee also meets the financial literacy and sophistication requirements of the listing standards of Nasdaq. In addition, our Board of Directors has determined that Ms. Whitman and Messrs. Blair and Mylod are audit committee financial experts within the meaning of Item 407(d) of Regulation S-K under the Securities Act. Following the completion of this offering, our audit committee will be responsible for, among other things:

- selecting a qualified firm to serve as the independent registered public accounting firm to audit our financial statements;

- helping to ensure the independence and overseeing performance of the independent registered public accounting firm;

- reviewing and discussing the scope and results of the audit with the independent registered public accounting firm, and reviewing, with management and the independent registered public accounting firm, our interim and year-end operating results;

- reviewing our financial statements and our critical accounting policies and estimates;

- reviewing the adequacy and effectiveness of our internal controls;

- developing procedures for employees to submit concerns anonymously about questionable accounting, internal accounting controls, or audit matters;

- overseeing our policies on risk assessment and risk management;

- overseeing compliance with our code of business conduct and ethics;

- reviewing related party transactions; and

- pre-approving all audit and all permissible non-audit services, other than de minimis non-audit services, to be performed by the independent registered public accounting firm.

Our audit committee will operate under a written charter, to be effective prior to the completion of this offering, that satisfies the applicable rules and regulations of the SEC and the listing standards of Nasdaq.

Compensation committee

Following the completion of this offering, our compensation committee will consist of Ms. Rice and Messrs. Mylod and Schreier, with Ms. Rice serving as Chairperson, each of whom will meet the requirements for

141

229

independence under the listing standards of Nasdaq and SEC rules and regulations. Each member of our compensation committee will also be a non-employee director, as defined pursuant to Rule 16b-3 promulgated under the Exchange Act, or Rule 16b-3. Following the completion of this offering, our compensation committee will be responsible for, among other things:

- reviewing, approving, and determining, or making recommendations to our Board of Directors regarding, the compensation of our executive officers, including our CEO;

- administering our equity compensation plans;

- reviewing, approving, and administering incentive compensation and equity compensation plans;

- reviewing and approving our overall compensation philosophy; and

- making recommendations regarding non-employee director compensation to our full Board of Directors.

Our compensation committee will operate under a written charter, to be effective prior to the completion of this offering, that satisfies the applicable rules and regulations of the SEC and the listing standards of Nasdaq.

Nominating and corporate governance committee

Following the completion of this offering, our nominating and corporate governance committee will consist of Ms. Whitman and Mr. Jacobs, with Ms. Whitman serving as Chairperson, each of whom will meet the requirements for independence under the listing standards of Nasdaq and SEC rules and regulations. Following the completion of this offering, our nominating and corporate governance committee will be responsible for, among other things:

- identifying, evaluating, and selecting, or making recommendations to our Board of Directors regarding, nominees for election to our Board of Directors and its committees;

- overseeing the evaluation the performance of our Board of Directors and of individual directors;

- considering and making recommendations to our Board of Directors regarding the composition of our Board of Directors and its committees;

- overseeing our corporate governance practices;

- contributing to succession planning; and

- developing and making recommendations to our Board of Directors regarding corporate governance guidelines and matters.

Our nominating and corporate governance committee will operate under a written charter, to be effective prior to the completion of this offering, that satisfies the applicable listing standards of Nasdaq.

Compensation Committee Interlocks and Insider Participation

None of the members of our compensation committee is or has been an officer or employee of our company. None of our executive officers currently serves, or in the past year has served, as a member of the board of directors or compensation committee (or other board committee performing equivalent functions) of any entity that has one or more of its executive officers serving on our Board of Directors or compensation committee.

Non-Employee Director Compensation

Our employee directors, Messrs. Houston and Ferdowsi, have not received any compensation as directors.

142

The following table provides information regarding compensation of our non-employee directors for service as directors, for the year ended December 31, 2017. In 2017, we did not pay any compensation to any person who served as a non-employee member of our Board of Directors who is affiliated with our greater than 5% stockholders.

Name	Stock awards($)(1)	Total($)
Donald W. Blair(2)	—	—
Paul E. Jacobs	—	—
Robert J. Mylod, Jr.	—	—
Condoleezza Rice	—	—
Margaret C. Whitman(3)	908,800	908,800
R. Bryan Schreier	—	—

(1) The amounts reported represent the aggregate grant-date fair value of the RSUs awarded to the director in 2017, calculated in accordance with ASC Topic 718. The assumptions used in calculating the grant-date fair value of the RSUs reported in this column are set forth in the section titled "Management's Discussion and Analysis of Financial Condition and Results of Operations—Critical Accounting Policies and Judgments."
(2) Mr. Blair became a member of our Board of Directors in December 2017.
(3) Ms. Whitman became a member of our Board of Directors in September 2017.

The following table lists all outstanding equity awards held by non-employee directors as of December 31, 2017:

Name	Date of grant	Number of shares underlying unvested stock awards(1)
Donald W. Blair(2)	—	—
Paul E. Jacobs	5/24/16(3)	26,667
Robert J. Mylod, Jr.	10/27/14(4)	24,433
	5/24/16(5)	53,333
Condoleezza Rice	7/29/14(6)	24,433
	5/24/16(7)	53,333
Margaret C. Whitman	9/8/17(8)	53,333
R. Bryan Schreier	—	—

(1) As further described in the footnotes below, the RSUs granted prior to August 1, 2015, which we refer to as two-tier RSUs, will generally vest upon the satisfaction of a service-based vesting condition and the occurrence of the Performance Vesting Condition. The Performance Vesting Condition occurs on the earlier of (i) an acquisition or change in control of the Company or (ii) the earlier of (a) six months after our initial public offering or (b) March 15 of the year following our initial public offering. Our Board of Directors has approved the acceleration of the Performance Vesting Condition such that it will occur upon the effectiveness of our registration statement of which this prospectus forms a part.
(2) Mr. Blair became a member of our Board of Directors in December 2017.
(3) 50% of the shares of our Class B common stock underlying the RSUs vested on each of May 1, 2017 and the remainder will vest on May 1, 2018, subject to continued service through such vesting date; provided, however, that as a result of amendments approved by our Board of Directors on September 8, 2017 applicable to all RSUs, or the September 2017 RSU Amendment, the May 1, 2018 vesting date is being accelerated to February 15, 2018.
(4) The service condition was satisfied as to 100% of the shares of Class B common stock underlying the RSUs on September 1, 2016. The Performance Vesting Condition has not been satisfied.
(5) 100% of the shares of our Class B common stock underlying the RSUs vest on September 1, 2018, subject to continued service through such vesting date; provided, however, that as a result of the September 2017 RSU Amendment, the September 1, 2018 vesting date is being accelerated to August 15, 2018.
(6) The service condition was satisfied as to 100% of the shares of Class B common stock underlying the RSUs on May 15, 2016. The Performance Vesting Condition has not been satisfied.
(7) 100% of the shares of our Class B common stock underlying the RSUs vest on May 15, 2018, subject to continued service through such vesting date.
(8) Ms. Whitman became a member of our Board of Directors in September 2017. 50% of the shares of our Class A common stock underlying the RSUs vest on each of August 15, 2018 and August 15, 2019, subject to continued service through each such vesting date.

143

In February 2018, our Board of Directors approved new awards of RSUs with a value of $300,000 to the non-employee directors listed below on the terms set forth below. In determining the size and terms of these awards, our Board of Directors considered such factors as it determined appropriate, including, the vested status of each of these non-employee director's current company equity awards, the compensation level of directors at comparable companies, the expected timing of the issuance of future equity awards to them under the director compensation policy described below, and the past and expected future contributions of these directors to our company.

- Ms. Rice and Messrs. Jacobs, Mylod, and Schreier: an award of RSUs with a value of $300,000 that vests on May 15, 2019 or the next annual meeting of our stockholders, if earlier, subject to the director's continued service with us. The award will be subject to vesting acceleration on a "change in control", as set forth in our director compensation policy described below. The award will be effective as of immediately prior to the effectiveness of our registration statement related to this offering, subject to their approval by our stockholders and the director's continued service with us. The number of RSUs subject to the award shall equal $300,000 divided by the per share price of Class A common stock listed on the cover of the registration statement related to this offering.

- Mr. Blair: an award of 53,333 RSUs that vests in two equal installments on November 15, 2018 and November 15, 2019, subject to his continued service with us. The award will be subject to vesting acceleration on a "change in control", as set forth in our director compensation policy described below. This award was provided to Mr. Blair as part of his recruitment to join our Board of Directors.

Prior to this offering, we did not have a formal policy with respect to compensation payable to our non-employee directors for service as directors. From time to time, we have granted equity awards to certain non-employee directors to entice them to join our Board of Directors and for their continued service on our Board of Directors. We also have reimbursed our directors for expenses associated with attending meetings of our Board of Directors and committees of our Board of Directors. In February 2018, our Board of Directors adopted a new compensation policy for our non-employee directors that will be effective as of the date of the effectiveness of the registration statement related to this offering. This policy was developed, with input from our independent compensation consultant firm, Compensia, Inc., regarding practices and compensation level at comparable companies. It is designed to attract, retain, and reward non-employee directors.

Under this director compensation policy, each non-employee director will receive the cash and equity compensation for board services described below. We also will continue to reimburse our non-employee directors for reasonable, customary, and documented travel expenses to board meetings.

The director compensation policy includes a maximum annual limit of $1,200,000 of cash compensation and equity awards that may be paid, issued, or granted to a non-employee director in any fiscal year. For purposes of this limitation, the value of equity awards is based on the grant date fair value (determined in accordance with GAAP). Any cash compensation paid or equity awards granted to a person for his or her services as an employee, or for his or her services as a consultant (other than as a non-employee director), will not count for purposes of the limitation. The maximum limit does not reflect the intended size of any potential compensation or equity awards to our non-employee directors.

Cash Compensation

Following the completion of this offering, non-employee directors will be entitled to receive the following cash compensation for their services:

- $50,000 per year for service as a board member;
- $20,000 per year for service as a lead independent director;
- $25,000 per year for service as chair of the audit committee;
- $12,500 per year for service as a member of the audit committee;

144

- $20,000 per year for service as chair of the compensation committee;
- $10,000 per year for service as a member of the compensation committee;
- $10,000 per year for service as chair of the nominating and governance committee; and
- $5,000 per year for service as a member of the nominating and governance committee.

Each non-employee director who serves as the chair of a committee will receive both the additional annual fee as the chair of the committee and the additional annual fee as a member of the committee. All cash payments to non-employee directors are paid quarterly in arrears on a prorated basis.

Equity Compensation

Initial Award. Each person who first becomes a non-employee director will receive, on the first trading date on or after the date on which the person first becomes a non-employee director, an initial award of RSUs, or the Initial Award, covering a number of shares of our Class A common stock having a grant date fair value (determined in accordance with GAAP) equal to $300,000 multiplied by the fraction obtained by dividing (1) the number of full months during the period beginning on the date the person first becomes a non-employee director and ending on the one-year anniversary of the date of the then-most recent annual meeting of the company's stockholders, or the Initial Award Vesting Period by (2) 12, rounded to the nearest whole share. The Initial Award will vest on the last day of the Initial Award Vesting Period or, if earlier, on the day before the annual meeting of our stockholders that follows the grant date of the Initial Award, subject to the non-employee director continuing to provide services to us through the applicable vesting date. If the person was a member of the Board of Directors and also an employee, becoming a non-employee director due to termination of employment will not entitle the non-employee director to an Initial Award.

Annual Award. Each non-employee director automatically will receive, on the date of each annual meeting of the Company's stockholders following the effective date of the policy, an annual award of RSUs, each of which we refer to as an Annual Award, covering a number of shares of our Class A common stock having a grant date fair value (determined in accordance with GAAP) of $300,000, rounded to the nearest whole share. The Annual Award will vest on the one-year anniversary of the grant date of the Annual Award or, if earlier, the day before our annual meeting of stockholders that follows the grant date of the Annual Award, subject to the non-employee director continuing to provide services to us through the applicable vesting date

In the event of a "change in control" (as defined in our 2018 Plan), each non-employee director will fully vest in his or her outstanding company equity awards, including any Initial Award or Annual Award, provided that the non-employee director continues to be a non-employee director through such date.

145

EXECUTIVE COMPENSATION

Summary Compensation Table

Our named executive officers, consisting of our principal executive officer and the next two most highly compensated executive officers, as of December 31, 2017, were:

- Andrew W. Houston, our Chief Executive Officer and co-founder;

- Arash Ferdowsi, our co-founder; and

- Quentin J. Clark, our Senior Vice President of Engineering, Product, and Design.

The amounts below represent the compensation paid to our named executive officers for 2017.

2017 Summary Compensation Table

Name and principal position	Year	Salary($)	Bonus($)	Stock awards($)	Non-equity incentive plan compensation ($)(1)	All other compensation ($)(6)	Total($)
Andrew W. Houston *Chief Executive Officer and Co-Founder*	2017	400,000	—	109,569,500(2)	260,000	3,000	110,232,500
Arash Ferdowsi *Co-Founder*	2017	400,000	—	46,655,400(2)	260,000	3,000	47,318,400
Quentin J. Clark(3) *Senior Vice President of Engineering, Product, and Design*	2017	130,513	340,000(4)	34,080,000(5)	84,055	16,136	34,650,704

(1) The amounts reported represent the amounts payable in 2017 under our 2017 Cash Bonus Plan, as described in greater detail under "—Non-Equity Incentive Plan Compensation."

(2) The amounts reported represent the aggregate grant-date fair value of restricted stock awards, or RSAs, calculated in accordance with ASC Topic 718. The RSAs are eligible to vest over a period of up to ten years based on the achievement of certain stock price goals measured over a consecutive thirty-day trading period during a performance period. We calculated the grant date fair value based on multiple stock price paths developed through the use of a Monte Carlo simulation. The assumptions used in calculating the grant-date fair value of the RSAs reported in this column are set forth in the section titled "Management's Discussion and Analysis of Financial Condition and Results of Operations—Critical Accounting Policies and Judgements". See "—Co-Founder Restricted Stock Awards" for additional information.

(3) Mr. Clark joined us in September 2017 and therefore his salary and non-equity incentive plan compensation set forth in the table above were prorated for the portion of 2017 in which he was employed with us.

(4) Amount represents a one-time signing bonus paid in connection with Mr. Clark's hiring in 2017. Mr. Clark must repay the bonus if, before the first anniversary of his employment start date, his employment ends voluntarily or involuntarily under certain specified circumstances.

(5) The amounts reported represent the aggregate grant-date fair value of RSUs calculated in accordance with ASC Topic 718. The assumptions used in calculating the grant-date fair value of the RSUs reported in this column are set forth in the section titled "Management's Discussion and Analysis of Financial Condition and Results of Operations—Critical Accounting Policies and Judgments."

(6) Amounts represent matching 401(k) contributions of $3,000 and, in the case of Mr. Clark, transportation reimbursements (to and from work) of $13,136.

Non-Equity Incentive Plan Compensation

Each of our named executive officers participated in our 2017 Cash Bonus Plan, or the 2017 Bonus Plan, which provides for cash bonus amounts based on our achievements of key company performance metrics.

Under the 2017 Bonus Plan, a cash bonus pool under our 2017 Bonus Plan is established if we achieve certain corporate financial performance measures based on revenue and free cash flow. Our Board of Directors retains the discretion to increase or decrease the cash bonus pool under the 2017 Bonus Plan based on our achievements of those corporate financial performance measures in 2017. In addition, the actual bonus amount payable under the 2017 Bonus Plan may be modified based on individual performance for 2017.

146

Following the end of 2017, our compensation committee reviewed our achievements against the revenue and free cash flow corporate financial performance measures and determined that we exceeded target levels of achievement for each of these performance measures. Accordingly, the annual bonus payment for each of our named executive officers was calculated based on 100% of his target bonus amount, which is described under "—Executive Employment Arrangements." Mr. Clark's amount is pro-rated based on his length of service with us in 2017. The actual bonus amounts payable to our named executive officers under the 2017 Bonus Plan are set forth in the "2017 Summary Compensation Table."

Outstanding Equity Awards at 2017 Year-End

The following table sets forth information regarding outstanding equity awards held by our named executive officers as of December 31, 2017.

| | | Stock awards | |
Name	Grant date	Number of shares or units of stock that have not vested	Market value of shares or units of stock that have not vested ($)(1)
Andrew W. Houston	12/12/17(2)	10,333,333	196,333,327
Arash Ferdowsi	12/12/17(2)	4,400,000	83,600,000
Quentin J. Clark	9/8/17(3)	2,000,000	38,000,000

(1) The market price for our Class A common stock is based upon the assumed initial public offering price of $19.00 per share, which is the midpoint of the estimated offering price range set forth on the cover page of this prospectus.

(2) This award represents RSAs granted to each of Messrs. Houston and Ferdowsi pursuant to a stand-alone restricted stock award agreement. The shares underlying the RSAs are Class A common stock. The RSAs vest over a period of up to ten years upon achievement of service-based, market-based, and liquidity event-related performance vesting conditions. See "—Co-Founder Restricted Stock Awards" for additional information.

(3) This award represents RSUs granted to Mr. Clark pursuant to our 2017 Plan. 25% of the shares of our Class A common stock underlying the RSUs vest on August 15, 2018, and an additional 3/48th of the total number of shares of our Class A common stock underlying the RSUs vests in equal quarterly installments, each subject to continued service through each such vesting date.

Co-Founder Restricted Stock Awards

In December 2017, our Board of Directors approved a grant to our co-founders, Messrs. Houston and Ferdowsi, of RSAs with respect to 14.7 million shares of Class A common stock in the aggregate, or, collectively, the Co-Founder Grants, of which 10.3 million RSAs were granted to Mr. Houston, our co-founder and Chief Executive Officer, and 4.4 million RSAs were granted to Mr. Ferdowsi, our co-founder and Director. The Co-Founder Grants vest upon the satisfaction of the service condition and achievement of certain stock price goals, as described below. These Co-Founder Grants have certain stockholder rights, such as the right to vote the shares immediately upon grant and prior to their vesting.

In determining the terms and conditions of these Co-Founder Grants, the Board of Directors considered that neither co-founder had received an equity award since founding the Company and wanted to provide a meaningful incentive to the co-founders to continue to drive the growth of the business following the completion of this offering. The Board of Directors thought it was important for the Co-Founder Grants to not simply vest based on the passage of time while our co-founders provide service to us. Rather, the Co-Founder Grants will vest only if we achieve certain stock price goals, which if achieved, would allow our other stockholders to benefit tremendously from such increases in our stock price.

The Co-Founder Grants are eligible to vest over the ten-year period following the closing of this offering. The Co-Founder Grants comprise nine tranches that are eligible to vest based on the achievement of stock price

147

goals, or each, a Stock Price Target, measured over a consecutive thirty-day trading period during the performance period as follows:

	Company Stock Price Target*	Shares Eligible to Vest for Mr. Houston	Shares Eligible to Vest for Mr. Ferdowsi
1.	$ 30.00	2,066,667	880,000
2.	$ 37.50	1,033,334	440,000
3.	$ 45.00	1,033,334	440,000
4.	$ 52.50	1,033,333	440,000
5.	$ 60.00	1,033,333	440,000
6.	$ 67.50	1,033,333	440,000
7.	$ 75.00	1,033,333	440,000
8.	$ 82.50	1,033,333	440,000
9.	$ 90.00	1,033,333	440,000

Measurement of our stock price for purposes of achievement of the Stock Price Targets will not commence until the later of the expiration of the lock-up period following the completion of this offering or January 1, 2019. In addition, the Stock Price Targets will be adjusted to reflect any stock splits, stock dividends, combinations, reorganizations, reclassifications, or similar event.

During the first four years of the performance period, no more than 20% of the shares subject to each Co-Founder Grant would be eligible to vest in any calendar year. This ensures that to fully vest in the Co-Founder Grants, any increase in our stock price must be sustained over a long period of time and not allow any short-term, unsustained increases in our stock price to result in a vesting event for either co-founder.

Further, the co-founders will only vest in the awards if they continue as the Chief Executive Officer or Executive Chairman, with respect to Mr. Houston, and as a member of the senior management team, with respect to Mr. Ferdowsi, or the Executive Service Requirement, at the time a Stock Price Target is achieved. Upon a co-founder's no longer satisfying the Executive Service Requirement, any portion of the Co-Founder Grant for which a Stock Price Target has not been achieved would terminate and be cancelled. By requiring that each continue in a senior executive role with us as a condition to vesting, the Board of Directors sought to ensure that each must be providing significant contributions to us that drive any future growth that would allow the Co-Founder Grants to vest.

Lastly, the Board of Directors considered the impact these grants would have on the co-founders' voting control of the Company. The Board of Directors determined that it was in our and our stockholders' best interests to issue the Co-Founder Grants because the receipt of the Co-Founder Grants would not materially impact the voting control of the Company, but would still provide the co-founders with meaningful incentives as described above, and thereby align their interests with those of our other stockholders.

In the event of an acquisition of the Company following the closing of this offering, but before the end of the performance period, the Co-Founder Grants may be eligible to vest in additional tranche(s) of shares if the per share deal price in the acquisition causes a Stock Price Target that has not previously been achieved to be satisfied, in which case the tranche(s) of shares corresponding to that Stock Price Target will vest. Additionally, if the acquisition price falls between a Stock Price Target that has been achieved and one that has not, then a portion of that tranche of shares will vest based on a linear interpolation between each of these Stock Price Targets.

Executive Employment Arrangements

Andrew W. Houston

We have entered into an employment letter with Andrew W. Houston, our Chief Executive Officer and one of our co-founders. The employment letter does not have a specific term and provides that Mr. Houston is an

148

at-will employee. Mr. Houston's current annual base salary is $400,000, and he is eligible for an annual target cash incentive payment equal to 65% of his annual base salary.

Arash Ferdowsi

We have entered into an employment letter with Arash Ferdowsi, one of our co-founders. The employment letter does not have a specific term and provides that Mr. Ferdowsi is an at-will employee. Mr. Ferdowsi's current annual base salary is $400,000, and he is eligible for an annual target cash incentive payment equal to 65% of his annual base salary.

Quentin J. Clark

We have entered into an employment letter with Quentin J. Clark, our Senior Vice President of Engineering, Product, and Design. The employment letter does not have a specific term and provides that Mr. Clark is an at-will employee. Mr. Clark's current annual base salary is $400,000, and he is eligible for an annual target cash incentive payment equal to 65% of his annual base salary.

Potential Payments upon Termination or Change in Control

We expect to enter into a change in control and severance agreement with each of our named executive officers that provides for the severance and change in control benefits described below. Each change in control and severance agreement will supersede any existing agreement or arrangement the named executive officers may have with us that provides for severance and/or change in control payments or benefits, except that the change in control and severance agreements with Messrs. Houston and Ferdowsi will not have any effect on the Co-Founder Grants.

If the named executive officer's employment is terminated by us other than for "cause," death, or "disability" or he resigns for "good reason" (as such terms are defined in his change in control and severance agreement), in either case, outside the Change in Control Period (as defined below), he will be eligible to receive the following payments and benefits:

- a lump-sum payment equal to 50% of annual base salary as of immediately before his termination (or if the termination is due to a resignation for good reason based on a material reduction in base salary, then as of immediately before such reduction); and

- if he elects to continue health insurance coverage for him and his eligible dependents under COBRA, our payment of the monthly premium for such COBRA continuation coverage for up to 6 months (or monthly taxable payments to him in lieu of our payment of such premiums).

If, within the three-month period before or after the 12-month period following a change in control (such period, the Change in Control Period), the named executive officer's employment is terminated by us other than for cause, death, or disability or he resigns for "good reason" (as defined in his change in control and severance agreement), he will be entitled to the following benefits:

- a lump-sum payment equal to 100% of his annual base salary as of immediately before his termination (or if the termination is due to a resignation for good reason based on a material reduction in base salary, then as of immediately before such reduction) or, if such amount is greater, as of immediately before the change in control;

- a lump-sum payment equal to 100% of his target annual bonus (for the year of his termination);

- if he elects to continue health insurance coverage for him and his eligible dependents under COBRA, our payment of the monthly premium for such COBRA continuation coverage for up to 12 months (or monthly taxable payments to him in lieu of our payment of such premiums); and

- 100% accelerated vesting of all outstanding equity awards, and, with respect to equity awards with performance-based vesting, unless otherwise specified in the award agreements governing such equity

149

awards, all performance goals or other vesting criteria will be deemed achieved at 100% of target levels.

The receipt of the payments and benefits above is conditioned on the named executive officer timely signing and not revoking a release of claims, returning all documents and property belonging to us, and resigning from all officer and director positions with us.

In addition, if any of the payments or benefits provided for under a change in control and severance agreement or otherwise payable to a named executive officer would constitute "parachute payments" within the meaning of Section 280G of the Internal Revenue Code and could be subject to the related excise tax, the named executive officer would be entitled to receive either full payment of such payments and benefits or such lesser amount that would result in no portion of the payments and benefits being subject to the excise tax, whichever results in the greater amount of after-tax benefits to him. The change in control and severance agreements do not require us to provide any tax gross-up payments to the named executive officers.

Employee Benefits and Stock Plans

2018 Equity Incentive Plan

In February 2018, our Board of Directors adopted, and in March 2018 our stockholders approved, our 2018 Plan. We expect that our 2018 Plan will be effective on the business day immediately prior to the effective date of our registration statement related to this offering. Our 2018 Plan will provide for the grant of incentive stock options, within the meaning of Section 422 of the Internal Revenue Code, or Code, to our employees, and for the grant of nonstatutory stock options, restricted stock, restricted stock units, stock appreciation rights, performance units, and performance shares to our employees, directors, and consultants.

Authorized shares. A total of 41,368,326 shares of our Class A common stock will be reserved for issuance pursuant to our 2018 Plan. In addition, the shares reserved for issuance under our 2018 Plan will also include (i) shares that, as of the effective date of the registration statement relating to the offering, were reserved but unissued under our 2017 Plan and are not subject to awards granted thereunder, plus (ii) Shares subject to stock options, restricted stock units, or similar awards granted under the 2017 Plan that, on or after the effective date of the registration statement relating to the offering, expire or otherwise terminate without having been exercised in full, are tendered to or withheld by us for payment of an exercise price or for tax withholding obligations, or are forfeited to or repurchased by us due to failure to vest, plus (iii) a number of shares equal to the shares of the Class B common stock subject to stock options, restricted stock units, or similar awards granted under the 2008 Plan that, on or after the effective date of the registration statement relating to the offering, expire or otherwise terminate without having been exercised in full, are tendered to or withheld by us for payment of an exercise price or for tax withholding obligations (including, for the avoidance of doubt, shares withheld on or after the effective date of the registration statement relating to the offering, to satisfy tax withholding obligations with respect to restricted stock units vesting on the effective date of the registration statement relating to the offering), or are forfeited to or repurchased by us due to failure to vest, (provided that the maximum number of shares that may be added to our 2018 Plan from the Prior Plans under clauses (i) through (iii) is 68,824,856 shares). The number of shares of our Class A common stock available for issuance under our 2018 Plan will also include an annual increase on the first day of each fiscal year beginning on January 1, 2019, equal to the least of:

- 41,368,326 shares of our Class A common stock;

- five percent (5%) of the outstanding shares of our capital stock as of the last day of the immediately preceding fiscal year; or

- such other amount as our Board of Directors may determine.

If an award expires or becomes unexercisable without having been exercised in full, is surrendered pursuant to an exchange program, or, with respect to restricted stock, restricted stock units, performance units, or

150

performance shares, is forfeited to or repurchased due to failure to vest, the unpurchased shares (or for awards other than stock options or stock appreciation rights, the forfeited or repurchased shares) will become available for future grant or sale under the 2018 Plan. With respect to stock appreciation rights, only the net shares actually issued will cease to be available under the 2018 Plan and all remaining shares under stock appreciation rights will remain available for future grant or sale under the 2018 Plan. Shares that have actually been issued under the 2018 Plan under any award will not be returned to the 2018 Plan; provided, however, that if shares issued pursuant to awards of restricted stock, restricted stock units, performance shares, or performance units are repurchased or forfeited, such shares will become available for future grant under the 2018 Plan. Shares used to pay the exercise price of an award or satisfy the tax withholding obligations related to an award will become available for future grant or sale under the 2018 Plan. To the extent an award is paid out in cash rather than shares, such cash payment will not result in a reduction in the number of shares available for issuance under the 2018 Plan.

Plan administration. Our Board of Directors or one or more committees appointed by our Board of Directors will administer our 2018 Plan. Our compensation committee is expected to administer our 2018 Plan. In addition, if we determine it is desirable to qualify transactions under our 2018 Plan as exempt under Rule 16b-3 of the Exchange Act, such transactions will be structured to satisfy the requirements for exemption under Rule 16b-3. Subject to the provisions of our 2018 Plan, the administrator has the power to administer our 2018 Plan and make all determinations deemed necessary or advisable for administering the 2018 Plan, including but not limited to, the power to determine the fair market value of our Class A common stock, select the service providers to whom awards may be granted, determine the number of shares covered by each award, approve forms of award agreements for use under the 2018 Plan, determine the terms and conditions of awards (including, but not limited to, the exercise price, the times or times at which the awards may be exercised, any vesting acceleration or waiver or forfeiture restrictions, and any restriction or limitation regarding any award or the shares relating thereto), construe and interpret the terms of our 2018 Plan and awards granted under it, to prescribe, amend, and rescind rules relating to our 2018 Plan, including creating sub-plans, and to modify or amend each award, including but not limited to the discretionary authority to extend the post-termination exercisability period of awards (provided that no option or stock appreciation right will be extended past its original maximum term), and to allow a participant to defer the receipt of payment of cash or the delivery of shares that would otherwise be due to such participant under an award. The administrator also has the authority to allow participants the opportunity to transfer outstanding awards to a financial institution or other person or entity selected by the administrator and to institute an exchange program by which outstanding awards may be surrendered or cancelled in exchange for awards of the same type which may have a higher or lower exercise price and/or different terms, awards of a different type and/or cash, or by which the exercise price of an outstanding award is increased or reduced. The administrator's decisions, interpretations, and other actions are final and binding on all participants.

Stock options. Stock options may be granted under our 2018 Plan. The exercise price of options granted under our 2018 Plan must at least be equal to the fair market value of our Class A common stock on the date of grant. The term of an option may not exceed ten years. With respect to any participant who owns more than 10% of the voting power of all classes of our outstanding stock, the term of an incentive stock option granted to such participant must not exceed five years and the exercise price must equal at least 110% of the fair market value on the grant date. The administrator will determine the methods of payment of the exercise price of an option, which may include cash, shares, or other property acceptable to the administrator, as well as other types of consideration permitted by applicable law. After the termination of service of an employee, director, or consultant, he or she may exercise his or her option for the period of time stated in his or her option agreement. In the absence of a specified time in an award agreement, if termination is due to death or disability, the option will remain exercisable for 12 months. In all other cases, in the absence of a specified time in an award agreement, the option will remain exercisable for three months following the termination of service. An option may not be exercised later than the expiration of its term. Subject to the provisions of our 2018 Plan, the administrator determines the other terms of options.

151

Stock appreciation rights. Stock appreciation rights may be granted under our 2018 Plan. Stock appreciation rights allow the recipient to receive the appreciation in the fair market value of our Class A common stock between the exercise date and the date of grant. Stock appreciation rights may not have a term exceeding ten years. After the termination of service of an employee, director, or consultant, he or she may exercise his or her stock appreciation right for the period of time stated in his or her stock appreciation rights agreement. In the absence of a specified time in an award agreement, if termination is due to death or disability, the stock appreciation rights will remain exercisable for 12 months. In all other cases, in the absence of a specified time in an award agreement, the stock appreciation rights will remain exercisable for three months following the termination of service. However, in no event may a stock appreciation right be exercised later than the expiration of its term. Subject to the provisions of our 2018 Plan, the administrator determines the other terms of stock appreciation rights, including when such rights become exercisable and whether to pay any increased appreciation in cash or with shares of our Class A common stock, or a combination thereof, except that the per share exercise price for the shares to be issued pursuant to the exercise of a stock appreciation right will be no less than 100% of the fair market value per share on the date of grant.

Restricted stock. Restricted stock may be granted under our 2018 Plan. Restricted stock awards are grants of shares of our Class A common stock that vest in accordance with terms and conditions established by the administrator. The administrator will determine the number of shares of restricted stock granted to any employee, director, or consultant and, subject to the provisions of our 2018 Plan, will determine the terms and conditions of such awards. The administrator may impose whatever conditions to vesting it determines to be appropriate (for example, the administrator may set restrictions based on the achievement of specific performance goals or continued service to us); provided, however, that the administrator, in its sole discretion, may accelerate the time at which any restrictions will lapse or be removed. Recipients of restricted stock awards generally will have voting and dividend rights with respect to such shares upon grant without regard to vesting, unless the administrator provides otherwise. Shares of restricted stock that do not vest are subject to our right of repurchase or forfeiture.

RSUs. RSUs may be granted under our 2018 Plan. Each RSU represents an amount equal to the fair market value of one share of our Class A common stock. Subject to the provisions of our 2018 Plan, the administrator determines the terms and conditions of RSUs, including the vesting criteria and the form and timing of payment. The administrator may set vesting criteria based upon the achievement of company-wide, divisional, business unit, or individual goals (including, but not limited to, continued employment or service), applicable federal or state securities laws, or any other basis determined by the administrator in its discretion. The administrator, in its sole discretion, may pay earned restricted stock units in the form of cash, in shares, or in some combination thereof. Notwithstanding the foregoing, the administrator, in its sole discretion, may accelerate the time at which any restrictions will lapse or be removed.

Performance units and performance shares. Performance units and performance shares may be granted under our 2018 Plan. Performance units and performance shares are awards that will result in a payment to a participant only if performance goals established by the administrator are achieved or the awards otherwise vest. The administrator will establish performance objectives or other vesting criteria in its discretion, which, depending on the extent to which they are met, will determine the number and/or the value of performance units and performance shares to be paid out to participants. The administrator may set performance objectives based on the achievement of company-wide, divisional, business unit, or individual goals (including, but not limited to, continued employment or service), applicable federal or state securities laws, or any other basis determined by the administrator in its discretion. After the grant of a performance unit or performance share, the administrator, in its sole discretion, may reduce or waive any performance criteria or other vesting provisions for such performance units or performance shares. Performance units shall have an initial dollar value established by the administrator on or prior to the grant date. Performance shares shall have an initial value equal to the fair market value of our Class A common stock on the grant date. The administrator, in its sole discretion, may pay earned performance units or performance shares in the form of cash, in shares, or in some combination thereof.

152

Outside Directors. Our 2018 Plan includes a maximum annual limit of $1,200,000 of cash compensation and equity awards that may be paid, issued, or granted to an outside (non-employee) director in any fiscal year. For purposes of this limitation, the value of equity awards is based on the grant date fair value (determined in accordance with GAAP). Any cash compensation paid or equity awards granted to a person for his or her services as an employee, or for his or her services as a consultant (other than as a non-employee director), will not count for purposes of the limitation. The maximum limit does not reflect the intended size of any potential compensation or equity awards to our outside (non-employee) directors.

Non-transferability of awards. Unless the administrator provides otherwise, our 2018 Plan generally does not allow for the transfer of awards and only the recipient of an award may exercise an award during his or her lifetime. If the administrator makes an award transferrable, such award will contain such additional terms and conditions as the administrator deems appropriate.

Certain adjustments. In the event of certain changes in our capitalization, to prevent diminution or enlargement of the benefits or potential benefits available under our 2018 Plan, the administrator will adjust the number and class of shares that may be delivered under our 2018 Plan and/or the number, class, and price of shares covered by each outstanding award, and the numerical share limits set forth in our 2018 Plan.

Dissolution or liquidation. In the event of our proposed liquidation or dissolution, the administrator will notify participants as soon as practicable and all awards will terminate immediately prior to the consummation of such proposed transaction.

Merger or change in control. Our 2018 Plan provides that in the event of a merger or change in control, as defined under our 2018 Plan, each outstanding award will be treated as the administrator determines, without a requirement to obtain a participant's consent. The administrator is not required to treat all awards, all awards held by a participant, or all awards of the same type, similarly.

In the event that a successor corporation or its parent or subsidiary does not assume or substitute an equivalent award for any outstanding award, then such award will fully vest, all restrictions on such award will lapse, all performance goals or other vesting criteria applicable to such award will be deemed achieved at 100% of target levels and such award will become fully exercisable, if applicable, for a specified period prior to the transaction, unless specifically provided for otherwise under the applicable award agreement or other written agreement with the participant. The award will then terminate upon the expiration of the specified period of time. If an option or stock appreciation right is not assumed or substituted, the administrator will notify the participant in writing or electronically that such option or stock appreciation right will be exercisable for a period of time determined by the administrator in its sole discretion and the option or stock appreciation right will terminate upon the expiration of such period.

If an outside director's awards are assumed or substituted for in a merger or change in control and the service of such outside director is terminated on or following a change in control, other than pursuant to a voluntary resignation, his or her options and stock appreciation rights, if any, will vest fully and become immediately exercisable, all restrictions on his or her restricted stock and restricted stock units will lapse and all performance goals or other vesting requirements for his or her performance shares and units will be deemed achieved at 100% of target levels, and all other terms and conditions met.

Clawback. Awards will be subject to any clawback policy of ours, and the administrator also may specify in an award agreement that the participant's rights, payments, and/or benefits with respect to an award will be subject to reduction, cancellation, forfeiture, and/or recoupment upon the occurrence of certain specified events. Our Board of Directors may require a participant to forfeit, return, or reimburse us all or a portion of the award and/or shares issued under the award, any amounts paid under the award, and any payments or proceeds paid or provided upon disposition of the shares issued under the award in order to comply with such clawback policy or applicable laws.

153

Amendment; termination. The administrator has the authority to amend, suspend, or terminate our 2018 Plan provided such action does not impair the existing rights of any participant. Our 2018 Plan automatically will terminate in 2028, unless we terminate it sooner.

2018 Class C Stock Incentive Plan

In February 2018, our Board of Directors adopted, and in March 2018 our stockholders approved, our 2018 Class C Plan. Our 2018 Class C Plan will be effective on the business day immediately prior to the effective date of our registration statement related to this offering and is not expected to be used immediately. A total of 41,368,326 shares of our Class C common stock will be reserved for issuance pursuant to our 2018 Class C Plan. If and when authorized by our Board of Directors, the number of shares available for issuance under our 2018 Class C Plan will be increased on the first day of each fiscal year following the year of such authorization, in an amount equal to the least of (i) 41,368,326 shares of our Class C common stock, (ii) five percent (5%) of the outstanding shares of all classes of the Company's common stock on the last day of the immediately preceding fiscal year, or (iii) such number of shares of our Class C common stock determined by our Board of Directors. Our 2018 Class C Plan will provide for the same types of grants and will include the same terms and conditions as those described above for our 2018 Plan.

2018 Employee Stock Purchase Plan

In February 2018, our Board of Directors adopted, and in March 2018 our stockholders approved, our Employee Stock Purchase Plan, or the ESPP. Our ESPP will be effective on the business day immediately prior to the effective date of the registration statement of which this prospectus forms a part. However, no offering period or purchase period under the ESPP will begin unless and until determined by our Board of Directors.

Authorized shares. A total of 4,136,832 shares of our Class A common stock will be available for sale under our ESPP. The number of shares of our Class A common stock that will be available for sale under our ESPP also includes an annual increase on the first day of each fiscal year beginning for the fiscal year following the fiscal year in which the first offering period enrollment date (if any) occurs, equal to the least of:

- 4,136,832 shares of our Class A common stock;

- one and a half percent (1.5%) of the outstanding shares of our capital stock as of the last day of the immediately preceding fiscal year; or

- such other amount as the administrator may determine.

Plan administration. Our Board of Directors, or a committee appointed by our Board of Directors will administer our ESPP, and have full but non-exclusive authority to interpret the terms of our ESPP and determine eligibility to participate, subject to the conditions of our ESPP, as described below. We expect our compensation committee to administer our ESPP. The administrator will have full and exclusive discretionary authority to construe, interpret, and apply the terms of the ESPP, to delegate ministerial duties to any of our employees, to designate separate offerings under the ESPP, to designate our subsidiaries and affiliates as participating in the ESPP, to determine eligibility, to adjudicate all disputed claims filed under the ESPP and to establish procedures that it deems necessary or advisable for the administration of the ESPP, including, but not limited to, adopting such procedures, sub-plans, and appendices to the enrollment agreement as are necessary or appropriate to permit participation in the ESPP by employees who are foreign nationals or employed outside the U.S. The administrator's findings, decisions, and determinations are final and binding on all participants to the full extent permitted by law.

Eligibility. Generally, all of our employees will be eligible to participate if they are customarily employed by us, or any participating subsidiary, for at least 20 hours per week and more than five months in any calendar year. The administrator, in its discretion, may, prior to an enrollment date for all options granted on such

154

enrollment date in an offering, determine that an employee who (i) has not completed at least two years of service (or a lesser period of time determined by the administrator) since his or her last hire date, (ii) customarily works not more than 20 hours per week (or a lesser period of time determined by the administrator), (iii) customarily works not more than five months per calendar year (or a lesser period of time determined by the administrator), (iv) is a highly compensated employee within the meaning of Section 414(q) of the Code, and (v) is a highly compensated employee within the meaning of Section 414(q) of the Code with compensation above a certain level or is an officer or subject to disclosure requirements under Section 16(a) of the Exchange Act, is or is not eligible to participate in such offering period.

However, an employee may not be granted rights to purchase shares of our Class A common stock under our ESPP if such employee:

- immediately after the grant would own capital stock possessing 5% or more of the total combined voting power or value of all classes of our capital stock; or
- hold rights to purchase shares of our Class A common stock under all of our employee stock purchase plans that accrue at a rate that exceeds $25,000 worth of shares of our Class A common stock for each calendar year.

Offering periods; purchase periods. Our ESPP includes a component that allows us to make offerings intended to qualify under Section 423 of the Code and a component that allows us to make offerings not intended to qualify under Section 423 of the Code to designated companies, as described in our ESPP. No offerings have been authorized to date by our Board of Directors under the ESPP. If our Board of Directors authorizes an offering period under the ESPP, our Board of Directors is authorized to establish the duration of offering periods and purchase periods, including the starting and ending dates of offering periods and purchase periods, provided that no offering period may have a duration exceeding 27 months.

Contributions. Our ESPP permits participants to purchase shares of our Class A common stock through contributions (in the form of payroll deductions or otherwise to the extent permitted by the administrator) of up to 15% of their eligible compensation. A participant may purchase a maximum of 2,500 shares of our Class A common stock during a purchase period.

Exercise of purchase right. If our Board of Directors authorizes an offering and purchase period under the ESPP, amounts contributed and accumulated by the participant during any offering period will be used to purchase shares of our Class A common stock at the end of each purchase period established by our Board of Directors. The purchase price of the shares will be 85% of the lower of the fair market value of our Class A common stock on the first trading day of each offering period or on the exercise date. Participants may end their participation at any time during an offering period and will be paid their accrued contributions that have not yet been used to purchase shares of our Class A common stock. Participation ends automatically upon termination of employment with us.

Non-transferability. A participant may not transfer rights granted under our ESPP. If our compensation committee permits the transfer of rights, it may only be done by will, the laws of descent and distribution, or as otherwise provided under our ESPP.

Merger or change in control. Our ESPP provides that in the event of a merger or change in control, as defined under our ESPP, a successor corporation may assume or substitute each outstanding purchase right. If the successor corporation refuses to assume or substitute for the outstanding purchase right, the offering period then in progress will be shortened, and a new exercise date will be set that will be before the date of the proposed merger or change in control. The administrator will notify each participant that the exercise date has been changed and that the participant's option will be exercised automatically on the new exercise date unless prior to such date the participant has withdrawn from the offering period.

155

Amendment; termination. The administrator has the authority to amend, suspend, or terminate our ESPP, except that, subject to certain exceptions described in our ESPP, no such action may adversely affect any outstanding rights to purchase shares of our Class A common stock under our ESPP. Our ESPP automatically will terminate in 2038, unless we terminate it sooner.

2018 Class C Employee Stock Purchase Plan

In February 2018, our Board of Directors adopted, and in March 2018 our stockholders approved, our 2018 Class C ESPP. Our 2018 Class C ESPP will be effective on the business day immediately prior to the effective date of our registration statement related to this offering. No offering period or purchase period under the ESPP will begin unless and until determined by our Board of Directors. A total of 4,136,832 shares of our Class C common stock will be reserved for sale pursuant to our 2018 Class C ESPP. The number of shares available for sale under our 2018 Class C ESPP will be increased on the first day of each fiscal year beginning for the fiscal year following the commencement of the first offering period under our 2018 Class C ESPP, in an amount equal to the least of (i) 4,136,832 shares of our Class C common stock, (ii) one and a half percent (1.5%) of the outstanding shares of our Class C common stock on the last day of the immediately preceding fiscal year or (iii) such number of shares of our Class C common stock determined by our Board of Directors. Our 2018 Class C ESPP will include the same terms and conditions as those described above for our ESPP. Our 2018 Class C ESPP will automatically terminate in 2038, unless we terminate it sooner.

2017 Equity Incentive Plan

Our Board of Directors and stockholders adopted our 2017 Plan on March 8, 2017. Our 2017 Plan allows for the grant of incentive stock options to our employees, and for the grant of nonqualified stock options and restricted stock awards, RSUs, and stock appreciation rights to employees, officers, directors, and certain of our consultants.

Authorized shares. Our 2017 Plan will be terminated immediately prior to the effectiveness of our 2018 Plan, and accordingly, no shares will be available for issuance under the 2017 Plan following its termination. Our 2017 Plan will continue to govern outstanding awards granted thereunder. As of December 31, 2017, 8,979,801 shares of our Class A common stock were reserved for future issuance under our 2017 Plan and RSUs covering 16,707,823 shares of our Class A common stock remained outstanding under our 2017 Plan.

Plan administration. Our Board of Directors or one or more committees appointed by our Board of Directors may administer our 2017 Plan. Our compensation committee currently administers our 2017 Plan. Subject to the provisions of our 2017 Plan, the administrator has the power to construe and interpret our 2017 Plan and any agreement thereunder and to determine the form and terms of awards (including the participants), the number of shares subject to each award, the exercise price (if any), the fair market value of a share of our Class A common stock, if such stock is not publicly-traded, listed, or admitted to trading on a national securities exchange, nor reported in any newspaper or other source, the vesting, exercisability, and payment of awards granted under our 2017 Plan, whether an award has been earned, and whether awards will be granted singly, in combination with, in tandem with, in replacement of, or as alternatives to, other awards. The administrator may correct, prescribe, amend, expand, modify, rescind, or terminate rules and regulations relating to our 2017 Plan. The administrator may, at any time, authorize the issuance of new awards in exchange for the surrender and cancellation of any or all outstanding awards with the consent of a participant. The administrator may also buy out an award previously granted for cash, shares, or other consideration as the administrator and the participant may agree.

Options. Stock options may be granted under our 2017 Plan. The exercise price per share of all options must equal at least the fair market value per share of our Class A common stock on the date of grant, unless otherwise expressly determined in writing by the administrator on the grant date. The term of an option may not exceed ten years. An incentive stock option granted to a participant who owns more than 10% of the total combined voting

156

power of all classes of our stock on the date of grant, or any parent or subsidiary corporations, may not have a term in excess of five years and must have an exercise price of at least 110% of the fair market value per share of our common stock on the grant date. The methods of payment of the exercise price of an option include cash (by check) or shares or certain other property or other consideration acceptable to the administrator and otherwise permitted under our 2017 Plan. After a participant's termination of service for reasons other than for death, disability, or cause, the participant generally may exercise his or her options, to the extent vested as of such date of termination, for three months after termination. After a participant's termination of service for death or disability, the option generally will remain exercisable, to the extent vested as of such date of termination, for 12 months after such termination. In no event may an option be exercised later than the expiration of its term. After a participant's termination of service for cause, the option generally will expire on the date of such termination.

Restricted stock. Restricted stock awards may be granted under our 2017 Plan. Restricted stock awards are offers by us to sell to an eligible person shares that are subject to certain specified restrictions, including restrictions on transferability and forfeiture provisions. Restricted stock awards will be entitled to receive all dividends or other distributions paid with respect to such shares, unless the administrator provides otherwise at the time of the award.

RSUs. RSUs may be granted under our 2017 Plan. RSUs are awards covering a number of shares that may be settled in cash, or by issue of those shares at a date in the future. No purchase price shall apply to an RSU settled in shares. The administrator may permit an RSU holder to defer payment under an RSU to a date or dates after the RSU is earned subject to certain restrictions set forth in our 2017 Plan. The administrator may permit holders of RSUs to receive dividend equivalent payments on outstanding RSUs if and when dividends are paid to stockholders in accordance with the terms of our 2017 Plan.

Stock appreciation rights. Stock appreciation rights may be granted under our 2017 Plan. Stock appreciation rights allow the participant to receive the appreciation in the fair market value of Class A common stock between the exercise date and the date of grant. Subject to the provisions of our 2017 Plan, the administrator determines the terms of stock appreciation rights, including when such rights become exercisable and whether to pay any increased appreciation in cash or shares. The per share exercise price for the shares to be issued pursuant to the exercise of a stock appreciation right must equal at least the fair market value per share of our Class A common stock on the date of grant. The term of a stock appreciation right may not exceed 10 years from the date the stock appreciation right is signed. The administrator will determine the period of time after a participant's termination of service during which the participant may exercise his or her stock appreciation right, subject to the same terms and conditions as applicable to options as described above.

Transferability or assignability of awards. Our 2017 Plan generally does not allow for the transfer or assignment of awards, other than by will or by the laws of descent and distribution and, with respect to nonqualified options, by instrument to an inter vivos or testamentary trust in which the options are to be passed to beneficiaries upon the death of the trustor (settlor) or by gift to "family member," and awards under our 2017 Plan may not be made subject to execution, attachment, or similar process. An award under our 2017 Plan generally is only exercisable by the participant or the participant's legal representative during the participant's lifetime.

Certain adjustments. In the event of certain changes in our capitalization, the administrator will proportionally adjust the number of shares that may be delivered under our 2017 Plan and/or the number and price of shares covered by each outstanding award subject to any required action by our Board of Directors or stockholders.

Dissolution or liquidation. In the event of our proposed liquidation or dissolution, our Board of Directors may terminate any and all outstanding awards followed by the payment of creditors and the distribution of any remaining funds to the our stockholders.

157

Acquisition or other combination. If we are subject to an acquisition, consolidation, or merger, or similar conversion event, outstanding awards under our 2017 Plan shall be subject to the agreement evidencing such transaction. The agreement may provide for the continuation, assumption, or substitution of outstanding awards by us (if we are the surviving corporation) or the successor or acquiring entity (if any), or the full or partial exercisability or vesting and accelerated expiration of awards, or the settlement of the full value of outstanding awards in cash, cash equivalents, or securities of the successor or its parent followed by the cancellation of such awards. If an outstanding award is not continued, assumed, or substituted, the award will terminate and cease to be outstanding immediately following the occurrence of the applicable transaction.

Amendment; termination. Our Board of Directors may terminate or amend our 2017 Plan at any time, provided that such amendment does not impair the rights under outstanding options without the participant's written consent. As noted above, prior to the adoption of our 2018 Plan in connection with this offering, our 2017 Plan will be terminated and no further awards will be granted thereunder. All outstanding awards will continue to be governed by their existing terms.

2008 Equity Incentive Plan, As Amended

Our Board of Directors and stockholders adopted our 2008 Plan in January 2008. Our 2008 Plan was most recently amended in November 2016. Our 2008 Plan was terminated in connection with our adoption of our 2017 Plan. As of December 31, 2017, options to purchase 4,959,492 shares of our Class B common stock remained outstanding under our 2008 Plan at a weighted-average exercise price of approximately $10.52 per share and RSUs covering 38,219,737 shares of our Class B common stock remained outstanding under our 2008 Plan. Awards granted under the 2008 Plan generally are subject to terms similar to those described above with respect to options and RSUs granted under the 2017 Plan. Our 2008 Plan provides that if there is (i) a dissolution or liquidation of the Company, (ii) any reorganization, consolidation, merger, or similar transaction or series of related transactions resulting in a significant change in our voting securities as described in our 2008 Plan, or (iii) a sale of all or substantially all of our assets followed by the distribution of the proceeds to our stockholders, any or all outstanding awards may be assumed, converted, replaced, or substituted by the successor or acquiring corporation (if any). If a successor or acquiring corporation refuses to assume, convert, replace, or substitute awards, vesting of awards will accelerate and options will become exercisable in full prior to the consummation of event on such terms as determined by the administrator, and all options that are not exercised prior to the consummation of the transaction and all other awards will terminate. Our 2008 Plan generally does not allow for the transfer or assignment of awards, other than by will or by the laws of descent and distribution and, with respect to nonqualified options, by instrument to an inter vivos or testamentary trust in which the options are to be passed to beneficiaries upon the death of the trustor (settlor) or by gift to "immediate family," and awards may not be made subject to execution, attachment, or similar process. An award is only exercisable by the participant or the participant's legal representative during the participant's lifetime. Our Board of Directors may amend our 2008 Plan at any time, provided that such amendment does not impair the rights under outstanding awards without the participant's written consent.

Cash Bonus Plan

Our Board of Directors has adopted a cash bonus plan, or our Cash Bonus Plan, that allows us to financially incentivize and reward our employees, including our executive officers, based upon our performance and their individual contributions to our success.

Our Cash Bonus Plan is administered by our Compensation Committee. Our Compensation Committee has the discretionary authority to interpret and administer our Cash Bonus Plan, including all terms defined therein, and to adopt rules and regulations to implement our Cash Bonus Plan, as it deems necessary. Our Compensation Committee has delegated to our Chief Financial Officer and our Vice President of People the day-to-day implementation and interpretation of our Cash Bonus Plan, including the approval of individual payouts under our Cash Bonus Plan to employees other than our executive management team. However, approval of our

158

Compensation Committee is required for any material amendments to our Cash Bonus Plan, approval of the aggregate payout under our Cash Bonus Plan, and approval of individual payouts under the Plan to the executive management team.

Unless otherwise determined by our Compensation Committee, all of our employees, including our named executive officers, who (i) are employed by us before November 1 of the applicable calendar year and (ii) not covered by any other performance bonus, commission, or incentive plan, are eligible to participate in our Cash Bonus Plan. Participation in our Cash Bonus Plan is effective on the later of January 1 or the applicable subsequent calendar year or the day (prior to November 1) that the eligible employee commences as a full-time/part-time regular employee of ours.

Our Cash Bonus Plan features annual performance periods. For each performance period, our Compensation Committee, in its sole discretion, will establish a bonus pool, which may be established before, during or after the applicable performance period. Our Compensation Committee may, in its sole discretion and at any time, increase, reduce, or eliminate the amount allocated to the bonus pool. Actual awards will be paid from the bonus pool subject to the terms and conditions set forth in our Cash Bonus Plan.

Our Compensation Committee will, in its sole discretion, determine the performance goals applicable to any award. The goals may be based on any such factors our Compensation Committee determines relevant, and may be on an individual, divisional, business unit, or company-wide basis. Performance goals may be measured over the period of time determined by our Compensation Committee in its sole discretion. A performance period may be divided into one or more shorter periods if, for example, but not by way of limitation, our Compensation Committee desires to measure some performance criteria over 12 months and other criteria over fewer months. The performance goals may differ from eligible employee to eligible employee and from award to award. Failure to meet the goals will result in a failure to earn the award, except as provided in our Cash Bonus Plan. As determined by our Compensation Committee, the performance goals may be based on GAAP or non-GAAP results and any actual results may be adjusted by our Compensation Committee for one-time items, unbudgeted or unexpected items, acquisition-related activities, or changes in applicable accounting rules when determining whether the performance goals have been met. Our Compensation Committee retains the sole discretion to make or not make any such equitable adjustments.

An eligible employee's bonus target is the percentage of his or her "eligible earnings" to be paid out at 100% performance achievement, determined by his or her position and communicated at the time of hire or as amended in writing. The bonus may be weighted based on individual performance to measurable objectives and company performance. The bonus can provide for payout above target for performance in excess of the individual performance factors and/or company performance factors. "Eligible earnings" means base salary as of December 31 of the applicable performance period, prorated for hire date and leaves of absence (proration based on the number of days in the performance period, as permitted by applicable law) that occur in the performance period. Eligible earnings exclude Company payments that are in addition to base salary, including, but not limited to, overtime, payments for moving or relocation allowances, or other wages (including but not limited to bonuses or commissions).

Bonuses are earned on the date of payment and not sooner, either in whole or in part. Bonuses will be paid in cash as soon as practicable after we determine our financial results for the performance period, which generally occurs in the fiscal quarter immediately following the end of the performance period. Achieved bonuses, if any, will be paid before March 15 of such succeeding calendar year. Unless otherwise determined by the plan administrator, an eligible employee must be employed by us through the date the bonus is paid.

We reserve the right, in our sole discretion, to modify or terminate the Cash Bonus Plan in total or in part, at any time. Any such change must be in writing and approved by the compensation committee. However, no modification or termination shall apply retroactively as to cause a forfeiture of an earned bonus.

159

401(k) plan

We maintain a tax-qualified 401(k) retirement plan for all U.S. employees who satisfy certain eligibility requirements, including requirements relating to age and length of service. Under our 401(k) plan, employees may elect to defer up to all eligible compensation, subject to applicable annual Internal Revenue Code limits. We match a portion of contributions made by our employees, including executives. We intend for our 401(k) plan to qualify under Section 401(a) and 501(a) of the Code so that contributions by employees to our 401(k) plan, and income earned on those contributions, are not taxable to employees until withdrawn from our 401(k) plan.

CERTAIN RELATIONSHIPS, RELATED PARTY TRANSACTIONS, AND OTHER TRANSACTIONS

In addition to the compensation arrangements, including employment, termination of employment, and change in control arrangements, discussed in the sections titled "Management" and "Executive Compensation", the following is a description of each transaction since January 1, 2015, and each currently proposed transaction in which:

- we have been or are to be a participant;

- the amount involved exceeded or exceeds $120,000; and

- any of our directors, executive officers, or holders of more than 5% of our outstanding capital stock, or any immediate family member of, or person sharing the household with, any of these individuals or entities, had or will have a direct or indirect material interest.

Amended and Restated Investors' Rights Agreement

We are party to our Amended and Restated Investors' Rights Agreement, or IRA, dated as of January 30, 2014, which provides, among other things, that certain holders of our capital stock, including entities affiliated with each of Sequoia Capital, Accel, and T. Rowe Price, be covered by a registration statement that we are otherwise filing. R. Bryan Schreier, a member of our Board of Directors, is affiliated with Sequoia Capital. See the section titled "Description of Capital Stock—Registration Rights" for additional information regarding these registration rights.

Right of First Refusal

Pursuant to certain of our bylaws, equity compensation plans, and certain agreements with our stockholders, including our Amended and Restated Right of First Refusal and Co-Sale Agreement, dated January 30, 2014, we or our assignees have a right to purchase shares of our capital stock which stockholders propose to sell to other parties. This right will terminate immediately prior to the completion of this offering.

Amended and Restated Voting and Drag-Along Agreement

We are party to our Amended and Restated Voting and Drag-Along Agreement, or Voting Agreement, dated as of April 21, 2016, under which certain holders of our capital stock, including entities affiliated with each of Sequoia Capital, Accel, and T. Rowe Price, have agreed to vote their shares of our capital stock on certain matters, including with respect to the election of directors. R. Bryan Schreier, a member of our Board of Directors, is affiliated with Sequoia Capital. Immediately prior to the completion of this offering, the Voting Agreement will terminate and none of our stockholders will have any special rights regarding the election or designation of members of our Board of Directors.

Commercial Arrangement

We previously had a commercial relationship with Hewlett-Packard Company, of which Ms. Whitman, a member of our Board of Directors, served as the Chief Executive Officer from September 2011 to November 2015. During 2015, we made payments of $37.3 million for capital leases and commercial products and services provided by the Hewlett-Packard Company.

We also have a commercial relationship with HPE, of which Ms. Whitman served as Chief Executive Officer from November 2015 to January 2018. These commercial relationships include infrastructure equipment under capital leases, the purchase of commercial products and other services, and a multi-year subscription agreement for access to the Dropbox platform. During 2016, we received payments of $1.0 million for services rendered to HPE. During 2015, 2016, and 2017, we made payments of $10.9 million, $79.7 million, and $81.7 million, respectively, for capital leases and commercial products and services provided by HPE.

161

Employment Arrangement

Sheila Vashee, who is the wife of Ajay Vashee, our Chief Financial Officer, was employed by us in a non-executive capacity. Her total compensation received in 2015, 2016, and 2017, which is comprised of a base salary and bonus, as applicable, was $234,228, $249,064, and $349,888, respectively, and was in line with similar roles at the Company. Additionally, we granted Ms. Vashee equity awards covering 46,652 shares of our Class B common stock during this time.

Dropbox Charitable Foundation

During 2016, two of our controlling stockholders formed the Dropbox Charitable Foundation, a Delaware non-stock corporation, or the Foundation. The primary purpose of the Foundation is to engage in charitable and educational activities within the meaning of Section 501(c)(3) of the Code. The Foundation is governed by a board of directors, a majority of which are independent. Both stockholders made contributions to the Foundation during 2016, comprised entirely of shares of Dropbox common stock. As of December 31, 2016, we had not made any contributions to the Foundation. We have not consolidated the Foundation in the accompanying consolidated financial statements, as we do not have control of the entity.

During the year ended December 31, 2017, we incurred total expense of $11.3 million, which included $9.4 million of expense for a non-cash charitable contribution, whereby we donated Class B common shares to initially fund the Foundation, and cash contributions of $1.9 million to the Foundation.

Executive and Director Compensation

We have granted stock options and RSUs to our executive officers and certain of our directors. See the sections titled "Executive Compensation—Outstanding Equity Awards at 2017 Year-End" and "Management—Non-Employee Director Compensation" for a description of these stock options and RSUs.

Other than as described above under this section titled "Certain Relationships and Related Party Transactions," since January 1, 2015, we have not entered into any transactions, nor are there any currently proposed transactions, between us and a related party where the amount involved exceeds, or would exceed, $120,000, and in which any related person had or will have a direct or indirect material interest. We believe the terms of the transactions described above were comparable to terms we could have obtained in arm's-length dealings with unrelated third parties.

From time to time, we do business with other companies affiliated with certain holders of our capital stock. We believe that all such arrangements have been entered into in the ordinary course of business and have been conducted on an arm's-length basis.

Limitation of Liability and Indemnification of Officers and Directors

We expect to adopt an amended and restated certificate of incorporation, which will become effective immediately prior to the completion of this offering, and which will contain provisions that limit the liability of our directors for monetary damages to the fullest extent permitted by Delaware law. Consequently, our directors will not be personally liable to us or our stockholders for monetary damages for any breach of fiduciary duties as directors, except liability for the following:

- any breach of their duty of loyalty to our company or our stockholders;

- any act or omission not in good faith or that involves intentional misconduct or a knowing violation of law;

- unlawful payments of dividends or unlawful stock repurchases or redemptions as provided in Section 174 of the Delaware General Corporation Law; or

- any transaction from which they derived an improper personal benefit.

162

Any amendment to, or repeal of, these provisions will not eliminate or reduce the effect of these provisions in respect of any act, omission, or claim that occurred or arose prior to that amendment or repeal. If the Delaware General Corporation Law is amended to provide for further limitations on the personal liability of directors of corporations, then the personal liability of our directors will be further limited to the greatest extent permitted by the Delaware General Corporation Law.

In addition, we expect to adopt amended and restated bylaws, which will become effective immediately prior to the completion of this offering, and which will provide that we will indemnify, to the fullest extent permitted by law, any person who is or was a party or is threatened to be made a party to any action, suit, or proceeding by reason of the fact that he or she is or was one of our directors or officers or is or was serving at our request as a director or officer of another corporation, partnership, joint venture, trust, or other enterprise. Our amended and restated bylaws are expected to provide that we may indemnify to the fullest extent permitted by law any person who is or was a party or is threatened to be made a party to any action, suit, or proceeding by reason of the fact that he or she is or was one of our employees or agents or is or was serving at our request as an employee or agent of another corporation, partnership, joint venture, trust, or other enterprise. Our amended and restated bylaws will also provide that we must advance expenses incurred by or on behalf of a director or officer in advance of the final disposition of any action or proceeding, subject to limited exceptions.

Further, we have entered into or will enter into indemnification agreements with each of our directors and executive officers that may be broader than the specific indemnification provisions contained in the Delaware General Corporation Law. These indemnification agreements require us, among other things, to indemnify our directors and executive officers against liabilities that may arise by reason of their status or service. These indemnification agreements also require us to advance all expenses incurred by the directors and executive officers in investigating or defending any such action, suit, or proceeding. We believe that these agreements are necessary to attract and retain qualified individuals to serve as directors and executive officers.

The limitation of liability and indemnification provisions that are expected to be included in our amended and restated certificate of incorporation, amended and restated bylaws, and in indemnification agreements that we have entered into or will enter into with our directors and executive officers may discourage stockholders from bringing a lawsuit against our directors and executive officers for breach of their fiduciary duties. They may also reduce the likelihood of derivative litigation against our directors and executive officers, even though an action, if successful, might benefit us and other stockholders. Further, a stockholder's investment may be adversely affected to the extent that we pay the costs of settlement and damage awards against directors and executive officers as required by these indemnification provisions. At present, we are not aware of any pending litigation or proceeding involving any person who is or was one of our directors, officers, employees, or other agents or is or was serving at our request as a director, officer, employee, or agent of another corporation, partnership, joint venture, trust, or other enterprise, for which indemnification is sought, and we are not aware of any threatened litigation that may result in claims for indemnification.

We have obtained insurance policies under which, subject to the limitations of the policies, coverage is provided to our directors and executive officers against loss arising from claims made by reason of breach of fiduciary duty or other wrongful acts as a director or executive officer, including claims relating to public securities matters, and to us with respect to payments that may be made by us to these directors and executive officers pursuant to our indemnification obligations or otherwise as a matter of law.

Certain of our non-employee directors may, through their relationships with their employers, be insured and/or indemnified against certain liabilities incurred in their capacity as members of our Board of Directors.

The underwriting agreement will provide for indemnification by the underwriters of us and our officers and directors for certain liabilities arising under the Securities Act or otherwise.

Insofar as indemnification for liabilities arising under the Securities Act may be permitted to directors, officers or persons controlling our company pursuant to the foregoing provisions, we have been informed that, in

163

251

the opinion of the SEC, such indemnification is against public policy as expressed in the Securities Act and is therefore unenforceable.

Policies and Procedures for Related Party Transactions

Following the completion of this offering, our audit committee will have the primary responsibility for reviewing and approving or disapproving "related party transactions," which are transactions between us and related persons in which the aggregate amount involved exceeds or may be expected to exceed $120,000 and in which a related person has or will have a direct or indirect material interest. Upon completion of this offering, our policy regarding transactions between us and related persons will provide that a related person is defined as a director, executive officer, nominee for director, or greater than 5% beneficial owner of our common stock, in each case since the beginning of the most recently completed year, and any of their immediate family members. Our audit committee charter that will be in effect upon completion of this offering will provide that our audit committee shall review and approve or disapprove any related party transactions.

164

PRINCIPAL AND SELLING STOCKHOLDERS

The following table sets forth certain information with respect to the beneficial ownership of our capital stock as of January 31, 2018, and as adjusted to reflect the sale of our common stock offered by us and the selling stockholders in this offering and the concurrent private placement assuming no exercise of the underwriters' option to purchase additional shares of our common stock from us and the selling stockholders, for:

- each of our named executive officers;

- each of our directors;

- all of our current directors and executive officers as a group;

- each person known by us to be the beneficial owner of more than 5% of the outstanding shares of each of our Class A common stock and Class B common stock; and

- all selling stockholders.

We have determined beneficial ownership in accordance with the rules of the SEC, and thus it represents sole or shared voting or investment power with respect to our securities. Unless otherwise indicated below, to our knowledge, the persons and entities named in the table have sole voting and sole investment power with respect to all shares that they beneficially owned, subject to community property laws where applicable. The information does not necessarily indicate beneficial ownership for any other purpose, including for purposes of Sections 13(d) and 13(g) of the Securities Act.

We have based our calculation of the percentage of beneficial ownership prior to this offering and the concurrent private placement on 26,989,114 shares of our Class A common stock, 348,933,885 shares of our Class B common stock, and no shares of our Class C common Stock outstanding as of January 31, 2018, and reflected:

- (i) 258,620 shares of preferred stock and 2,609,951 shares of Class B common stock that will convert into Class A common stock immediately prior to the completion of this offering pursuant to the terms of certain transfer agreements, and (ii) 147,310,563 shares of preferred stock that will automatically convert into shares of Class B common stock immediately prior to the completion of this offering pursuant to the terms of our amended and restated certificate of incorporation;

- 16,010,519 shares of our Class B common stock subject to RSUs, for which the service condition was satisfied as of January 31, 2018, and for which we expect the Performance Vesting Condition to be satisfied upon the effectiveness of our registration statement related to this offering (after repurchasing 10,236,235 shares of our Class B common stock subject to RSUs to satisfy tax withholding obligations at an assumed tax rate of 39%); and

- 14,733,333 shares of our Class A common stock subject to RSAs that were granted pursuant to our Co-Founder Grants, and vest upon the satisfaction of the service condition and achievement of certain stock price goals.

We have based our calculation of the percentage of beneficial ownership after this offering and the concurrent private placement on 32,085,567 shares of our Class A common stock issued by us in our initial public offering and the concurrent private placement and 68,252,272 shares of Class A common stock and 339,756,294 shares of Class B common stock outstanding immediately after the completion of this offering and the concurrent private placement, assuming that the underwriters will not exercise their option to purchase up to an additional 5,400,000 shares of our Class A common stock from us in full. We have deemed shares of our common stock subject to stock options that are currently exercisable or exercisable within 60 days of January 31, 2018, or issuable pursuant to RSUs which are subject to vesting and settlement conditions expected to occur within 60 days of January 31, 2018, to be outstanding and to be beneficially owned by the person holding the stock option or RSU for the purpose of computing the percentage ownership of that person. We did not deem these shares outstanding, however, for the purpose of computing the percentage ownership of any other person.

165

Unless otherwise indicated, the address of each beneficial owner listed in the table below is c/o Dropbox, Inc., 333 Brannan Street, San Francisco, California 94107.

Name of beneficial owner	Shares beneficially owned prior to this offering and the concurrent private placement				% of total outstanding	% of total voting power before offering and the concurrent private placement#	# of shares being sold	Shares beneficially owned after this offering and the concurrent private placement (assuming no exercise of option to purchase additional shares)				% of total outstanding (assuming no exercise of option to purchase additional shares)	% of total voting power after offering and the concurrent private placement (assuming no exercise of option to purchase additional shares)#	Shares beneficially o... offering and the con... placement (assumi... option to purchase ad...	
	Class A shares	%	Class B shares†	%				Class A shares	%	Class B shares†	%			Class A shares	%
Named executive officers and directors:															
Andrew W. Houston(1)	10,333,333	38.3%	84,763,454	24.3%	25.3%	24.4%	2,333,333	10,333,333	15.1%	82,430,121	24.3%	22.7%	24.1%	10,333,333	14.0%
Arash Ferdowsi(2)	4,400,000	16.3%	34,270,718	9.8%	10.3%	9.9%	2,333,333	4,400,000	6.4%	31,937,385	9.4%	8.9%	9.3%	4,400,000	6.0%
Quentin J. Clark	—	*	—	*	*	*	*	—	*	—	*	*	*	—	*
Donald W. Blair	—	*	—	*	*	*	*	—	*	—	*	*	*	—	*
Paul E. Jacobs(3)	—	*	226,044	*	*	*	—	—	*	226,044	*	*	*	—	*
Robert J. Mylod, Jr.(4)	122,698	*	24,433	*	*	*	—	122,698	*	24,433	*	*	*	122,698	*
Condoleezza Rice(5)	—	*	24,433	*	*	*	—	—	*	24,433	*	*	*	—	*
R. Bryan Schreier(6)	—	*	—	*	*	*	—	—	*	—	*	*	*	—	*
Margaret C. Whitman(7)	—	*	—	*	*	*	—	—	*	—	*	*	*	—	*
All executive officers and directors as a group (12 persons)(8)	14,862,638	55.1%	122,610,899	35.1%	36.6%	35.3%	4,666,666	14,862,638	21.8%	117,944,233	34.7%	32.5%	34.5%	14,862,638	20.2%
Greater than 5% stockholders															
Entities affiliated with Sequoia Capital(9)	—	*	87,171,450	25.0%	23.2%	24.8%	—	—	*	87,171,450	25.7%	21.4%	25.2%	—	*
Entities affiliated with Accel(10)	—	*	18,752,565	5.4%	5.0%	5.3%	—	—	*	18,752,565	5.5%	4.6%	5.4%	—	*
Entities advised by T. Rowe Price(11)	6,002,953	22.2%	7,064,283	2.0%	3.5%	2.2%	—	6,002,953	8.8%	7,064,283	2.1%	3.2%	2.2%	6,002,953	8.2%
Entities affiliated with Green Bay Advisors or Green Bay Generations Fund(12)	2,215,542	8.2%	558,428	*	*	*	—	2,215,542	3.2%	558,428	*	*	*	2,215,542	3.0%
Selling stockholders:															
Hadi Partovi(13)	—	*	3,520,333	1.0%	*	1.0%	3,520,333	—	*	—	*	*	*	—	*
Sujay Jaswa	—	*	2,148,289	*	*	*	433,333	—	*	1,714,956	*	*	*	—	*
Aditya Agarwal(14)	—	*	5,900,842	1.7%	1.6%	1.7%	275,740	—	*	5,625,102	1.7%	1.4%	1.6%	—	*
J. Rothschild Investments 1 Limited(15)	—	*	2,573,920	*	*	*	40,519	—	*	2,533,401	*	*	*	—	*
Rian Hunter	—	*	2,320,608	*	*	*	241,000	—	*	2,079,608	*	*	*	—	*

† The Class B common stock is convertible at any time by the holder into shares of Class A common stock on a share-for-share basis, such that each holder of Class B common stock beneficially owns an equivalent number of Class A common stock.

Percentage total voting power represents voting power with respect to all shares of our Class A common stock and Class B common stock, as a single class. Each holder of Class B common stock shall be entitled to ten votes per share of Class B common stock and each holder of Class A common stock shall be entitled to one vote per share of

166

Class A common stock on all matters submitted to our stockholders for a vote. The Class A common stock and Class B common stock vote together as a single class on all matters submitted to a vote of our stockholders, except as may otherwise be required by law.

* Represents beneficial ownership of less than one percent (1%) of the outstanding shares of our common stock.

(1) Consists of (i) 8,781,548 shares of Class B common stock held by the Houston Remainder Trust dated 12/30/2010, for which Mr. Houston serves as trustee, (ii) 75,481,406 shares of Class B common stock held by the Andrew W. Houston Revocable Trust dated 9/7/2011, for which Mr. Houston serves as trustee, (iii) 500,500 shares of Class B common stock held by the Houston 2012 Irrevocable Children's Trust dated 4/12/2012, for which Mr. Houston serves as trustee, and (iv) 10,333,333 shares of Class A common stock underlying RSAs. Prior to the effectiveness of our registration statement related to this offering, Mr. Houston and Mr. Ferdowsi are expected to enter into voting agreements with certain of our stockholders for up to 7% of the voting power of our outstanding capital stock following the completion of this offering and the concurrent private placement.

(2) Consists of (i) 2,900,802 shares of Class B common stock held by the Arash Ferdowsi Remainder Trust dated 3/21/2011, for which Mr. Ferdowsi serves as trustee, (ii) 31,369,916 shares of Class B common stock held by the Arash Ferdowsi Revocable Trust dated 4/20/2012, for which Mr. Ferdowsi serves as trustee, and (iii) 4,400,000 shares of Class A common stock underlying RSAs. Prior to the effectiveness of our registration statement related to this offering, Mr. Houston and Mr. Ferdowsi are expected to enter into voting agreements with certain of our stockholders for up to 7% of the voting power of our outstanding capital stock following the completion of this offering and the concurrent private placement.

(3) Consists of (i) 172,711 shares of Class B common stock held by the Paul E. Jacobs Trust dated November 7, 2014, for which Mr. Jacobs serves as trustee, (ii) 26,666 shares of Class B common stock held by Mr. Jacobs, and (iii) 26,667 shares of Class B common stock that will be issued upon the vesting of RSUs within 60 days of January 31, 2018.

(4) Consists of (i) 122,698 shares of Class B common stock held by Annox Capital, LLC, or Annox, which will convert into an equivalent number of shares of Class A common stock in connection with the Capital Stock Conversion and (ii) consists of 24,433 shares of Class B common stock that will be issued upon the vesting of RSUs within 60 days of January 31, 2018. Mr. Mylod, a member of our Board of Directors, is the managing member of Annox and has sole voting and investment control over the shares held by Annox.

(5) Consists of 24,433 shares of Class B common stock that will be issued upon the vesting of RSUs within 60 days of January 31, 2018.

(6) Excludes shares listed in footnote 9 below, which are held by entities affiliated with Sequoia Capital. Mr. Schreier, one of our directors, is a non-managing member of SC XII LLC.

(7) Margaret Whitman was elected to the Board of Directors in September 2017.

(8) Consists of (i) 121,366,947 shares of Class B common stock beneficially owned by our executive officers and directors, (ii) 90,884 shares of Class B common stock subject to options that are immediately exercisable within 60 days of January 31, 2018, and (iii) 1,123,609 shares of Class B common stock that will be net issued upon the vesting of RSUs within 60 days of January 31, 2018.

(9) Consists of (i) 76,179,144 shares of Class B common stock held by Sequoia Capital XII, L.P., or SC XII, (ii) 8,141,812 shares of Class B common stock held by Sequoia Capital XII Principals Fund, LLC, or SC XII PF, and (iii) 2,850,494 shares of Class B common stock held by Sequoia Technology Partners XII, L.P., or STP XII. SC XII Management, LLC, or SC XII LLC, is the general partner of each of SC XII and STP XII, and the managing member of SC XII PF. As a result, and by virtue of the relationships described in this footnote, SC XII LLC may be deemed to share beneficial ownership of the shares held by SC XII, SC XII PF, and STP XII. The address for these entities is 2800 Sand Hill Road #101, Menlo Park, California 94025.

(10) Consists of (i) 1,635,668 shares of Class B common stock held by Accel Investors 2008 L.L.C., or AI 2008, (ii) 14,772 shares of Class B common stock held by Accel Investors 2010 L.L.C., or AI 2010, (iii) 10,497 shares of Class B common stock held by Accel Investors 2013 L.L.C., or AI 2013, (iv) 98,854 shares of Class B common stock held by Accel XI L.P., or Accel XI, (v) 7,425 shares of Class B common stock held by Accel XI Strategic Partners L.P., or Accel XI Strategic, (vi) 15,788,974 shares of Class B common stock held by Accel X L.P., or Accel X, and (vii) 1,196,375 shares of Class B common stock held by Accel X Strategic Partners L.P., or Accel X Strategic, and together with AI 2008, AI 2010, AI 2013, Accel XI, Accel XI Strategic, and Accel X, the Accel Entities. Accel X Associates L.L.C., or Accel X Associates, is the general partner of Accel X and Accel X Strategic and has the sole voting and investment power. Andrew G. Braccia, Kevin Efrusy, Sameer K. Gandhi, Ping Li, Tracy L. Sedlock, and Richard P. Wong are the managing members of Accel X Associates, AI 2008, and AI 2010 and share voting and investment powers over such shares. Accel XI Associates L.L.C., or Accel XI Associates, is the general partner of Accel XI and Accel Strategic and has the sole voting and investment power. Andrew G. Braccia, Sameer K. Gandhi, Ping Li, Tracy L. Sedlock, and Richard P. Wong are the managing members of Accel XI Associates and AI 2013 and share voting and investment powers over such shares. The address for these entities and individuals is 428 University Ave., Palo Alto, California 94301.

(11) Consists of (i) 6,002,953 shares of Class A common stock held of record by 63 funds and accounts advised or sub-advised by T. Rowe Price Associates, Inc., or TRPA; and (ii) 7,064,283 shares of Class B common stock held of record by 62 funds and accounts advised or sub-advised by TRPA. TRPA serves as investment adviser with power to direct investments and/or sole power to vote the securities owned by these funds and accounts. The T. Rowe Price Proxy Committee develops the firm's positions on all major proxy voting issues, creates guidelines, and oversees the voting process. Once the Proxy Committee establishes its recommendations, they are distributed to the firm's portfolio managers as voting guidelines. Ultimately, the portfolio managers for each account decide how to vote on the proxy proposals of companies in their portfolios. More information on the T. Rowe Price proxy voting guidelines is available on its website at troweprice.com. The T. Rowe Price portfolio managers of the funds and accounts that hold our securities are collectively listed as follows: Joseph B. Fath,

167

255

Taymour R. Tamaddon, Paul D. Greene, Donald J. Peters, Henry M. Ellenbogen, Brian W. H. Berghuis, Kennard W. Allen, Joshua K. Spencer, and Justin White. For purposes of reporting requirements of the Securities Exchange Act of 1934, TRPA may be deemed to be the beneficial owner of all the shares listed above. T. Rowe Price Associates, Inc. is the wholly owned subsidiary of T. Rowe Price Group, Inc., which is a publicly traded financial services holding company. The address for T. Rowe Price Associates, Inc. is 100 East Pratt Street, Baltimore, Maryland 21202. T. Rowe Price Investment Services, Inc., or TRPIS, a registered broker-dealer, is a subsidiary of T. Rowe Price Associates, Inc. TRPIS was formed primarily for the limited purpose of acting as the principal underwriter of shares of the funds in the T. Rowe Price fund family. TRPIS does not engage in underwriting or market-making activities involving individual securities.

(12) Consists of (i) 1,073,999 shares of Class A common stock held by Green Bay - DX, LLC, (ii) 443,507 shares of Class A common stock held by Green Bay - DX II, LLC, (iii) 698,036 shares of Class A common stock held by Cloudy Sky, LLC, and (iv) 558,428 shares of Class B common stock held by D5X, LLC. Green Bay Generations Fund, LLC , or GBGF, is the investment adviser to Green Bay - DX, LLC, Green Bay - DX II, LLC and Cloudy Sky, LLC. Its address is 915 Broadway, Suite 1206, New York, New York 10010. Green Bay Advisors, LLC is the investment adviser to D5X, LLC, and its address is 480 Pacific Avenue, Suite 200, San Francisco, California 94133.

(13) Consists of (i) 293,672 shares of Class B common stock held by Mr. Partovi in his individual capacity and (ii) 3,226,661 shares of Class B common stock beneficially owned by Mr. Partovi through various trusts and related entities.

(14) Consists of (i) 634,353 shares of Class B common stock held by Mr. Agarwal in his individual capacity and (ii) 5,266,489 shares of Class B common stock beneficially owned by Mr. Agarwal through various trusts and related entities.

(15) Consists of 2,573,920 shares of Class B common stock held by J. Rothschild Investments 1 Limited. Anthony D. Holt, Emmalene Holden, and Kelvin J. Whelan are directors of J. Rothschild Investments 1 Limited and share voting and investment powers over the shares. The address for this entity is Newport House, 15 The Grange, St. Peter Port, Guernsey.

DESCRIPTION OF CAPITAL STOCK

General

The following description summarizes certain important terms of our capital stock, as they are expected to be in effect immediately prior to the completion of this offering and the concurrent private placement. We expect to adopt an amended and restated certificate of incorporation and amended and restated bylaws that will become effective immediately prior to the completion of this offering, and this description summarizes the provisions that are expected to be included in such documents. Because it is only a summary, it does not contain all the information that may be important to you. For a complete description of the matters set forth in this section titled "Description of Capital Stock," you should refer to our amended and restated certificate of incorporation, amended and restated bylaws and amended and restated investors' rights agreement, which are included as exhibits to the registration statement of which this prospectus forms a part, and to the applicable provisions of Delaware law.

Immediately following the completion of this offering, our authorized capital stock will consist of 3,915,000,000 shares of capital stock, $0.00001 par value per share, of which:

- 2,400,000,000 shares are designated as Class A common stock;

- 475,000,000 shares are designated as Class B common stock;

- 800,000,000 shares are designated as Class C common stock; and

- 240,000,000 shares are designated as preferred stock.

Assuming the conversion of all outstanding shares of our convertible preferred stock into shares of our Class B common stock, which will occur immediately prior to the completion of this offering, as of December 31, 2017, there were 11,817,248 shares of our Class A common stock outstanding (including the Capital Stock Conversions), held by 1,310 stockholders of record, 348,501,449 shares of our Class B common stock outstanding (including the Capital Stock Conversions and the RSU Settlement), held by 2,658 stockholders of record, and no shares of our Class C common stock outstanding. Pursuant to our amended and restated certificate of incorporation, our Board of Directors will have the authority, without stockholder approval except as required by the listing standards of Nasdaq, to issue additional shares of our Class A common stock and Class C common stock. Until the final conversion of all outstanding shares of Class B common stock pursuant to the terms of the amended and restated certificate of incorporation, or the Final Conversion Date, any issuance of additional shares of Class B common stock, other than shares issued pursuant to the exercise or conversion of options or warrants or the settlement of RSUs, in each case, outstanding as of the date the shares of Class A common stock are listed for issuance on Nasdaq, requires the approval of the holders of a majority of the outstanding shares of Class B common stock.

Common Stock

We have three classes of authorized common stock, Class A common stock, Class B common stock, and Class C common stock. The rights of the holders of Class A common stock, Class B common stock, and Class C common stock are identical, except with respect to voting and conversion.

Dividend Rights

Subject to preferences that may apply to any shares of preferred stock outstanding at the time, the holders of our common stock are entitled to receive dividends out of funds legally available if our Board of Directors, in its discretion, determines to issue dividends and then only at the times and in the amounts that our Board of Directors may determine. See the section titled "Dividend Policy" for additional information.

169

Voting Rights

Holders of our Class A common stock are entitled to one vote for each share held on all matters submitted to a vote of stockholders, holders of our Class B common stock are entitled to ten votes for each share held, and holders of our Class C common stock are not entitled to vote on any matter that is submitted to a vote of stockholders, except as otherwise required by law. The holders of our Class A common stock and Class B common stock vote together as a single class, unless otherwise required by law. Under our amended and restated certificate of incorporation, approval of the holders of a majority of the Class B common stock is required to increase the number of authorized shares of our Class B common stock. In addition, Delaware law could require either holders of our Class A common stock, our Class B common stock, or our Class C common stock to vote separately as a single class in the following circumstances:

- if we were to seek to amend our amended and restated certificate of incorporation to increase or decrease the par value of a class of stock, then that class would be required to vote separately to approve the proposed amendment; and

- if we were to seek to amend our amended and restated certificate of incorporation in a manner that alters or changes the powers, preferences, or special rights of a class of stock in a manner that affected its holders adversely, then that class would be required to vote separately to approve the proposed amendment.

Until the Final Conversion Date, our Class B common stock will have the right to vote as a separate class to:

- amend or modify any provision of the amended and restated certificate of incorporation inconsistent with, or otherwise alter, any provision of amended and restated certificate of incorporation to modify the voting, conversion or other rights, powers, preferences, privileges or restrictions of the Class B common stock;

- reclassify any outstanding shares of Class A common stock or Class C common stock into shares having rights as to dividends or liquidation that are senior to the Class B common stock or, in the case of Class A common stock, the right to have more than one (1) vote for each share thereof and, in the case of Class C common stock, the right to have any vote for any share thereof, except as required by law;

- issue any shares of Class B common stock (other than shares of Class B Common Stock originally issued after the date of this offering pursuant to the exercise or conversion of options or warrants or settlement of RSUs that, in each case, are outstanding as of the date of this offering);

- authorize, or issue any shares of, any class or series of capital stock of the Corporation having the right to more than (1) vote for each share thereof; or

- consummate a Liquidation Event (as defined in the amended and restated certificate of incorporation).

Our amended and restated certificate of incorporation and amended and restated bylaws that will be in effect at the closing of our initial public offering will provide that from and after the Voting Threshold Date, we will have a classified Board of Directors consisting of three classes of approximately equal size, each serving staggered three-year terms. Only the directors in one class will be subject to election by a plurality of the votes cast at each annual meeting of stockholders, with the directors in the other classes continuing for the remainder of their respective three-year terms. Until the Voting Threshold Date, our directors will be elected annually for one-year terms. Stockholders do not have the ability to cumulate votes for the election of directors.

No Preemptive or Similar Rights

Our common stock is not entitled to preemptive rights, and is not subject to conversion, redemption, or sinking fund provisions.

170

Right to Receive Liquidation Distributions

If we become subject to a liquidation, dissolution, or winding-up, the assets legally available for distribution to our stockholders would be distributable ratably among the holders of our common stock and any participating preferred stock outstanding at that time, subject to prior satisfaction of all outstanding debt and liabilities and the preferential rights of and the payment of liquidation preferences, if any, on any outstanding shares of preferred stock.

Conversion of Class B Common Stock

Each share of Class B common stock is convertible at any time at the option of the holder into one share of Class A common stock. Following the completion of this offering, shares of Class B common stock will automatically convert into shares of Class A common stock upon sale or transfer certain transfers described in our amended and restated certificate of incorporation, including estate planning transfers where sole dispositive power and exclusive voting control with respect to the shares of Class B common stock are retained by the transferring holder and transfers between our co-founders. In addition, each outstanding share of Class B common stock held by a stockholder who is a natural person, or held by the permitted entities and permitted transferees of such natural person (as described in our amended and restated certificate of incorporation), will convert automatically into one share of Class A common stock upon the death of such natural person. In the event of the death or permanent and total disability of a co-founder, shares of Class B common stock held by such co-founder, his permitted entities or permitted transferees will convert to Class A common stock, provided that the conversion will be deferred for nine months, or up to 18 months if approved by a majority of our independent directors, following his death or permanent and total and permanent disability. Transfers between our co-founders are permitted transfers and will not result in conversion of the shares of Class B common stock that are transferred; however, upon the death or total and permanent disability of the transferring co-founder, the transferred shares would convert to Class A common stock following the deferral period of nine months, or up to 18 months if approved by a majority of our independent directors.

Each share of Class B common stock will convert automatically into one share of Class A common stock upon (i) the date specified by affirmative vote of the holders of two-thirds of the then outstanding shares of Class B common stock, (ii) the date on which the outstanding shares of Class B common stock represent less than five percent of the aggregate number of shares of the then outstanding Class A common stock and Class B common stock, or (iii) nine months after the death or total disability of the last to die or become disabled of our co-founders, or such later date not to exceed a total period of 18 months after such death or disability as may be approved by a majority of our independent directors.

Additionally, pursuant to transfer agreements with certain of our stockholders, 2,609,951 shares of our Class B common stock will automatically convert into an equivalent number of shares of Class A common stock immediately prior to the completion of this offering.

Conversion of Class C Common Stock

Shares of Class C common stock will convert automatically into Class A common stock, on a share-for-share basis, following the conversion of all outstanding shares of Class B common stock into shares of Class A common stock, on the date or time specified by the holders of a majority of the outstanding shares of Class A common stock, voting as a separate class.

Fully Paid and Non-Assessable

In connection with this offering, our legal counsel will opine that the shares of our Class A common stock to be issued in this offering will be fully paid and non-assessable.

171

Preferred Stock

Our Board of Directors is authorized, subject to limitations prescribed by Delaware law, to issue preferred stock in one or more series, to establish from time to time the number of shares to be included in each series, and to fix the designation, powers, preferences, and rights of the shares of each series and any of its qualifications, limitations, or restrictions, in each case without further vote or action by our stockholders. Our Board of Directors can also increase or decrease the number of shares of any series of preferred stock, but not below the number of shares of that series then outstanding, without any further vote or action by our stockholders. Our Board of Directors may authorize the issuance of preferred stock with voting or conversion rights that could adversely affect the voting power or other rights of the holders of our common stock. The issuance of preferred stock, while providing flexibility in connection with possible acquisitions and other corporate purposes, could, among other things, have the effect of delaying, deferring, or preventing a change in control of our company and might adversely affect the market price of our common stock and the voting and other rights of the holders of our common stock. We have no current plan to issue any shares of preferred stock.

RSAs

As of December 31, 2017, we had outstanding 14,733,333 shares of our Class A common stock subject to RSAs, which were granted pursuant to the Co-Founder Grants. The Co-Founder Grants vest upon the satisfaction of the service condition and achievement of certain stock price goals. These Co-Founder Grants provide the holders with certain stockholder rights, such as the right to vote the shares immediately upon grant and prior to their vesting. See "Executive Compensation—Co-Founder Restricted Stock Awards" for additional information.

Options

As of December 31, 2017, we had outstanding options to purchase an aggregate of 4,959,492 shares of our Class B common stock, with a weighted-average exercise price of $10.52 per share, under our equity compensation plans.

RSUs

As of December 31, 2017, we had outstanding 38,219,737 shares of our Class B common stock subject to RSUs under our 2008 Plan and 16,707,823 shares of our Class A common stock subject to RSUs under our 2017 Plan. RSUs granted on and after August 1, 2015, which we refer to as one-tier RSUs, generally vest upon the satisfaction of a service-based vesting condition. The service-based vesting condition generally is satisfied over a four-year period. 25% of the one-tier RSUs vest upon completion of one year of service measured from the vesting commencement date, and as to the balance in successive equal quarterly installments, subject to continued service through each such vesting date. Our RSUs granted prior to August 1, 2015, which we refer to as two-tier RSUs, generally vest upon the satisfaction of both a service-based vesting condition and the Performance Vesting Condition occurring before these two-tier RSUs expire. The service-based vesting condition generally is satisfied over a four-year period. 25% of the two-tier RSUs service-based vesting condition is satisfied upon completion of one year of service measured from the vesting commencement date, and the balance generally vests in successive equal monthly installments prior to the occurrence of the Performance Vesting Condition and in successive equal quarterly installments after the occurrence of the Performance Vesting Condition, but, in all cases, subject to continued service through each applicable vesting date. The Performance Vesting Condition occurs on the earlier of (i) an acquisition or change in control of us or (ii) the earlier of (a) six months after our initial public offering or (b) March 15 of the year following our initial public offering. As a result of the September 2017 RSU Amendment, all RSUs were amended to provide that the quarterly dates for satisfying the service-based vesting condition shall be February 15, May 15, August 15, or November 15, each of which we refer to as a New Quarterly Date. This amendment will result in a partial acceleration of any RSUs that were scheduled to satisfy the service-based vesting condition on a date following a New Quarterly Date but before the next New Quarterly Date, such that these RSUs now will satisfy the service-based vesting condition

172

on the first of those New Quarterly Dates. For one-tier RSUs, this amendment will be effective as of February 15, 2018, and for two-tier RSUs, this amendment will be effective as of the satisfaction of the Performance Vesting Condition. In addition, as a result of the September 2017 RSU Amendment, any two-tier RSUs that are scheduled to satisfy the service-based vesting condition on the first day of any month now will satisfy this condition on the 15th day of the prior month until the date that the Performance Vesting Condition is satisfied. Our Board of Directors has approved the acceleration of the Performance Vesting Condition associated with the two-tier RSUs to occur upon the effectiveness of the registration statement of which this prospectus forms a part. All other significant terms of the two-tier RSUs will remain unchanged.

Voting Agreements

Prior to the effectiveness of our registration statement related to this offering, Mr. Houston and Mr. Ferdowsi are expected to enter into voting agreements with certain of our stockholders, which voting agreements will remain in effect after the completion of this offering. These voting agreements may cover an aggregate of up to 7% of the voting power of our outstanding capital stock after our initial public offering and the concurrent private placement. We are not a party to these voting agreements. Under these voting agreements, the proxyholder, either Mr. Houston or Mr. Ferdowsi, has the authority (and irrevocable proxy) to direct the vote and vote these shares at his discretion on all matters to be voted upon by stockholders.

Shares subject to the voting agreements will no longer be subject to the provisions of the voting agreement if an investor sells, transfers, assigns, pledges, or otherwise disposes of or encumbers the shares subject to the voting agreements after the completion of our initial public offering, except for permitted transfers under the amended and restated certificate of incorporation. The voting agreements will terminate on our dissolution, the express written consent of the proxyholder, the date on which the Final Conversion Date occurs as a result of the death or disability of both Mr. Houston and Mr. Ferdowsi or the date on which the stockholder and any of such stockholder's permitted transferees ceases to own any of the shares subject to the applicable voting agreement.

Registration Rights

After the completion of this offering and the concurrent private placement, certain holders of our Class B common stock will be entitled to rights with respect to the registration of their shares under the Securities Act. These registration rights are contained in our IRA. We and certain holders of our preferred stock are parties to the IRA. Immediately prior to the completion of this offering and the concurrent private placement, each share of outstanding preferred stock will convert automatically into one share of Class B common stock. The registration rights set forth in the IRA will expire five years following the completion of this offering, or, with respect to any particular stockholder, when such stockholder is able to sell all of its shares on any one day pursuant to Rule 144 of the Securities Act or a similar exemption. We will pay the registration expenses (other than underwriting discounts, selling commissions, and transfer taxes) of the holders of the shares registered pursuant to the registrations described below. In an underwritten offering, the managing underwriter, if any, has the right, subject to specified conditions, to limit the number of shares such holders may include. We expect that our stockholders will waive their rights under the IRA (i) to notice of this offering and (ii) to include their registrable shares in this offering. In addition, in connection with this offering, we expect that each stockholder that has registration rights will agree not to sell or otherwise dispose of any securities without the prior written consent of the company and the underwriters for a period of 180 days after the date of this prospectus, subject to certain terms and conditions and early release of certain holders in specified circumstances. See the section titled "Shares Eligible for Future Sale—Lock-Up and Market Standoff Agreements" for additional information regarding such restrictions.

Demand Registration Rights

After the completion of this offering and the concurrent private placement, the holders of up to 144,907,822 shares of our Class B common stock and 5,521,778 shares of our Class A common stock will be entitled to certain demand registration rights. At any time beginning six months after the effective date of this

173

offering, the holders of at least 40% of these shares then outstanding can request that we register the offer and sale of their shares, or such request must cover securities in which the anticipated aggregate public offering price, before payment of underwriting discounts and commissions, is at least $10,000,000. We are obligated to effect only two such registrations. If we determine that it would be seriously detrimental to us and our stockholders to effect such a demand registration, we have the right to defer such registration, not more than once in any 12-month period, for a period of up to 120 days.

Piggyback Registration Rights

After the completion of this offering and the concurrent private placement, if we propose to register the offer and sale of our Class A common stock under the Securities Act, in connection with the public offering of such Class A common stock, the holders of up to 144,907,822 shares of our Class B common stock and 5,521,778 shares of our Class A common stock will be entitled to certain "piggyback" registration rights allowing the holders to include their shares in such registration, subject to certain marketing and other limitations. As a result, whenever we propose to file a registration statement under the Securities Act, other than with respect to (1) a registration in which the only Class A common stock being registered is Class A common stock issuable upon conversion of debt securities that are also being registered, (2) a registration related to any employee benefit plan or a corporate reorganization or other transaction covered by Rule 145 promulgated under the Securities Act, or (3) a registration on any registration form which does not permit secondary sales or does not include substantially the same information as would be required to be included in a registration statement covering the public offering of our Class A common stock, the holders of these shares are entitled to notice of the registration and have the right, subject to certain limitations, to include their shares in the registration.

S-3 Registration Rights

After the completion of this offering and the concurrent private placement, the holders of up to 144,907,822 shares of our Class B common stock and 5,521,778 shares of our Class A common stock will be entitled to certain Form S-3 registration rights. The holders of at least 40% of these shares then outstanding may make a written request that we register the offer and sale of their shares on a registration statement on Form S-3 if we are eligible to file a registration statement on Form S-3 so long as the request covers securities the anticipated aggregate public offering price of which, before payment of underwriting discounts and commissions, is at least $3,000,000. These stockholders may make an unlimited number of requests for registration on Form S-3; however, we will not be required to effect a registration on Form S-3 if we have effected two such registrations within the 12-month period preceding the date of the request. Additionally, if we determine that it would be seriously detrimental to the Company and our stockholders to effect such a registration, we have the right to defer such registration, not more than once in any 12-month period, for a period of up to 120 days.

Anti-Takeover Provisions

Certain provisions of Delaware law, our amended and restated certificate of incorporation, and our amended and restated bylaws, which are summarized below, may have the effect of delaying, deferring, or discouraging another person from acquiring control of us. They are also designed, in part, to encourage persons seeking to acquire control of us to negotiate first with our Board of Directors. We believe that the benefits of increased protection of our potential ability to negotiate with an unfriendly or unsolicited acquirer outweigh the disadvantages of discouraging a proposal to acquire us because negotiation of these proposals could result in an improvement of their terms.

Delaware Law

We will be governed by the provisions of Section 203 of the Delaware General Corporation Law. In general, Section 203 prohibits a public Delaware corporation from engaging in a "business combination" with an

174

"interested stockholder" for a period of three years after the date of the transaction in which the person became an interested stockholder, unless:

- the transaction was approved by the board of directors prior to the time that the stockholder became an interested stockholder;

- upon consummation of the transaction which resulted in the stockholder becoming an interested stockholder, the interested stockholder owned at least 85% of the voting stock of the corporation outstanding at the time the transaction commenced, excluding shares owned by directors who are also officers of the corporation and shares owned by employee stock plans in which employee participants do not have the right to determine confidentially whether shares held subject to the plan will be tendered in a tender or exchange offer; or

- at or subsequent to the time the stockholder became an interested stockholder, the business combination was approved by the board of directors and authorized at an annual or special meeting of the stockholders, and not by written consent, by the affirmative vote of at least two-thirds of the outstanding voting stock which is not owned by the interested stockholder.

In general, Section 203 defines a "business combination" to include mergers, asset sales, and other transactions resulting in financial benefit to a stockholder and an "interested stockholder" as a person who, together with affiliates and associates, owns, or, within three years, did own, 15% or more of the corporation's outstanding voting stock. These provisions may have the effect of delaying, deferring, or preventing changes in control of our company.

Amended and Restated Certificate of Incorporation and Amended and Restated Bylaw Provisions

Our amended and restated certificate of incorporation and our amended and restated bylaws will include a number of provisions that could deter hostile takeovers or delay or prevent changes in control of our Board of Directors or management team, including the following:

Multi-class stock. As described above in "—Common Stock—Voting Rights," our amended and restated certificate of incorporation provides for a multi-class common stock structure, which will provide our pre-offering investors, which includes our executive officers, employees, directors, and their affiliates, with significant influence over matters requiring stockholder approval, including the election of directors and significant corporate transactions, such as a merger or other sale of our company or its assets.

Separate Class B Vote for Certain Transactions. Until the Final Conversion Date, our Class B common stock will have the right to vote as a separate class on amendments to our amended and restated certificate of incorporation that affect the rights of our Class B common stock, certain reclassifications and changes in voting rights of our Class A common stock or Class C common stock, issuances of Class B common stock other than pursuant to existing rights and equity awards, authorization of stock with more than one (1) vote per share and liquidation events. See the section titled "Description of Capital Stock—Voting Rights."

Board of Directors vacancies. Our amended and restated certificate of incorporation and amended and restated bylaws will authorize only our Board of Directors to fill vacant directorships, including newly created seats. In addition, the number of directors constituting our Board of Directors will be permitted to be set only by a resolution adopted by a majority vote of our entire Board of Directors. These provisions would prevent a stockholder from increasing the size of our Board of Directors and then gaining control of our Board of Directors by filling the resulting vacancies with its own nominees. This will make it more difficult to change the composition of our Board of Directors and will promote continuity of management.

Classified Board of Directors. Our amended and restated certificate of incorporation and amended and restated bylaws will provide that, from and after the time that the Class B common stock no longer represents a majority of the combined voting power of our Class A common stock and Class B common stock, or the Voting Threshold Date, our Board of Directors will be classified into three classes of directors. A third party may be

175

discouraged from making a tender offer or otherwise attempting to obtain control of us as it is more difficult and time consuming for stockholders to replace a majority of the directors on a classified Board of Directors. See the section titled "Management—Classified Board of Directors."

Stockholder action; special meeting of stockholders. Our amended and restated certificate of incorporation will provide that until the Voting Threshold Date, our stockholders may only take action by written consent if such action is first recommended or approved by the Board of Directors. Following the Voting Threshold Date, our stockholders will not be able to take action by written consent for any matter and may only take action at annual or special meetings. As a result, a holder controlling a majority of our capital stock would not be able to amend our amended and restated bylaws or remove directors without holding a meeting of our stockholders called in accordance with our amended and restated bylaws, unless previously approved by our Board of Directors. Our amended and restated bylaws will further provide that special meetings of our stockholders may be called only by a majority of our Board of Directors, the Chairman of our Board of Directors, our Chief Executive Officer or, until the Final Conversion Date, holders of 30% of the combined voting power of our Class A common stock and Class B common stock, thus limiting the ability of a stockholder to call a special meeting. These provisions might delay the ability of our stockholders to force consideration of a proposal or for stockholders controlling a majority of our capital stock to take any action, including the removal of directors.

Advance notice requirements for stockholder proposals and director nominations. Our amended and restated bylaws will provide advance notice procedures for stockholders seeking to bring business before our annual meeting of stockholders or to nominate candidates for election as directors at our annual meeting of stockholders. Our amended and restated bylaws will also specify certain requirements regarding the form and content of a stockholder's notice. These provisions might preclude our stockholders from bringing matters before our annual meeting of stockholders or from making nominations for directors at our annual meeting of stockholders if the proper procedures are not followed. We expect that these provisions may also discourage or deter a potential acquirer from conducting a solicitation of proxies to elect the acquirer's own slate of directors or otherwise attempting to obtain control of our company.

No cumulative voting. The Delaware General Corporation Law provides that stockholders are not entitled to cumulate votes in the election of directors unless a corporation's certificate of incorporation provides otherwise. Our amended and restated certificate of incorporation does not provide for cumulative voting.

Amendment of charter and bylaws provisions. Prior to the Final Conversion Date, any amendment of our amended and restated certificate of incorporation will require approval by holders of at least two-thirds of the voting power of our then outstanding capital stock. From and after the Final Conversion Date, certain amendments to our amended and restated certificate of incorporation will require the approval of two-thirds of the outstanding voting power of our common stock. Our amended and restated bylaws will provide that approval of stockholders holding two-thirds of our outstanding voting power voting as a single class is required for stockholders to amend or adopt any provision of our bylaws.

Issuance of undesignated preferred stock. Our Board of Directors will have the authority, without further action by our stockholders, to issue up to 240,000,000 shares of undesignated preferred stock with rights and preferences, including voting rights, designated from time to time by our Board of Directors. The existence of authorized but unissued shares of preferred stock would enable our Board of Directors to render more difficult or to discourage an attempt to obtain control of us by means of a merger, tender offer, proxy contest, or other means.

Exclusive Forum

Our amended and restated bylaws will provide that, unless we consent in writing to the selection of an alternative forum, the sole and exclusive forum for (1) any derivative action or proceeding brought on our behalf, (2) any action asserting a claim of breach of a fiduciary duty owed by any of our directors, officers, or other employees to us or our stockholders, (3) any action arising pursuant to any provision of the Delaware General

176

Corporation Law or our certificate of incorporation or bylaws, or (4) any other action asserting a claim that is governed by the internal affairs doctrine shall be the Court of Chancery of the State of Delaware (or, if the Court of Chancery does not have jurisdiction, the federal district court for the District of Delaware), in all cases subject to the court having jurisdiction over indispensable parties named as defendants. Any person or entity purchasing or otherwise acquiring any interest in our securities shall be deemed to have notice of and consented to this provision. Although we believe these provisions benefit us by providing increased consistency in the application of Delaware law for the specified types of actions and proceedings, the provisions may have the effect of discouraging lawsuits against us or our directors and officers. Our amended and restated bylaws will also provide that the federal district courts of the United States will be the exclusive forum for resolving any complaint asserting a cause of action arising under the Securities Act.

Transfer Agent and Registrar

Upon completion of this offering, the transfer agent and registrar for our common stock will be Computershare Trust Company, N.A. The transfer agent and registrar's address is 144 Fernwood Avenue, Edison, NJ 08837.

Limitations of Liability and Indemnification

See the section titled "Certain Relationships and Related Party Transactions—Limitation of Liability and Indemnification of Officers and Directors."

Listing

We have been approved to list our Class A common stock on Nasdaq under the symbol "DBX".

177

SHARES ELIGIBLE FOR FUTURE SALE

Prior to this offering, there has been no public market for our Class A common stock, and we cannot predict the effect, if any, that market sales of shares of our Class A common stock or the availability of shares of our Class A common stock for sale will have on the market price of our Class A common stock prevailing from time to time. Future sales of our common stock in the public market, or the availability of such shares for sale in the public market, could adversely affect market prices prevailing from time to time. As described below, only a limited number of shares of our Class A common stock will be available for sale shortly after this offering due to contractual and legal restrictions on resale. Nevertheless, sales of our Class A common stock in the public market after such restrictions lapse, or the perception that those sales may occur, could adversely affect the prevailing market price at such time and our ability to raise equity capital in the future.

Following the completion of this offering and the concurrent private placement, based on the number of shares of our capital stock outstanding as of December 31, 2017, we will have a total of 53,080,406 shares of our Class A common stock outstanding, 339,323,858 shares of our Class B common stock outstanding, and no shares of Class C common stock outstanding. Of these outstanding shares, all 36,000,000 shares of our Class A common stock sold in this offering will be freely tradable, except that any shares purchased in this offering by our affiliates, as that term is defined in Rule 144 under the Securities Act, would only be able to be sold in compliance with the Rule 144 limitations described below.

The remaining outstanding shares of our common stock will be deemed "restricted securities" as defined in Rule 144 under the Securities Act. Restricted securities may be sold in the public market only if they are registered under the Securities Act or if they qualify for an exemption from registration under Rule 144 or Rule 701 under the Securities Act, which rules are summarized below. As a result of the lock-up and market standoff agreements described below and the provisions of our IRA described under the section titled "Description of Capital Stock—Registration Rights," and subject to the provisions of Rule 144 or Rule 701, shares of our Class A common stock will be available for sale in the public market as follows:

- beginning on the date of this prospectus, all 36,000,000 shares of our Class A common stock sold in this offering will be immediately available for sale in the public market; and

- beginning 181 days after the date of this prospectus (subject to the terms of the lock-up and market standoff agreements described below) 356,404,264 additional shares will become eligible for sale in the public market, of which 258,718,600 shares will be held by affiliates and subject to the volume and other restrictions of Rule 144, as described below.

Lock-Up and Market Standoff Agreements

Our executive officers, directors, and certain other holders of our capital stock and securities convertible into or exchangeable for our capital stock have agreed that, subject to certain exceptions, for a period of 180 days after the date of this prospectus, or lock-up period, we and they will not, without the prior written consent of Goldman Sachs & Co. LLC and J.P. Morgan Securities LLC, dispose of or hedge any shares or any securities convertible into or exchangeable for shares of our capital stock; provided that if (i) at least 120 days have elapsed since the date of this prospectus, (ii) we have publicly released our earnings results for the quarterly period during which this offering occurred, and (iii) such lock-up period is scheduled to end during or within five trading days prior to a broadly applicable period during which trading in our securities would not be permitted under our insider trading policy, or a blackout period, such lock-up period will end ten trading days prior to the commencement of such blackout period. Goldman Sachs & Co. LLC and J.P. Morgan Securities LLC may, in their discretion, release any of the securities subject to these lock-up agreements at any time. In addition, our executive officers, directors, and holders of our capital stock and securities convertible into or exchangeable for our capital stock have entered into market standoff agreements with us under which they have agreed that, subject to certain exceptions, for a period of 180 days after the date of this prospectus, they will not, without our prior written consent, dispose of or hedge any shares or any securities convertible into or exchangeable for shares of our common stock.

178

In addition, we will enter into a lock-up agreement with the underwriters under which we will agree not to sell any of our stock for 180 days following the date of this prospectus, subject to certain exceptions including, but not limited to, our issuance of shares of common stock or certain other securities in connection with our acquisition of the securities, business, technology, property, or other assets of another person or entity or pursuant to an employee benefit plan that we assumed in connection with such acquisition, or our joint ventures, commercial relationships and other strategic transactions, provided that the aggregate number of shares of Class A common stock (including with respect to securities to be granted pursuant to any assumed employee benefit plans covered by a registration statement on Form S-8) issued pursuant to this exception will not exceed 10% of the total number of shares of Class A common stock outstanding immediately following this offering, and provided that each recipient executes and delivers a lock-up agreement with substantially the same restrictions to which our executive officers, directors, and certain other holders of our capital stock and securities convertible into or exchangeable for our capital stock are subject.

Rule 144

In general, Rule 144 provides that once we have been subject to the public company reporting requirements of Section 13 or Section 15(d) of the Exchange Act for at least 90 days, a person who is not deemed to have been one of our affiliates for purposes of the Securities Act at any time during the 90 days preceding a sale and who has beneficially owned the shares of our Class A common stock proposed to be sold for at least six months is entitled to sell those shares without complying with the manner of sale, volume limitation, or notice provisions of Rule 144, subject to compliance with the public information requirements of Rule 144. If such a person has beneficially owned the shares proposed to be sold for at least one year, including the holding period of any prior owner other than our affiliates, then that person would be entitled to sell those shares without complying with any of the requirements of Rule 144.

In general, Rule 144 provides that our affiliates or persons selling shares of our Class A common stock on behalf of our affiliates are entitled to sell upon expiration of the market standoff agreements and lock-up agreements described above, within any three-month period, a number of shares of our Class A common stock that does not exceed the greater of:

- 1% of the number of shares of our Class A common stock then outstanding, which will equal 530,804 shares immediately after the completion of this offering and the concurrent private placement; or
- the average weekly trading volume of our Class A common stock during the four calendar weeks preceding the filing of a notice on Form 144 with respect to that sale.

Sales of Class A common stock made in reliance upon Rule 144 by our affiliates or persons selling shares of our Class A common stock on behalf of our affiliates are also subject to certain manner of sale provisions and notice requirements and to the availability of current public information about us.

Rule 701

Rule 701 generally allows a stockholder who purchased shares of our capital stock pursuant to a written compensatory plan or contract and who is not deemed to have been an affiliate of our company during the immediately preceding 90 days to sell these shares in reliance upon Rule 144, but without being required to comply with the public information, holding period, volume limitation, or notice provisions of Rule 144. Rule 701 also permits affiliates of our company to sell their Rule 701 shares under Rule 144 without complying with the holding period requirements of Rule 144. All holders of Rule 701 shares, however, are required to wait until 90 days after the date of this prospectus before selling those shares pursuant to Rule 701.

Registration Rights

Pursuant to our IRA, after the completion of this offering and the concurrent private placement, the holders of up to 144,907,822 shares of our Class B common stock and 5,521,778 shares of our Class A common stock,

179

or certain transferees, will be entitled to certain rights with respect to the registration of the offer and sale of those shares, as converted into an equivalent number of shares of our Class A common stock upon such offer and sale, under the Securities Act. See the section titled "Description of Capital Stock—Registration Rights" for a description of these registration rights. If the offer and sale of these shares of our Class A common stock are registered, the shares will be freely tradable without restriction under the Securities Act, subject to the Rule 144 limitations applicable to affiliates, and a large number of shares may be sold into the public market.

Registration Statement

We intend to file a registration statement on Form S-8 under the Securities Act promptly after the completion of this offering to register shares of our common stock subject to RSUs and options outstanding, as well as reserved for future issuance, under our equity compensation plans. The registration statement on Form S-8 is expected to become effective immediately upon filing, and shares of our common stock covered by the registration statement will then become eligible for sale in the public market, subject to the Rule 144 limitations applicable to affiliates, vesting restrictions, and any applicable market standoff agreements and lock-up agreements. See the section titled "Executive Compensation—Employee Benefit and Stock Plans" for a description of our equity compensation plans.

MATERIAL U.S. FEDERAL INCOME TAX CONSEQUENCES TO NON-U.S. HOLDERS OF OUR CLASS A COMMON STOCK

The following is a summary of the material U.S. federal income tax consequences to certain non-U.S. holders (as defined below) of the ownership and disposition of our Class A common stock but does not purport to be a complete analysis of all the potential tax considerations relating thereto. This summary is based upon the provisions of the Internal Revenue Code of 1986, as amended, or the Code, Treasury Regulations promulgated thereunder, administrative rulings, and judicial decisions, all as of the date hereof. These authorities may be changed, possibly retroactively, so as to result in U.S. federal income tax consequences different from those set forth below. No ruling from the Internal Revenue Service, or the IRS, has been, or will be, sought with respect to the tax consequences discussed herein, and there can be no assurance that the IRS will not take a position contrary to the tax consequences discussed below or that any position taken by the IRS would not be sustained.

This summary does not address the tax considerations arising under the laws of any non-U.S., state, or local jurisdiction, or under U.S. federal gift and estate tax laws, except to the limited extent set forth below. In addition, this discussion does not address the application of the Medicare contribution tax on net investment income or any tax considerations applicable to a non-U.S. holder's particular circumstances or non-U.S. holders that may be subject to special tax rules, including, without limitation:

- banks, insurance companies or other financial institutions (except to the extent specifically set forth below), regulated investment companies, or real estate investment trusts;

- persons subject to the alternative minimum tax;

- tax-exempt organizations or governmental organizations;

- controlled foreign corporations, passive foreign investment companies, or corporations that accumulate earnings to avoid U.S. federal income tax;

- brokers or dealers in securities or currencies;

- traders in securities or other persons that elect to use a mark-to-market method of accounting for their holdings in our stock;

- U.S. expatriates or certain former citizens or long-term residents of the United States;

- partnerships or entities classified as partnerships for U.S. federal income tax purposes or other pass-through entities (and investors therein);

- persons who hold our Class A common stock as a position in a hedging transaction, "straddle," "conversion transaction," or other risk reduction transaction or integrated investment;

- persons who hold or receive our Class A common stock pursuant to the exercise of any employee stock option or otherwise as compensation;

- persons who do not hold our Class A common stock as a capital asset within the meaning of Section 1221 of the Code;

- persons deemed to sell our Class A common stock under the constructive sale provisions of the Code;

- persons that own, or are deemed to own, more than five percent of our Class A common stock (except to the extent specifically set forth below); or

- persons that own, or are deemed to own, our Class B common stock.

In addition, if a partnership or entity classified as a partnership for U.S. federal income tax purposes holds our Class A common stock, the tax treatment of a partner generally will depend on the status of the partner and upon the activities of the partnership. Accordingly, partnerships that hold our Class A common stock, and partners in such partnerships, should consult their tax advisors.

You are urged to consult your tax advisor with respect to the application of the U.S. federal income tax laws to your particular situation, as well as any tax consequences of the acquisition, ownership, and disposition of our common stock arising under the U.S. federal estate or gift tax rules, under the laws of any state, local, non-U.S., or other taxing jurisdiction, or under any applicable tax treaty.

Non-U.S. Holder Defined

For purposes of this discussion, you are a non-U.S. holder if you are a holder of our common stock that is not a partnership (or entity or arrangement treated as a partnership for U.S. federal income tax purposes) and is not any of the following:

- an individual who is a citizen or resident of the United States (for U.S. federal income tax purposes);

- a corporation or other entity taxable as a corporation created or organized in the United States or under the laws of the United States or any political subdivision thereof or other entity treated as such for U.S. federal income tax purposes;

- an estate whose income is subject to U.S. federal income tax regardless of its source; or

- a trust (x) whose administration is subject to the primary supervision of a U.S. court and which has one or more "U.S. persons" (within the meaning of Section 7701(a)(3) of the Code) who have the authority to control all substantial decisions of the trust or (y) which has made a valid election to be treated as a U.S. person.

Distributions

As described in the section titled "Dividend Policy," we have never declared or paid cash dividends on our capital stock and do not anticipate paying any dividends on our capital stock in the foreseeable future. However, if we do make distributions on our Class A common stock, those payments will constitute dividends for U.S. tax purposes to the extent paid from our current or accumulated earnings and profits, as determined under U.S. federal income tax principles. To the extent those distributions exceed both our current and our accumulated earnings and profits, they will constitute a return of capital and will first reduce your basis in our Class A common stock, but not below zero, and then will be treated as gain from the sale of stock as described below under "—Gain on Disposition of Our Class A Common Stock."

Except as otherwise described below in the discussions of effectively connected income (in the next paragraph), backup withholding and FATCA, any dividend paid to you generally will be subject to U.S. withholding tax either at a rate of 30% of the gross amount of the dividend or such lower rate as may be specified by an applicable income tax treaty. In order to receive a reduced treaty rate, you must provide us with an IRS Form W-8BEN, IRS Form W-8BEN-E, or other appropriate version of IRS Form W-8, including any required attachments and your taxpayer identification number, certifying qualification for the reduced rate; additionally you will be required to update such Forms and certifications from time to time as required by law. A non-U.S. holder of shares of our Class A common stock eligible for a reduced rate of U.S. withholding tax pursuant to an income tax treaty may obtain a refund of any excess amounts withheld by timely filing an appropriate claim for refund with the IRS. If the non-U.S. holder holds the stock through a financial institution or other agent acting on the non-U.S. holder's behalf, the non-U.S. holder will be required to provide appropriate documentation to the agent, which then will be required to provide certification to us or our paying agent, either directly or through other intermediaries. Non-U.S. holders should consult their tax advisors regarding their entitlement to benefits under an applicable income tax treaty.

Dividends received by you that are effectively connected with your conduct of a U.S. trade or business (and, if required by an applicable income tax treaty, attributable to a permanent establishment maintained by you in the United States) are generally exempt from such withholding tax. In order to obtain this exemption, you must provide us with an IRS Form W-8ECI or other applicable IRS Form W-8, including any required attachments

182

and your taxpayer identification number; additionally you will be required to update such forms and certifications from time to time as required by law. Such effectively connected dividends, although not subject to withholding tax, are includable on your U.S. income tax return and generally taxed to you at the same graduated rates applicable to U.S. persons, net of certain deductions and credits. If you are a corporate non-U.S. holder, dividends you receive that are effectively connected with your conduct of a U.S. trade or business may also be subject to a branch profits tax at a rate of 30% or such lower rate as may be specified by an applicable income tax treaty. You should consult your tax advisor regarding any applicable tax treaties that may provide for different rules.

Gain on Disposition of Our Class A Common Stock

Except as otherwise described below in the discussions of backup withholding and FATCA, you generally will not be subject to U.S. federal income tax on any gain realized upon the sale or other disposition of our Class A common stock unless:

- the gain is effectively connected with your conduct of a U.S. trade or business (and, if required by an applicable income tax treaty, the gain is attributable to a permanent establishment maintained by you in the United States);

- you are a non-resident alien individual who is present in the United States for a period or periods aggregating 183 days or more during the calendar year in which the sale or disposition occurs, and other conditions are met; or

- our Class A common stock constitutes a United States real property interest by reason of our status as a "United States real property holding corporation," or USRPHC, for U.S. federal income tax purposes at any time within the shorter of the five-year period preceding your disposition of, or your holding period for, our Class A common stock, and, in the case where shares of our Class A common stock are regularly traded on an established securities market, you own, or are treated as owning, more than 5% of our Class A common stock at any time during the foregoing period.

Generally, a corporation is a "United States real property holding corporation" if the fair market value of its United States real property interests equals or exceeds 50% of the sum of the fair market value of its worldwide real property interests and its other assets used or held for use in a trade or business (all as determined for United States federal income tax purposes). We believe that we are not currently and will not become a USRPHC for U.S. federal income tax purposes, and the remainder of this discussion assumes this is the case. However, because the determination of whether we are a USRPHC depends on the fair market value of our U.S. real property relative to the fair market value of our other business assets, there can be no assurance that we will not become a USRPHC in the future. Even if we become a USRPHC, however, as long as our Class A common stock is regularly traded on an established securities market, such Class A common stock will be treated as U.S. real property interests only if you actually or constructively hold more than 5% of such regularly traded Class A common stock at any time during the shorter of the five-year period preceding your disposition of, or your holding period for, our Class A common stock. No assurance can be provided that our Class A common stock will be regularly traded on an established securities market at all times for purposes of the rules described above.

If you are a non-U.S. holder described in the first bullet above, you will generally be required to pay tax on the net gain derived from the sale under regular graduated U.S. federal income tax rates (and a corporate non-U.S. holder described in the first bullet above also may be subject to the branch profits tax at a 30% rate), unless otherwise provided by an applicable income tax treaty. If you are a non-U.S. holder described in the second bullet above, you will generally be required to pay a flat 30% tax (or such lower rate specified by an applicable income tax treaty) on the gain derived from the sale, which gain may be offset by U.S. source capital losses for the year (provided you have timely filed U.S. federal income tax returns with respect to such losses). You should consult your tax advisor with respect to whether any applicable income tax or other treaties may provide for different rules.

183

Federal Estate Tax

Our Class A common stock beneficially owned by an individual who is not a citizen or resident of the United States (as defined for U.S. federal estate tax purposes) at the time of their death will generally be includable in the decedent's gross estate for U.S. federal estate tax purposes, unless an applicable estate tax treaty provides otherwise.

Backup Withholding and Information Reporting

Generally, we must report annually to the IRS the amount of dividends paid to you, your name and address, and the amount of tax withheld, if any. A similar report will be sent to you. Pursuant to applicable income tax treaties or other agreements, the IRS may make these reports available to tax authorities in your country of residence.

Payments of dividends or of proceeds on the disposition of stock made to you may be subject to information reporting and backup withholding at a current rate of 28% unless you establish an exemption, for example, by properly certifying your non-U.S. status on an IRS Form W-8BEN, IRS Form W-8BEN-E, or another appropriate version of IRS Form W-8. Notwithstanding the foregoing, backup withholding and information reporting may apply if either we our paying agent has actual knowledge, or reason to know, that you are a United States person as defined under the Code.

Backup withholding is not an additional tax; rather, the U.S. federal income tax liability of persons subject to backup withholding will be reduced by the amount of tax withheld. If withholding results in an overpayment of taxes, a refund or credit may generally be obtained from the IRS, provided that the required information is furnished to the IRS in a timely manner.

FATCA

The Foreign Account Tax Compliance Act and the rules and regulations promulgated thereunder, or collectively, FATCA, generally impose withholding tax at a rate of 30% on dividends on and gross proceeds from the sale or other disposition of our Class A common stock paid to "foreign financial institutions" (as specially defined under these rules), unless such institution enters into an agreement with the U.S. government to withhold on certain payments and to collect and provide to the U.S. tax authorities substantial information regarding the U.S. account holders of such institution (which includes certain equity and debt holders of such institution, as well as certain account holders that are foreign entities with U.S. owners) or otherwise establishes an exemption. FATCA also generally imposes a U.S. federal withholding tax of 30% on dividends on and gross proceeds from the sale or other disposition of our Class A common stock paid to a "non-financial foreign entities" (as specially defined under these rules) unless such entity provides the withholding agent with a certification identifying certain substantial direct and indirect U.S. owners of the entity, certifies that there are none, or otherwise establishes and certifies to an exemption. The withholding provisions under FATCA generally apply to dividends on our Class A common stock, and under current transition rules, are expected to apply with respect to the gross proceeds from the sale or other disposition of our Class A common stock on or after January 1, 2019. An intergovernmental agreement between the United States and your country of tax residence may modify the requirements described in this paragraph. If a dividend payment is both subject to withholding under FATCA and subject to the withholding tax discussed above under "—Distributions," the withholding under FATCA may be credited against, and therefore reduce, such other withholding tax. Non-U.S. holders should consult their own tax advisors regarding the possible implications of FATCA on their investment in our Class A common stock.

Each prospective investor should consult its own tax advisor regarding the particular U.S. federal, state, and local, and non-U.S. tax consequences of purchasing, holding, and disposing of our common stock, including the consequences of any proposed change in applicable laws.

184

UNDERWRITING (CONFLICTS OF INTEREST)

We, the selling stockholders and the underwriters named below will enter into an underwriting agreement with respect to the shares being offered. Subject to certain conditions, each underwriter will severally agree to purchase the number of shares indicated in the following table. Goldman Sachs & Co. LLC and J.P. Morgan Securities LLC are the representatives of the underwriters.

Underwriters	Number of shares
Goldman Sachs & Co. LLC	
J.P. Morgan Securities LLC	
Deutsche Bank Securities Inc.	
Allen & Company LLC	
Merrill Lynch, Pierce, Fenner & Smith Incorporated	
RBC Capital Markets, LLC	
Jefferies LLC	
Macquarie Capital (USA) Inc.	
Canaccord Genuity LLC	
JMP Securities LLC	
KeyBanc Capital Markets Inc.	
Piper Jaffray & Co.	
Total	36,000,000

The underwriters will be committed to take and pay for all of the shares being offered, if any are taken, other than the shares covered by the option described below, unless and until this option is exercised.

The underwriters will have an option to buy up to an additional 5,400,000 shares from us to cover sales by the underwriters of a greater number of shares than the total number set forth in the table above. They may exercise that option for 30 days. If any shares are purchased pursuant to this option, the underwriters will severally purchase shares in approximately the same proportion as set forth in the table above.

The following tables show the per share and total underwriting discounts and commissions to be paid to the underwriters by us and the selling stockholders. Such amounts are shown assuming both no exercise and full exercise of the underwriters' option to purchase 5,400,000 additional shares.

Paid by us

	No exercise	Full exercise
Per share	$	$
Total	$	$

Paid by the selling stockholders

	No exercise	Full exercise
Per share	$	$
Total	$	$

Shares sold by the underwriters to the public will initially be offered at the initial public offering price set forth on the cover of this prospectus. Any shares sold by the underwriters to securities dealers may be sold at a discount of up to $ per share from the initial public offering price. After the initial offering of the shares,

185

the representatives may change the offering price and the other selling terms. The offering of the shares by the underwriters is subject to receipt and acceptance and subject to the underwriters' right to reject any order in whole or in part.

Our executive officers, directors, and certain other holders of our capital stock and securities convertible into or exchangeable for our capital stock have agreed that, subject to certain exceptions, for a period of 180 days after the date of this prospectus, or lock-up period, they will not, without the prior written consent of Goldman Sachs & Co. LLC and J.P. Morgan Securities LLC, dispose of or hedge any shares or any securities convertible into or exchangeable for shares of our capital stock; provided that if (i) at least 120 days have elapsed since the date of this prospectus, (ii) we have publicly released our earnings results for the quarterly period during which this offering occurred, and (iii) such lock-up period is scheduled to end during or within five trading days prior to a blackout period, such lock-up period will end ten trading days prior to the commencement of such blackout period. In addition, we will enter into a lock-up agreement with the underwriters under which we will agree not to sell any of our stock for 180 days following the date of this prospectus, subject to certain exceptions including, but not limited to, our issuance of shares of common stock or certain other securities in connection with our acquisition of the securities, business, technology, property, or other assets of another person or entity or pursuant to an employee benefit plan that we assumed in connection with such acquisition, or our joint ventures, commercial relationships, and other strategic transactions, provided that the aggregate number of shares of Class A common stock (including with respect to securities to be granted pursuant to any assumed employee benefit plans covered by a registration statement on Form S-8) issued pursuant to this exception will not exceed 10% of the total number of shares of Class A common stock outstanding immediately following this offering, and provided that each recipient executes and delivers a lock-up agreement with substantially the same restrictions to which our executive officers, directors, and certain holders of our capital stock and securities convertible into or exchangeable for our capital stock are subject. Goldman Sachs & Co. LLC and J.P. Morgan Securities LLC may, in their discretion, release any of the securities subject to these lock-up agreements at any time. See "Shares Available for Future Sale" for a discussion of certain transfer restrictions, including market standoff agreements between us and each of our executive officers, directors, and holders of our capital stock and securities convertible into or exchangeable for our capital stock.

Prior to the offering, there has been no public market for the shares. The initial public offering price has been negotiated among us, the selling stockholders, and the representatives. Among the factors to be considered in determining the initial public offering price of the shares, in addition to prevailing market conditions, will be our historical performance, estimates of our business potential and earnings prospects, an assessment of our management, and the consideration of the above factors in relation to market valuation of companies in related businesses.

We have been approved to list our Class A common stock on the Nasdaq Global Select Market under the symbol "DBX".

In connection with the offering, the underwriters may purchase and sell shares of Class A common stock in the open market. These transactions may include short sales, stabilizing transactions, and purchases to cover positions created by short sales. Short sales involve the sale by the underwriters of a greater number of shares than they are required to purchase in the offering, and a short position represents the amount of such sales that have not been covered by subsequent purchases. A "covered short position" is a short position that is not greater than the amount of additional shares for which the underwriters' option described above may be exercised. The underwriters may cover any covered short position by either exercising their option to purchase additional shares or purchasing shares in the open market. In determining the source of shares to cover the covered short position, the underwriters will consider, among other things, the price of shares available for purchase in the open market as compared to the price at which they may purchase additional shares pursuant to the option described above. "Naked" short sales are any short sales that create a short position greater than the amount of additional shares for which the option described above may be exercised. The underwriters must cover any such naked short position by purchasing shares in the open market. A naked short position is more likely to be created if the

186

underwriters are concerned that there may be downward pressure on the price of the Class A common stock in the open market after pricing that could adversely affect investors who purchase in the offering. Stabilizing transactions consist of various bids for or purchases of common stock made by the underwriters in the open market prior to the completion of the offering.

The underwriters may also impose a penalty bid. This occurs when a particular underwriter repays to the underwriters a portion of the underwriting discount received by it because the representatives have repurchased shares sold by or for the account of such underwriter in stabilizing or short covering transactions.

Purchases to cover a short position and stabilizing transactions, as well as other purchases by the underwriters for their own accounts, may have the effect of preventing or retarding a decline in the market price of our stock, and together with the imposition of the penalty bid, may stabilize, maintain, or otherwise affect the market price of the common stock. As a result, the price of our Class A common stock may be higher than the price that otherwise might exist in the open market. The underwriters are not required to engage in these activities and may end any of these activities at any time. These transactions may be effected on Nasdaq, in the over-the-counter market or otherwise

The underwriters do not expect sales to discretionary accounts to exceed five percent of the total number of shares of Class A common stock offered.

We and the selling stockholders estimate that our share of the total expenses of the offering, excluding underwriting discounts and commissions, will be approximately $7.0 million. The underwriters have agreed to reimburse us, or will pay and not seek reimbursement from us, for certain expenses incurred by us in connection with this offering.

We and the selling stockholders have agreed to indemnify the several underwriters against certain liabilities, including liabilities under the Securities Act of 1933. In addition, we and the selling stockholders have agreed to reimburse the underwriters for certain expenses in connection with this offering.

The underwriters and their respective affiliates are full service financial institutions engaged in various activities, which may include sales and trading, commercial and investment banking, advisory, investment management, investment research, principal investment, hedging, market making, brokerage, and other financial and non-financial activities and services. Certain of the underwriters and their respective affiliates have provided, and may in the future provide, a variety of these services to the issuer and to persons and entities with relationships with the issuer, for which they received or will receive customary fees and expenses. In 2014, we entered into a revolving credit agreement with affiliates of Goldman Sachs & Co. LLC, J.P. Morgan Securities LLC, Deutsche Bank Securities Inc., Merrill Lynch, Pierce, Fenner & Smith Incorporated, RBC Capital Markets, LLC, and Macquarie Capital (USA) Inc., under which these underwriters and their respective affiliates have been, and may be in the future, paid customary fees. For additional information on our revolving credit facility, see the section titled "Management's Discussion and Analysis of Financial Condition and Results of Operations—Liquidity and Capital Resources."

In September 2011, affiliates of Goldman Sachs & Co. LLC, one of the underwriters, purchased an aggregate of 1,837,199 shares of our Series B Preferred Stock, all of which shares will automatically convert into an aggregate of 1,837,199 shares of Class B common stock in connection with this offering. In November 2011, Allen & Company LLC, one of the underwriters, and certain of its affiliates and employees purchased an aggregate of 184,180 shares of our Series B preferred stock, which shares will automatically convert into an aggregate of 184,180 shares of Class B common stock in connection with this offering.

Pursuant to the concurrent private placement, Salesforce Ventures LLC will purchase from us in a private placement $100.0 million of our Class A common stock at a price per share equal to the initial public offering price. Based on an assumed initial public offering price of $19.00 per share, which is the midpoint of the estimated offering price range set forth on the cover page of this prospectus, this would be 5,263,158 shares.

187

Goldman Sachs & Co. LLC, J.P. Morgan Securities LLC, Deutsche Bank Securities Inc., Merrill Lynch, Pierce, Fenner & Smith Incorporated, Allen & Company LLC, RBC Capital Markets, LLC, Jefferies LLC, and Canaccord Genuity LLC, or certain of their respective affiliates beneficially own shares of salesforce.com, inc. As a result of this ownership, these underwriters would be deemed to beneficially own 192,106 shares of our Class A common stock. These shares of Class A common stock would be deemed underwriting compensation pursuant to FINRA Rule 5110, but meet an exception to the lock-up restriction pursuant to FINRA Rule 5110(g)(2)(A)(iii).

In addition, certain of our employees who are considered associated persons of some of the underwriters have been granted RSUs as part of our ordinary course employee compensation practices. These grants are deemed to be underwriting compensation pursuant to FINRA Rule 5110.

In the ordinary course of their various business activities, the underwriters and their respective affiliates, officers, directors, and employees may purchase, sell, or hold a broad array of investments and actively trade securities, derivatives, loans, commodities, currencies, credit default swaps, and other financial instruments for their own account and for the accounts of their customers, and such investment and trading activities may involve or relate to assets, securities, and/or instruments of the issuer (directly, as collateral securing other obligations or otherwise), and/or persons and entities with relationships with the issuer. The underwriters and their respective affiliates may also communicate independent investment recommendations, market color or trading ideas and/or publish or express independent research views in respect of such assets, securities, or instruments and may at any time hold, or recommend to clients that they should acquire, long, and/or short positions in such assets, securities and instruments.

Affiliates of Goldman Sachs & Co. LLC, J.P. Morgan Securities LLC, Deutsche Bank Securities Inc., and Merrill Lynch, Pierce, Fenner & Smith Incorporated, underwriters in this offering, will receive at least 5% of the net proceeds of this offering in connection with the repayment of $193.1 million that is expected to be outstanding immediately prior to the completion of this offering under our revolving credit facility. See "Use of Proceeds." Accordingly, this offering is being made in compliance with the requirements of FINRA Rule 5121. This rule requires, among other things, that a "qualified independent underwriter" has participated in the preparation of, and has exercised the usual standards of "due diligence" with respect to, the registration statement. Allen & Company LLC has agreed to act as qualified independent underwriter for this offering and to undertake the legal responsibilities and liabilities of an underwriter under the Securities Act. Allen & Company LLC will not receive any additional fees for serving as qualified independent underwriter in connection with this offering. We have agreed to indemnify Allen & Company LLC against liabilities incurred in connection with acting as qualified independent underwriter, including liabilities under the Securities Act. Pursuant to FINRA Rule 5121, Goldman Sachs & Co. LLC, J.P. Morgan Securities LLC, Deutsche Bank Securities Inc., and Merrill Lynch, Pierce, Fenner & Smith Incorporated will not confirm sales of securities to any account over which it exercises discretionary authority without the prior written approval of the customer.

European Economic Area

In relation to each Member State of the European Economic Area which has implemented the Prospectus Directive (each, a Relevant Member State), with effect from and including the date on which the Prospectus Directive is implemented in that Relevant Member State, no offer of shares of Class A common stock which are the subject of the offering contemplated by this prospectus may be made to the public in that Relevant Member State other than:

(a) to any legal entity which is a "qualified investor" as defined in the Prospectus Directive;

(b) to fewer than 150 natural or legal persons (other than "qualified investors" as defined in the Prospectus Directive), per Relevant Member State, subject to obtaining the prior consent of the underwriters; or

(c) in any other circumstances falling within Article 3(2) of the Prospectus Directive,

provided that no such offer of shares of our Class A common stock shall result in a requirement for us or any underwriter to publish a prospectus pursuant to Article 3 of the Prospectus Directive or a supplemental prospectus pursuant to Article 16 of the Prospectus Directive and each person who initially acquires any shares of our Class A common stock or to whom any offer is made will be deemed to have represented, warranted, and

188

agreed to and with each of the underwriters and us that it is a "qualified investor" within the meaning of the law in that Relevant Member State implementing Article 2(1)(e) of the Prospectus Directive.

For the purposes of this provision, the expression an "offer of shares to the public" in relation to any shares of our Class A common stock in any Relevant Member State means the communication in any form and by any means of sufficient information on the terms of the offer and the shares of our Class A common stock to be offered so as to enable an investor to decide to purchase or subscribe for the shares of our Class A common stock, as the same may be varied in that Relevant Member State by any measure implementing the Prospectus Directive in that Relevant Member State. The expression "Prospectus Directive" means Directive 2003/71/EC (as amended, including by Directive 2010/73/EU), and includes any relevant implementing measure in the Relevant Member State.

United Kingdom

In the United Kingdom, this prospectus in relation to the shares of Class A common stock described herein is being directed only at persons who are "qualified investors" (as defined in the Prospectus Directive) who are (i) persons having professional experience in matters relating to investments falling within Article 19(5) of the Financial Services and Markets Act 2000 Order 2005, or (ii) high net worth entities falling within Article 49(2)(a) to (d) of the Order, or (iii) persons to whom it would otherwise be lawful to distribute it, all such persons together being referred to as "Relevant Persons." The shares of Class A common stock described herein are only available to, and any invitation, offer, or agreement to subscribe, purchase, or otherwise acquire such shares of Class A common stock will be engaged in only with, Relevant Persons. This prospectus and its contents are confidential and should not be distributed, published, or reproduced (in whole or in part), or disclosed by any recipients to any other person in the United Kingdom. Any person in the United Kingdom that is not a Relevant Person should not act or rely on this prospectus or its contents.

Canada

The shares of Class A common stock may be sold in Canada only to purchasers purchasing, or deemed to be purchasing, as principal that are accredited investors, as defined in National Instrument 45-106 Prospectus Exemptions or subsection 73.3(1) of the Securities Act (Ontario), and are permitted clients, as defined in National Instrument 31-103 Registration Requirements, Exemptions, and Ongoing Registrant Obligations. Any resale of the shares of Class A common stock must be made in accordance with an exemption form, or in a transaction not subject to, the prospectus requirements of applicable securities laws.

Securities legislation in certain provinces or territories of Canada may provide a purchaser with remedies for rescission or damages if this offering memorandum (including any amendment thereto) contains a misrepresentation, provided that the remedies for rescission or damages are exercised by the purchaser within the time limit prescribed by the securities legislation of the purchaser's province or territory. The purchaser should refer to any applicable provisions of the securities legislation of the purchaser's province or territory of these rights or consult with a legal advisor.

Pursuant to section 3A.3 of National Instrument 33-105 Underwriting Conflicts (NI 33-105), the underwriters are not required to comply with the disclosure requirements of NI 33-105 regarding underwriter conflicts of interest in connection with this offering.

Hong Kong

The shares of Class A common stock may not be offered or sold in Hong Kong by means of any document other than (i) in circumstances which do not constitute an offer to the public within the meaning of the Companies (Winding Up and Miscellaneous Provisions) Ordinance (Cap. 32 of the Laws of Hong Kong), or Companies (Winding Up and Miscellaneous Provisions) Ordinance, or which do not constitute an invitation to the public within the meaning of the Securities and Futures Ordinance (Cap. 571 of the Laws of Hong Kong), or

189

Securities and Futures Ordinance, or (ii) to "professional investors" as defined in the Securities and Futures Ordinance and any rules made thereunder, or (iii) in other circumstances which do not result in the document being a "prospectus" as defined in the Companies (Winding Up and Miscellaneous Provisions) Ordinance, and no advertisement, invitation, or document relating to the shares of Class A common stock may be issued or may be in the possession of any person for the purpose of issue (in each case whether in Hong Kong or elsewhere), which is directed at, or the contents of which are likely to be accessed or read by, the public in Hong Kong (except if permitted to do so under the laws of Hong Kong) other than with respect to shares of Class A common stock which are or are intended to be disposed of only to persons outside Hong Kong or only to "professional investors" in Hong Kong within the meaning of the Securities and Futures Ordinance and any rules made thereunder.

Singapore

This prospectus has not been registered as a prospectus with the Monetary Authority of Singapore. Accordingly, this prospectus and any other document or material in connection with the offer or sale, or invitation for subscription or purchase, of the shares of Class A common stock may not be circulated or distributed, nor may the shares of Class A common stock be offered or sold or be made the subject of an invitation for subscription or purchase, whether directly or indirectly, to persons in Singapore other than (i) to an institutional investor under Section 274 of the Securities and Futures Act, Chapter 289 of Singapore, or the SFA, (ii) to a relevant person, or any person pursuant to Section 275(1A), and in accordance with the conditions, specified in Section 275 of the SFA, or (iii) otherwise pursuant to, and in accordance with the conditions of, any other applicable provision of the SFA.

Where the shares of Class A common stock are subscribed or purchased under Section 275 by a relevant person which is: (a) a corporation (which is not an accredited investor) the sole business of which is to hold investments and the entire share capital of which is owned by one or more individuals, each of whom is an accredited investor; or (b) a trust (where the trustee is not an accredited investor) whose sole purpose is to hold investments and each beneficiary is an accredited investor, shares, debentures, and units of shares and debentures of that corporation or the beneficiaries' rights and interest in that trust shall not be transferable for six months after that corporation or that trust has acquired the shares of Class A common stock under Section 275 except: (1) to an institutional investor under Section 274 of the SFA or to a relevant person, or any person pursuant to Section 275(1A), and in accordance with the conditions, specified in Section 275 of the SFA; (2) where no consideration is given for the transfer; or (3) by operation of law.

Japan

The securities have not been and will not be registered under the Financial Instruments and Exchange Law of Japan, or the Financial Instruments and Exchange Law, and the securities may not be offered or sold, directly or indirectly, in Japan or to, or for the benefit of, any resident of Japan (which term as used herein means any person resident in Japan, including any corporation or other entity organized under the laws of Japan), or to others for re-offering or resale, directly or indirectly, in Japan or to a resident of Japan, except pursuant to an exemption from the registration requirements of, and otherwise in compliance with, the Financial Instruments and Exchange Law and any other applicable laws, regulations, and ministerial guidelines of Japan.

Switzerland

The shares of Class A common stock may not be publicly offered in Switzerland and will not be listed on the SIX Swiss Exchange, or SIX, or on any other stock exchange or regulated trading facility in Switzerland. This document does not constitute a prospectus within the meaning of, and has been prepared without regard to the disclosure standards for issuance prospectuses under art. 652a or art. 1156 of the Swiss Code of Obligations or the disclosure standards for listing prospectuses under art. 27 ff. of the SIX Listing Rules or the listing rules of any other stock exchange or regulated trading facility in Switzerland. Neither this document nor any other

190

278

offering or marketing material relating to the shares of Class A common stock or the offering may be publicly distributed or otherwise made publicly available in Switzerland.

Neither this document nor any other offering or marketing material relating to the offering, the Company, or the shares of Class A common stock have been or will be filed with or approved by any Swiss regulatory authority. In particular, this document will not be filed with, and the offer of shares of Class A common stock will not be supervised by, the Swiss Financial Market Supervisory Authority FINMA, or FINMA, and the offer of shares of Class A common stock has not been and will not be authorized under the Swiss Federal Act on Collective Investment Schemes, or CISA. The investor protection afforded to acquirers of interests in collective investment schemes under the CISA does not extend to acquirers of the shares of Class A common stock.

Dubai International Financial Centre

This document relates to an Exempt Offer in accordance with the Markets Rules 2012 of the Dubai Financial Services Authority, or DFSA. This document is intended for distribution only to persons of a type specified in the Markets Rules 2012 of the DFSA. It must not be delivered to, or relied on by, any other person. The DFSA has no responsibility for reviewing or verifying any documents in connection with Exempt Offers. The DFSA has not approved this prospectus supplement nor taken steps to verify the information set forth herein and has no responsibility for this document. The securities to which this document relates may be illiquid and/or subject to restrictions on their resale. Prospective purchasers of the securities offered should conduct their own due diligence on the securities. If you do not understand the contents of this document you should consult an authorized financial advisor.

In relation to its use in the Dubai International Financial Centre, or DIFC, this document is strictly private and confidential and is being distributed to a limited number of investors and must not be provided to any person other than the original recipient, and may not be reproduced or used for any other purpose. The interests in the securities may not be offered or sold, directly or indirectly, to the public in the DIFC.

United Arab Emirates

The shares of Class A common stock have not been, and are not being, publicly offered, sold, promoted, or advertised in the United Arab Emirates (including the Dubai International Financial Centre) other than in compliance with the laws of the United Arab Emirates (and the Dubai International Financial Centre) governing the issue, offering and sale of securities. Further, this prospectus does not constitute a public offer of securities in the United Arab Emirates (including the Dubai International Financial Centre) and is not intended to be a public offer. This prospectus has not been approved by or filed with the Central Bank of the United Arab Emirates, the Securities and Commodities Authority, or the Dubai Financial Services Authority.

Australia

This prospectus:

- does not constitute a product disclosure document or a prospectus under Chapter 6D.2 of the Corporations Act 2001 (Cth), or the Corporations Act;

- has not been, and will not be, lodged with the Australian Securities and Investments Commission, or ASIC, as a disclosure document for the purposes of the Corporations Act and does not purport to include the information required of a disclosure document under Chapter 6D.2 of the Corporations Act;

- does not constitute or involve a recommendation to acquire, an offer or invitation for issue or sale, an offer or invitation to arrange the issue or sale, or an issue or sale, of interests to a "retail client" (as defined in section 761G of the Corporations Act and applicable regulations) in Australia; and

- may only be provided in Australia to select investors who are able to demonstrate that they fall within one or more of the categories of investors, or Exempt Investors, available under section 708 of the Corporations Act.

191

279

The shares of Class A common stock may not be directly or indirectly offered for subscription or purchased or sold, and no invitations to subscribe for or buy the shares of Class A common stock may be issued, and no draft or definitive offering memorandum, advertisement, or other offering material relating to any shares of Class A common stock may be distributed in Australia, except where disclosure to investors is not required under Chapter 6D of the Corporations Act or is otherwise in compliance with all applicable Australian laws and regulations. By submitting an application for the shares of Class A common stock, you represent and warrant to us that you are an Exempt Investor.

As any offer of shares of Class A common stock under this document will be made without disclosure in Australia under Chapter 6D.2 of the Corporations Act, the offer of those securities for resale in Australia within 12 months may, under section 707 of the Corporations Act, require disclosure to investors under Chapter 6D.2 if none of the exemptions in section 708 applies to that resale. By applying for the shares of Class A common stock you undertake to us that you will not, for a period of 12 months from the date of issue of the shares of Class A common stock, offer, transfer, assign, or otherwise alienate those securities to investors in Australia except in circumstances where disclosure to investors is not required under Chapter 6D.2 of the Corporations Act or where a compliant disclosure document is prepared and lodged with ASIC.

Bermuda

The shares of Class A common stock may be offered or sold in Bermuda only in compliance with the provisions of the Investment Business Act of 2003 of Bermuda which regulates the sale of securities in Bermuda. Additionally, non-Bermudian persons (including companies) may not carry on or engage in any trade or business in Bermuda unless such persons are permitted to do so under applicable Bermuda legislation.

Saudi Arabia

This document may not be distributed in the Kingdom of Saudi Arabia except to such persons as are permitted under the Offers of Securities Regulations as issued by the board of the Saudi Arabian Capital Market Authority, or CMA, pursuant to resolution number 2-11-2004 dated 4 October 2004 as amended by resolution number 1-28-2008, as amended, or the CMA Regulations. The CMA does not make any representation as to the accuracy or completeness of this document and expressly disclaims any liability whatsoever for any loss arising from, or incurred in reliance upon, any part of this document. Prospective purchasers of the securities offered hereby should conduct their own due diligence on the accuracy of the information relating to the securities. If you do not understand the contents of this document, you should consult an authorized financial adviser.

British Virgin Islands

This prospectus has not been, and will not be, registered with the Financial Services Commission of the British Virgin Islands. No registered prospectus has been or will be prepared in respect of the shares of Class A common stock for the purposes of the Securities and Investment Business Act, 2010, or SIBA, or the Public Issuers Code of the British Virgin Islands.

The shares of Class A common stock may be offered to persons located in the British Virgin Islands who are "qualified investors" for the purposes of SIBA. Qualified investors include (i) certain entities which are regulated by the Financial Services Commission in the British Virgin Islands, including banks, insurance companies, licensees under SIBA, and public, professional, and private mutual funds; (ii) a company, any securities of which are listed on a recognised exchange; and (iii) persons defined as "professional investors" under SIBA, which is any person (a) whose ordinary business involves, whether for that person's own account or the account of others, the acquisition or disposal of property of the same kind as the property, or a substantial part of the property of the Company; or (b) who has signed a declaration that he, whether individually or jointly with his spouse, has net worth in excess of US$1,000,000 and that he consents to being treated as a professional investor.

192

China

This prospectus does not constitute a public offer of shares of Class A common stock, whether by sale or subscription, in the People's Republic of China, or the PRC. The shares of Class A common stock are not being offered or sold, directly or indirectly, in the PRC to or for the benefit of, legal or natural persons of the PRC.

Further, no legal or natural persons of the PRC may directly or indirectly purchase any of the shares of Class A common stock or any beneficial interest therein without obtaining all prior PRC's governmental approvals that are required, whether statutorily or otherwise. Persons who come into possession of this document are required by the issuer and its representatives to observe these restrictions.

Korea

The shares of Class A common stock have not been and will not be registered under the Financial Investments Services and Capital Markets Act of Korea and the decrees and regulations thereunder, or the FSCMA, and the shares of Class A common stock have been and will be offered in Korea as a private placement under the FSCMA. None of the shares of Class A common stock may be offered, sold, or delivered, directly or indirectly, or offered or sold to any person for re-offering or resale, directly or indirectly, in Korea or to any resident of Korea except pursuant to the applicable laws and regulations of Korea, including the FSCMA and the Foreign Exchange Transaction Law of Korea and the decrees and regulations thereunder, or the FETL. Furthermore, the purchaser of the shares of Class A common stock shall comply with all applicable regulatory requirements (including but not limited to requirements under the FETL) in connection with the purchase of the shares of Class A common stock. By the purchase of the shares of Class A common stock, the relevant holder thereof will be deemed to represent and warrant that if it is in Korea or is a resident of Korea, it purchased the shares of Class A common stock pursuant to the applicable laws and regulations of Korea.

Malaysia

No prospectus or other offering material or document in connection with the offer and sale of the shares of Class A common stock has been or will be registered with the Securities Commission of Malaysia, or Commission, for the Commission's approval pursuant to the Capital Markets and Services Act 2007. Accordingly, this prospectus and any other document or material in connection with the offer or sale, or invitation for subscription or purchase, of the shares of Class A common stock may not be circulated or distributed, nor may the shares of Class A common stock be offered or sold, or be made the subject of an invitation for subscription or purchase, whether directly or indirectly, to persons in Malaysia other than (i) a closed end fund approved by the Commission; (ii) a holder of a Capital Markets Services Licence; (iii) a person who acquires the shares of Class A common stock, as principal, if the offer is on terms that the shares of Class A common stock may only be acquired at a consideration of not less than RM250,000 (or its equivalent in foreign currencies) for each transaction; (iv) an individual whose total net personal assets or total net joint assets with his or her spouse exceeds RM3 million (or its equivalent in foreign currencies), excluding the value of the primary residence of the individual; (v) an individual who has a gross annual income exceeding RM300,000 (or its equivalent in foreign currencies) per annum in the preceding twelve months; (vi) an individual who, jointly with his or her spouse, has a gross annual income of RM400,000 (or its equivalent in foreign currencies), per annum in the preceding twelve months; (vii) a corporation with total net assets exceeding RM10 million (or its equivalent in a foreign currencies) based on the last audited accounts; (viii) a partnership with total net assets exceeding RM10 million (or its equivalent in foreign currencies); (ix) a bank licensee or insurance licensee as defined in the Labuan Financial Services and Securities Act 2010; (x) an Islamic bank licensee or takaful licensee as defined in the Labuan Financial Services and Securities Act 2010; and (xi) any other person as may be specified by the Commission; provided that, in the each of the preceding categories (i) to (xi), the distribution of the shares of Class A common stock is made by a holder of a Capital Markets Services Licence who carries on the business of dealing in securities. The distribution in Malaysia of this prospectus is subject to Malaysian laws. This prospectus does not constitute and may not be used for the purpose of public offering or an issue, offer for subscription or purchase, or invitation to subscribe for or purchase any securities requiring the registration of a prospectus with the Commission under the Capital Markets and Services Act 2007.

Taiwan

The shares of Class A common stock have not been and will not be registered with the Financial Supervisory Commission of Taiwan pursuant to relevant securities laws and regulations and may not be sold, issued, or offered within Taiwan through a public offering or in circumstances which constitutes an offer within the meaning of the Securities and Exchange Act of Taiwan that requires a registration or approval of the Financial Supervisory Commission of Taiwan. No person or entity in Taiwan has been authorised to offer, sell, give advice regarding, or otherwise intermediate the offering and sale of the shares of Class A common stock in Taiwan.

South Africa

Due to restrictions under the securities laws of South Africa, the shares of Class A common stock are not offered, and the offer shall not be transferred, sold, renounced, or delivered, in South Africa or to a person with an address in South Africa, unless one or other of the following exemptions applies:

(i)   the offer, transfer, sale, renunciation, or delivery is to:

(a) persons whose ordinary business is to deal in securities, as principal or agent;

(b) the South African Public Investment Corporation;

(c) persons or entities regulated by the Reserve Bank of South Africa;

(d) authorised financial service providers under South African law;

(e) financial institutions recognised as such under South African law;

(f) a wholly-owned subsidiary of any person or entity contemplated in (c), (d), or (e), acting as agent in the capacity of an authorised portfolio manager for a pension fund or collective investment scheme (in each case duly registered as such under South African law); or

(g) any combination of the person in (a) to (f); or

(ii)   the total contemplated acquisition cost of the securities, for any single addressee acting as principal is equal to or greater than ZAR1,000,000.

No "offer to the public" (as such term is defined in the South African Companies Act, No. 71 of 2008 (as amended or re-enacted), or the South African Companies Act) in South Africa is being made in connection with the issue of the shares of Class A common stock. Accordingly, this document does not, nor is it intended to, constitute a "registered prospectus" (as that term is defined in the South African Companies Act) prepared and registered under the South African Companies Act and has not been approved by, and/or filed with, the South African Companies and Intellectual Property Commission or any other regulatory authority in South Africa. Any issue or offering of the shares of Class A common stock in South Africa constitutes an offer of the shares of Class A common stock in South Africa for subscription or sale in South Africa only to persons who fall within the exemption from "offers to the public" set out in section 96(1)(a) of the South African Companies Act. Accordingly, this document must not be acted on or relied on by persons in South Africa who do not fall within section 96(1)(a) of the South African Companies Act, or such persons being referred to as SA Relevant Persons. Any investment or investment activity to which this document relates is available in South Africa only to SA Relevant Persons and will be engaged in South Africa only with SA relevant persons.

194

CONCURRENT PRIVATE PLACEMENT

Immediately subsequent to the closing of this offering, Salesforce Ventures LLC will purchase from us in a private placement $100.0 million of our Class A common stock at a price per share equal to the initial public offering price. Based on an assumed initial public offering price of $19.00 per share, which is the midpoint of the estimated offering price range set forth on the cover page of this prospectus, this would be 5,263,158 shares. We will receive the full proceeds and will not pay any underwriting discounts or commissions with respect to the shares that are sold in the private placement. The sale of the shares in the private placement is contingent upon the completion of this offering. The sale of these shares to Salesforce Ventures LLC will not be registered in this offering and will be subject to a market standoff agreement with us and a lock-up agreement with the underwriters for a period of up to 180 days after the date of this prospectus.

LEGAL MATTERS

Wilson Sonsini Goodrich & Rosati, P.C., Palo Alto, California, which has acted as our counsel in connection with this offering, will pass upon the validity of the shares of our Class A common stock being offered by this prospectus. The underwriters have been represented by Simpson Thacher & Bartlett LLP, Palo Alto, California.

EXPERTS

The consolidated financial statements of Dropbox, Inc. at December 31, 2016 and 2017, and for each of the three years in the period ended December 31, 2017, appearing in this prospectus and Registration Statement have been audited by Ernst & Young LLP, independent registered public accounting firm, as set forth in their report thereon appearing elsewhere herein, and are included in reliance upon such report given on the authority of such firm as experts in accounting and auditing.

WHERE YOU CAN FIND ADDITIONAL INFORMATION

We have filed with the SEC a registration statement on Form S-1 under the Securities Act with respect to the shares of our Class A common stock offered by this prospectus. This prospectus, which constitutes a part of the registration statement, does not contain all of the information set forth in the registration statement, some of which is contained in exhibits to the registration statement as permitted by the rules and regulations of the SEC. For further information with respect to us and our Class A common stock, we refer you to the registration statement, including the exhibits filed as a part of the registration statement. Statements contained in this prospectus concerning the contents of any contract or any other document is not necessarily complete. If a contract or document has been filed as an exhibit to the registration statement, please see the copy of the contract or document that has been filed. Each statement in this prospectus relating to a contract or document filed as an exhibit is qualified in all respects by the filed exhibit. You may obtain copies of this information by mail from the Public Reference Section of the SEC, 100 F Street, N.E., Room 1580, Washington, D.C. 20549, at prescribed rates. You may obtain information on the operation of the public reference rooms by calling the SEC at 1-800-SEC-0330. The SEC also maintains an Internet website that contains reports, proxy statements, and other information about issuers, like us, that file electronically with the SEC. The address of that website is www.sec.gov.

As a result of this offering, we will become subject to the information and reporting requirements of the Exchange Act and, in accordance with this law, will file periodic reports, proxy statements, and other information with the SEC. These periodic reports, proxy statements, and other information will be available for inspection and copying at the SEC's public reference facilities and the website of the SEC referred to above. We also

195

maintain a website at www.dropbox.com. Upon completion of this offering, you may access these materials free of charge as soon as reasonably practicable after they are electronically filed with, or furnished to, the SEC. Information contained on our website is not a part of this prospectus and the inclusion of our website address in this prospectus is an inactive textual reference only.

196

DROPBOX, INC.
INDEX TO CONSOLIDATED FINANCIAL STATEMENTS

	Page
Report of Ernst & Young LLP, Independent Registered Public Accounting Firm	F-2
Consolidated Balance Sheets	F-3
Consolidated Statements of Operations	F-4
Consolidated Statements of Comprehensive Loss	F-5
Consolidated Statements of Stockholders' Equity	F-6
Consolidated Statements of Cash Flows	F-7
Notes to Consolidated Financial Statements	F-8

F-1

285

REPORT OF ERNST & YOUNG LLP, INDEPENDENT REGISTERED PUBLIC ACCOUNTING FIRM

To the Stockholders and the Board of Directors of Dropbox, Inc.

Opinion on the Financial Statements

We have audited the accompanying consolidated balance sheets of Dropbox, Inc. (the Company) as of December 31, 2016 and 2017, the related consolidated statements of operations, comprehensive loss, stockholders' equity and cash flows for each of the three years in the period ended December 31, 2017, and the related notes (collectively referred to as the "financial statements"). In our opinion, the financial statements present fairly, in all material respects, the consolidated financial position of the Company at December 31, 2016 and 2017, and the consolidated results of its operations and its cash flows for each of the three years in the period ended December 31, 2017, in conformity with U.S. generally accepted accounting principles.

Basis for Opinion

These financial statements are the responsibility of the Company's management. Our responsibility is to express an opinion on the Company's financial statements based on our audits. We are a public accounting firm registered with the Public Company Accounting Oversight Board (United States) (PCAOB), and are required to be independent with respect to the Company in accordance with the U.S. federal securities laws and the applicable rules and regulations of the Securities and Exchange Commission and the PCAOB.

We conducted our audits in accordance with the standards of the PCAOB. Those standards require that we plan and perform the audit to obtain reasonable assurance about whether the financial statements are free of material misstatement, whether due to error or fraud. The Company is not required to have, nor were we engaged to perform, an audit of its internal control over financial reporting. As part of our audits we are required to obtain an understanding of internal control over financial reporting but not for the purpose of expressing an opinion on the effectiveness of the Company's internal control over financial reporting. Accordingly, we express no such opinion.

Our audits included performing procedures to assess the risks of material misstatement of the financial statements, whether due to error or fraud, and performing procedures that respond to those risks. Such procedures included examining, on a test basis, evidence regarding the amounts and disclosures in the financial statements. Our audits also included evaluating the accounting principles used and significant estimates made by management, as well as evaluating the overall presentation of the financial statements. We believe that our audits provide a reasonable basis for our opinion.

/s/ Ernst & Young LLP

We have served as the Company's auditor since 2013.

San Francisco, California
February 23, 2018, (except as to the eleventh paragraph of Note 1, as to which the date is March 7, 2018)

F-2

DROPBOX, INC.
CONSOLIDATED BALANCE SHEETS
(In millions, except for par value)

	As of December 31,		Pro forma stockholders' equity (deficit) as of December 31,
	2016	2017	2017
			(unaudited)
Assets			
Current assets:			
Cash and cash equivalents	$ 352.7	$ 430.0	
Trade and other receivables, net	13.2	29.3	
Prepaid expenses and other current assets	47.5	58.8	
Total current assets	413.4	518.1	
Property and equipment, net	444.0	341.9	
Intangible assets, net	24.2	17.0	
Goodwill	96.0	98.9	
Other assets	26.6	44.0	
Total assets	$1,004.2	$ 1,019.9	
Liabilities and stockholders' equity (deficit)			
Current liabilities:			
Accounts payable	$ 15.5	$ 31.9	
Accrued and other current liabilities	97.9	129.8	
Accrued compensation and benefits	41.3	56.1	
Capital lease obligation[1]	127.6	102.7	
Deferred revenue	353.0	417.9	
Total current liabilities	635.3	738.4	
Capital lease obligation, non-current[1]	129.6	71.6	
Deferred rent, non-current	72.5	69.8	
Other non-current liabilities	44.0	37.2	
Total liabilities	881.4	917.0	
Commitments and contingencies (Note 10)			
Stockholders' equity (deficit):			
Convertible preferred stock, $0.00001 par value; 151.2 shares authorized as of December 31, 2016 and 2017; 147.6 shares issued and outstanding as of December 31, 2016 and 2017; no shares authorized, issued and outstanding pro forma (unaudited); liquidation preference of $624.7 as of December 31, 2016 and 2017	615.3	615.3	$ —
Common stock $0.00001 par value; 1,000.0 shares authorized; Class A common stock - 533.3 shares authorized; 5.5 and 8.9 shares[2] issued and outstanding as of December 31, 2016 and 2017, respectively; 11.8 shares issued and outstanding pro forma (unaudited); Class B common stock - 466.7 shares authorized, 181.6 and 187.9 shares issued and outstanding as of December 31, 2016 and 2017, respectively; 348.5 shares issued and outstanding pro forma (unaudited)	—	—	—
Additional paid-in capital	446.0	533.1	1,370.9
Accumulated deficit	(937.5)	(1,049.7)	(1,465.3)
Accumulated other comprehensive income (loss)	(1.0)	4.2	4.2
Total stockholders' equity (deficit)	122.8	102.9	$ (90.2)
Total liabilities and stockholders' equity	$1,004.2	$ 1,019.9	

[1] Includes amounts attributable to related party transactions. See Note 15 for further details.
[2] Class A shares issued and outstanding as of December 31, 2017 exclude 14.7 million unvested restricted stock awards granted to the Company's co-founders. See Note 11 for further details.

See accompanying Notes to Consolidated Financial Statements.

F-3

DROPBOX, INC.
CONSOLIDATED STATEMENTS OF OPERATIONS
(In millions, except per share data)

	Year ended December 31,		
	2015	2016	2017
Revenue	$ 603.8	$ 844.8	$1,106.8
Cost of revenue[1]	407.4	390.6	368.9
Gross profit	196.4	454.2	737.9
Operating expenses[1]:			
Research and development	201.6	289.7	380.3
Sales and marketing	193.1	250.6	314.0
General and administrative[2]	107.9	107.4	157.3
Total operating expenses	502.6	647.7	851.6
Loss from operations	(306.2)	(193.5)	(113.7)
Interest expense, net	(15.2)	(16.4)	(11.0)
Other income (expense), net	(4.2)	4.9	13.2
Loss before income taxes	(325.6)	(205.0)	(111.5)
Provision for income taxes	(0.3)	(5.2)	(0.2)
Net loss	$(325.9)	$(210.2)	$ (111.7)
Net loss per share attributable to common stockholders, basic and diluted	$ (1.77)	$ (1.11)	$ (0.57)
Weighted-average shares used in computing net loss per share attributable to common stockholders, basic and diluted	184.5	189.1	195.9
Pro forma net loss per share attributable to common stockholders, basic and diluted (unaudited)			$ (0.31)
Weighted-average shares used in computing pro forma net loss per share attributable to common stockholders, basic and diluted (unaudited)			358.6

[1] Includes stock-based compensation as follows (in millions):

	Year ended December 31,		
	2015	2016	2017
Cost of revenue	$ 2.6	$ 8.2	$ 12.2
Research and development	36.1	72.7	93.1
Sales and marketing	19.8	44.6	33.7
General and administrative	7.6	22.1	25.6

[2] 2017 general and administrative expense includes $9.4 million for a non-cash charitable contribution and $1.9 million of cash contributions to the Dropbox Charitable Foundation, a related party. See Note 15 for further details.

See accompanying Notes to Consolidated Financial Statements.

F-4

DROPBOX, INC.
CONSOLIDATED STATEMENTS OF COMPREHENSIVE LOSS
(In millions)

	Year ended December 31,		
	2015	2016	2017
Net loss	$(325.9)	$(210.2)	$(111.7)
Other comprehensive income (loss):			
Change in cumulative foreign currency translation adjustments	0.1	(1.3)	5.2
Comprehensive loss	$(325.8)	$(211.5)	$(106.5)

See accompanying Notes to Consolidated Financial Statements.

F-5

DROPBOX, INC.
CONSOLIDATED STATEMENTS OF STOCKHOLDERS' EQUITY
(In millions)

	Convertible preferred stock		Common stock		Additional paid-in capital	Accumulated deficit	Accumulated other comprehensive income (loss)	Total stockholders' equity
	Shares	Amount	Shares	Amount				
Balance at December 31, 2014	147.6	$ 615.3	187.5	$ —	$ 192.3	$ (399.7)	$ 0.2	$ 408.1
Cumulative-effect adjustment from adoption of Topic 606	—	—	—	—	—	(1.7)	—	(1.7)
Vesting of early exercised stock options	—	—	—	—	2.2	—	—	2.2
Issuance of common stock, options and awards related to acquisitions	—	—	0.7	—	35.2	—	—	35.2
Exercise of stock options and awards	—	—	0.4	—	2.8	—	—	2.8
Repurchase of unvested common stock (related to early exercised stock options)	—	—	(1.3)	—	(1.3)	—	—	(1.3)
Stock-based compensation	—	—	—	—	66.1	—	—	66.1
Other comprehensive income	—	—	—	—	—	—	0.1	0.1
Net loss	—	—	—	—	—	(325.9)	—	(325.9)
Balance at December 31, 2015	147.6	615.3	187.3	—	297.3	(727.3)	0.3	185.6
Vesting of early exercised stock options	—	—	—	—	0.5	—	—	0.5
Issuance of common stock, options and awards related to acquisitions	—	—	0.1	—	0.7	—	—	0.7
Repurchase of unvested common stock (related to early exercised stock options)	—	—	(0.3)	—	(0.1)	—	—	(0.1)
Stock-based compensation	—	—	—	—	147.6	—	—	147.6
Other comprehensive loss	—	—	—	—	—	—	(1.3)	(1.3)
Net loss	—	—	—	—	—	(210.2)	—	(210.2)
Balance at December 31, 2016	147.6	615.3	187.1	—	446.0	(937.5)	(1.0)	122.8
Cumulative-effect adjustment from adoption of ASU 2016-09	—	—	—	—	0.5	(0.5)	—	—
Release of restricted stock units	—	—	14.6	—	—	—	—	—
Shares repurchased for tax withholdings on release of restricted stock	—	—	(5.5)	—	(87.9)	—	—	(87.9)
Donation of common stock to charitable foundation	—	—	0.6	—	9.4	—	—	9.4
Exercise of stock options and awards	—	—	0.2	—	0.5	—	—	0.5
Repurchase of unvested common stock (related to early exercised stock options)	—	—	(0.2)	—	—	—	—	—
Stock-based compensation	—	—	—	—	164.6	—	—	164.6
Other comprehensive income	—	—	—	—	—	—	5.2	5.2
Net loss	—	—	—	—	—	(111.7)	—	(111.7)
Balance at December 31, 2017	147.6	$ 615.3	196.8	$ —	$ 533.1	$ (1,049.7)	$ 4.2	$ 102.9

See accompanying Notes to Consolidated Financial Statements.

F-6

DROPBOX, INC.
CONSOLIDATED STATEMENTS OF CASH FLOWS
(In millions)

	Year ended December 31,		
	2015	2016	2017
Cash flow from operating activities			
Net loss	$(325.9)	$(210.2)	$(111.7)
Adjustments to reconcile net loss to net cash provided by operating activities:			
Depreciation and amortization	149.6	191.6	181.8
Stock-based compensation	66.1	147.6	164.6
Amortization of deferred commissions	0.6	3.7	6.6
Donation of common stock to charitable foundation	—	—	9.4
Other	0.8	1.1	(1.7)
Changes in operating assets and liabilities:			
Trade and other receivables, net	(9.9)	1.0	(14.4)
Prepaid expenses and other current assets	(1.8)	—	(18.2)
Other assets	2.5	(7.8)	(10.6)
Accounts payable	9.2	5.5	16.2
Accrued and other current liabilities	21.7	(12.4)	34.0
Accrued compensation and benefits	(9.0)	35.6	14.4
Deferred revenue	82.0	87.6	64.3
Non-current liabilities	28.9	9.3	(4.4)
Net cash provided by operating activities	14.8	252.6	330.3
Cash flow from investing activities			
Capital expenditures	(78.7)	(115.2)	(25.3)
Purchase of intangible assets	(4.6)	(8.5)	(0.8)
Cash received from equipment rebates	—	3.6	2.2
Business acquisitions, net of cash acquired	(2.3)	—	—
Cash received from sales of equipment	—	2.1	—
Net cash used in investing activities	(85.6)	(118.0)	(23.9)
Cash flow from financing activities			
Principal payments on capital lease obligations(1)	(101.2)	(137.9)	(133.0)
Principal payments against note payable	—	(3.8)	(3.9)
Principal payments against financing lease obligation	(1.8)	(1.6)	(2.3)
Proceeds from sale-leaseback agreement	—	8.8	—
Proceeds from issuance of note payable	11.9	—	—
Fees paid for revolving credit facility	—	—	(2.6)
Shares repurchased for tax withholdings on release of restricted stock	—	—	(87.9)
Proceeds from issuance of common stock, net of repurchases	1.5	—	0.5
Payments of deferred offering costs	—	—	(2.5)
Net cash used in financing activities	(89.6)	(134.5)	(231.7)
Effect of exchange rate changes on cash and cash equivalents	(0.9)	(4.3)	2.6
Change in cash, cash equivalents, and restricted cash	(161.3)	(4.2)	77.3
Cash, cash equivalents, and restricted cash—beginning of period	518.2	356.9	352.7
Cash, cash equivalents, and restricted cash—end of period	$ 356.9	$ 352.7	$ 430.0
Supplemental cash flow data:			
Cash paid during the period for:			
Interest	$ 13.2	$ 14.9	$ 10.8
Income taxes	$ 0.2	$ 1.5	$ 3.4
Non-cash investing and financing activities:			
Property and equipment received and accrued in accounts payable and accrued liabilities	$ 23.8	$ 7.6	$ 2.4
Property and equipment acquired under capital leases	$ 226.3	$ 92.2	$ 44.9
Fair value of shares issued related to acquisitions of businesses and other assets	$ 35.2	$ 0.7	$ —
Deferred offering costs accrued in accounts payable and accrued liabilities	$ —	$ —	$ 1.6

(1) Includes amounts attributable to related party transactions. See Note 15 for further details.

See accompanying Notes to Consolidated Financial Statements.

F-7

DROPBOX, INC.
NOTES TO CONSOLIDATED FINANCIAL STATEMENTS

(Amounts in tables are in millions except per share data, or as otherwise noted)

Note 1. Description of the Business and Summary of Significant Accounting Policies

Business

Dropbox, Inc. (the "Company" or "Dropbox") is a global collaboration platform. Dropbox was incorporated in May 2007 as Evenflow, Inc., a Delaware corporation, and changed its name to Dropbox, Inc. in October 2009. The Company is headquartered in San Francisco, California.

Basis of presentation and consolidation

The accompanying consolidated financial statements have been prepared in accordance with the United States of America generally accepted accounting principles ("GAAP"). The accompanying consolidated financial statements include the accounts of Dropbox and its wholly owned subsidiaries. All intercompany balances and transactions have been eliminated in consolidation. Certain prior year non-current liability balances have been reclassified to conform to the current year presentation.

On January 1, 2017, the Company adopted the requirements of Accounting Standards Update ("ASU") No. 2014-09, *Revenue from Contracts with Customers* (*Topic 606*) as discussed further in *Recently adopted accounting pronouncements* below ("Topic 606"). Topic 606 establishes a principle for recognizing revenue upon the transfer of promised goods or services to customers, in an amount that reflects the expected consideration received in exchange for those goods or services. Topic 606 also includes Subtopic 340-40, *Other Assets and Deferred Costs—Contracts with Customers*, which requires the deferral of incremental costs of obtaining a contract with a customer. Collectively, references to Topic 606 used herein refer to both Topic 606 and Subtopic 340-40. The Company adopted Topic 606 with retrospective application to the beginning of the earliest period presented.

Unaudited pro forma stockholders' equity (deficit)

Subject to the satisfaction of certain conditions, immediately prior to the completion of the Company's initial public offering, all of the 147,310,563 shares of convertible preferred stock will convert into an equivalent number of shares of Class B common stock. Further, pursuant to transfer agreements with certain of the Company's stockholders, 258,620 shares of the Company's convertible preferred stock and 2,609,951 shares of the Company's Class B common stock will automatically convert into an equivalent numbers of shares of Class A common stock. The unaudited pro forma stockholders' equity (deficit) information gives effect to these conversions as of December 31, 2017.

As described in detail in "Stock-Based Compensation" below, the Company has granted restricted stock units ("RSUs") that generally vest upon the satisfaction of a service-based vesting condition, and with respect to RSUs granted prior to August 2015, ("two-tier RSUs"), upon the satisfaction of both a service-based vesting condition and a liquidity event-related performance vesting condition (the "Performance Vesting Condition"). The Performance Vesting Condition is satisfied on the earlier of (i) an acquisition or change in control of the Company or (ii) the earlier of (a) six months after our initial public offering or (b) March 15 of the year following our initial public offering. At the time the Performance Vesting Condition becomes probable, the Company will recognize the cumulative stock-based compensation expense for the two-tier RSUs that have met their service-based vesting condition using the accelerated attribution method. Accordingly, the unaudited pro forma stockholders' equity (deficit) information as of December 31, 2017, gives effect to stock-based compensation expense of approximately $415.6 million associated with two-tier RSUs using the accelerated attribution method. This pro forma adjustment related to stock-based compensation expense of approximately $415.6 million has been reflected as an increase to additional paid-in capital and accumulated deficit.

F-8

The Company's Board of Directors has approved the acceleration of the Performance Vesting Condition for two-tier RSUs for which the service condition was satisfied as of December 31, 2017, to occur upon the effectiveness of its registration statement related to this offering. Accordingly, to satisfy the tax withholding and remittance obligations related to the two-tier RSUs, the Company will repurchase the number of shares necessary to satisfy the tax withholding obligations, based on the fair value of its common stock on the date of the initial public offering. The Company currently expects that the average of these withholding tax rates will be approximately 39%. Based upon the assumed initial public offering price of $19.00 per share, which is the midpoint of the estimated offering price range set forth on the cover page of this prospectus, the Company estimates that its tax withholding and remittance obligation would be approximately $193.1 million in the aggregate. Such amount is included as a decrease in additional paid-in capital in the pro forma stockholders' equity (deficit) as of December 31, 2017. The unaudited pro forma stockholders' equity (deficit) gives effect to the assumed conversion of the two-tier RSUs that had satisfied the service-based vesting condition and the Performance Vesting Condition as of December 31, 2017, and will convert into 15,897,254 shares of Class B common stock, net of 10,163,817 shares repurchased for tax withholding obligations.

The shares of common stock issuable and the proceeds expected to be received upon the completion of an initial public offering are excluded from the pro forma stockholders' equity (deficit).

Use of estimates

The preparation of financial statements in conformity with GAAP requires management to make estimates and assumptions that affect the amounts reported and disclosed in the Company's consolidated financial statements and accompanying notes. These estimates are based on information available as of the date of the consolidated financial statements. On a regular basis, management evaluates these estimates and assumptions. Actual results may differ materially from these estimates.

The Company's most significant estimates and judgments involve recognition of revenue, the measurement of the Company's stock-based compensation, including the estimation of the underlying deemed fair value of common stock, the estimation of the fair value of market-based awards, and the valuation of acquired intangible assets and goodwill from business combinations.

Financial information about segments and geographic areas

The Company manages its operations and allocates resources as a single operating segment. Further, the Company manages, monitors, and reports its financials as a single reporting segment. The Company's chief operating decision-maker is its Chief Executive Officer, who reviews financial information presented on a consolidated basis for purposes of making operating decisions, assessing financial performance, and allocating resources. For information regarding the Company's long-lived assets and revenue by geographic area, see Note 16.

Stock Split

On March 7, 2018, the Company effected a 1-for-1.5 reverse stock split of its capital stock. All of the share and per share information referenced throughout the consolidated financial statements and notes to the consolidated financial statements have been retroactively adjusted to reflect this reverse stock split.

Foreign currency transactions

The assets and liabilities of the Company's foreign subsidiaries are translated from their respective functional currencies into U.S. dollars at the rates in effect at the balance sheet date and revenue and expense amounts are translated at the average exchange rate for the period. Foreign currency translation gains and losses are recorded in other comprehensive income (loss).

F-9

Gains and losses realized from foreign currency transactions (those transactions denominated in currencies other than the foreign subsidiaries' functional currency) are included in other income (expense), net. Monetary assets and liabilities are remeasured using foreign currency exchange rates at the end of the period, and non-monetary assets are remeasured based on historical exchange rates. The Company recorded $4.6 million and $3.6 million in net foreign currency transaction losses in the years ended December 31, 2015 and 2016, respectively, and $5.0 million in net foreign currency gains in the year ended December 31, 2017.

Revenue recognition

The Company adopted the requirements of Topic 606 as of January 1, 2017, utilizing the full retrospective method of transition. The impact of adopting Topic 606 on the Company's revenue is not material to any of the periods presented. The primary impact of adopting Topic 606 relates to the deferral of incremental costs of obtaining customer contracts and the amortization of those costs over a longer period of benefit.

The Company derives its revenue from subscription fees from customers for access to its platform. The Company's policy is to exclude sales and other indirect taxes when measuring the transaction price of its subscription agreements. The Company accounts for revenue contracts with customers by applying the requirements of Topic 606, which includes the following steps:

- Identification of the contract, or contracts, with a customer
- Identification of the performance obligations in the contract
- Determination of the transaction price
- Allocation of the transaction price to the performance obligations in the contract
- Recognition of revenue when, or as, the Company satisfies a performance obligation

The Company's subscription agreements generally have monthly or annual contractual terms and a small percentage have multi-year contractual terms. Revenue is recognized ratably over the related contractual term beginning on the date that the platform is made available to a customer. Access to the platform represents a series of distinct services as the Company continually provides access to, and fulfills its obligation to the end customer over the subscription term. The series of distinct services represents a single performance obligation that is satisfied over time. The Company recognizes revenue ratably because the customer receives and consumes the benefits of the platform throughout the contract period. The Company's contracts are generally non-cancelable.

The Company bills in advance for monthly contracts and typically bills annually in advance for contracts with terms of one year or longer. The Company also recognizes an immaterial amount of contract assets, or unbilled receivables, primarily relating to rights to consideration for services completed but not billed at the reporting date. Unbilled receivables are classified as receivables when the Company has the right to invoice the customer.

The Company records contract liabilities when cash payments are received or due in advance of performance to deferred revenue. Deferred revenue primarily relates to the advance consideration received from the customer.

The price of subscriptions is generally fixed at contract inception and therefore, the Company's contracts do not contain a significant amount of variable consideration. As a result, the amount of revenue recognized in the periods presented from performance obligations satisfied (or partially satisfied) in previous periods was not material.

The Company recognized $184.7 million, $266.9 million, and $353.0 million of revenue during 2015, 2016 and 2017, respectively, that was included in the deferred revenue balances at the beginning of the respective periods.

F-10

As of December 31, 2017, future estimated revenue related to performance obligations that are unsatisfied or partially unsatisfied at the end of the reporting period was $467.8 million. The substantial majority of the unsatisfied performance obligations will be satisfied over the next twelve months.

The Company applied the practical expedient in Topic 606 and did not evaluate contracts of one year or less for the existence of a significant financing component. Multi-year contracts were not significant.

Stock-based compensation

The Company has granted RSUs to its employees and members of the Board of Directors under the 2008 Equity Incentive Plan ("2008 Plan") and the 2017 Equity Incentive Plan ("2017 Plan"). The Company had two types of RSUs outstanding as of December 31, 2017:

- One-tier RSUs, which have a service-based vesting condition over a four year period. These awards typically have a cliff vesting period of one year and continue to vest quarterly thereafter. The Company began granting one-tier RSUs under its 2008 Plan in August 2015 and it continues to grant one-tier RSUs under its 2017 Plan. The Company recognizes compensation expense associated with one-tier RSUs ratably on a straight-line basis over the requisite service period.

- Two-tier RSUs, which have both a service-based vesting condition and the Performance Vesting Condition. The service-based vesting period for these awards is typically four years with a cliff vesting period of one year and continue to vest monthly thereafter. Upon satisfaction of the Performance Vesting Condition, these awards will vest quarterly. The Performance Vesting Condition is satisfied on the earlier of (i) an acquisition or change in control of the Company or (ii) the earlier of (a) six months after the Company's initial public offering or (b) March 15 of the year following the Company's initial public offering. Prior to August 2015, the Company granted two-tier RSUs under the 2008 Plan. The Company's Board of Directors has approved the acceleration of the Performance Vesting Condition for two-tier RSUs, for which the service condition was satisfied as of December 31, 2017, to occur upon the effectiveness of its registration statement related to this offering. The last grant date for two-tier RSUs was in May 2015.

As of December 31, 2017, all compensation expense related to two-tier RSUs remained unrecognized because the Performance Vesting Condition was not satisfied. At the time the Performance Vesting Condition becomes probable, the Company will recognize the cumulative stock-based compensation expense for the two-tier RSUs that have met their service-based vesting condition using the accelerated attribution method. If the Performance Vesting Condition had occurred on December 31, 2017, the Company would have recorded $415.6 million of stock-based compensation expense using the accelerated attribution method. As of December 31, 2017, 28.2 million two-tier RSUs were outstanding, of which 26.1 million had met their service condition. If the Performance Vesting Condition had been satisfied on these two-tier RSUs as of December 31, 2017, unamortized stock-based compensation expense of $5.6 million would be recognized over a weighted-average period of approximately one year if the requisite service is provided. See Note 11, "Stockholders' Equity" for further discussion.

Since August 2015, the Company has granted RSUs as the only stock-based payment awards to its employees, excluding to its co-founders, and has not granted any stock options since then. The fair values of the common stock underlying the RSUs were determined by the Board of Directors, with input from management and contemporaneous third-party valuations, which were performed at least quarterly.

In December 2017, the Board of Directors approved a grant to the Company's co-founders of restricted stock awards ("RSAs") with respect to 14.7 million shares of Class A Common Stock in the aggregate (collectively, the "Co-Founder Grants"), of which 10.3 million RSAs were granted to Mr. Houston, the Company's co-founder and Chief Executive Officer, and 4.4 million RSAs were granted to Mr. Ferdowsi, the Company's co-founder and Director. These Co-Founder Grants have service-based, market-based, and performance-based vesting conditions.

F-11

The Co-Founder Grants comprise nine tranches that are eligible to vest based on the achievement of stock price goals, or, each, a Stock Price Target. The Company estimated the grant date fair value of the Co-Founder Grants using a model based on multiple stock price paths developed through the use of a Monte Carlo simulation that incorporates into the valuation the possibility that the Stock Price Targets may not be satisfied. The average grant date fair value of each Co-Founder Grant was estimated to be $10.60 per share, and the Company will recognize aggregate stock-based compensation expense of $156.2 million over the requisite service period of each tranche, which ranged from 2.9 to 6.9 years, using the accelerated attribution method. If the Stock Price Targets are met sooner than the derived service period, the Company will adjust its stock-based compensation to reflect the cumulative expense associated with the vested awards. The Company will recognize expense if the requisite service is provided, regardless of whether the market conditions are achieved.

The Co-Founder Grants contain an implied performance-based vesting condition satisfied upon the Company's shares being traded on an established national securities exchange or automated quotation system, because no shares subject to the Co-Founder Grants will vest until then. Accordingly, as of December 31, 2017, all compensation expense related to the Co-Founder Grants remained unrecognized because the performance-based vesting condition was not deemed probable of being achieved. See Note 11, "Stockholders' Equity" for further discussion.

The Company has outstanding stock options that will continue to vest through 2019 if the requisite service is provided. The Company used the Black-Scholes Merton Option ("BSM") pricing model to determine the fair value of stock options granted on the date of grant. This valuation model for stock-based compensation expense requires the Company to make assumptions and judgments about the variables used in the BSM model, including the fair value of its common stock, expected term, expected volatility, risk-free interest rate, and dividend yield. These judgments are made as follows:

- *Fair value of common stock.* The absence of an active market for the Company's common stock requires it to estimate the fair value of its common stock for purposes of granting stock options, granting RSUs, and for determining stock-based compensation expense for the periods presented. The Company obtained contemporaneous third-party valuations to assist in determining the fair value of its common stock. These contemporaneous third-party valuations used the methodologies, approaches, and assumptions consistent with the American Institute of Certified Public Accountants Practice Guide, *Valuation of Privately-Held-Company Equity Securities Issued as Compensation.*

The Company considered numerous factors in assessing the fair value of its common stock including:

- The results of contemporaneous valuations of its common stock by unrelated third parties;

- The rights, preferences, and privileges of its convertible preferred stock relative to those of its common stock;

- Market multiples of comparable public companies in its industry as indicated by their market capitalization and guideline merger and acquisition transactions;

- The Company's performance and market position relative to its competitors, who may change from time to time;

- The Company's historical financial results and estimated trends and prospects for its future performance;

- Valuations published by institutional investors that hold investments in the Company's capital stock;

- The economic and competitive environment;

- The likelihood and timeline of achieving a liquidity event, such as an initial public offering or sale of Dropbox, given prevailing market conditions;

- Any adjustments necessary to recognize a lack of marketability for its common stock; and

- Precedent sales of or offers to purchase its capital stock.

- *Expected term*. The Company determines the expected term based on the average period the stock options are expected to remain outstanding, generally calculated as the midpoint of the stock options' vesting term and contractual expiration period, as the Company does not have sufficient historical information to develop reasonable expectations about future exercise patterns and post-vesting employment termination behavior.

- *Expected volatility*. The expected volatility rate is based on an average of the historical volatilities of the common stock of several entities with publicly traded equity securities with characteristics similar to those of Dropbox.

- *Risk-free interest rate*. The risk-free interest rate is based on the U.S. Treasury security in effect at the time of grant for maturities corresponding with the expected term of the option.

- *Expected dividend yield*. The Company has not paid and does not expect to pay dividends. Consequently, the Company uses an expected dividend yield of zero.

The Company did not grant stock options during 2016 or 2017. The fair values of stock options granted to employees in 2015 were calculated using the following assumptions:

	Year ended December 31, 2015
Expected volatility	51% - 57%
Risk-free interest rate	1.4% - 1.9%
Expected term (in years)	6.0 - 6.1
Expected dividend yield	—
Fair value of common stock	$24.24 - $25.23

On January 1, 2017, the Company adopted ASU No. 2016-09: *Improvement to Employee Share-based Payment Accounting (Topic 718)* issued by the Financial Accounting Standards Board, which among other items, provides an accounting policy election to account for forfeitures as they occur, rather than to account for them based on an estimate of expected forfeitures. The Company elected to account for forfeitures as they occur and therefore, stock-based compensation expense for the year ended December 31, 2017, has been calculated based on actual forfeitures in the Company's consolidated statements of operations, rather than the Company's previous approach which was net of estimated forfeitures. The net cumulative effect of this change as of January 1, 2017, was not material. Stock-based compensation expense for the years ended December 31, 2015 and 2016, were recorded net of estimated forfeitures, which were based on historical forfeitures and adjusted to reflect changes in facts and circumstances, if any.

Cost of revenue

Cost of revenue consists primarily of expenses associated with the storage, delivery, and distribution of the Company's platform for both paying users and Basic users. These costs, which are referred to as infrastructure costs, include depreciation of servers located in co-location facilities that the Company leases and operates, rent and facilities expense for those datacenters, network and bandwidth costs, support and maintenance costs for infrastructure equipment, and payments to third-party datacenter service providers. Cost of revenue also includes costs, such as salaries, bonuses, benefits, travel-related expenses, and stock-based compensation, which are referred to as employee-related costs, for employees whose primary responsibilities relate to supporting the Company's infrastructure and delivering user support. Other non-employee costs included in cost of revenue include credit card fees related to processing customer transactions and allocated overhead, such as facilities, including rent, utilities, depreciation on leasehold improvements and other equipment shared by all departments, and shared information technology costs. In addition, cost of revenue includes amortization of developed technologies, professional fees related to user support initiatives, and property taxes related to the datacenters.

F-13

Advertising and promotional expense

Advertising and promotional expenses are included in sales and marketing expenses within the consolidated statements of operations and are expensed when incurred. Advertising and promotional expenses were $59.5 million, $46.6 million, and $80.1 million in the years ended December 31, 2015, 2016, and 2017, respectively.

Cash and cash equivalents

Cash consists primarily of cash on deposit with banks. Cash equivalents include highly liquid investments purchased with an original maturity date of 90 days or less from the date of purchase and primarily consist of money market funds. Cash equivalents also include amounts in transit from payment processors for credit and debit card transactions, which typically settle within five days. Cash and cash equivalents are recorded at cost, which approximates fair value.

Trade and other receivables, net

Trade and other receivables, net consists primarily of trade receivables that are recorded at the invoice amount, net of an allowance for doubtful accounts.

Trade and other receivables, net consisted of the following as of December 31, 2016 and 2017:

	December 31,	
	2016	2017
Trade accounts receivables	$13.1	$29.7
Other receivables	0.1	0.6
Less: Allowance for doubtful accounts	—	(1.0)
Trade and other receivables, net	$13.2	$29.3

The allowance for doubtful accounts is based on the Company's assessment of the collectability of accounts. The Company regularly reviews the adequacy of the allowance for doubtful accounts by considering the age of each outstanding invoice, the collection history of each customer, and other relevant factors to determine the appropriate amount of the allowance. Accounts receivable deemed uncollectable are charged against the allowance for doubtful accounts when identified.

Concentrations of credit risk

Financial instruments that potentially subject the Company to significant concentrations of credit risk consist primarily of cash, cash equivalents, and accounts receivable. The Company places its cash and cash equivalents with well-established financial institutions. Cash equivalents consist primarily of highly rated money market funds.

Trade accounts receivables are typically unsecured and are derived from revenue earned from customers located around the world. Two customers accounted for 11% and 12% of total trade and other receivables, net as of December 31, 2016. Two customers accounted for 18% and 27% of total trade and other receivables, net as of December 31, 2017. No customer accounted for more than 10% of the Company's revenue in the periods presented.

Non-trade receivables

The Company records non-trade receivables to reflect amounts due for activities outside of its subscription agreements. Historically, the Company's non-trade receivables have related primarily to receivables resulting

F-14

from tenant improvement allowances. Non-trade receivables totaled $3.0 million and $5.2 million, as of December 31, 2016 and 2017, respectively, and are classified within prepaid expenses and other current assets in the accompanying consolidated balance sheets.

Deferred commissions, net

Deferred commissions, net is stated at gross deferred commissions less accumulated amortization. Sales commissions earned by the Company's sales force and third-party resellers, as well as related payroll taxes, are considered to be incremental and recoverable costs of obtaining a contract with a customer. As a result, these amounts have been capitalized as deferred commissions within prepaid and other current assets and other assets on the consolidated balance sheet. The Company deferred incremental costs of obtaining a contract of $17.2 million and $19.4 million during the years ended December 31, 2016 and 2017, respectively.

Deferred commissions, net included in prepaid and other current assets were $3.7 million and $8.1 million as of December 31, 2016 and 2017, respectively. Deferred commissions, net included in other assets were $16.4 million and $24.8 million as of December 31, 2016 and 2017, respectively.

Deferred commissions are amortized over a period of benefit of five years. The period of benefit was estimated by considering factors such as historical customer attrition rates, the useful life of the Company's technology, and the impact of competition in its industry. Amortized costs were $0.6 million, $3.7 million, and $6.6 million for the years ended December 31, 2015, 2016, and 2017, respectively. Amortized costs are included in sales and marketing expense in the accompanying consolidated statements of operations. There was no impairment loss in relation to the deferred costs for any period presented.

Property and equipment, net

Equipment is stated at cost less accumulated depreciation. Depreciation is computed using the straight-line method over the estimated useful life of the related asset, which is generally three to seven years. Leasehold improvements are amortized on a straight-line basis over the shorter of their estimated useful lives or the initial term of the related lease.

The following table presents the estimated useful lives of property and equipment:

Property and equipment	Useful life
Buildings	20 to 30 years
Datacenter and other computer equipment	3 to 5 years
Office equipment and other	3 to 7 years
Leasehold improvements	Lesser of estimated useful life or remaining lease term

Lease obligations

The Company leases office space, datacenters, and equipment under non-cancelable capital and operating leases with various expiration dates through 2033. Certain of the Company's operating lease agreements contain tenant improvement allowances from its landlords. These allowances are accounted for as lease incentive obligations, and are amortized as reductions to rent expense over the lease term. In addition, certain of the operating lease agreements contain rent concession, rent escalation, and options to renew. Rent concession and rent escalation provisions are considered in determining the straight-line rent expense to be recorded over the lease term. The lease term begins on the date the Company has the right to use the leased property for purposes of recognizing lease expense on a straight-line basis over the term of the lease. The Company does not assume renewals in its determination of the lease term unless the renewals are deemed to be reasonably assured at lease inception.

The Company leases certain equipment from various third parties, including from a related party, through equipment financing leases under capital leases. See Note 15, "Related Party Transactions" for additional details. These leases either include a bargain purchase option, a full transfer of ownership at the completion of the lease term, or the terms of the leases are at least 75 percent of the useful lives of the assets and are therefore classified as a capital leases. These leases are capitalized in property and equipment and the related amortization of assets under capital leases is included in depreciation and amortization expense in the Company's consolidated statements of operations. Initial asset values and lease obligations are based on the present value of future minimum lease payments.

Internal use software

The Company capitalizes certain costs related to developed or modified software solely for its internal use and cloud based applications used to deliver its platform. The Company capitalizes costs during the application development stage once the preliminary project stage is complete, management authorizes and commits to funding the project, and it is probable that the project will be completed and that the software will be used to perform the function intended. Costs related to preliminary project activities and post implementation activities are expensed as incurred. Capitalized internal use software costs were not material to the Company's consolidated financial statements during the years ended December 31, 2015, 2016, and 2017.

Business combinations

The Company uses best estimates and assumptions to assign a fair value to the tangible and intangible assets acquired and liabilities assumed in business combinations as of the acquisition date. These estimates are inherently uncertain and subject to refinement. During the measurement period, which may be up to one year from the acquisition date, adjustments to the fair value of these tangible and intangible assets acquired and liabilities assumed may be recorded, with the corresponding offset to goodwill. Upon the conclusion of the measurement period or final determination of the fair value of assets acquired or liabilities assumed, whichever comes first, any subsequent adjustments are recorded to the Company's consolidated statements of operations.

Long-lived assets, including goodwill and other acquired intangible assets, net

The Company evaluates the recoverability of property and equipment and finite-lived intangible assets for possible impairment whenever events or circumstances indicate that the carrying amount of such assets may not be recoverable. The evaluation is performed at the lowest level for which identifiable cash flows are largely independent of the cash flows of other assets and liabilities. Recoverability of these assets is measured by a comparison of the carrying amounts to the future undiscounted cash flows the assets are expected to generate. If such review determines that the carrying amount of specific property and equipment or intangible assets is not recoverable, the carrying amount of such assets is reduced to its fair value.

The Company reviews goodwill for impairment at least annually in the fourth quarter, or more frequently if events or changes in circumstances would more likely than not reduce the fair value of its single reporting unit below its carrying value.

The Company has not recorded impairment charges on property and equipment, goodwill, or intangible assets for the periods presented in these consolidated financial statements.

Acquired property and equipment and finite-lived intangible assets are amortized over their useful lives. The Company evaluates the estimated remaining useful life of these assets when events or changes in circumstances warrant a revision to the remaining period of amortization. If the Company reduces the estimated useful life assumption for any asset, the remaining unamortized balance is amortized or depreciated over the revised estimated useful life on a prospective basis.

F-16

Deferred offering costs

Deferred offering costs, which consist of direct incremental legal, accounting, and consulting fees relating to the initial public offering, are capitalized. The deferred offering costs will be offset against initial public offering proceeds upon the consummation of the offering. In the event the offering is terminated, the deferred offering costs will be expensed. As of December 31, 2017, the Company had capitalized approximately $4.1 million of deferred offering costs within other assets on the consolidated balance sheet.

Income taxes

Deferred income tax balances reflect the effects of temporary differences between the financial reporting and tax bases of the Company's assets and liabilities using enacted tax rates expected to apply when taxes are actually paid or recovered. In addition, deferred tax assets are recorded for net operating loss and credit carryforwards.

A valuation allowance is provided against deferred tax assets unless it is more likely than not that they will be realized based on all available positive and negative evidence. Such evidence includes, but is not limited to, recent cumulative earnings or losses, expectations of future taxable income by taxing jurisdiction, and the carry-forward periods available for the utilization of deferred tax assets.

The Company uses a two-step approach to recognizing and measuring uncertain income tax positions. The first step is to evaluate the tax position for recognition by determining if the weight of available evidence indicates it is more likely than not that the position will be sustained on audit. The second step is to measure the tax benefit as the largest amount, which is more than 50% likely of being realized upon ultimate settlement. The Company recognizes interest and penalties related to unrecognized tax benefits as income tax expense. Significant judgment is required to evaluate uncertain tax positions.

Although the Company believes that it has adequately reserved for its uncertain tax positions, it can provide no assurance that the final tax outcome of these matters will not be materially different. The Company evaluates its uncertain tax positions on a regular basis and evaluations are based on a number of factors, including changes in facts and circumstances, changes in tax law, such as the Tax Cuts and Jobs Act, correspondence with tax authorities during the course of an audit, and effective settlement of audit issues.

To the extent that the final tax outcome of these matters is different than the amounts recorded, such differences will affect the provision for income taxes in the period in which such determination is made and could have a material impact on the Company's financial condition and results of operations.

Fair value measurement

The Company applies fair value accounting for all financial assets and liabilities and non-financial assets and liabilities that are recognized or disclosed at fair value in the financial statements on a recurring basis. The Company defines fair value as the price that would be received from selling an asset or paid to transfer a liability in an orderly transaction between market participants at the measurement date. When determining fair value measurements for assets and liabilities, the Company considers the principal or most advantageous market in which it would transact and the market-based risk measurements or assumptions that market participants would use in pricing the asset or liability, such as risks inherent in valuation techniques, transfer restrictions, and credit risk. Fair value is estimated by applying the following hierarchy, which prioritizes the inputs used to measure fair value into three levels and bases the categorization within the hierarchy upon the lowest level of input that is available and significant to the fair value measurement:

Level 1—Quoted prices in active markets for identical assets or liabilities.

Level 2—Observable inputs other than quoted prices in active markets for identical assets and liabilities, quoted prices for identical or similar assets or liabilities in inactive markets, or other inputs that are observable or can be corroborated by observable market data for substantially the full term of the assets or liabilities.

Level 3—Inputs that are generally unobservable and typically reflect management's estimate of assumptions that market participants would use in pricing the asset or liability.

Recently issued accounting pronouncements not yet adopted

In October 2016, the FASB issued ASU No. 2016-16, *Income Taxes: Intra-Entity Transfers Other than Inventory (Topic 740)*, which requires entities to recognize the income tax consequences of an intra-entity transfer of an asset other than inventory when the transfer occurs. ASU 2016-16 is effective for fiscal years beginning after December 15, 2018. Early adoption is permitted. The Company does not expect the adoption to have a material impact on its consolidated financial statements.

In February 2016, the FASB issued ASU No. 2016-02, *Leases (Topic 842)*. Most prominent among the changes in the standard is the recognition of right of use assets and lease liabilities by lessees for those leases classified as operating leases under current GAAP. Under the standard, disclosures are required to meet the objective of enabling users of financial statements to assess the amount, timing, and uncertainty of cash flows arising from leases. The Company will be required to recognize and measure leases existing at, or entered into after, the beginning of the earliest comparative period presented using a modified retrospective approach, with certain practical expedients available. The new standard is effective for fiscal years beginning after December 15, 2018. Early adoption by public entities is permitted. The Company is in the initial stage of its assessment of the new standard and is currently evaluating the timing of adoption, the quantitative impact of adoption, and the related disclosure requirements. The Company anticipates the adoption of this standard will result in a substantial increase in its non-current assets and liabilities recorded on the consolidated balance sheets. The adoption of the standard is not expected to have a material impact on the consolidated statement of operations. While the Company is assessing all potential impacts of the adoption of the standard, it currently expects the most significant impact to be the capitalization of right-to-use assets and lease liabilities for its office space and datacenter operating leases. The Company expects its accounting for capital leases related to infrastructure equipment to remain substantially unchanged under the new standard.

Recently adopted accounting pronouncements

In May 2014, the FASB issued ASU No. 2014-09, *Revenue from Contracts with Customers (Topic 606)* and Subtopic 340-40, *Other Assets and Deferred Costs—Contracts with Customers (Subtopic 340-40)*. Topic 606 supersedes the revenue recognition requirements in Accounting Standards Codification Topic 605, *Revenue Recognition (Topic 605)*, and requires the recognition of revenue when promised goods or services are transferred to customers in an amount that reflects the considerations to which the entity expects to be entitled to in exchange for those goods or services. Subtopic 340-40 requires the deferral of incremental costs of obtaining a contract with a customer. Collectively, reference to Topic 606 used herein refers to both Topic 606 and Subtopic 340-40.

The Company adopted the requirements of Topic 606 as of January 1, 2017, utilizing the full retrospective method of transition. The adoption of Topic 606 resulted in changes to accounting policies for revenue recognition, trade and other receivables, and deferred commissions.

The impact of adopting Topic 606 on the Company's revenue is not material to any of the periods presented. The primary impact of adopting Topic 606 relates to the deferral of incremental costs of obtaining customer contracts and the amortization of those costs over a longer period of benefit. Under Topic 606, the Company defers all incremental costs to obtain the contract, which primarily include sales commissions and related payroll taxes. The Company amortizes these costs over a period of benefit of five years.

In May 2017, the FASB issued ASU No. 2017-09, *Compensation-Stock Compensation (Topic 718): Scope of Modification Accounting*, which amends the guidance in ASC Topic 718. The standard provides clarity and

F-18

reduces the cost and complexity when applying the guidance in ASC Topic 718 to a change to the terms or conditions of a share-based payment award. ASU No. 2017-09 is effective for fiscal years beginning after December 15, 2017, and interim periods within those years, with early adoption permitted. The Company elected to adopt ASU No. 2017-09 in the fourth quarter of 2017 on a prospective basis. The adoption of the guidance did not have a material impact on the consolidated financial statements.

In January 2017, the FASB issued ASU No. 2017-04, *Goodwill and Other, Simplifying the Test for Goodwill Impairment (Topic 350)*, which amends the guidance in ASC Topic 350 to eliminate Step 2 from the goodwill impairment test. The updated guidance requires an entity to perform its annual or interim goodwill impairment test by comparing the fair value of a reporting unit with its carrying amount and recognize an impairment charge for the amount by which the carrying amount exceeds the reporting unit's fair value not to exceed the total amount of goodwill allocated to that reporting unit. ASU No. 2017-04 is effective for fiscal years beginning after December 15, 2019, and is applied prospectively when adopted. Early adoption is permitted. The Company elected to adopt ASU No. 2017-04 as of January 1, 2017. The adoption of the guidance did not have an impact on the consolidated financial statements.

In January 2017, the FASB issued ASU No. 2017-01, *Business Combinations, Clarifying the Definition of a Business (Topic 805)*, which clarifies the definition of a business with the objective of adding guidance to assist entities with evaluating whether transactions should be accounted for as acquisitions or disposals of assets or businesses. ASU No. 2017-01 is effective for fiscal years beginning after December 15, 2017, and interim periods within those years, and is applied prospectively when adopted. Early adoption is permitted. The Company elected to adopt ASU No. 2017-01 as of January 1, 2017. The adoption of the guidance did not have an impact on the consolidated financial statements.

In March 2016, the FASB issued ASU No. 2016-09, *Improvements to Employee Share-Based Payment Accounting (Topic 718)*, which aligns with the FASB's current simplification initiatives. The major areas for simplification in ASU No. 2016-09 involve several aspects of the accounting for stock-based payment transactions, including income tax consequences, classification of awards as either equity or liabilities, and classification on the statement of cash flows. Specifically, ASU No. 2016-09 has introduced updates to minimum statutory tax withholding requirements, policy elections surrounding forfeitures, expected term, intrinsic values, and changes to the classification of certain stock-based payment related transactions on the statement of cash flows. The Company elected to adopt ASU No. 2016-09 effective as of January 1, 2017. The adoption of the guidance did not have a material impact on the consolidated financial statements.

In November 2016, the FASB issued ASU No. 2016-18, *Statement of Cash Flows, Restricted Cash (Topic 230)*, which amends the guidance in ASC Topic 230, *Statement of Cash Flows,* and requires that entities show the changes in total of cash, cash equivalents, restricted cash, and restricted cash equivalents in their statement of cash flows. As a result, entities will no longer present transfers between cash and cash equivalents and restricted cash and restricted cash equivalents in the statement of cash flows. ASU No. 2016-18 is effective for fiscal years beginning after December 15, 2017, and interim periods within those years, and is applied retrospectively when adopted. Early adoption is permitted. The Company elected to adopt ASU No. 2016-18 effective January 1, 2016. The adoption of the guidance did not have a material impact on the consolidated financial statements.

In April 2015, the FASB issued ASU No. 2015-05, *Intangibles—Goodwill and Other—Internal-Use Software: Customer's Accounting for Fees Paid in a Cloud Computing Arrangement (Subtopic 350-40),* which provides guidance to customers about whether a cloud computing arrangement includes a software license. If a cloud computing arrangement includes a software license, then the customer should account for the software license element of the arrangement consistent with the acquisition of other software licenses. If a cloud computing arrangement does not include a software license, the customer should account for the arrangement as a service contract. The Company adopted ASU No. 2015-05 in 2016. The adoption of the guidance did not have a material impact on the consolidated financial statements.

Note 2. Cash and Cash Equivalents

Cash and cash equivalents consisted of the following:

	As of December 31,	
	2016	2017
Cash	$ 93.7	$ 62.9
Money market mutual funds	259.0	367.1
Total cash and cash equivalents	$352.7	$430.0

Included in cash and cash equivalents are cash in transit from payment processors for credit and debit card transactions of $8.4 million and $13.3 million as of December 31, 2016 and 2017, respectively.

Note 3. Fair Value Measurements

The Company's cash equivalents primarily consist of money market funds. The total cash equivalents held by the Company in money market funds as of December 31, 2016 and 2017, were $259.0 million and $367.1 million, respectively. The Company's cash equivalents are classified within Level 1 of the fair value hierarchy. See Note 1, "Description of the Business and Summary of Significant Accounting Policies" for additional details.

Note 4. Property and Equipment, Net

Property and equipment, net consisted of the following:

	As of December 31,	
	2016	2017
Building	$ 36.6	$ 36.6
Datacenter and other computer equipment	608.4	663.1
Furniture and fixtures	21.0	21.2
Leasehold improvements	114.1	118.6
Construction in process	0.5	7.2
Total property and equipment	780.6	846.7
Accumulated depreciation and amortization	(336.6)	(504.8)
Property and equipment, net	$ 444.0	$ 341.9

In 2012, the Company undertook a series of structural improvements to the floor that it occupied in its previous corporate headquarters. As a result of the requirement to fund construction costs and its responsibility for cost overruns during the construction period, the Company was considered the deemed owner of the floor for accounting purposes. Due to the presence of a standby letter of credit as a security deposit, the Company was deemed to have continuing involvement after the construction period. As such, it accounted for this arrangement as owned real estate and recorded an imputed financing obligation for its obligation to the legal owners. The net book value of the asset was $27.7 million and $25.9 million as of December 31, 2016 and 2017, respectively. The accumulated depreciation of the building totaled $8.9 million and $10.8 million as of December 31, 2016 and 2017, respectively. See Note 10, "Commitments and Contingencies," for additional details.

The Company leases certain infrastructure from various third parties, including from a related party, through equipment financing leases under capital leases. See Note 15, "Related Party Transactions" for additional details. Infrastructure assets as of December 31, 2016 and 2017, respectively, included a total of $474.2 million and $417.9 million acquired under capital lease agreements. These leases are capitalized in property and equipment,

F-20

304

and the related amortization of assets under capital leases is included in depreciation and amortization expense. The accumulated depreciation of the infrastructure under capital leases totaled $224.9 million and $259.0 million as of December 31, 2016 and 2017, respectively.

Construction in process includes costs primarily related to construction of leasehold improvements for office buildings and datacenters.

Depreciation expense related to property and equipment was $127.3 million, $173.8 million, and $170.7 million for the years ended December 31, 2015, 2016, and 2017, respectively.

Note 5. Business Combinations

The Company did not complete any business combinations during the years ended December 31, 2016 and 2017. During the year ended December 31, 2015, the Company completed the business combination described below. The results of operations for this business combination were included in the accompanying consolidated statements of operations since its acquisition date. The impact of its results to the periods presented was not material. Pro forma results of operations have not been presented because the effects of the acquisition were not material to the consolidated financial statements.

In January 2015, the Company acquired all of the outstanding shares of CloudOn, Inc ("CloudOn") for total consideration of $31.4 million, which was comprised solely of shares of Dropbox common stock. CloudOn was an Israel-based developer of mobile software that allowed users to edit, create, organize, and share Microsoft Office documents. The fair value of the net assets acquired from the CloudOn business combination was not material.

Note 6. Intangible Assets, Net

Intangible assets consisted of the following:

	As of December 31,		Weighted-average remaining useful life (In years)
	2016	2017	
Developed technology	$ 50.6	$ 50.9	0.5
Patents	13.0	13.0	8.7
Software	14.7	17.8	2.5
Assembled workforce in asset acquisitions	10.1	10.1	1.3
Licenses	4.6	4.6	3.3
Non-compete agreements, trademarks and other	4.1	4.0	6.8
Total intangibles	97.1	100.4	
Accumulated amortization	(72.9)	(83.4)	
Intangible assets, net	$ 24.2	$ 17.0	

Amortization expense was $22.2 million, $17.3 million, and $10.5 million for the years ended December 31, 2015, 2016, and 2017, respectively.

F-21

Expected future amortization expense for intangible assets as of December 31, 2017 is as follows:

2018	$ 5.2
2019	3.5
2020	2.5
2021	1.1
2022	0.7
Thereafter	4.0
Total	$17.0

Note 7. Goodwill

Goodwill represents the excess of the purchase price in a business combination over the fair value of net tangible and intangible assets acquired. Goodwill amounts are not amortized, but tested for impairment on an annual basis. There was no impairment of goodwill as of December 31, 2016 and 2017. Goodwill consisted of the following:

Balance at December 31, 2015	96.1
Effect of foreign currency translation	(0.1)
Balance at December 31, 2016	96.0
Effect of foreign currency translation	2.9
Balance at December 31, 2017	$98.9

Note 8. Accrued and Other Current Liabilities

Accrued and other current liabilities consisted of the following:

	As of December 31,	
	2016	2017
Non-income taxes payable	$ 49.4	$ 69.7
Accrued legal and other external fees	11.9	21.3
Deferred rent	11.0	14.6
Financing obligations, current	11.4	9.7
Accrued infrastructure costs	1.9	2.6
Accrued property and equipment purchases	5.8	1.8
Income taxes payable	2.2	0.4
Other accrued and current liabilities	4.3	9.7
Total accrued and other current liabilities	$ 97.9	$129.8

Note 9. Revolving Credit Agreement

On April 3, 2017, the Company entered into an amended and restated credit and guaranty agreement which currently provides for a $600.0 million revolving loan facility (the "revolving credit facility"). The revolving credit facility has an accordion option, which, if exercised, would allow the Company to increase the aggregate commitments up to $150.0 million, subject to obtaining additional lender commitments and satisfying certain conditions. The revolving credit facility replaced the Company's existing $500.0 million revolving credit facility that was set to expire on March 20, 2018 (the "2014 revolving credit facility"). In conjunction with the revolving credit facility, the Company paid upfront issuance fees of $2.6 million, which are being amortized over the five-year term of the agreement.

F-22

Pursuant to the terms of the revolving credit facility, the Company may issue letters of credit under the revolving credit facility, which reduce the total amount available for borrowing. Pursuant to the terms of the revolving credit facility, the Company is required to pay an annual commitment fee that accrues at a rate of 0.20% per annum on the unused portion of the borrowing commitments under the revolving credit facility. In addition, the Company is required to pay a fee in connection with letters of credit issued under the revolving credit facility, which accrues at a rate of 1.5% per annum on the amount to be drawn under such letters of credit outstanding. There is an additional fronting fee of 0.125% per annum multiplied by the average aggregate daily maximum amount available to be drawn under all letters of credit. Borrowings under the revolving credit facility bear interest, at the Company's option, at an annual rate based on LIBOR plus a spread of 1.50% or at an alternative base rate plus a spread of 0.50%.

The revolving credit facility contains customary conditions to borrowing, events of default and covenants, including covenants that restrict the Company's ability to incur indebtedness, grant liens, make distributions to holders of the Company or its subsidiaries' equity interests, make investments, or engage in transactions with its affiliates. In addition, the revolving credit facility contains financial covenants, including a consolidated leverage ratio covenant and a minimum liquidity balance of $100.0 million, which includes any available borrowing capacity. The Company was in compliance with the covenants of the 2014 revolving credit facility as of December 31, 2016, and the revolving credit facility as of December 31, 2017.

As of December 31, 2016, the Company had an aggregate of $48.7 million of letters of credit outstanding under the 2014 revolving credit facility. As of December 31, 2017, the Company had an aggregate of $82.6 million of letters of credit outstanding under the revolving credit facility. The Company's total available borrowing capacity under the 2014 revolving credit facility was $451.3 million as of December 31, 2016. The Company's total available borrowing capacity under the revolving credit facility was $517.4 million as of December 31, 2017. The Company's letters of credit expire between April of 2019 and April of 2022.

Note 10. Commitments and Contingencies

Leases

The Company has entered into various non-cancelable operating lease agreements for certain offices and datacenters with contractual lease periods expiring at various dates through 2033. The facility lease agreements generally provide for escalating rental payments and for options to renew, which could increase future minimum lease payments if exercised. The Company recognizes rent expense on a straight-line basis over the lease period and accounts for the difference between straight-line rent and actual lease payments as deferred rent.

Gross rent expense was $49.7 million, $67.9 million, $71.0 million for the years ended December 31, 2015, 2016, and 2017, respectively. Sublease income, which is recorded as a reduction of rental expense, was $0.1 million, $4.5 million, and $10.6 million for the years ended December 31, 2015, 2016, and 2017, respectively. Sublease income in excess of the Company's original lease obligation is split with the original lessor per the terms of the sublease agreement, with the Company's portion recorded to other income (expense), net.

Other commitments include payments to third-party vendors for services related to the Company's infrastructure, infrastructure warranty contracts, payments related to the imputed financing obligation for its previous headquarters, asset retirement obligations for office modifications, and a note payable related to financing of infrastructure. As described in Note 4, "Property and Equipment", the Company is considered the deemed owner of a floor in its previous corporate headquarters, for accounting purposes, as part of a build-to-suit lease agreement. In June 2011, the Company initially recorded a building asset and an imputed financing obligation for its obligation to the legal owner in the amount of $36.6 million. In connection with this lease, the Company is obligated to pay $8.6 million in lease payments over the next two years as of December 31, 2017. The imputed financing obligation on the Company's consolidated balance sheets totaled $29.5 million and

F-23

$27.4 million at December 31, 2016 and 2017, respectively. The current portion of the imputed financing obligation totaled $2.4 million and $2.6 million as of December 31, 2016 and 2017, respectively, and is classified within accrued and other current liabilities. The non-current portion of the imputed financing obligation totaled $27.1 million and $24.8 million as of December 31, 2016 and 2017, respectively, and is classified within other non-current liabilities.

In 2015, the Company entered into a note payable arrangement with a vendor to finance infrastructure totaling $11.9 million. The note payable is classified within accrued and other current liabilities. The term of the arrangement is thirty-six months and will end in the fourth quarter of 2018. Payments including interest towards the note payable totaled $4.3 million in each of the years ended December 31, 2016 and 2017. The total remaining obligation including interest was $7.5 million and $3.6 million as of December 31, 2016 and 2017, respectively. The note payable is included in other commitments in the table below.

In 2016, the Company entered into a sale-leaseback agreement with a vendor for infrastructure. As a result of the transaction, it received $8.8 million in proceeds. Payments including interest towards the leaseback arrangement totaled $1.3 million and $2.5 million for the years ended December 31, 2016 and 2017, respectively. The total remaining obligation including interest was $8.8 million and $6.3 million as of December 31, 2016 and 2017, respectively. The obligation is included in capital lease commitments in the table below.

In 2017, the Company entered into a new lease agreement for office space in San Francisco, California, to serve as its new corporate headquarters. The Company expects to start making recurring rental payments under the lease in the third quarter of 2019. Included in the operating lease commitments below are total expected minimum obligations under the lease agreement of $827.0 million, which exclude expected tenant improvement reimbursements from the landlord of approximately $73.6 million and variable operating expenses. The Company's obligations under the lease are supported by a $34.2 million letter of credit, which reduced the borrowing capacity under the revolving credit facility.

Future minimum payments under the Company's non-cancelable leases, financing obligations, and other commitments as of December 31, 2017, are as follows, and exclude non-cancelable rent payments from the Company's sub-tenants:

	Capital lease commitments	Operating lease commitments[1]	Other commitments
Year ended December 31:			
2018	$ 108.3	$ 91.5	$ 64.0
2019	54.9	94.9	49.9
2020	18.4	126.0	34.7
2021	0.4	115.9	1.7
2022	—	109.0	—
Thereafter	—	812.6	4.8
Future minimum payments	182.0	$ 1,349.9	$ 155.1
Less interest and taxes	(7.7)		
Less current portion of the present value of minimum lease payments	(102.7)		
Capital lease obligations, net of current portion	$ 71.6		

[1] Consists of future non-cancelable minimum rental payments under operating leases for the Company's offices and datacenters, excluding rent payments from the Company's sub-tenants and variable operating expenses. Non-cancelable rent payments from the Company's sub-tenants as of December 31, 2017, are expected to be $72.1 million through 2023.

F-24

Legal matters

From time to time, the Company is a party to a variety of claims, lawsuits, and proceedings which arise in the ordinary course of business, including claims of alleged infringement of intellectual property rights. The Company records a liability when it believes that it is probable that a loss will be incurred and the amount of loss or range of loss can be reasonably estimated. In its opinion, resolution of pending matters is not likely to have a material adverse impact on its consolidated results of operations, cash flows, or its financial position. Given the unpredictable nature of legal proceedings, the Company bases its estimate on the information available at the time of the assessment. As additional information becomes available, the Company reassesses the potential liability and may revise the estimate.

Indemnification

The Company's arrangements generally include certain provisions for indemnifying customers against liabilities if its products or services infringe a third party's intellectual property rights. It is not possible to determine the maximum potential amount under these indemnification obligations due to the limited history of prior indemnification claims.

Note 11. Stockholders' Equity

Common stock

The Company's amended and restated certificate of incorporation authorizes the issuance of Class A common stock and Class B common stock. The Company is authorized to issue 533,333,333 shares of Class A common stock and 466,666,666 shares of Class B common stock. Holders of Class A common stock and Class B common stock are entitled to dividends on a pro rata basis, when, as, and if declared by the Company's Board of Directors, subject to the rights of the holders of the Company's preferred stock. Holders of Class A common stock are entitled to one vote per share, and holders of Class B common stock are entitled to 10 votes per share. Upon a liquidation event, as defined in the amended and restated certificate of incorporation, after payments are made to holders of the Company's preferred stock, any distribution of proceeds to common stockholders will be made on a pro rata basis to the holders of Class A common stock and Class B common stock. Following the completion of an initial public offering of the Company, shares of Class B common stock will automatically convert into shares of Class A common stock upon a sale or transfer (other than with respect to certain estate planning transfers).

Convertible preferred stock

The Company is authorized to issue 151,212,292 shares of preferred stock. The following table summarizes the convertible preferred stock outstanding and liquidation preferences as of December 31, 2017:

	Shares		Per share price at issuance	Aggregate liquidation preference	Dividend per share amount
	Authorized	Outstanding			
			(In millions, except for per share amounts)		
Series A	63.9	63.9	$ 0.09	$ 6.0	$ 0.02
Series A-1	52.0	51.9	0.03	1.3	0.02
Series B	19.5	19.5	13.58	264.8	1.08
Series C	15.8	12.3	$ 28.65	352.6	$ 2.30
	151.2	147.6		$ 624.7	

F-25

Significant terms of the convertible preferred stock are as follows:

Liquidation preference

Upon a liquidation event, as defined in the amended and restated certificate of incorporation, the holders of Series A, Series A-1, Series B, and Series C convertible preferred stock are entitled to receive, prior to and in preference to any distribution of the proceeds of such liquidation to common stockholders, an amount per share equal to $0.09, $0.03, $13.58 and $28.65, respectively, plus any declared but unpaid dividends on such shares. If the proceeds distributed among the holders of the preferred stock are insufficient to permit the Series A, Series A-1, Series B, and Series C convertible preferred stock holders to receive the full payment noted above, then the entire proceeds legally available for distribution shall be distributed ratably among the holders of the preferred stock in proportion to the full preferential amount that each such holder is otherwise entitled to receive.

Dividends

Holders of the Company's preferred stock are entitled to receive dividends, when, as and if declared by the Company's Board of Directors, at the applicable dividend rate of $0.02, $0.02, $1.08, and $2.30 for each share of Series A, Series A-1, Series B, and Series C convertible preferred stock, respectively, prior to and in preference of any dividend paid to holders of the Company's common stock (other than a stock dividend declared and paid on the Class A common stock that is payable in shares of Class A common stock or on the Class B common stock that is payable in shares of Class B common stock). Such dividends shall not be cumulative or mandatory. No dividends have been declared in any period presented.

Voting

Each holder of preferred stock shall have the right to 10 votes for each share of Class B common stock into which the shares of preferred stock held by such holder could then be converted. In addition, so long as at least 30.0 million shares of preferred stock are outstanding, the holders of the preferred stock shall be entitled to elect one director of Dropbox. The holders of the shares of outstanding Class A common stock and Class B common stock representing at least a majority in voting power of the then-issued common stock shall be entitled to elect seven directors of Dropbox.

Conversion

At the option of the holder thereof, each share of preferred stock is convertible into a number of shares of Class B common stock that results from dividing the applicable original issue price for such series by the applicable conversion price in effect on the date of conversion (the "Conversion Rate"). Each share of preferred stock will be automatically converted into shares of Class B common stock at the Conversion Rate at the time in effect for such series of preferred stock upon the earlier of (i) immediately prior to the closing of a firm commitment underwritten public offering of Dropbox's common stock on an internationally recognized securities exchange or trading system pursuant to a registration statement under the Securities Act of 1933, as amended, with gross proceeds of not less than $35.0 million in the aggregate (a "Qualified IPO"), or (ii) the date specified by written consent or agreement of the holders of a majority of the outstanding preferred stock, voting together as a single class; *provided*, that other than pursuant to a Qualified IPO (x) so long as a majority of the shares of Series B convertible preferred stock originally issued remains outstanding, the consent of the holders of 70% of the shares of the Series B convertible preferred stock, voting together as a single class, is required to convert any shares of Series B convertible preferred stock into Class B common stock and (y) so long as a majority of the shares of Series C convertible preferred stock originally issued remains outstanding, the consent of the holders of a majority of the shares of the Series C convertible preferred stock, voting together as a single class, is required to convert any shares of Series C convertible preferred stock into Class B common stock.

F-26

Equity incentive plans

Under the Company's 2017 Equity Incentive Plan (the "Plan"), the Company may grant stock-based awards to purchase or directly issue shares of common stock to employees, directors, and consultants. Options are granted at a price per share equal to the fair market value of Dropbox's common stock at the date of grant. Options granted are exercisable over a maximum term of 10 years from the date of grant and generally vest over a period of four years. No options have been granted since August of 2015. RSUs and RSAs are also granted under the Plan. The Plan will terminate 10 years after the later of (i) its adoption or (ii) the most recent stockholder-approved increase in the number of shares reserved under the Plan, unless terminated earlier by the Dropbox Board of Directors. This Plan was adopted on March 8, 2017, and replaced the Company's 2008 Equity Incentive Plan (the "Prior Plan"). In August 2017, the Company increased the number of shares of common stock reserved for grant under the 2017 Plan by 6,666,666 shares. As of December 31, 2017, there were 59.9 million shares issued and outstanding under the Plan and the Prior Plan. Shares available for issuance under the Plans were 9.0 million as of December 31, 2017.

Stock option and restricted stock activity for the Plans was as follows for the years ended December 31, 2015, 2016, and 2017:

	Number of shares available for issuance under the Plans	Options outstanding			Restricted stock outstanding	
		Number of shares outstanding under the Plans	Weighted-average exercise price per share	Weighted-average remaining contractual term (In years)	Number of Plan shares outstanding	Weighted-average grant date fair value per share
		(In millions, except per share amounts)				
Balance at December 31, 2014	0.4	13.5	$ 15.92	8.9	27.1	$ 13.70
Additional shares authorized	30.7	—	—		—	—
Options granted	(2.0)	2.0	25.23		—	—
Restricted stock granted	(21.0)	—	—		21.0	22.74
Options and RSAs exercised	—	(0.4)	6.77		—	—
Options and RSUs canceled	6.3	(1.7)	16.31		(4.6)	17.36
Repurchased under the Plan	0.2	—	—		—	—
Balance at December 31, 2015	14.6	13.4	$ 17.51	8.1	43.5	$ 17.67
Options and RSUs canceled	14.1	(8.0)	22.04		(6.1)	20.06
Restricted stock granted	(16.6)	—	—		16.6	15.59
Balance at December 31, 2016	12.1	5.4	$ 10.68	6.5	54.0	$ 16.41
Additional shares authorized	6.7	—	—		—	—
Options exercised and RSUs released	—	(0.1)	6.00		(14.6)	17.12
Options and RSUs canceled	6.2	(0.3)	17.44		(6.0)	17.96
Shares repurchased for tax withholdings on release of restricted stock	5.5	—	—		—	17.09
Restricted stock granted	(21.5)	—	—		21.5	15.70
Balance at December 31, 2017	9.0	5.0	$ 10.52	5.5	54.9	$ 15.60
Vested at December 31, 2017		4.8	$ 10.11	5.5	—	$ —
Unvested at December 31, 2017		0.2	$ 21.11		54.9	$ 15.60

Two-tier RSUs are included in the unvested share counts in the table above as the Performance Vesting Condition was not probable.

F-27

The following table summarizes information about the pre-tax intrinsic value of options exercised and the weighted-average grant date fair value per share of options granted during the years ended December 31, 2015, 2016, and 2017:

	Year ended December 31,		
	2015	2016	2017
Intrinsic value of options exercised	$ 7.4	$—	$ 1.2
Weighted-average grant date fair value per share of stock options granted(1)	$12.27	$—	$—

(1) The weighted-average grant date fair value per share of stock options granted is calculated, as of the stock option grant date, using the BSM option pricing model. The Company did not grant stock options during the years ended December 31, 2016 and 2017.

As of December 31, 2017, unamortized stock-based compensation expense related to unvested stock options, restricted stock awards (excluding the Co-Founder Grants), and one-tier RSUs was $386.8 million. The weighted-average period over which such compensation expense will be recognized if the requisite service is provided is approximately 2.8 years as of December 31, 2017.

As of December 31, 2017, all compensation expense related to the Company's two-tier RSUs remained unrecognized because the Performance Vesting Condition was not satisfied. Approximately 26.1 million two-tier RSUs had met their service-based vesting condition as of December 31, 2017, but not the Performance Vesting Condition. If the Performance Vesting Condition had been satisfied on December 31, 2017, the Company would have recorded $415.6 million of stock-based compensation expense using the accelerated attribution method related to the two-tier RSUs. As of December 31, 2017, approximately 2.1 million two-tier RSUs had not met their service-based vesting condition. If the Performance Vesting Condition had been satisfied on these two-tier RSUs as of December 31, 2017, unamortized stock-based compensation expense of $5.6 million would be recognized over a weighted-average period of approximately one year if the requisite service is provided.

Co-Founder Grants

In December 2017, the Board of Directors approved a grant to the Company's co-founders of non-Plan RSAs with respect to 14.7 million shares of Class A Common Stock in the aggregate (collectively, the "Co-Founder Grants"), of which 10.3 million RSAs were granted to Mr. Houston, the Company's co-founder and Chief Executive Officer, and 4.4 million RSAs were granted to Mr. Ferdowsi, the Company's co-founder and Director. These Co-Founder Grants have service-based, market-based, and performance-based vesting conditions. The Co-Founder Grants are excluded from Class A common stock issued and outstanding within these financial statements until the satisfaction of these vesting conditions. The Co-Founder Grants also provide the holders with certain stockholder rights, such as the right to vote the shares with the other holders of Class A common stock and a right to cumulative declared dividends. However, the Co-Founder Grants are not considered a participating security for purposes of calculating net loss per share attributable to common stockholders in Note 12 as the right to the cumulative declared dividends is forfeitable if the service condition is not met.

The Co-Founder Grants are eligible to vest over the ten-year period following the closing of this offering. The Co-Founder Grants comprise nine tranches that are eligible to vest based on the achievement of stock price goals, or, each, a Stock Price Target, measured over a consecutive thirty-day trading period during the Performance Period. The Performance Period begins on the first trading day following the later of (a) the expiration of the lock-up period following the first date the Company's shares are traded on an established national securities exchange or automated quotation system (the "IPO Date") and (b) January 1, 2019 and ends on the earliest to occur of: (i) the date on which all shares subject to the Co-Founder Grants vest, (ii) the date the applicable co-founder ceases to satisfy the service-based vesting condition, (iii) the tenth anniversary of the IPO Date, and (iv) the occurrence of an acquisition of the Company prior to the IPO Date.

During the first four years of the Performance Period, no more than 20% of the shares subject to each Co-Founder Grant would be eligible to vest in any calendar year. After the first four years, all shares are eligible to vest based on the achievement of the Stock Price Targets.

The Co-Founder Grants contain an implied performance-based vesting condition satisfied upon the IPO Date, because no shares subject to the Co-Founder Grants will vest unless the IPO Date occurs. Accordingly, as of December 31, 2017, all compensation expense related to the Co-Founder Grants remained unrecognized because the performance-based vesting condition was not deemed probable of being achieved.

The Company calculated the grant date fair value of the Co-Founder Grants based on multiple stock price paths developed through the use of a Monte Carlo simulation. A Monte Carlo simulation also calculates a derived service period for each of the nine vesting tranches, which is the measure of the expected time to achieve each Stock Price Target. A Monte Carlo simulation requires the use of various assumptions, including the underlying stock price, volatility, and the risk-free interest rate as of the valuation date, corresponding to the length of time remaining in the performance period, and expected dividend yield. The weighted-average grant date fair value of each Co-Founder Grant was estimated to be $10.60 per share. The weighted-average derived service period of each Co-Founder Grant was estimated to be 5.2 years, and ranged from 2.9 - 6.9 years. The Company will recognize aggregate stock-based compensation expense of $156.2 million over the derived service period of each tranche using the accelerated attribution method as long as the co-founders satisfy their service-based vesting conditions. If the Stock Price Targets are met sooner than the derived service period, the Company will adjust its stock-based compensation to reflect the cumulative expense associated with the vested awards. The Company will recognize expense if the requisite service is provided, regardless of whether the market conditions are achieved.

Award modifications

During the year ended December 31, 2016, the Company's Board of Directors voted to approve the exchange of stock options previously granted to an executive officer under the Plan for one-tier RSUs. In total, options to purchase 4.3 million shares of common stock were exchanged for 2.2 million RSUs. Total compensation expense for the modified awards is $37.7 million, of which $18.8 million in stock-based compensation expense was recognized on the date of exchange representing the portion that vested immediately. Out of the total $37.7 million in stock-based compensation expense, $8.9 million was incremental to what would have been recognized related to the original stock option award. The Company will recognize approximately $2.4 million in stock-based compensation expense per quarter related to these awards. As of December 31, 2017, the total unamortized expense relating to these awards was $2.4 million.

Additionally, during the year ended December 31, 2016, the Board of Directors voted to approve a continuation of vesting upon change in employment status clause for an executive officer who had previously provided services to the Company. Under this clause, 0.4 million RSUs previously granted to the former executive officer will continue to vest for a pre-determined period of time. The continuation of vesting was accounted for as a modification of the terms of the original award. As a result, the Company recognized an incremental $4.2 million of stock-based compensation expense. An additional $1.5 million of stock-based compensation expense may be recognized in future periods for the former executive officers' two-tier RSUs if the initial qualifying liquidity event defined under the award agreement occurs.

During the year ended December 31, 2017, the Company's Board of Directors voted to approve a modification of vesting schedules for certain unvested one-tier and two-tier RSUs to align the vesting schedules for all RSUs to vest once per quarter. As a result of this modification, the Company's unamortized stock-based compensation expense related to one-tier RSUs increased by $3.2 million, which will be recognized over a weighted-average period of 2.8 years if and when the awards vest. The total unamortized stock-based compensation expense related to two-tier RSUs decreased by $9.5 million. The unamortized amount will be recognized over a period of 0.9 years if and when the awards vest.

Note 12. Net Loss Per Share

The following table sets forth the calculation of basic and diluted net loss per share attributable to common stockholders during the periods presented:

	Year ended December 31,					
	2015		2016		2017	
	(In millions, except per share amounts)					
	Class A	Class B	Class A	Class B	Class A	Class B
Numerator:						
Net loss attributable to common stockholders	$ (9.7)	$(316.2)	$ (6.1)	$(204.1)	$ (3.6)	$(108.1)
Denominator:						
Weighted-average number of common shares outstanding used in computing basic and diluted net loss per common share	5.5	179.0	5.5	183.6	6.3	189.6
Net loss per common share, basic and diluted	$(1.77)	$ (1.77)	$(1.11)	$ (1.11)	$(0.57)	$ (0.57)

Since the Company was in a loss position for all periods presented, basic net loss per share attributable to common stockholders is the same as diluted net loss per share for all periods as the inclusion of all potential common shares outstanding would have been anti-dilutive. The weighted-average impact of potentially dilutive securities that were not included in the diluted per share calculations because they would be anti-dilutive were as follows:

	Year ended December 31,		
	2015	2016	2017
	(Shares in millions)		
Convertible preferred stock	147.6	147.6	147.6
Restricted stock units	34.1	47.9	52.7
Options to purchase shares of common stock	14.0	7.9	5.1
Co-Founder Grants[1]	—	—	0.8
Shares subject to repurchase from early-exercised options and unvested restricted stock	3.6	0.9	0.2
Total	199.3	204.3	206.4

[1] A total of 14.7 million shares of Class A common stock associated with the Co-Founder Grants could potentially dilute earnings per share in the future if the requisite vesting conditions are met.

Note 13. Unaudited Pro Forma Net Loss Per Share

Pro forma net loss per share was computed to give effect to the automatic conversion of all series of convertible preferred stock using the if-converted method as though the conversion had occurred as of the beginning of the period or the date of issuance, if later. Subject to the satisfaction of certain conditions, immediately prior to the completion of the Company's initial public offering, 147,310,563 shares of convertible preferred stock will convert into an equivalent number of shares of Class B common stock. Further, pursuant to transfer agreements with certain of the Company's stockholders, 258,620 shares of the Company's preferred stock and 2,609,951 shares of the Company's Class B common stock will automatically convert into an equivalent number of shares of Class A common stock. In addition, the pro forma share amounts give effect to the weighted-average issuance of two-tier RSUs that have satisfied the service-based vesting condition and the Performance Vesting Condition as of December 31, 2017. The Company's Board of Directors has approved the acceleration of the Performance Vesting Condition for two-tier RSUs for which the service condition was

F-30

satisfied as of December 31, 2017, to occur upon the effectiveness of its registration statement related to this offering. The Company will repurchase the number of shares necessary to satisfy the tax withholding obligations, based on the fair value of its common stock on the date of the initial public offering. The Company currently expects that the average of these withholding tax rates will be approximately 39%. For two-tier RSUs for which the service-based vesting condition and the Performance Vesting Condition was satisfied as of December 31, 2017, the pro forma shares outstanding for the year ended December 31, 2017 includes the weighted-average issuance of 15,897,254 shares of Class B common stock, net of 10,163,817 shares repurchased to satisfy tax withholding obligations.

The net loss used in computing pro forma net loss per share amount in the table below does not give effect to the stock-based compensation expense associated with two-tier RSUs that have both a service-based vesting condition and the Performance Vesting Condition. If an initial public offering had been completed on December 31, 2017, the Company would have recognized approximately $415.6 million of stock-based compensation expense on the effective date, and would have approximately $5.6 million of additional future period expense that would be recognized over a weighted-average period of approximately one year if the requisite service is provided.

The following table presents the calculation of pro forma net loss attributable to common stockholders per share, basic and diluted:

| | Year ended December 31, 2017 | |
| | (In millions, except per share amounts) | |
	Class A	Class B
Numerator:		
Net loss as reported	$ (3.6)	$ (108.1)
Reallocation of net loss due to pro forma adjustments	0.7	(0.7)
Net loss attributable to common stockholders for pro forma net loss per share computation, basic and diluted	$ (2.9)	$ (108.8)
Denominator:		
Weighted-average shares of common stock used in computing net loss per share attributable to common stockholders, basic and diluted	6.3	189.6
Weighted-average pro forma adjustment to reflect conversion of convertible preferred stock	0.3	147.3
Weighted-average pro forma adjustment to reflect assumed vesting of two-tier RSUs, net of shares repurchased to satisfy tax withholding obligations	—	15.1
Weighted-average pro forma adjustment of conversions of Class B to Class A common stock	2.6	(2.6)
Weighted-average shares used in computing pro forma net loss per share attributable to common stockholders, basic and diluted	9.2	349.4
Pro forma net loss attributable to common stockholders per share, basic and diluted	$ (0.31)	$ (0.31)

F-31

Note 14. Income Taxes

For the years ended December 31, 2015, 2016, and 2017 the Company's loss from continuing operations before provision for income taxes was as follows:

	Year ended December 31,		
	2015	2016	2017
Domestic	$(176.9)	$ (94.4)	$ (76.9)
Foreign	(148.7)	(110.6)	(34.6)
Loss before income taxes	$(325.6)	$(205.0)	$(111.5)

The components of the provision for income taxes in the years ended December 31, 2015, 2016, and 2017 were as follows:

	Year ended December 31,		
	2015	2016	2017
Current:			
Federal	$ —	$ (1.5)	$ 0.1
State	—	(0.6)	(0.3)
Foreign	(0.5)	(2.9)	(2.3)
Deferred:			
Federal	—	—	1.4
State	—	—	—
Foreign	0.2	(0.2)	0.9
Provision for income taxes	$ (0.3)	$ (5.2)	$ (0.2)

Income tax benefit attributable to loss from continuing operations differed from the amounts computed by applying the statutory U.S. federal income tax rate of 34% to pretax loss from continuing operations as a result of the following:

	Year ended December 31,		
	2015	2016	2017
Tax benefit at federal statutory rate of 34%	$ 110.7	$ 69.7	$ 37.9
State taxes, net of federal benefit	4.5	2.2	1.7
Foreign rate differential	(50.7)	(38.8)	(12.3)
Research and other credits	12.7	12.6	25.4
Permanent differences	(4.8)	(3.5)	(9.0)
Tax Cuts and Jobs Act impact	—	—	(61.7)
Change in valuation allowance	(71.2)	(40.7)	38.9
Stock-based compensation	(6.1)	(4.8)	(20.1)
Other nondeductible items	4.6	(1.9)	(1.0)
Provision for income taxes	$ (0.3)	$ (5.2)	$ (0.2)

F-32

The significant components of the Company's deferred tax assets and liabilities as of December 31, 2016 and 2017 were as follows:

| | As of December 31, | |
	2016	2017
Deferred tax assets:		
Net operating loss carryforwards	$ 127.9	$ 119.6
Research credit carryforwards	41.3	67.9
Stock-based compensation	70.3	20.0
Accruals and reserves	43.9	34.0
Gross deferred tax assets	283.4	241.5
Valuation allowance	(259.7)	(233.7)
Total deferred tax assets, net of valuation allowance	23.7	7.8
Deferred tax liabilities:		
Fixed assets and intangible assets	20.3	6.6
Other	3.5	0.4
Total deferred tax liability	23.8	7.0
Net deferred tax assets (liabilities)	$ (0.1)	$ 0.8

For the years ended December 31, 2016 and 2017, based on all available objective evidence, including the existence of cumulative losses, the Company determined that it was not more likely than not that the U.S., Ireland, and Israel net deferred tax assets were fully realizable as of December 31, 2016 and 2017. Accordingly, the Company established a full valuation allowance against its U.S. and Ireland deferred tax assets and a partial valuation allowance against its Israeli deferred tax assets.

As of December 31, 2017, the Company had $312.2 million of federal and $143.0 million of state net operating loss carryforwards available to reduce future taxable income, which will begin to expire in 2031 for federal and 2030 for state tax purposes.

As of December 31, 2017, the Company had research credit carryforwards of $59.2 million and $34.6 million for federal and state income tax purposes, respectively, of which $14.7 million and $8.6 million is the unrecognized tax benefit portion related to the research credit carryforwards for federal and state, respectively. The federal credit carryforward will begin to expire in 2027. The state research credits have no expiration date. The Company also had $3.7 million of state enterprise zone credit carryforwards, which will begin to expire in 2023.

As of December 31, 2017, the Company also had $289.3 million of foreign net operating loss carryforwards available to reduce future taxable income, which will carryforward indefinitely. In addition, the Company had $22.9 million of foreign acquired net operating losses, which will carryforward indefinitely.

Under Section 382 and 383 of the Internal Revenue Code of 1986, as amended, or the Code, if a corporation undergoes an "ownership change," the corporation's ability to use its pre-change net operating loss carryforwards and other pre-change attributes, such as research tax credits, to offset its post-change income may be limited. In general, an "ownership change" will occur if there is a cumulative change in our ownership by "5-percent shareholders" that exceeds 50 percentage points over a rolling three-year period. Similar rules may apply under state tax laws. The Company performed a study for the period through December 31, 2017, and determined that no ownership changes exceeding 50 percentage points have occurred. The Company's ability to use net operating loss and tax credit carryforwards to reduce future taxable income and liabilities may be subject to annual limitations as a result of ownership changes from January 1, 2018, and subsequent years or as a result of this offering.

F-33

As of December 31, 2017, the balance of unrecognized tax benefits was $25.6 million of which $2.3 million, if recognized, would affect the effective tax rate and $23.3 million would result in adjustment to deferred tax assets with corresponding adjustments to the valuation allowance.

A reconciliation of the beginning and ending amount of unrecognized tax benefit is as follows:

	Year ended December 31,		
	2015	2016	2017
Balance of gross unrecognized tax benefits at the beginning of the fiscal year	$ 3.1	$ 7.9	$ 15.7
Gross increases related to prior period tax positions	1.1	2.2	—
Gross increases related to current period tax positions	3.7	5.6	9.9
Balance of gross unrecognized tax benefits at the end of the fiscal year	$ 7.9	$ 15.7	$ 25.6

The Company recognizes interest and/or penalties related to income tax matters as a component of income tax expense. As of December 31, 2017, the amount of accrued interest and penalties related to uncertain tax positions was $0.6 million. Interest and penalties recognized for the year ended December 31, 2016 and 2017, was $0.4 million and $0.2 million, respectively, and the Company did not recognize any interest and penalties for the year ended December 31, 2015.

The Company files income tax returns in the U.S. federal, multiple states, and foreign jurisdictions. All of the Company's tax years from 2007 remain open for examination by the federal and state authorities, and from 2013 by foreign authorities.

The Company generally does not provide deferred income taxes for the undistributed earnings of its foreign subsidiaries as the Company intends to reinvest such earnings indefinitely. Should circumstances change and it becomes apparent that some or all of the undistributed earnings will no longer be indefinitely reinvested, the Company will accrue for income taxes not previously recognized. As of December 31, 2017, there were no cumulative undistributed earnings in its Irish subsidiary and, as a result, there were no unrecorded deferred tax liabilities. The amount of undistributed earnings in the Company's other foreign subsidiaries, if any, are immaterial.

Impact of The Tax Cuts and Jobs Act

The Tax Cuts and Jobs Act (the "Tax Reform Act") was enacted on December 22, 2017 and provides for significant changes to U.S. tax law. Among other provisions, the Tax Reform Act reduces the U.S. corporate income tax rate to 21% effective in 2018. The Tax Reform Act also contains a number of provisions that may impact the Company in future years. Since the Tax Reform Act was recently finalized and ongoing guidance and accounting interpretation is expected over the next twelve months, the Company has made certain provisional accounting estimates, as permitted under Staff Accounting Bulletin No. 118, and continues to analyze its accounting policies in this area. The U.S. Treasury Department, the IRS, and other standard-setting bodies could interpret or issue guidance on how provisions of the Tax Reform Act will be applied or otherwise administered that is different from the Company's interpretation. As the Company completes its analysis of the Tax Reform Act, collects and prepares necessary data, and interprets any additional guidance, the Company may make adjustments to provisional amounts that it has recorded that may be material in the period in which the adjustments are made. The final accounting analysis will occur no later than one year from the date the Tax Reform Act was enacted.

As a result of the reduction in the corporate rate, the Company has remeasured its U.S. deferred tax assets and liabilities as of December 31, 2017 to reflect the lower rate expected to apply when these temporary differences reverse. The Company provisionally estimates that the remeasurement resulted in a reduction in deferred tax assets of $63.1 million, which was fully offset by a corresponding change to the Company's

F-34

valuation allowance. Although the tax rate reduction is known, the Company has not collected all of the necessary data to complete its analysis of the effect of the Tax Reform Act on the underlying deferred taxes and as such, the amounts recorded as of December 31, 2017 are provisional. However, the Company anticipates that any adjustment to provisional amounts recorded would be fully offset by a corresponding change to the Company's valuation allowance.

The Tax Reform Act repeals the corporate alternative minimum tax ("AMT") effective beginning in 2018 and permits AMT credit carryforwards to be refunded to the extent unused through 2021. Since the Company does not anticipate the use of these credits to reduce future federal taxes, it recognized an income tax benefit and established an income tax receivable to reflect anticipated refunds of $1.4 million for its 2016 AMT credit carryforward during the year ended December 31, 2017. The Company has not collected all of the necessary data to complete its analysis of the classification of the AMT tax credit as a receivable and as such, the amounts recorded as an income tax receivable as of December 31, 2017 are provisional.

The Tax Reform Act also provides for a transition to a new territorial system of taxation and generally requires companies to include certain untaxed foreign earnings of non-U.S. subsidiaries into taxable income in 2017 ("Transition Tax"). As a result of the cumulative deficits in the Company's foreign subsidiaries, the Company estimates that it will have no Transition Tax inclusion.

The Company continues to evaluate its accounting policy for recording deferred taxes, if any, that would arise as a result of other new provisions including the global intangible low-taxed income tax and the base erosion tax regimes established under the Tax Reform Act. This evaluation will be completed no later than one year from the date the Tax Reform Act was enacted.

Note 15. Related Party Transactions

Dropbox Charitable Foundation

During the year ended December 31, 2016, two of the Company's controlling shareholders formed the Dropbox Charitable Foundation, a Delaware non-stock corporation (the "Foundation"). The primary purpose of the Foundation is to engage in charitable and educational activities within the meaning of Section 501(c)(3) of the Code. The Foundation is governed by a Board of Directors, a majority of which are independent. Both shareholders made contributions to the Foundation during the year ended December 31, 2016, comprised entirely of shares of Dropbox common stock. The Company has not consolidated the Foundation in the accompanying consolidated financial statements, as the Company does not have control of the entity.

During the year ended December 31, 2017, the Company recorded $9.4 million of expense for a non-cash charitable contribution, whereby the Company donated Class B common shares to initially fund the Foundation. The expense was recorded to general and administrative expenses based on the Company's estimate of the then current fair value of the contributed shares. Additionally, during the year ended December 31, 2017, the Company made cash contributions of $1.9 million to the Foundation.

Hewlett Packard Enterprise

The Company has engaged in various commercial relationships with Hewlett Packard Enterprise ("HPE"), whose chief executive officer was appointed to the Dropbox Board of Directors in September 2017. These commercial relationships include infrastructure equipment under capital leases, the purchase of commercial products and other services, and a multi-year subscription agreement for access to the Dropbox platform. From the date of appointment of HPE's chief executive officer to the Dropbox Board of Directors through December 31, 2017, the Company made payments of $18.4 million for infrastructure equipment under capital leases and commercial products and services provided by HPE. As of December 31, 2017, the Company had a remaining obligation of $87.1 million for equipment under capital lease from HPE. Related to the multi-year

F-35

319

subscription agreement, the Company recognized an immaterial amount of revenue from the date of appointment of HPE's chief executive officer to the Dropbox Board of Directors through December 31, 2017, and had an immaterial balance of deferred revenue and outstanding trade receivables as of December 31, 2017.

Note 16. Geographic Areas

Long-lived assets

The following table sets forth long-lived assets by geographic area:

	As of December 31,	
	2016	2017
United States	$425.1	$ 323.7
International[1]	18.9	18.2
Total property and equipment, net	$444.0	$ 341.9

[1] No single country other than the United States had a property and equipment balance greater than 10% of total property and equipment, net, as of December 31, 2016 and 2017.

Revenue

Revenue by geography is generally based on the address of the customer as defined in the Company's subscription agreement. The following table sets forth revenue by geographic area for the years ended December 31, 2015, 2016, and 2017.

	Year ended December 31,		
	2015	2016	2017
United States	$ 326.1	$ 455.9	$ 575.7
International[1]	277.7	388.9	531.1
Total revenue	$ 603.8	$ 844.8	$1,106.8

[1] No single country outside of the United States accounted for more than 10 percent of total revenue during the years ended December 31, 2015, 2016, and 2017

Note 17. Subsequent Events

The Company has evaluated subsequent events through February 23, 2018, the date that the independent auditor's report as of and for the year ended December 31, 2017 was originally issued and the audited annual consolidated financial statements were available for issuance.

In February 2018, the Company amended its revolving credit facility to, among other things, permit the Company to make certain investments, enter into an unsecured standby letter of credit facility, and increase its standby letter of credit sublimit to $187.5 million. The Company also increased its borrowing capacity under the revolving credit facility from $600.0 million to $725.0 million. The Company may from time to time request increases in its borrowing capacity under its revolving credit facility of up to $275.0 million, provided no event of default has occurred or is continuing or would result from such increase.

In February 2018, the Board of Directors approved grants of 9,909,986 RSUs. These RSUs will result in estimated stock-based compensation of $170.2 million, which is expected to be recognized over a weighted-average period of 3.9 years from the grant date.

In February 2018, the Company's Board of Directors also approved the acceleration of the Performance Vesting Condition for two-tier RSUs for which the service condition was satisfied, to occur upon the effectiveness of the registration statement related to this offering.

F-36

Note 18. Subsequent Events (unaudited)

The Company has evaluated subsequent events through March 21, 2018, the date the consolidated financial statements as of and for the years ended December 31, 2017 were available for issuance.

In March 2018, the Board of Directors approved grants of 1,011,430 RSUs. These RSUs will result in estimated stock-based compensation of $17.4 million, which is expected to be recognized over a weighted-average period of 3.8 years from the grant date.

In March 2018, the Company entered into a purchase agreement with Salesforce Ventures LLC to purchase $100.0 million of the Company's Class A common stock in a private placement at a price per share equal to the initial public offering price. The purchase of the Company's Class A shares will occur immediately subsequent to the closing of the Company's initial public offering.

In February 2018, the Board of Directors approved, and in March 2018 the Company's stockholders approved, grants of RSUs with an aggregate value of $1.2 million to four of the Company's non-employee directors. The awards will be effective as of immediately prior to the effectiveness of the registration statement related to this offering, subject to each director's continued service with the Company. The number of RSUs subject to the award will equal the value of the award divided by the per share price of Class A common stock listed on the cover of the registration statement related to this offering.

Additionally, in February 2018, the Board of Directors approved, and in March 2018 the Company's stockholders approved, the Company's amended and restated certificate of incorporation, which will become effective immediately prior to the completion of this offering, the increase in the total number of shares of Class A common stock reserved for issuance under the 2017 Plan by 1,333,333 shares, and the adoption of the 2018 Equity Incentive Plan, the 2018 Class C Stock Incentive Plan, the 2018 Employee Stock Purchase Plan, the 2018 Class C Employee Stock Purchase Plan, and the form of indemnification agreement the Company has entered into with its directors and executive officers.

F-37

Table of Contents

322

PART II

INFORMATION NOT REQUIRED IN PROSPECTUS

ITEM 13. OTHER EXPENSES OF ISSUANCE AND DISTRIBUTION.

The following table sets forth all expenses to be paid by us, other than underwriting discounts and commissions, upon completion of this offering. All amounts shown are estimates except for the SEC registration fee, the FINRA filing fee and the exchange listing fee.

	Amount to be paid
SEC registration fee	$ 92,778
FINRA filing fee	124,700
Exchange listing fee	225,000
Printing and engraving expenses	875,000
Legal fees and expenses	2,500,000
Accounting fees and expenses	2,500,000
Transfer agent and registrar fees	10,000
Miscellaneous	672,522
Total	$ 7,000,000

ITEM 14. INDEMNIFICATION OF DIRECTORS AND OFFICERS.

Section 145 of the Delaware General Corporation Law authorizes a corporation's board of directors to grant, and authorizes a court to award, indemnity to officers, directors, and other corporate agents.

We expect to adopt an amended and restated certificate of incorporation, which will become effective immediately prior to the completion of this offering, and which will contain provisions that limit the liability of our directors for monetary damages to the fullest extent permitted by Delaware law. Consequently, our directors will not be personally liable to us or our stockholders for monetary damages for any breach of fiduciary duties as directors, except liability for the following:

- any breach of their duty of loyalty to our company or our stockholders;

- any act or omission not in good faith or that involves intentional misconduct or a knowing violation of law;

- unlawful payments of dividends or unlawful stock repurchases or redemptions as provided in Section 174 of the Delaware General Corporation Law; or

- any transaction from which they derived an improper personal benefit.

Any amendment to, or repeal of, these provisions will not eliminate or reduce the effect of these provisions in respect of any act, omission, or claim that occurred or arose prior to that amendment or repeal. If the Delaware General Corporation Law is amended to provide for further limitations on the personal liability of directors of corporations, then the personal liability of our directors will be further limited to the greatest extent permitted by the Delaware General Corporation Law.

In addition, we expect to adopt amended and restated bylaws, which will become effective immediately prior to the completion of this offering, and which will provide that we will indemnify, to the fullest extent permitted by law, any person who is or was a party or is threatened to be made a party to any action, suit, or

II-1

proceeding by reason of the fact that he or she is or was one of our directors or officers or is or was serving at our request as a director or officer of another corporation, partnership, joint venture, trust, or other enterprise. Our amended and restated bylaws are expected to provide that we may indemnify to the fullest extent permitted by law any person who is or was a party or is threatened to be made a party to any action, suit, or proceeding by reason of the fact that he or she is or was one of our employees or agents or is or was serving at our request as an employee or agent of another corporation, partnership, joint venture, trust, or other enterprise. Our amended and restated bylaws will also provide that we must advance expenses incurred by or on behalf of a director or officer in advance of the final disposition of any action or proceeding, subject to limited exceptions.

Further, we have entered into or will enter into indemnification agreements with each of our directors and executive officers that may be broader than the specific indemnification provisions contained in the Delaware General Corporation Law. These indemnification agreements require us, among other things, to indemnify our directors and executive officers against liabilities that may arise by reason of their status or service. These indemnification agreements also require us to advance all expenses incurred by the directors and executive officers in investigating or defending any such action, suit, or proceeding. We believe that these agreements are necessary to attract and retain qualified individuals to serve as directors and executive officers.

The limitation of liability and indemnification provisions that are expected to be included in our amended and restated certificate of incorporation, amended and restated bylaws, and the indemnification agreements that we have entered into or will enter into with our directors and executive officers may discourage stockholders from bringing a lawsuit against our directors and executive officers for breach of their fiduciary duties. They may also reduce the likelihood of derivative litigation against our directors and executive officers, even though an action, if successful, might benefit us and other stockholders. Further, a stockholder's investment may be adversely affected to the extent that we pay the costs of settlement and damage awards against directors and executive officers as required by these indemnification provisions. At present, we are not aware of any pending litigation or proceeding involving any person who is or was one of our directors, officers, employees, or other agents or is or was serving at our request as a director, officer, employee, or agent of another corporation, partnership, joint venture, trust, or other enterprise, for which indemnification is sought, and we are not aware of any threatened litigation that may result in claims for indemnification.

We have obtained insurance policies under which, subject to the limitations of the policies, coverage is provided to our directors and executive officers against loss arising from claims made by reason of breach of fiduciary duty or other wrongful acts as a director or executive officer, including claims relating to public securities matters, and to us with respect to payments that may be made by us to these directors and executive officers pursuant to our indemnification obligations or otherwise as a matter of law.

Certain of our non-employee directors may, through their relationships with their employers, be insured and/or indemnified against certain liabilities incurred in their capacity as members of our Board of Directors.

The underwriting agreement filed as Exhibit 1.1 to this registration statement will provide for indemnification by the underwriters of us and our officers and directors for certain liabilities arising under the Securities Act or otherwise.

ITEM 15. RECENT SALES OF UNREGISTERED SECURITIES.

Since January 1, 2014, we have issued the following unregistered securities:

Preferred Stock Issuances

From January 2014 through April 2014, we sold an aggregate of 12,307,226 shares of our Series C convertible preferred stock to 55 accredited investors at a purchase price of approximately $28.65 per share, for an aggregate purchase price of $352,625,362.

II-2

Option and RSU Issuances

From January 1, 2014 to December 31, 2017, we granted to our directors, officers, employees, consultants, and other service providers options to purchase an aggregate of 10,295,142 shares of our Class B common stock under our 2008 Plan at exercise prices ranging from approximately $20.76 to $25.23 per share.

From January 1, 2014 to December 31, 2017, we granted to our directors, officers, employees, consultants, and other service providers an aggregate of 19,186,292 RSUs to be settled in shares of our Class A common stock under our 2017 Plan and an aggregate of 51,321,122 RSUs to be settled in shares of our Class B common stock under our 2008 Plan.

RSA Grants

In December 2017, we granted RSAs with respect to 14.7 million shares of Class A common stock, of which 10.3 million RSAs were granted to Mr. Houston, our co-founder and Chief Executive Officer, and 4.4 million RSAs were granted to Mr. Ferdowsi, our co-founder and Director.

Shares Issued in Connection with Third-Party Tender Offer

From January 1, 2014 to December 31, 2017, we issued an aggregate of 5,452,108 shares of our Class A common stock in connection with a third-party tender offer to purchase shares of our capital stock from certain holders of our Class B common stock and convertible preferred stock. Each share of our Class B common stock and convertible preferred stock transferred in connection with the tender offer was automatically converted to one share of our Class A common stock.

Shares Issued in Connection with Acquisitions

From January 1, 2014 to December 31, 2017, we issued an aggregate of 4,177,085 shares of our Class B common stock in connection with our acquisitions of certain companies or their assets and as consideration to individuals and entities who were former service providers and/or stockholders of such companies.

None of the foregoing transactions involved any underwriters, underwriting discounts or commissions, or any public offering. We believe the offers, sales, and issuances of the above securities were exempt from registration under the Securities Act (or Regulation D or Regulation S promulgated thereunder) by virtue of Section 4(2) of the Securities Act because the issuance of securities to the recipients did not involve a public offering, or in reliance on Rule 701 because the transactions were pursuant to compensatory benefit plans or contracts relating to compensation as provided under such rule. The recipients of the securities in each of these transactions represented their intentions to acquire the securities for investment only and not with a view to or for sale in connection with any distribution thereof, and appropriate legends were placed upon the stock certificates issued in these transactions. All recipients had adequate access, through their relationships with us, to information about us. The sales of these securities were made without any general solicitation or advertising.

ITEM 16. EXHIBITS AND FINANCIAL STATEMENT SCHEDULES.

(a) Exhibits.

See the Exhibit Index immediately preceding the signature page hereto for a list of exhibits filed as part of this registration statement on Form S-1, which Exhibit Index is incorporated herein by reference.

(b) Financial statement schedules.

All financial statement schedules are omitted because the information called for is not required or is shown either in the consolidated financial statements or in the notes thereto.

II-3

ITEM 17. UNDERTAKINGS.

The undersigned Registrant hereby undertakes to provide to the underwriters at the closing specified in the underwriting agreement certificates in such denominations and registered in such names as required by the underwriters to permit prompt delivery to each purchaser.

Insofar as indemnification for liabilities arising under the Securities Act of 1933, as amended, or the Act, may be permitted to directors, officers, and controlling persons of the registrant pursuant to the foregoing provisions, or otherwise, the registrant has been advised that in the opinion of the Securities and Exchange Commission such indemnification is against public policy as expressed in the Act and is, therefore, unenforceable. In the event that a claim for indemnification against such liabilities (other than the payment by the registrant of expenses incurred or paid by a director, officer, or controlling person of the registrant in the successful defense of any action, suit, or proceeding) is asserted by such director, officer, or controlling person in connection with the securities being registered, the registrant will, unless in the opinion of its counsel the matter has been settled by controlling precedent, submit to a court of appropriate jurisdiction the question whether such indemnification by it is against public policy as expressed in the Act and will be governed by the final adjudication of such issue.

The undersigned Registrant hereby undertakes that:

(1)   For purposes of determining any liability under the Act, the information omitted from the form of prospectus filed as part of this registration statement in reliance upon Rule 430A and contained in a form of prospectus filed by the Registrant pursuant to Rule 424(b)(1) or (4) or 497(h) under the Securities Act shall be deemed to be part of this registration statement as of the time it was declared effective.

(2)   For the purpose of determining any liability under the Act, each post-effective amendment that contains a form of prospectus shall be deemed to be a new registration statement relating to the securities offered therein, and the offering of such securities at that time shall be deemed to be the initial bona fide offering thereof.

II-4

326

EXHIBIT INDEX

Exhibit Number	Description
1.1#	Form of Underwriting Agreement.
3.1#	Restated Certificate of Incorporation of the Registrant, as amended and currently in effect.
3.2#	Certificate of Amendment to the Restated Certificate of Incorporation, as filed on April 4, 2014.
3.3#	Certificate of Amendment to the Restated Certificate of Incorporation, as filed on April 21, 2016.
3.4#	Certificate of Amendment to the Restated Certificate of Incorporation, as filed on March 7, 2018.
3.5#	Form of Amended and Restated Certificate of Incorporation of the Registrant, to be in effect upon completion of this offering.
3.6#	Bylaws of the Registrant, as amended and currently in effect.
3.7#	Form of Amended and Restated Bylaws of the Registrant, to be in effect upon completion of this offering.
4.1#	Form of Class A common stock certificate of the Registrant.
4.2#	Amended and Restated Investors' Rights Agreement among the Registrant and certain holders of its capital stock, dated as of January 30, 2014, as amended.
5.1#	Opinion of Wilson Sonsini Goodrich & Rosati, P.C.
10.1+#	Form of Indemnification Agreement between the Registrant and each of its directors and executive officers.
10.2+	Dropbox, Inc. 2018 Equity Incentive Plan and related form agreements.
10.3+	Dropbox, Inc. 2018 Employee Stock Purchase Plan and related form agreements.
10.4+	Dropbox, Inc. 2018 Class C Stock Incentive Plan and related form agreements.
10.5+	Dropbox, Inc. 2018 Class C Employee Stock Purchase Plan and related form agreements.
10.6+	Dropbox, Inc. 2017 Equity Incentive Plan and related form agreements.
10.7+	Dropbox, Inc. 2008 Equity Incentive Plan, as amended, and related form agreements.
10.8+#	Dropbox, Inc. Amended and Restated Cash Bonus Plan.
10.9+#	Restricted Stock Agreement between the Registrant and Andrew W. Houston.
10.10+#	Restricted Stock Agreement between the Registrant and Arash Ferdowsi.
10.11+#	Form of Change of Control and Severance Agreement between the Registrant and certain executive officers.
10.12+#	Employment Letter between the Registrant and Andrew W. Houston.
10.13+#	Employment Letter between the Registrant and Arash Ferdowsi.
10.14+#	Employment Letter between the Registrant and Quentin J. Clark.
10.15#	Office Lease between the Registrant and Kilroy Realty Finance Partnership, L.P., dated as of January 31, 2014.
10.16#	First Amendment to Office Lease between the Registrant and Kilroy Realty Finance Partnership, L.P., dated as of June 5, 2015.
10.17#	Second Amendment to Office Lease between the Registrant and Kilroy Realty Finance Partnership, L.P., dated as of May 3, 2016.

II-5

Exhibit Number	Description
10.18#	Third Amendment to Office Lease between the Registrant and Kilroy Realty Finance Partnership, L.P., dated as of October 6, 2017.
10.19#	Office Lease between the Registrant and KR Mission Bay, LLC, dated as of October 6, 2017.
10.20#	Second Amendment and Restatement to the Revolving Credit and Guaranty Agreement among the Registrant, the lenders party thereto and JPMorgan Chase Bank, N.A., as Administrative Agent, dated as of April 3, 2017.
10.21#	Incremental Facility and Amendment Agreement among the Registrant, the lenders party thereto and JPMorgan Chase Bank, N.A., as Administrative Agent, dated as of February 9, 2018.
10.22#	Class A Common Stock Purchase Agreement by and among the Registrant, salesforce.com, inc. and Salesforce Ventures LLC, dated as of March 7, 2018.
10.23+#	Dropbox, Inc. Outside Director Compensation Policy and related form agreements.
21.1#	List of subsidiaries of the Registrant.
23.1	Consent of Ernst & Young LLP, Independent Registered Public Accounting Firm.
23.2#	Consent of Wilson Sonsini Goodrich & Rosati, P.C. (included in Exhibit 5.1).
24.1#	Power of Attorney (included on page II-7).

\# Previously filed.
+ Indicates management contract or compensatory plan.

SIGNATURES

Pursuant to the requirements of the Securities Act of 1933, as amended, the Registrant has duly caused this registration statement on Form S-1 to be signed on its behalf by the undersigned, thereunto duly authorized, in San Francisco, California, on the 21st day of March, 2018.

DROPBOX, INC.

By: /s/ Andrew W. Houston
_____
Andrew W. Houston
Chief Executive Officer

Pursuant to the requirements of the Securities Act of 1933, as amended, this registration statement on Form S-1 has been signed by the following persons in the capacities and on the dates indicated.

Signature	Title	Date
/s/ Andrew W. Houston Andrew W. Houston	Chief Executive Officer and Chairman *(Principal Executive Officer)*	March 21, 2018
/s/ Ajay V. Vashee Ajay V. Vashee	Chief Financial Officer *(Principal Financial Officer)*	March 21, 2018
/s/ Timothy J. Regan Timothy J. Regan	Chief Accounting Officer *(Principal Accounting Officer)*	March 21, 2018
* Donald W. Blair	Director	March 21, 2018
* Arash Ferdowsi	Director	March 21, 2018
* Paul E. Jacobs	Director	March 21, 2018
* Robert J. Mylod, Jr.	Director	March 21, 2018
* Condoleezza Rice	Director	March 21, 2018
* R. Bryan Schreier	Director	March 21, 2018
* Margaret C. Whitman	Director	March 21, 2018

*By: /s/ Andrew W. Houston
_____
Andrew W. Houston
Attorney-in-Fact

II-7

Exhibit 1.1

Dropbox, Inc.

Class A Common Stock, $0.00001 par value per share

Underwriting Agreement

[●], 2018

Goldman Sachs & Co. LLC
J.P. Morgan Securities LLC
As representatives of the several Underwriters named in Schedule I hereto,

c/o Goldman Sachs & Co. LLC
200 West Street
New York, New York 10282-2198

c/o J.P. Morgan Securities LLC
383 Madison Avenue
New York, New York 10179

Ladies and Gentlemen:

Dropbox, Inc., a Delaware corporation (the "Company"), proposes, subject to the terms and conditions stated in this agreement (this "Agreement"), to issue and sell to the Underwriters named in Schedule I hereto (the "Underwriters"), for whom Goldman Sachs & Co. LLC and J.P. Morgan Securities LLC are acting as representatives (the "Representatives"), an aggregate of [●] shares and, at the election of the Underwriters, up to [●] additional shares of Class A common stock (the "Stock") of the Company, and the stockholders of the Company named in Schedule II hereto (the "Selling Stockholders") propose, subject to the terms and conditions stated in this Agreement to sell to the Underwriters an aggregate of [●] shares. The aggregate of [●] shares to be sold by the Company and the Selling Stockholders is herein called the "Firm Shares" and the aggregate of [●] additional shares to be sold by the Company is herein called the "Optional Shares". The Firm Shares and the Optional Shares that the Underwriters elect to purchase pursuant to Section 2 hereof are herein collectively called the "Shares".

The Company and the Underwriters, in accordance with the requirements of Rule 5121 of Financial Industry Regulatory Authority Inc. ("Rule 5121") and subject to the terms and conditions stated herein, also hereby confirm the engagement of the services of Allen & Company LLC ("Allen & Co.") as a "qualified independent underwriter" (the "QIU") within the meaning of Rule 5121 in connection with the offering and sale of the Shares. No compensation will be paid to the QIU for its services.

1. (a) The Company represents and warrants to, and agrees with, each of the Underwriters that:

(i) A registration statement on Form S–1 (File No. 333-223182) (the "Initial Registration Statement") in respect of the Shares has been filed with the Securities and

330

Exchange Commission (the "Commission"); the Initial Registration Statement and any post-effective amendment thereto, each in the form heretofore delivered to the Representatives, have been declared effective by the Commission in such form; other than a registration statement, if any, increasing the size of the offering (a "Rule 462(b) Registration Statement"), filed pursuant to Rule 462(b) under the Securities Act of 1933, as amended (the "Act"), which became effective upon filing, no other document with respect to the Initial Registration Statement has been filed with the Commission; and no stop order suspending the effectiveness of the Initial Registration Statement, any post-effective amendment thereto or the Rule 462(b) Registration Statement, if any, has been issued and no proceeding for that purpose has been initiated or, to the Company's knowledge, threatened by the Commission (any preliminary prospectus included in the Initial Registration Statement or filed with the Commission pursuant to Rule 424(a) of the rules and regulations of the Commission under the Act is hereinafter called a "Preliminary Prospectus"; the various parts of the Initial Registration Statement and the Rule 462(b) Registration Statement, if any, including all exhibits thereto and including the information contained in the form of final prospectus filed with the Commission pursuant to Rule 424(b) under the Act in accordance with Section 5(a) hereof and deemed by virtue of Rule 430A under the Act to be part of the Initial Registration Statement at the time it was declared effective, each as amended at the time such part of the Initial Registration Statement became effective or such part of the Rule 462(b) Registration Statement, if any, became or hereafter becomes effective, are hereinafter collectively called the "Registration Statement"; the Preliminary Prospectus relating to the Shares that was included in the Registration Statement immediately prior to the Applicable Time (as defined in Section 1(a)(iii) hereof) is hereinafter called the "Pricing Prospectus"; such final prospectus, in the form first filed pursuant to Rule 424(b) under the Act, is hereinafter called the "Prospectus"; any oral or written communication with potential investors undertaken in reliance on Section 5(d) of the Act is hereinafter called a "Section 5(d) Communication"; and any Section 5(d) Communication that is a written communication within the meaning of Rule 405 under the Act is hereinafter called a "Section 5(d) Writing"; and any "issuer free writing prospectus" as defined in Rule 433 under the Act relating to the Shares is hereinafter called an "Issuer Free Writing Prospectus");

(ii)   (A) No order preventing or suspending the use of any Preliminary Prospectus or any Issuer Free Writing Prospectus has been issued by the Commission, and (B) each Preliminary Prospectus, at the time of filing thereof, conformed in all material respects to the requirements of the Act and the rules and regulations of the Commission thereunder, and did not contain an untrue statement of a material fact or omit to state a material fact required to be stated therein or necessary to make the statements therein, in the light of the circumstances under which they were made, not misleading; provided, however, that this representation and warranty shall not apply to any statements or omissions made in reliance upon and in conformity with the Underwriter Information (as defined in Section 9(c) of this Agreement) or any Selling Stockholder Information (as defined in Section 1(b)(vi) hereof);

(iii)   For the purposes of this Agreement, the "Applicable Time" is [___:___] (Eastern time) on the date of this Agreement; the Pricing Prospectus, as supplemented by the information listed on Schedule III(b) hereto, taken together (collectively, the "Pricing Disclosure Package"), as of the Applicable Time, did not include any untrue statement of a material fact or omit to state any material fact necessary in order to make the statements therein, in the light of the circumstances under which they were made, not misleading; and each Issuer Free Writing Prospectus and each Section 5(d) Writing listed on Schedule III(c) hereto does not conflict with the information contained in the Registration Statement, the Pricing Prospectus or the

Prospectus, and each Issuer Free Writing Prospectus and each Section 5(d) Writing listed on Schedule III(c) hereto, as supplemented by and taken together with the Pricing Disclosure Package, as of the Applicable Time, did not include any untrue statement of a material fact or omit to state any material fact necessary in order to make the statements therein, in the light of the circumstances under which they were made, not misleading; provided, however, that this representation and warranty shall not apply to statements or omissions made in reliance upon and in conformity with the Underwriter Information or the Selling Stockholder Information;

(iv)   The Registration Statement conforms, and the Prospectus and any further amendments or supplements to the Registration Statement and the Prospectus will conform, in all material respects to the requirements of the Act and the rules and regulations of the Commission thereunder and do not and will not, as of the applicable effective date as to each part of the Registration Statement, as of the applicable filing date as to the Prospectus and any amendment or supplement thereto, contain an untrue statement of a material fact or omit to state a material fact required to be stated therein or necessary to make the statements therein not misleading; provided, however, that this representation and warranty shall not apply to any statements or omissions made in reliance upon and in conformity with the Underwriter Information or the Selling Stockholder Information;

(v)   Neither the Company nor any of its subsidiaries has, since the date of the latest audited financial statements included in the Pricing Prospectus, (i) sustained any material loss or interference with its business from fire, explosion, flood or other calamity, whether or not covered by insurance, or from any labor dispute or court or governmental action, order or decree, or (ii) entered into any transaction or agreement (whether or not in the ordinary course of business) that is material to the Company and its subsidiaries taken as a whole or incurred any liability or obligation, direct or contingent, that is material to the Company and its subsidiaries taken as a whole, in each case, otherwise than as set forth or contemplated in the Pricing Prospectus; and, since the respective dates as of which information is given in the Registration Statement and the Pricing Prospectus, there has not been (x) any change in the capital stock (other than as a result of (i) the exercise or settlement (including any "net" or "cashless" exercises or settlements) of stock options or restricted stock units or the award, if any, of stock options or restricted stock units in the ordinary course of business, in each case pursuant to the Company's equity plans that are described in the Pricing Prospectus, (ii) the repurchase of shares of capital stock pursuant to agreements providing for an option to repurchase or a right of first refusal on behalf of the Company pursuant to the Company's repurchase rights or (iii) the issuance, if any, of stock upon conversion of Company securities as described in the Pricing Prospectus) or long-term debt of the Company or any of its subsidiaries or (y) any Material Adverse Effect (as defined below); as used in this Agreement, "Material Adverse Effect" shall mean any material adverse change or effect, or any development involving a prospective material adverse change or effect, in or affecting the business, management, consolidated financial position, consolidated stockholders' equity or consolidated results of operations of the Company and its subsidiaries, taken as a whole, except as set forth or contemplated in the Pricing Prospectus;

(vi)   The Company and its subsidiaries do not own any real property. Except as would not reasonably be expected to have a Material Adverse Effect, the Company and its subsidiaries have good and marketable title to all personal property owned by them (other than with respect to Intellectual Property, title to which is addressed exclusively in subsection (xxvi)), free and clear of all liens, encumbrances and defects, and any real property and buildings held under lease by the Company and its subsidiaries are held by them under, to the Company's knowledge, valid, subsisting and enforceable leases (subject to the effects of (i) bankruptcy, insolvency, fraudulent conveyance, fraudulent transfer, reorganization, moratorium or other similar laws relating to or affecting the rights or remedies of creditors generally; (ii) the application of general principles of equity (including without limitation, concepts of materiality, reasonableness, good faith and fair dealing, regardless of whether enforcement is considered in proceedings at law or in equity); and (iii) applicable law and public policy with respect to rights to indemnity and contribution);

(vii)   The Company has been (i) duly incorporated and is validly existing and in good standing under the laws of the state of Delaware, with power and authority (corporate and other) to own its properties and conduct its business as described in the Pricing Prospectus, and (ii) duly qualified as a foreign corporation for the transaction of business and is in good standing under the laws of each other jurisdiction in which it owns or leases properties or conducts any business so as to require such qualification, except, in the case of this clause (ii), where the failure to be so qualified or in good standing would not, individually or in the aggregate, reasonably be expected to have a Material Adverse Effect; and each of the Company's subsidiaries has been duly organized and is validly existing as a corporation or other entity, as applicable, and in good standing (or the foreign equivalent) under the laws of its jurisdiction of organization, with power and authority (corporate and otherwise) to own its properties and conduct its business as described in the Pricing Prospectus, except where the failure to be in good standing (or the foreign equivalent) would not, individually or in the aggregate, reasonably be expected to have a Material Adverse Effect;

(viii)   The Company has an authorized capitalization as set forth in the Pricing Prospectus and all of the issued shares of capital stock of the Company, including the Shares to be sold by the Selling Stockholders, have been duly and validly authorized and issued and are fully paid and non-assessable and conform in all material respects to the description of the Stock contained in the Pricing Disclosure Package and the Prospectus; and all of the issued shares of capital stock of each subsidiary of the Company have been duly and validly authorized and issued, are fully paid and non-assessable and (except, in the case of any foreign subsidiary, for directors' qualifying shares) are owned directly or indirectly by the Company, free and clear of all liens, encumbrances, equities or claims, except for such liens or encumbrances described in the Pricing Prospectus and the Prospectus;

(ix)   The Shares to be issued and sold by the Company to the Underwriters hereunder have been duly and validly authorized and, when issued and delivered against payment therefor as provided herein, will be duly and validly issued and fully paid and non-assessable and will conform in all material respects to the description of the Stock contained in the Pricing Prospectus and the Prospectus; and the issuance of the Shares is not subject to any preemptive, registration or similar rights, in each case other than rights which have been complied with or waived in writing;

(x)   The issue and sale of the Shares to be sold by the Company and the compliance by the Company with this Agreement and the consummation of the transactions contemplated in this Agreement and the Pricing Prospectus will not conflict with or result in a breach or violation of any of the terms or provisions of, or constitute a default under, (A) any indenture, mortgage, deed of trust, loan agreement, lease or other agreement or instrument to which the Company or any of its subsidiaries is a party or by which the Company or any of its subsidiaries is bound or to which any of the property or assets of the Company or any of its subsidiaries is subject, (B) the certificate of incorporation or by-laws of (1) the Company or (2) any of its subsidiaries, or (C) any statute or any judgment, order, rule or regulation of any court or governmental agency or body having jurisdiction over the Company or any of its subsidiaries or any of their properties, except in the case of (A), (B)(2) and (C) for such violations that would not individually or in the aggregate, reasonably be expected to have a Material Adverse Effect or materially impair the ability of the Company to perform its obligations under this Agreement, including the issuance and sale of the Shares, or to consummate the transactions contemplated in the Pricing Prospectus and the Prospectus; and no consent, approval, authorization, order, registration or qualification of or with any such court or governmental agency or body is required for the issue of the Shares to be sold by the Company and the sale of the Shares or the consummation by the Company of the transactions contemplated by this Agreement, except such as have been obtained under the Act, the approval by the Financial Industry Regulatory Authority ("FINRA") of the underwriting terms and arrangements, the approval for listing on the Nasdaq Stock Market Inc.'s National Market ("NASDAQ") and such consents, approvals, authorizations, orders, registrations or qualifications as may be required under state securities or Blue Sky laws in connection with the purchase and distribution of the Shares by the Underwriters;

(xi)   Neither the Company nor any of its subsidiaries is (i) in violation of its certificate of incorporation or by-laws or other applicable organizational document, as applicable (ii) in violation of any statute or any judgment, order, rule or regulation of any court or governmental agency or body having jurisdiction over the Company or any of its subsidiaries or any of their properties, or (iii) in default in the performance or observance of any obligation, agreement, covenant or condition contained in any indenture, mortgage, deed of trust, loan agreement, lease or other agreement or instrument to which it is a party or by which it or any of its properties may be bound, except, in the case of the foregoing clauses (ii) and (iii) and, with respect to the Company's subsidiaries in the case of clause (i), for such defaults as would not, individually or in the aggregate, reasonably be expected to have a Material Adverse Effect;

(xii)   The statements set forth in the Pricing Prospectus and the Prospectus under the caption "Description of Capital Stock", insofar as they purport to constitute a summary of the terms of the Stock, under the caption "Material U.S. Federal Income Tax Consequences to Non-U.S. Holders of Our Class A Common Stock", and under the caption "Underwriting (Conflicts of Interest)", insofar as they purport to describe the provisions of the laws and documents referred to therein, are accurate, complete and fair in all material respects;

(xiii)   Other than as set forth in the Pricing Prospectus, there are no legal or governmental proceedings pending to which the Company or any of its subsidiaries or, to the Company's knowledge, any officer or director of the Company is a party or of which any property or assets of the Company or any of its subsidiaries or, to the Company's knowledge, any officer or director of the Company is the subject which, if determined adversely to the Company or any of its subsidiaries (or such officer or director), would individually or in the aggregate have a Material Adverse Effect; and, to the Company's knowledge, no such proceedings are threatened or contemplated by governmental authorities or threatened by others;

(xiv)   The Company is not and, immediately after giving effect to the offering and sale of the Shares and the application of the proceeds thereof, will not be required to register as an "investment company", as such term is defined in the Investment Company Act of 1940, as amended (the "Investment Company Act");

(xv)   At the time of filing the Initial Registration Statement and at the date hereof, the Company was not and is not an "ineligible issuer," as defined under Rule 405 under the Act;

(xvi)   Ernst & Young LLP, who has certified certain financial statements of the Company and its subsidiaries, is an independent registered public accounting firm as required by the Act and the rules and regulations of the Commission thereunder;

(xvii)   The Company maintains a system of internal control over financial reporting (as such term is defined in Rule 13a-15(f) under the Securities Exchange Act of 1934, as amended (the "Exchange Act")) that (i) complies with the requirements of the Exchange Act applicable to the Company, (ii) has been designed by the Company's principal executive officer and principal financial officer, or under their supervision, to provide reasonable assurance regarding the reliability of financial reporting and the preparation of financial statements for external purposes in accordance with generally accepted accounting principles and (iii) is sufficient to provide reasonable assurance that (A) transactions are executed in accordance with management's general or specific authorization, (B) transactions are recorded as necessary to permit preparation of financial statements in conformity with generally accepted accounting principles and to maintain accountability for assets, (C) access to assets is permitted only in accordance with management's general or specific authorization and (D) the recorded accountability for assets is compared with the existing assets at reasonable intervals and appropriate action is taken with respect to any differences; and except as disclosed in the Pricing Prospectus, the Company is not aware of any material weaknesses in its internal control over financial reporting (it being understood that this subsection shall not require the Company to comply with Section 404 of the Sarbanes-Oxley Act of 2002 as of an earlier date than it would otherwise be required to so comply under applicable law);

(xviii)   Since the date of the latest audited financial statements included in the Pricing Prospectus, there has been no change in the Company's internal control over financial reporting that has materially and adversely affected, or is reasonably likely to materially and adversely affect, the Company's internal control over financial reporting;

(xix)   The Company maintains disclosure controls and procedures (as such term is defined in Rule 13a-15(e) under the Exchange Act) that comply with the requirements of the Exchange Act applicable to the Company; such disclosure controls and procedures have been designed to ensure that material information relating to the Company and its subsidiaries is made known to the Company's principal executive officer and principal financial officer by others within those entities; and such disclosure controls and procedures are effective;

(xx)   This Agreement has been duly authorized, executed and delivered by the Company;

(xxi)   None of the Company or any of its subsidiaries nor, to the knowledge of the Company, any director, officer, agent, employee, affiliate or other person, while acting on behalf of the Company or any of its subsidiaries has (i) made, offered, promised or authorized any unlawful contribution, gift, entertainment or other unlawful expense; (ii) made, offered, promised or authorized any direct or indirect unlawful payment to any foreign or domestic government official or employee (including any officer or employee of a government or government-owned or controlled entity or of a public international organization, or any person acting in an official capacity for or on behalf of any of the foregoing, or any political party or party official or candidate for political office) from corporate funds; or (iii) violated or is in violation of any provision of the Foreign Corrupt Practices Act of 1977, the Bribery Act 2010 of the United Kingdom or any other applicable anti-bribery or anti-corruption law applicable to the Company; and the Company and its subsidiaries conduct their business in compliance with applicable anti-corruption laws in all material respects and have instituted and maintained policies and procedures designed to promote and achieve compliance with such laws in all material respects;

(xxii) The operations of the Company and its subsidiaries are and have been conducted at all times in compliance with the requirements of applicable anti-money laundering laws, including, but not limited to, the Bank Secrecy Act of 1970, as amended by the USA PATRIOT ACT of 2001, and the rules and regulations promulgated thereunder, and the applicable anti-money laundering laws of the various jurisdictions in which the Company and its subsidiaries conduct business (collectively, the "Money Laundering Laws") and no action, suit or proceeding by or before any court or governmental agency, authority or body or any arbitrator involving the Company or any of its subsidiaries with respect to the Money Laundering Laws is pending or, to the knowledge of the Company, threatened;

(xxiii) None of the Company or any of its subsidiaries nor, to the knowledge of the Company, any director, officer, agent, employee or affiliate of the Company or any of its subsidiaries is currently the subject or the target of any sanctions administered or enforced by the U.S. Government, including, without limitation, the Office of Foreign Assets Control of the U.S. Department of the Treasury, or other relevant sanctions authority (collectively, "Sanctions"), and the Company will not directly or indirectly use the proceeds of the offering of the Shares hereunder, or lend, contribute or otherwise make available such proceeds to any subsidiary, joint venture partner or other person or entity (i) to fund or facilitate any activities of or business with any person, or in any country or territory, that, at the time of such funding, is the subject or the target of Sanctions or (ii) in any other manner that will result in a violation by any person (including any person participating in the transaction, whether as underwriter, advisor, investor or otherwise) of Sanctions. Except for any violations that have been disclosed in the Pricing Prospectus or are otherwise related to the Voluntary Self Disclosure filings that have been identified in the Pricing Prospectus, for the past five years, the Company and its subsidiaries have not engaged in and are not now knowingly engaged in any dealings or transactions in violation of U.S. Sanctions;

(xxiv) The financial statements, together with the related schedules and notes, included in the Registration Statement, the Pricing Prospectus and the Prospectus present fairly in all material respects the financial position of the Company and its subsidiaries at the dates indicated and the statement of operations, stockholders' equity and cash flows of the Company and its subsidiaries for the periods specified; said financial statements have been prepared in conformity with U.S. generally accepted accounting principles ("GAAP") applied on a consistent basis throughout the periods involved. The supporting schedules, if any, included in the Registration Statement, the Pricing Prospectus and the Prospectus, present fairly in all material respects the information required to be stated therein in accordance with GAAP. The selected financial data and the summary financial information included in the Registration Statement, the Pricing Prospectus and the Prospectus present fairly the information shown therein and have been compiled on a basis consistent with that of the audited financial statements included therein. No other historical or pro forma financial statements or supporting schedules are required to be included in the Registration Statement, the Pricing Prospectus or the Prospectus under the Act or the rules and regulations promulgated thereunder. All disclosures contained in the Registration Statement, the Pricing Prospectus and the Prospectus regarding "non-GAAP financial measures" (as such term is defined by the rules and regulations of the Commission) comply in all material respects with Regulation G of the Exchange Act and Item 10 of Regulation S-K of the Act, to the extent applicable;

(xxv)   At time of initial confidential submission of a registration statement relating to the Shares with the Commission (or, if earlier, the first date on which a Section 5(d) Communication was made), the Company was an "emerging growth company" as defined in Section 2(a)(19) of the Act (an "Emerging Growth Company"), and continued to be an "emerging growth company" through December 31, 2017;

(xxvi)   To the Company's knowledge (solely with respect to third party patents and patent rights), the Company and its subsidiaries own or possess, or can acquire on commercially reasonable terms, sufficient rights to use all patents, copyrights, know-how (including trade secrets and other unpatented and/or unpatentable proprietary or confidential information, systems or procedures), trademarks, service marks and trade names, Internet domain names and all goodwill associated therewith and other technology and intellectual property rights (collectively, the "Intellectual Property") used in the conduct of their respective businesses as currently conducted, except where the failure to own or possess any of the foregoing would not reasonably be expected to have a Material Adverse Effect. Except as disclosed in the Pricing Prospectus, neither the Company nor any of its subsidiaries has received any written notice of any claim of infringement, misappropriation or conflict with, asserted rights of others with respect to any Intellectual Property which, individually or in the aggregate, if the subject of an unfavorable decision, ruling or finding, would reasonably be expected to have a Material Adverse Effect; and except as would not reasonably be expected to have a Material Adverse Effect, to the Company's knowledge, (A) the conduct of the business of the Company and its subsidiaries does not infringe, misappropriate or violate the Intellectual Property of others and (B) no third party is infringing any Intellectual Property owned by the Company or its subsidiaries;

(xxvii)   No material labor disputes against the Company or any of its subsidiaries exists or, to the knowledge of the Company, is threatened;

(xxviii)   Except as would not, individually or in the aggregate, have a Material Adverse Effect, the Company reasonably believes that (i) the Company and its subsidiaries own or have a valid right to access and use all computer systems, networks, hardware, software, databases, websites, and equipment used to process, store, maintain and operate data, information, and functions used in connection with the business of the Company and its subsidiaries (the "Company IT Systems"), (ii) the Company IT Systems are adequate for, and operate and perform as required in connection with, the operation of the business of the Company and its subsidiaries as currently conducted and (iii) the Company and its subsidiaries have implemented reasonable backup, security and disaster recovery technology consistent with applicable regulatory standards;

(xxix)   Except as described in the Pricing Prospectus, the Company has not sold or issued any shares of capital stock during the six-month period preceding the date of the Prospectus, including any sales pursuant to Rule 144A under, or Regulations D or S of, the Act, other than shares issued pursuant to employee benefit plans, stock option plans or other employee compensation plans or pursuant to outstanding options, restricted stock units, rights or warrants;

(xxx)   The Company and its subsidiaries taken as a whole are insured by insurers of recognized financial responsibility against such losses and risks and in such amounts as are, in the Company's reasonable judgment, prudent and customary in the business in which it is engaged; and none of the Company or any of its subsidiaries has any reason to believe that it will not be able to renew its existing insurance coverage as and when such coverage expires or to obtain similar coverage from similar insurers as may be necessary to continue its business at a cost that would not have a Material Adverse Effect;

(xxxi)   The Company and each of its subsidiaries (i) are in compliance with all applicable laws, regulations, ordinances, rules, orders, judgments, decrees, permits or other legal requirements of any governmental authority, including without limitation any international, national, state, provincial, regional, or local authority, relating to the protection of human health or safety, the environment, or natural resources, or to hazardous or toxic substances or wastes, pollutants or contaminants ("Environmental Laws"), (ii) have received all permits, licenses or other approvals required of them under applicable Environmental Laws to conduct their respective businesses, (iii) are in compliance with all terms and conditions of any such permit, license or approval, and (iv) the Company has not received notice of any proceedings that are pending or threatened against the Company or any of its subsidiaries under Environmental Laws in which a governmental authority is also a party, except where such non-compliance with Environmental Laws, or where any claim, request, notice, proceeding, investigation, failure to receive required permits, licenses or other approvals or failure to comply with the terms and conditions of such permits, licenses or approvals would not individually or in the aggregate reasonably be expected to have a Material Adverse Effect;

(xxxii)   Except as would not, either individually or in the aggregate, have a Material Adverse Effect, the Company and its subsidiaries possess, and are in compliance with the terms of, all certificates, authorizations, franchises, licenses and permits ("Business Licenses") necessary to the conduct of the business now conducted and the Company and its subsidiaries have not received any notice of proceedings relating to the revocation or modification of any Business Licenses;

(xxxiii)   The statistical and market-related data included in the Pricing Prospectus and the Prospectus are based on or derived from estimates and sources that the Company believes to be reliable and accurate in all material respects;

(xxxiv)   The Company has not, directly or indirectly, including through any subsidiary, extended or maintained credit, or arranged for the extension of credit, or renewed any extension of credit, in the form of a personal loan to or for any of its directors or executive officers that was outstanding at or after the time of the first filing of the Registration Statement with the Commission;

(xxxv)   Except for cases in which the failure to file or pay would not, individually or in the aggregate, reasonably be expected to have a Material Adverse Effect, the Company and each of its subsidiaries have filed all federal, state, local and foreign income and franchise tax returns required to be filed through the date hereof, subject to permitted extensions, and have paid all taxes due thereon. Except for cases where a tax deficiency would not, individually or in the aggregate, reasonably be expected to have a Material Adverse Effect, (i) no tax deficiency has been determined adversely to the Company or any of its subsidiaries, and (ii) the Company has not received any written notice from any taxing authorities asserting any tax deficiency against the Company and its subsidiaries;

(xxxvi)   Neither the Company nor any of its subsidiaries has taken, directly or indirectly, any action that was designed to or that has constituted or that might reasonably be expected to cause or result in the manipulation of the price of any security of the Company to facilitate the sale of the Shares;

(xxxvii)   There are no contracts or other documents of a character required to be described in the Registration Statement, the Pricing Prospectus or the Prospectus or to be filed as an exhibit to the Registration Statement which are not described or filed as required pursuant to the requirements of Form S-1;

(xxxviii)   Except as would not, individually or in the aggregate, reasonably be expected to have a Material Adverse Effect, (i) the Company and its subsidiaries have (A) operated and currently operate their respective businesses in a manner compliant with all applicable foreign, federal, state and local laws and regulations, all contractual obligations and all Company policies (internal and posted) related to privacy and data security applicable to the Company's, and its subsidiaries', collection, use, handling, transfer, transmission, storage, disclosure and/or disposal of the data of their respective customers, employees and other third parties (the "Privacy and Data Security Laws") and (B) implemented, monitored and have been and are in compliance with, applicable administrative, technical and physical safeguards and policies and procedures designed to ensure compliance with Privacy and Data Security Laws and (ii) except as described in the Pricing Prospectus, there has been no loss or unauthorized access, use, modification or breach of security of customer, employee or third party data maintained by or on behalf of the Company and its subsidiaries, and neither the Company nor any of its subsidiaries has notified, nor has the current intention to notify, any customer, governmental entity or the media of any such event with regard to any material data breach;

(xxxix)   (i) Each employee benefit plan, within the meaning of Section 3(3) of the Employee Retirement Income Security Act of 1974, as amended ("ERISA"), for which the Company or any member of its "Controlled Group" (defined as any organization which is a member of a controlled group of corporations within the meaning of Section 414 of the Internal Revenue Code of 1986, as amended (the "Code")) may have any liability (each, a "Plan") has been maintained in compliance with its terms and the requirements of any applicable statutes, orders, rules and regulations, including but not limited to, ERISA and the Code, except for such noncompliance that, individually or in the aggregate, would not have a Material Adverse Effect; (ii) for each Plan that is subject to the funding rules of Section 412 of the Code or Section 302 of ERISA, the minimum funding standard of Section 412 of the Code or Section 302 of ERISA, as applicable, has been satisfied and is reasonably expected to be satisfied in the future (without taking into account any waiver thereof or extension of any amortization period); (iii) no "reportable event" (within the meaning of Section 4043(c) of ERISA) has occurred or is reasonably expected to occur with respect to any Plan that, individually or in the aggregate, would have a Material Adverse Effect; (iv) neither the Company nor any member of the Controlled Group has incurred, or reasonably expects to incur, any liability under Title IV of ERISA (other than for Pension Benefit Guaranty Corporation ("PBGC") premiums due but not delinquent under Section 4007 of ERISA) with respect to any Plan (including a "multiemployer plan", within the meaning of Section 4001(a)(3) of ERISA);(v) there is no pending or, to the Company's knowledge, threatened audit or investigation by the Internal Revenue Service, the U.S. Department of Labor, the PBGC or any other governmental agency or any foreign regulatory agency with respect to any Plan that, individually or in the aggregate, would have a Material Adverse Effect; and (vi) none of the following events has occurred or is reasonably likely to occur: (x) a material increase in the aggregate amount of contributions required to be made to all Plans by the Company in the current fiscal year of the Company compared to the amount of such contributions made in the Company's recently completed fiscal year; or (y) a material increase in the Company "accumulated post-retirement benefit obligations" (within the meaning of Statement of Financial Accounting Standards 106) compared to the amount of such obligations in the Company's most recently completed fiscal year;

(xl)   There are no debt securities or preferred stock of, or guaranteed by, the Company that are rated by a "nationally recognized statistical rating organization," as such term is defined in Section 3(a)(62) of the Exchange Act;

(xli)   Each of the holders listed on Schedule IV hereto represent over 0.125% of the outstanding equity securities of the Company or securities convertible into equity securities of the Company.

(b)   Each of the Selling Stockholders severally and not jointly represents and warrants to, and agrees with, each of the Underwriters and the Company that:

(i)   All consents, approvals, authorizations and orders necessary for the execution and delivery by such Selling Stockholder of this Agreement and the Power of Attorney and the Custody Agreement referred to below, and for the sale and delivery of the Shares to be sold by such Selling Stockholder hereunder, have been obtained (except for the registration under the Act of the Shares and such consents, approvals, authorizations and orders as may be required under state securities or Blue Sky laws, the rules and regulations of FINRA or the approval for listing on the NASDAQ); and such Selling Stockholder has full right, power and authority to enter into this Agreement, the Power of Attorney and the Custody Agreement and to sell, assign, transfer and deliver the Shares to be sold by such Selling Stockholder hereunder;

(ii)   The sale of the Shares to be sold by such Selling Stockholder hereunder and the compliance by such Selling Stockholder with this Agreement, the Power of Attorney and the Custody Agreement and the consummation of the transactions herein and therein contemplated will not (A) conflict with or result in a breach or violation of any of the terms or provisions of, or constitute a default under, any statute, indenture, mortgage, deed of trust, loan agreement, lease or other agreement or instrument to which such Selling Stockholder is a party or by which such Selling Stockholder is bound or to which any of the property or assets of such Selling Stockholder is subject, (B) result in any violation of the provisions of the organizational documents of any entity of such Selling Stockholder or (C) result in any violation of any statute or any judgment, order, rule or regulation of any court or governmental agency or body having jurisdiction over such Selling Stockholder or any of its subsidiaries or any property or assets of such Selling Stockholder, except in the case of (A) and (C), for such violations that individually or in the aggregate would not impair the ability of such Selling Stockholder to *consummate* the transactions contemplated by this Agreement; and no consent, approval, authorization, order, registration or qualification of or with any such court or governmental body or agency is required for the performance by such Selling Stockholder of its obligations under this Agreement, the Power of Attorney and the Custody Agreement and the consummation by such Selling Stockholder of the transactions contemplated by this Agreement, the Power of Attorney and the Custody Agreement in connection with the Shares to be sold by such Selling Stockholder hereunder, except the registration under the Act of the Shares, the approval by FINRA of the underwriting terms and arrangements, the approval for listing on the NASDAQ and such consents, approvals, authorizations, orders, registrations or qualifications as may be required under state securities or Blue Sky laws in connection with the purchase and distribution of the Shares by the Underwriters;

(iii)   Such Selling Stockholder has, and immediately prior to each Time of Delivery (as defined in Section 4 hereof) such Selling Stockholder will have, good and valid title to, or a valid "security entitlement" within the meaning of Section 8-501 of the New York Uniform Commercial Code in respect of, the Shares to be sold by such Selling Stockholder hereunder at such Time of Delivery, free and clear of all liens, encumbrances, equities or claims; and, upon delivery of such Shares and payment therefor pursuant hereto, good and valid title to such Shares, free and clear of all liens, encumbrances, equities or claims, will pass to the several Underwriters;

(iv)   On or prior to the date of the Pricing Prospectus, such Selling Stockholder has executed and delivered to the Underwriters an agreement substantially in the form of Annex IV hereto.

(v)   Such Selling Stockholder has not taken and will not take, directly or indirectly, any action that is designed to or that has constituted or might reasonably be expected to cause or result in stabilization or manipulation of the price of any security of the Company to facilitate the sale or resale of the Shares;

(vi)   The Registration Statement and Pricing Prospectus did, and the Prospectus and any further amendments or supplements to the Registration Statement and the Prospectus will, when they become effective or are filed with the Commission, as the case may be, conform in all material respects to the requirements of the Act and the rules and regulations of the Commission thereunder and not contain any untrue statement of a material fact or omit to state any material fact required to be stated therein or necessary to make the statements therein not misleading; provided that such representations and warranties set forth in this clause (vi) apply, with respect to a Selling Stockholder, only to statements or omissions made in the Registration Statement, the Pricing Prospectus, the Prospectus and any further amendments or supplements to the Registration Statement, the Pricing Prospectus and the Prospectus that are made in reliance upon and in conformity with written information furnished to the Company by such Selling Stockholder in writing expressly for use therein; provided, further, that it is agreed that such information furnished by such Selling Stockholder to the Company consists only of (A) the legal name, address and the number of Shares owned by such Selling Stockholder before and after the offering, (B) the other information with respect to such Selling Stockholder (excluding percentages) which appear in the table (and corresponding footnotes) under the caption "Principal and Selling Stockholders," and (C) with respect to any Selling Stockholder that is an executive officer of the Company or a member of the Company's board of directors, the biography of such Selling Stockholder set forth under the caption "Management" in the Pricing Prospectus or the Prospectus (with respect to such Selling Stockholder, the "Selling Stockholder Information");

(vii)   In order to document the Underwriters' compliance with the reporting and withholding provisions of the Tax Equity and Fiscal Responsibility Act of 1982 with respect to the transactions herein contemplated, such Selling Stockholder will deliver to you prior to or at the First Time of Delivery a properly completed and executed United States Treasury Department Form W-9 (or other applicable form or statement specified by Treasury Department regulations in lieu thereof);

(viii)   Certificates in negotiable form or book-entry securities entitlements representing the Shares to be sold by such Selling Stockholder hereunder have been placed in custody under a Custody Agreement, in the form heretofore furnished to you (the "Custody Agreement"), duly executed and delivered by such Selling Stockholder to Computershare Trust Company, N.A., as custodian (the "Custodian"), and such Selling Stockholder has duly executed and delivered a Power of Attorney, in the form heretofore furnished to you (the "Power of Attorney"), appointing the persons indicated in Schedule II hereto, and each of them, as such Selling Stockholder's attorneys-in-fact (the "Attorneys-in-Fact") with authority to execute and deliver this Agreement on behalf of such Selling Stockholder, to determine the purchase price to be paid by the Underwriters to the Selling Stockholders as provided in Section 2 hereof, to authorize the delivery of the Shares to be sold by such Selling Stockholder hereunder and otherwise to act on behalf of such Selling Stockholder in connection with the transactions contemplated by this Agreement and the Custody Agreement;

(ix)   The Shares held in custody for such Selling Stockholder under the Custody Agreement are subject to the interests of the Underwriters hereunder; the arrangements made by such Selling Stockholder for such custody, and the appointment by such Selling Stockholder of the Attorneys-in-Fact by the Power of Attorney, are to that extent irrevocable; the obligations of the Selling Stockholders hereunder shall not be terminated by operation of law, whether by the death or incapacity of any individual Selling Stockholder or, in the case of an estate or trust, by the death or incapacity of any executor or trustee or the termination of such estate or trust, or in the case of any other entity, by the dissolution of such entity, or by the occurrence of any other event; if any individual Selling Stockholder or any such executor or trustee should die or become incapacitated, or if any such estate or trust should be terminated, or if any such entity should be dissolved, or if any other such event should occur, before the delivery of the Shares to be sold by such Selling Stockholder hereunder, certificates representing the Shares to be sold by such Selling Stockholder hereunder shall be delivered by or on behalf of the Selling Stockholders in accordance with the terms and conditions of this Agreement and of the Custody Agreements; and actions taken by the Attorneys-in-Fact pursuant to the Powers of Attorney shall be as valid as if such death, incapacity, termination, dissolution or other event had not occurred, regardless of whether or not the Custodian, the Attorneys-in-Fact, or any of them, shall have received notice of such death, incapacity, termination, dissolution or other event;

(x)   Such Selling Stockholder is not prompted by any material non-public information concerning the Company or any of its subsidiaries that is not disclosed in the Pricing Prospectus to sell its Shares pursuant to this Agreement;

(xi)   Such Selling Stockholder is not (i) an employee benefit plan subject to Title I of ERISA, (ii) a plan or account subject to Section 4975 of the Code or (iii) an entity deemed to hold "plan assets" of any such plan or account under Section 3(42) of ERISA, 29 C.F.R. 2510.3-101, or otherwise; and

(xii)   Such Selling Stockholder will not directly or indirectly use the proceeds of the offering of the Shares hereunder, or lend, contribute or otherwise make available such proceeds to any subsidiary, joint venture partner or other person or entity (i) to fund or facilitate any activities of or business with any person, or in any country or territory, that, at the time of such funding, is the subject or the target of Sanctions or (ii) in any other manner that will result in a violation by any person (including any person participating in the transaction, whether as underwriter, advisor, investor or otherwise) of Sanctions.

2.   Subject to the terms and conditions herein set forth, (a) the Company and each of the Selling Stockholders agree, severally and not jointly, to sell to each of the Underwriters, and each of the Underwriters agrees, severally and not jointly, to purchase from the Company and each of the Selling Stockholders, at a purchase price per share of $[●], the number of Firm Shares (to be adjusted by you so as to eliminate fractional shares) determined by multiplying the aggregate number of Firm Shares to be sold by the Company and each of the Selling Stockholders as set forth opposite their respective names in Schedule II hereto by a fraction, the numerator of which is the aggregate number of Firm Shares to be purchased by such Underwriter as set forth opposite the name of such Underwriter in Schedule I hereto and the denominator of which is the aggregate number of Firm Shares to be purchased by all of the Underwriters from the Company and all of the Selling Stockholders hereunder and (b) in the event and to the extent that the Underwriters shall exercise the election to purchase Optional Shares as provided below, the Company agrees to sell to each of the Underwriters, and each of the Underwriters agrees, severally and not jointly, to purchase from the Company, at the purchase price per share set forth in clause (a) of this Section 2 (provided that the purchase price per Optional Share shall be reduced by an amount per share equal to any dividends or distributions declared by the Company and payable on the Firm Shares but not payable on the Optional Shares), that portion of the number of Optional Shares as to which such election shall have been exercised (to be adjusted by you so as to eliminate fractional shares) determined by multiplying such number of Optional Shares by a fraction, the numerator of which is the maximum number of Optional Shares which such Underwriter is entitled to purchase as set forth opposite the name of such Underwriter in Schedule I hereto and the denominator of which is the maximum number of Optional Shares that all of the Underwriters are entitled to purchase hereunder.

The Company hereby grants to the Underwriters the right to purchase at their election up to [●] Optional Shares, at the purchase price per share set forth in the paragraph above, for the sole purpose of covering sales of shares in excess of the number of Firm Shares, provided that the purchase price per Optional Share shall be reduced by an amount per share equal to any dividends or distributions declared by the Company and payable on the Firm Shares but not payable on the Optional Shares. Any such election to purchase Optional Shares may be exercised only by written notice from you to the Company, given within a period of 30 calendar days after the date of this Agreement, setting forth the aggregate number of Optional Shares to be purchased and the date on which such Optional Shares are to be delivered, as determined by you but in no event earlier than the First Time of Delivery (as defined in Section 4 hereof) or, unless you and the Company otherwise agree in writing, earlier than two or later than ten business days after the date of such notice.

3.   Upon the authorization by you of the release of the Firm Shares, the several Underwriters propose to offer the Firm Shares for sale upon the terms and conditions set forth in the Pricing Prospectus and the Prospectus.

4.   (a) The Shares to be purchased by each Underwriter hereunder, in definitive or book-entry form, and in such authorized denominations and registered in such names as the Representatives may request upon at least forty-eight hours' prior notice to the Company and the Selling Stockholders shall be delivered by or on behalf of the Company and the Selling Stockholders to the Representatives, through the facilities of the Depository Trust Company ("DTC"), for the account of such Underwriter, against payment by or on behalf of such Underwriter of the purchase price therefor by wire transfer of Federal (same-day) funds to the accounts specified by the Company and the Custodian to the Representatives at least forty-eight hours in advance. The time and date of such delivery and payment shall be, with respect to the Firm Shares, 9:30 a.m., New York City time, on [●], 2018 or such other time and date as the Representatives, the Company and the Attorneys-in-

Fact may agree upon in writing, and, with respect to the Optional Shares, 9:30 a.m., New York time, on the date specified by the Representatives in each written notice given by the Representatives of the Underwriters' election to purchase such Optional Shares, or such other time and date as the Representatives and the Company may agree upon in writing. Such time and date for delivery of the Firm Shares is herein called the "First Time of Delivery", each such time and date for delivery of the Optional Shares, if not the First Time of Delivery, is herein called the "Second Time of Delivery", and each such time and date for delivery is herein called a "Time of Delivery".

(b)   The documents to be delivered at each Time of Delivery by or on behalf of the parties hereto pursuant to Section 8 hereof, including the cross receipt for the Shares and any additional documents requested by the Underwriters pursuant to Section 8(j) hereof will be delivered at the offices of Simpson Thacher & Bartlett LLP, 2475 Hanover Street, Palo Alto, CA 94304 (the "Closing Location"), and the Shares will be delivered at the office of DTC or its designated custodian, all at such Time of Delivery. A meeting will be held at the Closing Location at [●] p.m., New York City time, on the New York Business Day next preceding such Time of Delivery, at which meeting the final drafts of the documents to be delivered pursuant to the preceding sentence will be available for review by the parties hereto. For the purposes of this Section 4, "New York Business Day" shall mean each Monday, Tuesday, Wednesday, Thursday and Friday which is not a day on which banking institutions in New York City are generally authorized or obligated by law or executive order to close.

5.   The Company agrees with each of the Underwriters:

(a)   To prepare the Prospectus in a form approved by you and to file such Prospectus pursuant to Rule 424(b) under the Act not later than the Commission's close of business on the second business day following the execution and delivery of this Agreement, or, if applicable, such earlier time as may be required by Rule 430A(a)(3) under the Act; to make no further amendment or any supplement to the Registration Statement or the Prospectus prior to the last Time of Delivery which shall be disapproved by you promptly after reasonable notice thereof; to advise you, promptly after it receives notice thereof, of the time when any amendment to the Registration Statement has been filed or becomes effective or any amendment or supplement to the Prospectus has been filed and to furnish you with copies thereof; to file promptly all materials required to be filed by the Company with the Commission pursuant to Rule 433(d) under the Act; to advise you, promptly after it receives notice thereof, of the issuance by the Commission of any stop order or of any order preventing or suspending the use of any Preliminary Prospectus or other prospectus in respect of the Shares, of the suspension of the qualification of the Shares for offering or sale in any jurisdiction, of the initiation or threatening of any proceeding for any such purpose, or of any request by the Commission for the amending or supplementing of the Registration Statement or the Prospectus or for additional information; and, in the event of the issuance of any stop order or of any order preventing or suspending the use of any Preliminary Prospectus or other prospectus or suspending any such qualification, to promptly use its best efforts to obtain the withdrawal of such order;

(b)   Promptly from time to time to take such action as you may reasonably request to qualify the Shares for offering and sale under the securities laws of such jurisdictions as you may reasonably request and to comply with such laws so as to permit the continuance of sales and dealings therein in such jurisdictions for as long as may be necessary to complete the distribution of the Shares, provided that in connection therewith the Company shall not be required to qualify as a foreign corporation where not otherwise required or to file a general consent to service of process in any jurisdiction where not otherwise required or subject itself to taxation for doing business in any jurisdiction in which it was not otherwise subject to taxation;

(c)   Prior to 10:00 a.m., New York City time, on the New York Business Day next succeeding the date of this Agreement (or such later time as may be agreed by the Company and the Representatives) and from time to time, to furnish the Underwriters with written and electronic copies of the Prospectus in New York City in such quantities as you may reasonably request, and, if the delivery of a prospectus (or in lieu thereof, the notice referred to in Rule 173(a) under the Act) is required at any time prior to the expiration of nine months after the time of issue of the Prospectus in connection with the offering or sale of the Shares and if at such time any event shall have occurred as a result of which the Prospectus as then amended or supplemented would include an untrue statement of a material fact or omit to state any material fact necessary in order to make the statements therein, in the light of the circumstances under which they were made when such Prospectus (or in lieu thereof, the notice referred to in Rule 173(a) under the Act) is delivered, not misleading, or, if for any other reason it shall be necessary during such same period to amend or supplement the Prospectus in order to comply with the Act, to notify you and upon your request to prepare and furnish without charge to each Underwriter and to any dealer (whose name and address the Underwriters shall furnish to the Company) in securities as many written and electronic copies as you may from time to time reasonably request of an amended Prospectus or a supplement to the Prospectus which will correct such statement or omission or effect such compliance; and in case any Underwriter is required to deliver a prospectus (or in lieu thereof, the notice referred to in Rule 173(a) under the Act) in connection with sales of any of the Shares at any time nine months or more after the time of issue of the Prospectus, upon your request but at the expense of such Underwriter, to prepare and deliver to such Underwriter as many written and electronic copies as you may request of an amended or supplemented Prospectus complying with Section 10(a)(3) of the Act;

(d)   To make generally available to its securityholders as soon as practicable (which may be satisfied by filing with the Commission's Electronic Data Gathering, Analysis and Retrieval System ("EDGAR"), but in any event not later than sixteen months after the effective date of the Registration Statement (as defined in Rule 158(c) under the Act), an earnings statement of the Company and its subsidiaries (which need not be audited) complying with Section 11(a) of the Act and the rules and regulations of the Commission thereunder (including, at the option of the Company, Rule 158);

(e)   (1) During the period beginning from the date hereof and continuing to and including the date 180 days after the date of the Prospectus (the "Company Lock-up Period") not to (i) offer, sell, contract to sell, pledge, grant any option to purchase, make any short sale or otherwise transfer or dispose of, directly or indirectly, or file with or confidentially submit to the Commission a registration statement under the Act relating to, any securities of the Company that are substantially similar to the Shares, including but not limited to any options or warrants to purchase shares of Stock or any securities that are convertible into or exchangeable for, or that represent the right to receive, Stock or any such substantially similar securities, or publicly disclose the intention to make any offer, sale, pledge, disposition or filing or (ii) enter into any swap or other agreement that transfers, in whole or in part, any of the economic consequences of ownership of the Stock or any such other securities, whether any such transaction described in clause (i) or (ii) above is to be settled by delivery of Stock or such other securities, in cash or otherwise (other than the Shares to be sold hereunder or pursuant to employee stock option plans existing on, or upon the conversion or exchange of convertible or exchangeable securities outstanding as of, the date of this Agreement), without the prior written consent of Goldman Sachs & Co. LLC and J.P. Morgan Securities LLC; provided, however, that the foregoing restrictions shall not apply to (i) Shares to be sold hereunder, (ii) the issuance by the Company of shares of Class A common stock, Class B common stock or Class C common stock upon the exercise of options, the settlement of restricted stock units or the conversion or exchange of convertible or exchangeable securities outstanding as of the date of this Agreement and described in the Pricing Prospectus, (iii) the issuance by the Company of shares of Class A common stock, Class B common stock or Class C common stock or securities convertible into, exchangeable for or that represent that right to receive shares of Class A common stock, Class B common stock or Class C common stock, in each case pursuant to the Company's stock plans that are described in the Pricing Prospectus, (iv) the issuance by the Company of shares of Class A common stock or Class C common stock or securities convertible into, exchangeable for or that represent the right to receive shares of Class A common stock or Class C common stock in connection with (x) the acquisition by the Company or any of its subsidiaries of the securities, business, technology, property or other assets of another person or entity or pursuant to an employee benefit plan assumed by the Company in connection with such acquisition, and the issuance of any such securities pursuant to any such agreement, or (y) the Company's joint ventures, commercial relationships and other strategic transactions, or (v) the filing of any registration statement on Form S-8 relating to securities granted or to be granted pursuant to (A) the Company's stock plans that are described in the Pricing Prospectus or (B) any assumed employee benefit plan contemplated by clause (iv); provided, that the aggregate number of shares of Stock that the Company may sell or issue or agree to sell or issue pursuant to clause (iv) and, with respect to securities to be granted pursuant to any assumed employee benefit plan pursuant to clause (v) shall not exceed 10% of the total number of shares of Stock outstanding immediately following the offering of the Shares contemplated by this Agreement; and provided, further, that in the case of clauses (ii) through (v), the Company shall (a) cause each recipient of such securities to execute and deliver to you, on or prior to the issuance of such securities, a lock-up agreement substantially to the effect set forth in Annex IV hereto to the extent not already executed and delivered by such recipients as of the date hereof; provided that in the case of clauses (ii), (iii) and (v)(A) such lock-up agreement shall only be required if the recipient of such securities is a member of the Company's board of directors, an executive officer or a beneficial holder of 0.125% of the capital stock of the Company and (b) enter stop transfer instructions with the Company's transfer agent and registrar on such securities with respect to all recipients of such securities, which the Company agrees it will not waive or amend without the prior written consent of Goldman Sachs & Co. LLC and J.P. Morgan Securities LLC;

(2) If Goldman Sachs & Co. LLC and J.P. Morgan Securities LLC, in their sole discretion, agree to release or waive the restrictions set forth in lock-up letters pursuant to Section 8(h) hereof, in each case for an officer or director of the Company, and provide the Company with notice of the impending release or waiver at least three business days before the effective date of the release or waiver, the Company agrees to announce the impending release or waiver by a press release substantially in the form of Annex III hereto through a major news service at least two business days before the effective date of the release or waiver, if required by FINRA Rule 5131;

(3) During the Company Lock-Up Period, to the extent that any agreement between the Company and any holder of Stock or any securities of the Company that are substantially similar to the Shares, including but not limited to any options to purchase shares of Stock or any securities that are convertible into or exchangeable for, or that represent the right to receive, Stock or any such substantially similar securities, contains or references any restriction similar to the restrictions contained in Annex IV or any other form of "lock up" or "market stand-off provision", the Company will not waive any such restriction with respect to any such holder without the prior written consent of Goldman Sachs & Co. LLC and J.P. Morgan Securities LLC and will take all reasonable actions necessary to enforce any such restriction, including imposing stop-transfer instructions with respect to such securities and instructing its transfer agent to place restrictive legends describing such restriction on the certificates or book-entries with respect to such securities;

(f)   During a period of three years from the effective date of the Registration Statement, so long as the Company is subject to the reporting requirements of either Section 13 or Section 15(d) of the Exchange Act, to furnish to its stockholders as soon as practicable after the end of each fiscal year an annual report (including a balance sheet and statements of income, stockholders' equity and cash flows of the Company and its consolidated subsidiaries certified by independent public accountants) and, as soon as practicable after the end of each of the first three quarters of each fiscal year (beginning with the fiscal quarter ending after the effective date of the Registration Statement), to make available to its stockholders consolidated summary financial information of the Company and its subsidiaries for such quarter in reasonable detail; provided that no reports, documents or other information need to be furnished pursuant to this Section 5(f) to the extent they are available on EDGAR;

(g)   During a period of three years from the effective date of the Registration Statement, so long as the Company is subject to the reporting requirements of either Section 13 or Section 15(d) of the Exchange Act, to furnish to you copies of all reports or other communications (financial or other) furnished to stockholders, and to deliver to you as soon as they are available, copies of any reports and financial statements furnished to or filed with the Commission or any national securities exchange on which any class of securities of the Company is listed (such financial statements to be on a consolidated basis to the extent the accounts of the Company and its subsidiaries are consolidated in reports furnished to its stockholders generally or to the Commission); provided that no reports, documents or other information need to be furnished pursuant to this Section 5(g) to the extent they are available on EDGAR or to the extent such provision of such reports, documents or other information would require public disclosure by the Company under Regulation FD;

(h)   To use the net proceeds received by it from the sale of the Shares pursuant to this Agreement in the manner specified in the Pricing Prospectus under the caption "Use of Proceeds";

(i)   To use its best efforts to list, subject to notice of issuance, the Shares on the NASDAQ;

(j)   To file with the Commission such information on Form 10-Q or Form 10-K as may be required by Rule 463 under the Act;

(k)   If the Company elects to rely upon Rule 462(b), the Company shall file a Rule 462(b) Registration Statement with the Commission in compliance with Rule 462(b) by 10:00 p.m., Washington, D.C. time, on the date of this Agreement, and the Company shall at the time of filing either pay to the Commission the filing fee for the Rule 462(b) Registration Statement or give irrevocable instructions for the payment of such fee pursuant to Rule 111(b) under the Act;

(l)   Upon request of any Underwriter, to furnish, or cause to be furnished, to such Underwriter an electronic version of the Company's trademarks, servicemarks and corporate logo for use on the website, if any, operated by such Underwriter for the purpose of facilitating the on-line offering of the Shares (the "License"); provided, however, that the License shall be used solely for the purpose described above, is granted without any fee and may not be assigned or transferred; and

6.   (a) The Company represents and agrees that, without the prior consent of the Representatives, it has not made and will not make any offer relating to the Shares that would constitute a "free writing prospectus" as defined in Rule 405 under the Act; each Selling Stockholder represents and agrees that, without the prior consent of the Company and the Representatives, it has not made and will not make any offer relating to the Shares that would constitute a free writing prospectus; and each Underwriter represents and agrees that, without the prior consent of the Company and the Representatives, it has not made and will not make any offer relating to the Shares that would constitute a free writing prospectus required to be filed with the Commission; any such free writing prospectus the use of which has been consented to by the Company and the Representatives is listed on Schedule III(a) hereto;   347

(b)   The Company has complied and will comply with the requirements of Rule 433 under the Act applicable to any Issuer Free Writing Prospectus, including timely filing with the Commission or retention where required and legending; and the Company represents that it has satisfied and agrees that it will satisfy the conditions under Rule 433 under the Act to avoid a requirement to file with the Commission any electronic road show;

(c)   The Company agrees that if at any time following issuance of an Issuer Free Writing Prospectus or Section 5(d) Writing prepared or authorized by it, any event occurred or occurs as a result of which such Issuer Free Writing Prospectus or Section 5(d) Writing prepared or authorized by it would conflict with the information in the Registration Statement, the Pricing Prospectus or the Prospectus or would include an untrue statement of a material fact or omit to state any material fact necessary in order to make the statements therein, in the light of the circumstances then prevailing, not misleading, the Company will give prompt notice thereof to the Representatives and, if requested by the Representatives, will prepare and furnish without charge to each Underwriter an Issuer Free Writing Prospectus, Section 5(d) Writing or other document which will correct such conflict, statement or omission; provided, however, that this representation and warranty shall not apply to any statements or omissions in an Issuer Free Writing Prospectus made in reliance upon and in conformity with the Underwriter Information or any Selling Stockholder Information;

(d)   The Company represents and agrees that (i) it has not engaged in, or authorized any other person to engage in, any Section 5(d) Communications, other than Section 5(d) Communications with the prior consent of the Representatives with entities that are qualified institutional buyers as defined in Rule 144A under the Act or institutions that are accredited investors as defined in Rule 501(a) under the Act; and (ii) it has not distributed, or authorized any other person to distribute, any Section 5(d) Writings, other than those distributed with the prior consent of the Representatives that are listed on Schedule III(c) hereto; and the Company reconfirms that the Underwriters have been authorized to act on its behalf in engaging in Section 5(d) Communications; and

(e)   Each Underwriter represents and agrees that any Section 5(d) Communications undertaken by it were with entities that are qualified institutional buyers as defined in Rule 144A under the Act or institutions that are accredited investors as defined in Rule 501(a) under the Act.

7.   The Company and each of the Selling Stockholders covenant and agree with one another and with the several Underwriters that (a) the Company will pay or cause to be paid the following: (i) the fees, disbursements and expenses of the Company's counsel, the Company's accountants in connection with the registration of the Shares under the Act and the expenses incurred in connection with the preparation, printing, reproduction and filing of the Registration Statement, any Preliminary Prospectus, any Section 5(d) Writing, any Issuer Free Writing Prospectus and the Prospectus and amendments and supplements thereto and the mailing and delivering of copies thereof to the Underwriters and dealers; (ii) the cost of printing or producing any Agreement among Underwriters, this Agreement, the Blue Sky Memorandum, closing documents and any other documents in connection with the offering, purchase, sale and delivery of the Shares; (iii) all expenses in connection with the qualification of the Shares for offering and sale under state securities laws as provided in Section 5(b) hereof, including the reasonable and documented fees and disbursements of counsel for the Underwriters in connection with such qualification and in connection with any Blue Sky survey; (iv) the expenses of the Company relating to any "road show" undertaken in connection with the marketing of the offering of the Shares, including, without limitation, expenses associated with the

preparation or dissemination of any electronic road show, expenses associated with the production of any road show presentation and related slides and graphics, fees and expenses of any consultants engaged in connection with any road show presentations, the lodging and meal expenses of the officers of the Company and one-third of the cost of any aircraft chartered in connection with any such road show, subject to the last sentence of this paragraph, (v) in connection with any testing-the-waters meetings, the expenses of the Company associated with the production of testing-the-waters investor presentations and related slides and graphics, fees and expenses of any consultants engaged in connection with such testing-the-waters presentations, the lodging and meal expenses of the officers of the Company, and one-third of the cost of any aircraft chartered in connection with such testing-the-waters meetings, subject to the last sentence of this paragraph, (vi) all fees and expenses in connection with listing the Shares on the NASDAQ; (vii) the filing fees incident to, and the reasonable and documented fees and disbursements of counsel for the Underwriters in connection with, any required review by FINRA of the terms of the sale of the Shares; (viii) the cost of preparing stock certificates; if applicable; (ix) the cost and charges of any transfer agent or registrar; (x) all other costs and expenses incident to the performance of its obligations hereunder which are not otherwise specifically provided for in this Section; (xi) each Selling Stockholder's pro rata share of the fees and expenses of the Attorneys-in-Fact and the Custodian; and (xii) the fees and disbursements of one counsel to the Selling Stockholders (the "Common Selling Stockholder Counsel") and all costs and expenses incident to the performance of each Selling Stockholder's obligations hereunder which are not otherwise specifically provided for in this Section, provided, however, that the amounts payable by the Company for the fees and disbursements of counsel to the Underwriters pursuant to subsections (iii) and (vii) shall not exceed $30,000 in the aggregate; and (b) each Selling Stockholder, severally and not jointly, will pay or cause to be paid all costs and expenses incident to the performance of such Selling Stockholder's obligations hereunder in connection with (i) any fees and expenses of counsel for such Selling Stockholder other than the fees and expenses of the Company's counsel and the Common Selling Stockholder Counsel being paid for by the Company, (ii) all stamp or transfer taxes incident to the sale and delivery of the Shares to be sold by such Selling Stockholder to the Underwriters hereunder and (iii) any underwriters' discounts and commissions relating to the Shares to be sold by such Selling Stockholder to the Underwriters hereunder. In connection with clause (b)(ii) of the preceding sentence, the Representatives agree to pay New York State stock transfer tax, and the Selling Stockholder agrees to reimburse the Representatives for associated carrying costs if such tax payment is not rebated on the day of payment and for any portion of such tax payment not rebated. It is understood, however, that the Company shall bear, and the Selling Stockholders shall not be required to pay or to reimburse the Company for, the cost of any other matters not directly relating to the sale and purchase of the Shares pursuant to this Agreement. Notwithstanding anything to the contrary herein, except as provided in this Section, and Sections 9 and 12 hereof, the Underwriters will pay (i) all of their own costs and expenses, including the fees of their counsel, stock transfer taxes on resale of any of the Shares by them, and any advertising expenses connected with any offers they may make, (ii) in connection with any "road show" undertaken in connection with the marketing of the offering of the Shares, the travel, lodging and meal expenses of the Representatives, the cost of all transportation of the officers of the Company and the Representatives other than the chartered aircraft and two-thirds of the cost of any aircraft chartered in connection with such road show and (iii) in connection with any testing-the-waters meetings, the travel, lodging and meal expenses of the Representatives, the cost of all transportation of the officers of the Company and the Representatives other than the chartered aircraft and two-thirds of the cost of any aircraft chartered in connection with such testing-the-waters meetings.

8.   The obligations of the Underwriters hereunder, as to the Shares to be delivered at each Time of Delivery, shall be subject, in their discretion, to the condition that all representations and warranties and other statements of the Company and the Selling Stockholders herein are, at and as of the Applicable Time and such Time of Delivery, true and correct, the condition that the Company and the Selling Stockholders shall have performed all of its and their obligations hereunder theretofore to be performed, and the following additional conditions:

(a)   The Prospectus shall have been filed with the Commission pursuant to Rule 424(b) under the Act within the applicable time period prescribed for such filing by the rules and regulations under the Act and in accordance with Section 5(a) hereof; all material required to be filed by the Company pursuant to Rule 433(d) under the Act shall have been filed with the Commission within the applicable time period prescribed for such filing by Rule 433; if the Company has elected to rely upon Rule 462(b) under the Act, the Rule 462(b) Registration Statement shall have become effective by 10:00 p.m., Washington, D.C. time, on the date of this Agreement; no stop order suspending the effectiveness of the Registration Statement or any part thereof shall have been issued and no proceeding for that purpose shall have been initiated or threatened by the Commission; no stop order suspending or preventing the use of the Pricing Prospectus, Prospectus or any Issuer Free Writing Prospectus shall have been initiated or threatened by the Commission; and all requests for additional information on the part of the Commission shall have been complied with to your reasonable satisfaction;

(b)   Simpson Thacher & Bartlett LLP, counsel for the Underwriters, shall have furnished to you such written opinion or opinions, dated such Time of Delivery, in form and substance satisfactory to you, with respect to the issuance and sale of the Shares, the Registration Statement and the Prospectus as well as such other related matters as you may reasonably request, and such counsel shall have received such papers and information as they may reasonably request to enable them to pass upon such matters;

(c)   (i) Wilson Sonsini Goodrich & Rosati, Professional Corporation, counsel for the Company and the Selling Stockholders, shall have furnished to you their written opinion and negative assurance letter (a form which is attached as Annex I hereto) with respect to the Company and (ii) counsel for the Selling Stockholders shall have furnished to you their written opinion with respect to each of the Selling Stockholders, in each case dated such Time of Delivery and in form and substance satisfactory to you;

(d)   On the date of the Prospectus on the effective date of any post-effective amendment to the Registration Statement filed subsequent to the date of this Agreement and also at each Time of Delivery, Ernst & Young LLP shall have furnished to you a letter or letters, dated the respective dates of delivery thereof, in form and substance satisfactory to you;

(e)   (i) Neither the Company nor any of its subsidiaries shall have sustained since the date of the latest audited financial statements included in the Pricing Prospectus any material loss or interference with its business from fire, explosion, flood or other calamity, whether or not covered by insurance, or from any labor dispute or court or governmental action, order or decree, otherwise than as set forth or contemplated in the Pricing Prospectus, and (ii) since the respective dates as of which information is given in the Pricing Prospectus there shall not have been any change in the capital stock (other than (A) as a result of the exercise or settlement (including any "net" or "cashless" exercises or settlements) of stock options or restricted stock units or the award of stock options or restricted stock units in the ordinary course of business, in each case pursuant to the Company's equity plans that are described in the Pricing Prospectus, (B) the repurchase of shares of common stock by the Company pursuant to agreements providing for an option to repurchase or a right of first refusal on behalf of the Company pursuant to the Company's repurchase rights, or (C) the issuance, if any, of stock upon conversion of Company securities as described in the Pricing Prospectus) or the issuance or incurrence of long-term debt of the Company or any of its subsidiaries or any change or effect, or any development involving a prospective change or effect, in or affecting the business, management, consolidated financial position, consolidated stockholders' equity or consolidated results of operations of the Company and its subsidiaries, taken as a whole, except as set forth or contemplated in the Pricing Prospectus and the Prospectus, the effect of which, in any such case described in clause (i) or (ii), is in your judgment so material and adverse as to make it impracticable or inadvisable to proceed with the public offering or the delivery of the Shares being delivered at such Time of Delivery on the terms and in the manner contemplated in the Pricing Prospectus and the Prospectus;

(f) On or after the Applicable Time there shall not have occurred any of the following: (i) a suspension or material limitation in trading in securities generally on the Exchange or on NASDAQ; (ii) a suspension or material limitation in trading in the Company's securities on the NASDAQ; (iii) a general moratorium on commercial banking activities declared by either Federal or New York State authorities or a material disruption in commercial banking or securities settlement or clearance services in the United States; (iv) the outbreak or escalation of hostilities involving the United States or the declaration by the United States of a national emergency or war or (v) the occurrence of any other calamity or crisis or any change in financial, political or economic conditions in the United States or elsewhere, if the effect of any such event specified in clause (iv) or (v) in your judgment makes it impracticable or inadvisable to proceed with the public offering or the delivery of the Shares being delivered at such Time of Delivery on the terms and in the manner contemplated in the Pricing Prospectus and the Prospectus;

(g) The Shares to be sold at such Time of Delivery shall have been duly listed for quotation on the NASDAQ;

(h) The Company shall have obtained and delivered to the Underwriters executed copies of an agreement from each member of the Company's board of directors, each executive officer of the Company and each of the other holders of the Company's securities listed on Schedule IV hereto, substantially to the effect set forth in Annex IV hereto in form and substance reasonably satisfactory to you;

(i) The Company shall have complied with the provisions of Section 5(c) hereof with respect to the furnishing of prospectuses on the New York Business Day next succeeding the date of this Agreement;

(j) The Company and the Selling Stockholders shall have furnished or caused to be furnished to you at such Time of Delivery certificates of officers of the Company and of the Selling Stockholders, respectively, satisfactory to you as to the accuracy of the representations and warranties of the Company and the Selling Stockholders, respectively, herein at and as of such Time of Delivery, as to the performance by the Company and the Selling Stockholders of all of their respective obligations hereunder to be performed at or prior to such Time of Delivery, as to such other matters as you may reasonably request, and the Company shall have furnished or caused to be furnished certificates as to the matters set forth in subsections (a) and (e) of this Section; and

(k) The chief financial officer of the Company shall have furnished to the Underwriters a certificate (a form of which is attached as Annex V), dated the date hereof and such Time of Delivery, respectively, in form and substance satisfactory to you.

9.   (a) The Company will indemnify and hold harmless each Underwriter against any losses, claims, damages or liabilities, joint or several, to which such Underwriter may become subject, under the Act or otherwise, insofar as such losses, claims, damages or liabilities (or actions in respect thereof) arise out of or are based upon an untrue statement or alleged untrue statement of a material fact contained in the Registration Statement, any Preliminary Prospectus, the Pricing Prospectus or the Prospectus, or any amendment or supplement thereto, any Issuer Free Writing Prospectus, any "roadshow" as defined in Rule 433(h) under the Act (a "roadshow"), any "issuer information" filed or required to be filed pursuant to Rule 433(d) under the Act or any Section 5(d) Writing prepared or authorized by the Company, or arise out of or are based upon the omission or alleged omission to state therein a material fact required to be stated therein or necessary to make the statements therein not misleading, and will reimburse each Underwriter for any legal or other expenses reasonably incurred by such Underwriter in connection with investigating or defending any such action or claim as such expenses are incurred; provided, however, that the Company shall not be liable in any such case to the extent that any such loss, claim, damage or liability arises out of or is based upon an untrue statement or alleged untrue statement or omission or alleged omission made in the Registration Statement, any Preliminary Prospectus, the Pricing Prospectus or the Prospectus, or any amendment or supplement thereto, or any Issuer Free Writing Prospectus or any Section 5(d) Writing, in reliance upon and in conformity with the Underwriter Information.

The Company also agrees to indemnify and hold harmless Allen & Co. and each person, if any, who controls Allen & Co. within the meaning of either Section 15 of the Securities Act or Section 20 of the Exchange Act from and against any and all losses, claims, damages, or liabilities (or actions in respect thereof) incurred as a result of Allen & Co.'s participation as a "qualified independent underwriter" within the meaning of Rule 5121 of the Financial Industry Regulatory Authority in connection with the offering of the Shares, except for any losses, claims, damages, or liabilities (or actions in respect thereof) resulting from Allen & Co.'s, or such controlling person's, willful misconduct.

(b)   Each Selling Stockholder will severally and not jointly indemnify and hold harmless each Underwriter against any losses, claims, damages or liabilities, joint or several, to which such Underwriter may become subject, under the Act or otherwise, insofar as such losses, claims, damages or liabilities (or actions in respect thereof) arise out of or are based upon an untrue statement or alleged untrue statement of a material fact contained in the Registration Statement, any Preliminary Prospectus, the Pricing Prospectus or the Prospectus, or any amendment or supplement thereto, any Issuer Free Writing Prospectus or arise out of or are based upon the omission or alleged omission to state therein a material fact required to be stated therein or necessary to make the statements therein not misleading, in each case to the extent, but only to the extent, that such untrue statement or alleged untrue statement or omission or alleged omission was made in the Registration Statement, any Preliminary Prospectus, the Pricing Prospectus or the Prospectus, or any amendment or supplement thereto or any Issuer Free Writing Prospectus, or any roadshow, or any Section 5(d) Writing, in reliance upon and in conformity with any Selling Stockholder Information furnished to the Company in writing by such Selling Stockholder expressly for use therein; and will reimburse each Underwriter for any legal or other expenses reasonably incurred by such Underwriter in connection with investigating or defending any such action or claim as such expenses are incurred; provided, however, that the Company and the Selling Stockholders shall not be liable in any such case to the extent that any such loss, claim, damage or liability arises out of or is based upon an untrue statement or alleged untrue statement or omission or alleged omission made in the Registration Statement, any Preliminary Prospectus, the Pricing Prospectus or the Prospectus, or any amendment or supplement thereto, or any Issuer Free Writing Prospectus or any Section 5(d) Writing, in reliance upon and in conformity with the Underwriter Information; and provided, further, that the liability of such Selling Stockholders pursuant to this subsection (b) shall not exceed the net proceeds (net of any underwriting discounts and commissions but before deducting expenses) from the sale of the Shares sold by the Selling Stockholder hereunder (the "Selling Stockholder Proceeds").

(c) Each Underwriter will indemnify and hold harmless the Company and each Selling Stockholder against any losses, claims, damages or liabilities to which the Company or such Selling Stockholder may become subject, under the Act or otherwise, insofar as such losses, claims, damages or liabilities (or actions in respect thereof) arise out of or are based upon an untrue statement or alleged untrue statement of a material fact contained in the Registration Statement, any Preliminary Prospectus, the Pricing Prospectus or the Prospectus, or any amendment or supplement thereto, or any Issuer Free Writing Prospectus, or any roadshow, or any Section 5(d) Writing, or arise out of or are based upon the omission or alleged omission to state therein a material fact required to be stated therein or necessary to make the statements therein not misleading, in each case to the extent, but only to the extent, that such untrue statement or alleged untrue statement or omission or alleged omission was made in the Registration Statement, any Preliminary Prospectus, the Pricing Prospectus or the Prospectus, or any amendment or supplement thereto, or any Issuer Free Writing Prospectus, or any roadshow, or any Section 5(d) Writing, in reliance upon and in conformity with the Underwriter Information; and will reimburse the Company and each Selling Stockholder for any legal or other expenses reasonably incurred by the Company or such Selling Stockholder in connection with investigating or defending any such action or claim as such expenses are incurred. As used in this Agreement with respect to an Underwriter and an applicable document, "Underwriter Information" shall mean the written information furnished to the Company by such Underwriter through the Representatives expressly for use therein; it being understood and agreed upon that the only such information furnished by any Underwriter consists of the following information in the Prospectus furnished on behalf of each Underwriter: the [fifth] paragraph of text under the caption "Underwriting (Conflicts of Interest)" concerning the terms of the offering by the Underwriters; the [ninth, tenth and eleventh] paragraphs of text under the caption "Underwriting (Conflicts of Interest)" concerning short sales, stabilizing transactions and purchases to cover positions created by short sales by the Underwriters; and the [twelfth] paragraph of text under the caption "Underwriting (Conflicts of Interest)" concerning sales to discretionary accounts by the Underwriters.

(d) Promptly after receipt by an indemnified party under subsection (a),(b) or (c) of this Section 9 of notice of the commencement of any action, such indemnified party shall, if a claim in respect thereof is to be made against the indemnifying party under such subsection, notify the indemnifying party in writing of the commencement thereof; provided that the failure to notify the indemnifying party shall not relieve it from any liability that it may have under the preceding paragraphs of this Section 9 except to the extent that it has been materially prejudiced (through the forfeiture of substantive rights or defenses) by such failure; and provided further that the failure to notify the indemnifying party shall not relieve it from any liability that it may have to an indemnified party otherwise than under the preceding paragraphs of this Section 9. In case any such action shall be brought against any indemnified party and it shall notify the indemnifying party of the commencement thereof, the indemnifying party shall be entitled to participate therein and, to the extent that it shall wish, jointly with any other indemnifying party similarly notified, to assume the defense thereof, with counsel reasonably satisfactory to such indemnified party (who shall not, except with the consent of the indemnified party, be counsel to the indemnifying party), and, after notice from the indemnifying party to such indemnified party of its election so to assume the defense thereof, the indemnifying party shall not be liable to such indemnified party under such subsection for any legal expenses of other counsel or any other expenses, in each case subsequently incurred by such indemnified party, in connection with the defense thereof other than reasonable costs of investigation. No indemnifying party shall, without the written consent of the indemnified party, effect the settlement or compromise of, or consent to the entry of any judgment with respect to, any pending or threatened action or claim in respect of which indemnification or contribution may be sought hereunder (whether or not the indemnified party is an actual or potential party to such action or claim) unless such settlement, compromise or judgment (i) includes an unconditional release of the indemnified party from all liability arising out of such action or claim and (ii) does not include a statement as to or an admission of fault, culpability or a failure to act, by or on behalf of any indemnified party.

(e)   If the indemnification provided for in this Section 9 is unavailable to or insufficient to hold harmless an indemnified party under subsection (a), (b) or (c) above in respect of any losses, claims, damages or liabilities (or actions in respect thereof) referred to therein, then each indemnifying party shall contribute to the amount paid or payable by such indemnified party as a result of such losses, claims, damages or liabilities (or actions in respect thereof) in such proportion as is appropriate to reflect the relative benefits received by the Company and the Selling Stockholders on the one hand and the Underwriters on the other from the offering of the Shares. If, however, the allocation provided by the immediately preceding sentence is not permitted by applicable law or if the indemnified party failed to give the notice required under subsection (d) above, then each indemnifying party shall contribute to such amount paid or payable by such indemnified party in such proportion as is appropriate to reflect not only such relative benefits but also the relative fault of the Company and the Selling Stockholders on the one hand and the Underwriters on the other in connection with the statements or omissions which resulted in such losses, claims, damages or liabilities (or actions in respect thereof), as well as any other relevant equitable considerations. The relative benefits received by the Company and the Selling Stockholders on the one hand and the Underwriters on the other shall be deemed to be in the same proportion as the total net proceeds from the offering (before deducting expenses) received by the Company and the Selling Stockholders bear to the total underwriting discounts and commissions received by the Underwriters, in each case as set forth in the table on the cover page of the Prospectus. Benefits, if any, received by the QIU in its capacity as such shall be deemed to be equal to the compensation, if any, received by the QIU for acting in such capacity. The relative fault shall be determined by reference to, among other things, whether the untrue or alleged untrue statement of a material fact or the omission or alleged omission to state a material fact relates to information supplied by the Company or the Selling Stockholders on the one hand or the Underwriters on the other and the parties' relative intent, knowledge, access to information and opportunity to correct or prevent such statement or omission. The Company, each of the Selling Stockholders and the Underwriters agree that it would not be just and equitable if contribution pursuant to this subsection (e) were determined by pro rata allocation (even if the Underwriters were treated as one entity for such purpose) or by any other method of allocation which does not take account of the equitable considerations referred to above in this subsection (e). The amount paid or payable by an indemnified party as a result of the losses, claims, damages or liabilities (or actions in respect thereof) referred to above in this subsection (e) shall be deemed to include any legal or other expenses reasonably incurred by such indemnified party in connection with investigating or defending any such action or claim. Notwithstanding the provisions of this subsection (e), (i) no Underwriter shall be required to contribute any amount in excess of the amount by which the total price at which the Shares underwritten by it and distributed to the public were offered to the public exceeds the amount of any damages which such Underwriter has otherwise been required to pay by reason of such untrue or alleged untrue statement or omission or alleged omission, (ii) the contribution by the Selling Stockholders pursuant to this subsection (e) shall not exceed the Selling Stockholder Proceeds (reduced by any amounts such Selling Stockholder has paid under subsection

(b) above), (iii) the Selling Stockholders shall be liable only to the extent that the relevant loss, claim, damage or liability arises out of or is based upon an untrue statement or alleged untrue statement or omission or alleged omission, in each case, which relates to the Selling Stockholder made in the Registration Statement, any Preliminary Prospectus, the Pricing Prospectus or the Prospectus, or any amendment or supplement thereto, or any Issuer Free Writing Prospectus, or any roadshow, or any Section 5(d) Writing, in reliance upon and in conformity with any Selling Stockholder Information furnished to the Underwriters in writing by the Selling Stockholder expressly for use therein and (iv) the QIU, in its capacity as such, shall not be responsible for any amount in excess of the compensation received by the QIU for acting in such capacity. No person guilty of fraudulent misrepresentation (within the meaning of Section 11(f) of the Act) shall be entitled to contribution from any person who was not guilty of such fraudulent misrepresentation. The Underwriters' obligations in this subsection (d) to contribute are several in proportion to their respective underwriting obligations and not joint.

Notwithstanding anything contained herein to the contrary, if indemnity may be sought pursuant to subsections (a) and (b) above, in respect of such action or proceeding, then in addition to such separate firm for the indemnified parties, the indemnifying party shall be liable for the reasonable fees and expenses of not more than one separate firm (in addition to any local counsel) for the QIU in its capacity as such and all persons, if any, who control such QIU within the meaning of either Section 15 of the Securities Act or Section 20 of the Exchange Act.

(f)   The obligations of the Company and the Selling Stockholders under this Section 9 shall be in addition to any liability which the Company and the Selling Stockholders may otherwise have and shall extend, upon the same terms and conditions, to each officer and director of each Underwriter and each person, if any, who controls any Underwriter within the meaning of the Act and each broker-dealer affiliate of any Underwriter; and the obligations of the Underwriters under this Section 9 shall be in addition to any liability which the respective Underwriters may otherwise have and shall extend, upon the same terms and conditions, to each officer and director of the Company and to each person, if any, who controls the Company or any Selling Stockholder within the meaning of the Act.

10.   (a) If any Underwriter shall default in its obligation to purchase the Shares which it has agreed to purchase hereunder at a Time of Delivery, you may in your discretion arrange for you or another party or other parties to purchase such Shares on the terms contained herein. If within thirty-six hours after such default by any Underwriter you do not arrange for the purchase of such Shares, then the Company and the Selling Stockholders shall be entitled to a further period of thirty-six hours within which to procure another party or other parties satisfactory to you to purchase such Shares on such terms. In the event that, within the respective prescribed periods, you notify the Company and the Selling Stockholders that you have so arranged for the purchase of such Shares, or the Company or a Selling Stockholder notifies you that it has so arranged for the purchase of such Shares, you or the Company or the Selling Stockholders shall have the right to postpone such Time of Delivery for a period of not more than seven days, in order to effect whatever changes may thereby be made necessary in the Registration Statement or the Prospectus, or in any other documents or arrangements, and the Company agrees to file promptly any amendments or supplements to the Registration Statement or the Prospectus which in your opinion may thereby be made necessary. The term "Underwriter" as used in this Agreement shall include any person substituted under this Section with like effect as if such person had originally been a party to this Agreement with respect to such Shares.

(b) If, after giving effect to any arrangements for the purchase of the Shares of a defaulting Underwriter or Underwriters by you, the Company and the Selling Stockholders as provided in subsection (a) above, the aggregate number of such Shares which remains unpurchased does not exceed one-eleventh of the aggregate number of all the Shares to be purchased at such Time of Delivery, then the Company and the Selling Stockholders shall have the right to require each non-defaulting Underwriter to purchase the number of Shares which such Underwriter agreed to purchase hereunder at such Time of Delivery and, in addition, to require each non-defaulting Underwriter to purchase its pro rata share (based on the number of Shares which such Underwriter agreed to purchase hereunder) of the Shares of such defaulting Underwriter or Underwriters for which such arrangements have not been made; but nothing herein shall relieve a defaulting Underwriter from liability for its default.

(c) If, after giving effect to any arrangements for the purchase of the Shares of a defaulting Underwriter or Underwriters by you, the Company and the Selling Stockholders as provided in subsection (a) above, the aggregate number of such Shares which remains unpurchased exceeds one-eleventh of the aggregate number of all the Shares to be purchased at such Time of Delivery, or if the Company and the Selling Stockholders shall not exercise the right described in subsection (b) above to require non-defaulting Underwriters to purchase Shares of a defaulting Underwriter or Underwriters, then this Agreement (or, with respect to a Second Time of Delivery, the obligations of the Underwriters to purchase and of the Company to sell the Optional Shares) shall thereupon terminate, without liability on the part of any non-defaulting Underwriter, the Company or the Selling Stockholders, except for the expenses to be borne by the Company, the Selling Stockholders and the Underwriters as provided in Section 7 hereof and the indemnity and contribution agreements in Section 9 hereof; but nothing herein shall relieve a defaulting Underwriter from liability for its default.

11. The respective indemnities, agreements, representations, warranties and other statements of the Company, the Selling Stockholders and the several Underwriters, as set forth in this Agreement or made by or on behalf of them, respectively, pursuant to this Agreement, shall remain in full force and effect, regardless of any investigation (or any statement as to the results thereof) made by or on behalf of any Underwriter or any controlling person of any Underwriter, or the Company, or any of the Selling Stockholders, or any officer or director or controlling person of the Company, or any controlling person of any Selling Stockholder, and shall survive delivery of and payment for the Shares.

12. If this Agreement shall be terminated pursuant to Section 10 hereof, neither the Company nor the Selling Stockholders shall then be under any liability to any Underwriter except as provided in Sections 7 and 9 hereof; but, if for any other reason (other than those set forth in clauses (i), (iii), (iv) and (v) of Section 8(f)), any Shares are not delivered by or on behalf of the Company and the Selling Stockholders as provided herein, the Company and each of the Selling Stockholders pro rata (based on the number of Shares to be sold by the Company and such Selling Stockholder hereunder) will reimburse the Underwriters through you for all documented out-of-pocket expenses approved in writing by you, including fees and disbursements of counsel, reasonably incurred by the Underwriters in making preparations for the purchase, sale and delivery of the Shares not so delivered, but the Company and the Selling Stockholders shall then be under no further liability to any Underwriter except as provided in Sections 7 and 9 hereof.

13. In all dealings hereunder, you shall act on behalf of each of the Underwriters, and the parties hereto shall be entitled to act and rely upon any statement, request, notice or agreement on behalf of any Underwriter made or given by you jointly or by Goldman Sachs & Co. LLC and J.P. Morgan Securities LLC on behalf of you as the representatives; and in all dealings with any Selling

Stockholder hereunder, you and the Company shall be entitled to act and rely upon any statement, request, notice or agreement on behalf of such Selling Stockholder made or given by any or all of the Attorneys-in-Fact for such Selling Stockholder.

In accordance with the requirements of the USA Patriot Act (Title III of Pub. L. 107-56 (signed into law October 26, 2001)), the Underwriters are required to obtain, verify and record information that identifies their respective clients, including the Company and the Selling Stockholders, which information may include the name and address of their respective clients, as well as other information that will allow the Underwriters to properly identify their respective clients.

All statements, requests, notices and agreements hereunder shall be in writing, and if to the Underwriters shall be delivered or sent by mail, telex or facsimile transmission to each of the representatives in care of (a) Goldman Sachs & Co. LLC, 200 West Street, New York, New York 10282-2198, Attention: Registration Department and (b) J.P. Morgan Securities LLC, 383 Madison Avenue, New York, New York 10179, Attention: Equity Syndicate Desk; if to any Selling Stockholder shall be delivered or sent by mail, telex or facsimile transmission to counsel for such Selling Stockholder at its address set forth in Schedule II hereto; if to the Company shall be delivered or sent by mail, telex or facsimile transmission to the address of the Company set forth in the Registration Statement, Attention: Secretary; and if to any stockholder that has delivered a lock-up letter described in Section 8(h) hereof shall be delivered or sent by mail to his or her respective address provided in such lock-up letter; provided, however, that any notice to an Underwriter pursuant to Section 9(d) hereof shall be delivered or sent by mail, telex or facsimile transmission to such Underwriter at its address set forth in its Underwriters' Questionnaire or telex constituting such Questionnaire, which address will be supplied to the Company or the Selling Stockholders by you on request; provided, however, that notices under subsection 5(e) shall be in writing, and if to the Underwriters shall be delivered or sent by mail, telex or facsimile transmission to you as the representatives at Goldman Sachs & Co. LLC, 200 West Street, New York, New York 10282-2198, Attention: Control Room. Any such statements, requests, notices or agreements shall take effect upon receipt thereof.

14.   This Agreement shall be binding upon, and inure solely to the benefit of, the Underwriters, the Company and the Selling Stockholders and, to the extent provided in Sections 9 and 11 hereof, the officers and directors of the Company and each person who controls the Company, any Selling Stockholder or any Underwriter, and their respective heirs, executors, administrators, successors and assigns, and no other person shall acquire or have any right under or by virtue of this Agreement. No purchaser of any of the Shares from any Underwriter shall be deemed a successor or assign by reason merely of such purchase.

15.   Time shall be of the essence of this Agreement. As used herein, the term "business day" shall mean any day when the Commission's office in Washington, D.C. is open for business.

16.   The Company and the Selling Stockholders acknowledge and agree that (i) the purchase and sale of the Shares pursuant to this Agreement is an arm's-length commercial transaction between the Company and the Selling Stockholders, on the one hand, and the several Underwriters, on the other, (ii) in connection therewith and with the process leading to such transaction each Underwriter is acting solely as a principal and not the agent or fiduciary of the Company or any Selling Stockholder, (iii) no Underwriter has assumed an advisory or fiduciary responsibility in favor of the Company or any Selling Stockholder with respect to the offering contemplated hereby or the process leading thereto (irrespective of whether such Underwriter has advised or is currently advising the Company or any Selling Stockholder on other matters) or any other obligation to the Company or any Selling Stockholder except the obligations expressly set forth in this Agreement and (iv) the Company and each Selling Stockholder has consulted its own legal and financial advisors to the extent it deemed

357

appropriate. The Company and each Selling Stockholder agrees that it will not claim that the Underwriters, or any of them, has rendered advisory services of any nature or respect, or owes a fiduciary or similar duty to the Company or any Selling Stockholder, in connection with such transaction or the process leading thereto.

17.   This Agreement supersedes all prior agreements and understandings (whether written or oral) between the Company, the Selling Stockholders and the Underwriters, or any of them, with respect to the subject matter hereof.

18.   This Agreement and any transaction contemplated by this Agreement shall be governed by and construed in accordance with the laws of the State of New York without regard to principles of conflict of laws that would results in the application of any other law than the laws of the State of New York. The Company and each Selling Stockholder agree that any suit or proceeding arising in respect of this Agreement or any transaction contemplated by this Agreement will be tried exclusively in the U.S. District Court for the Southern District of New York or, if that court does not have subject matter jurisdiction, in any state court located in The City and County of New York and the Company and each Selling Stockholder agree to submit to the jurisdiction of, and to venue in, such courts.

19.   The Company, each Selling Stockholder and each of the Underwriters hereby irrevocably waives, to the fullest extent permitted by applicable law, any and all right to trial by jury in any legal proceeding arising out of or relating to this Agreement or the transactions contemplated hereby.

20.   This Agreement may be executed by any one or more of the parties hereto in any number of counterparts, each of which shall be deemed to be an original, but all such counterparts shall together constitute one and the same instrument.

21.   Notwithstanding anything herein to the contrary, the Company and the Selling Stockholders are authorized to disclose to any persons the U.S. federal and state income tax treatment and tax structure of the potential transaction and all materials of any kind (including tax opinions and other tax analyses) provided to the Company and the Selling Stockholders relating to that treatment and structure, without the Underwriters imposing any limitation of any kind. However, any information relating to the tax treatment and tax structure shall remain confidential (and the foregoing sentence shall not apply) to the extent necessary to enable any person to comply with securities laws. For this purpose, "tax structure" is limited to any facts that may be relevant to that treatment.

If the foregoing is in accordance with your understanding, please sign and return to us counterparts hereof, and upon the acceptance hereof by you, on behalf of each of the Underwriters, this letter and such acceptance hereof shall constitute a binding agreement among each of the Underwriters, the Company and each of the Selling Stockholders. It is understood that your acceptance of this letter on behalf of each of the Underwriters is pursuant to the authority set forth in a form of Agreement among Underwriters, the form of which shall be submitted to the Company and the Selling Stockholders for examination, upon request, but without warranty on your part as to the authority of the signers thereof.

Very truly yours,

Dropbox, Inc.

By: _____
    Name:
    Title:

[Names of Selling Stockholders]

By: _____
    Name:
    Title:
    As Attorney-in-Fact on behalf of each of
      the Selling Stockholders named in
      Schedule II to this Agreement

Accepted as of the date hereof

in New York, New York

Goldman Sachs & Co. LLC

By: _____
    Name:
    Title:

J.P. Morgan Securities LLC

By: _____
    Name:
    Title:

On behalf of each of the Underwriters

[Signature Page to Underwriting Agreement]

SCHEDULE I

Underwriter	Total Number of Firm Shares to be Purchased	Number of Optional Shares to be Purchased if Maximum Option Exercised
Goldman Sachs & Co. LLC		
J.P. Morgan Securities LLC		
Deutsche Bank Securities Inc.		
Allen & Company LLC		
Merrill Lynch, Pierce, Fenner & Smith Incorporated		
RBC Capital Markets, LLC		
Jefferies LLC		
Macquarie Capital (USA) Inc.		
Canaccord Genuity Inc.		
JMP Securities LLC		
KeyBanc Capital Markets Inc.		
Piper Jaffray & Co.		
Total		

360

SCHEDULE II

	Total Number of Firm Shares to be Sold	Number of Optional Shares to be Sold if Maximum Option Exercised
The Company		
The Selling Stockholder(s):		
[Name of Selling Stockholder](a)		
[Name of Selling Stockholder](a)		
Total		

(a) Each Selling Stockholder is represented by Whalen LLP, 1601 Dove Street, Suite 270, Newport Beach, CA 92660 and has appointed Andrew W. Houston, Ajay V. Vashee and Bart E. Volkmer, and each of them, as the Attorneys-in-Fact for such Selling Stockholder.

SCHEDULE III

(a) Issuer Free Writing Prospectuses not included in the Pricing Disclosure Package

[   ]

(b) Information other than the Pricing Prospectus that comprise the Pricing Disclosure Package

The initial public offering price per share for the Shares is $ [●].

The number of Shares purchased by the Underwriters is [●].

[Add any other pricing disclosure.]

(c) Section 5(d) Writings

[   ]

[FORM OF PRESS RELEASE]

Dropbox, Inc.
[Date]

Dropbox, Inc. announced today that Goldman Sachs & Co. LLC and J.P. Morgan Securities LLC, the lead book-running managers in the Company's recent public sale of   shares of common stock, are [waiving] [releasing] a lock-up restriction with respect to   shares of the Company's common stock held by [certain officers or directors] [an officer or director] of the Company. The [waiver] [release] will take effect on   , 20   , and the shares may be sold on or after such date.

This press release is not an offer for sale of the securities in the United States or in any other jurisdiction where such offer is prohibited, and such securities may not be offered or sold in the United States absent registration or an exemption from registration under the United States Securities Act of 1933, as amended.

[FORM OF LOCK-UP AGREEMENT]

Dropbox, Inc.

Lock-Up Agreement

[Date]

Goldman Sachs & Co. LLC
J.P. Morgan Securities LLC

c/o Goldman Sachs & Co. LLC
200 West Street
New York, NY 10282-2198

c/o J.P. Morgan Securities LLC
383 Madison Avenue
New York, New York 10179

Re: Dropbox, Inc. - Lock-Up Agreement

Ladies and Gentlemen:

The undersigned understands that you, as representatives (the "Representatives"), propose to enter into an Underwriting Agreement (the "Underwriting Agreement") on behalf of the several Underwriters named in Schedule I to such agreement (collectively, the "Underwriters"), with Dropbox, Inc., a Delaware corporation (the "Company"), and the Selling Stockholders named in Schedule II to such agreement, if any, providing for a public offering (the "Public Offering") of shares (the "Shares") of the Class A common stock of the Company, par value $0.00001 per share (the "Class A Common Stock" and together with the Class B common stock of the Company, $0.00001 par value per share, the "Common Stock") pursuant to a Registration Statement on Form S-1 to be filed with the Securities and Exchange Commission (the "SEC").

In consideration of the agreement by the Underwriters to offer and sell the Shares, and of other good and valuable consideration the receipt and sufficiency of which is hereby acknowledged, the undersigned agrees that, during the period beginning from the date of this lock-up agreement (the "Lock-Up Agreement") and continuing to and including the date 180 days after the Public Offering date (the "Public Offering Date") set forth on the cover of the final prospectus (the "Prospectus") used to sell the Shares (the "Stockholder Lock-Up Period"), the undersigned will not offer, sell, contract to sell, pledge, grant any option to purchase, make any short sale or otherwise dispose of any shares of Common Stock of the Company, or any options or warrants to purchase any shares of Common Stock of the Company, or any securities convertible into, exchangeable for or that represent the right to receive shares of Common Stock of the Company, whether now owned or hereafter acquired, owned directly by the undersigned (including holding as a custodian) or with respect to which the undersigned has beneficial ownership within the rules and regulations of the SEC (collectively the

"Undersigned's Shares") other than any Shares sold to the Underwriters pursuant to the Underwriting Agreement or as otherwise provided herein. The foregoing restriction is expressly agreed to preclude the undersigned from engaging in any hedging or other transaction which is designed to or which reasonably could be expected to lead to or result in a sale or disposition of the Undersigned's Shares even if such shares of Common Stock would be disposed of by someone other than the undersigned. Such prohibited hedging or other transactions would include without limitation any short sale or any purchase, sale or grant of any right (including without limitation any put or call option) with respect to any of the Undersigned's Shares or with respect to any security that includes, relates to, or derives any significant part of its value from such shares of Common Stock.

If the undersigned is an officer or director of the Company, (1) the undersigned further agrees that the foregoing restrictions shall be equally applicable to any issuer-directed Shares the undersigned may purchase in connection with the Public Offering, (2) Goldman Sachs & Co. LLC and J.P. Morgan Securities LLC agree that, at least three business days before the effective date of any release or waiver of the foregoing restrictions in connection with a transfer of Common Stock, Goldman Sachs & Co. LLC and J.P. Morgan Securities LLC will notify the Company of the impending release or waiver and (3) the Company has agreed or will agree in the Underwriting Agreement to announce the impending release or waiver by press release through a major news service at least two business days before the effective date of the release or waiver in accordance with the requirements under FINRA Rule 5131 (or any successor provision thereto) (for the avoidance of doubt, the Blackout-Related Release (as defined below) shall not be deemed a release or waiver under this Lock-Up Agreement pursuant to FINRA Rule 5131, and is instead an expiration of the Lock-Up Agreement pursuant to its terms). Any release or waiver granted by Goldman Sachs & Co. LLC and J.P. Morgan Securities LLC hereunder to any such officer or director shall only be effective two business days after the publication date of such press release. The provisions of this paragraph will not apply if (a) the release or waiver is effected solely to permit a transfer not for consideration and (b) the transferee has agreed in writing to be bound by the same terms described in this Lock-Up Agreement to the extent and for the duration that such terms remain in effect at the time of the transfer.

Notwithstanding the foregoing, the undersigned may

(a) transfer the Undersigned's Shares:

    (i)   as a bona fide gift or gifts, or for bona fide estate planning purposes,

    (ii)   to any member of the undersigned's immediate family or to any trust for the direct or indirect benefit of the undersigned or the immediate family of the undersigned, or if the undersigned is a trust, to a trustor or beneficiary of the trust or to the estate of a beneficiary of such trust,

    (iii)   upon death or by will, testamentary document or the laws of intestate succession,

    (iv)   in connection with a sale of the Undersigned's Shares acquired (A) from the Underwriters in the Public Offering or (B) in open market transactions after the Public Offering Date,

(v)   if the undersigned is a corporation, partnership, limited liability company, trust or other business entity, (A) to another corporation, partnership, limited liability company, trust or other business entity that is an affiliate (as defined in Rule 405 promulgated under the Securities Act of 1933, as amended) of the undersigned, or to any investment fund or other entity controlling, controlled by, managing or managed by or under common control with the undersigned or affiliates of the undersigned (including, for the avoidance of doubt, where the undersigned is a partnership, to its general partner or a successor partnership or fund, or any other funds managed by such partnership), or (B) as part of a distribution, transfer or disposition without consideration by the undersigned to its stockholders, partners, members or other equity holders,

(vi)   (A) to the Company for the purposes of exercising (including for the payment of tax withholdings or remittance payments due as a result of such exercise) on a "net exercise" basis options to purchase shares of Common Stock to the extent such options would otherwise expire during the Stockholder Lock-Up Period and (B) in connection with the vesting or settlement of restricted stock units, including any transfer to the Company for the payment of tax withholdings or remittance payments due as a result of the vesting or settlement of such restricted stock units, and any transfer necessary to generate such amount of cash needed for the payment of taxes, including estimated taxes, due as a result of the vesting or settlement of restricted stock units whether by means of a "net settlement" or otherwise, provided that any such transfers described in this subclause (B) occurring within 90 days of the Public Offering Date shall be only to the Company, and in all such cases described in (A) and (B), provided that any such shares of Common Stock received upon such exercise, vesting or settlement shall be subject to the terms of this Lock-Up Agreement, and provided further that any such options and restricted stock units are held by the undersigned as of the Public Offering Date and were issued pursuant to equity awards granted under a stock incentive plan or other equity award plan, which plan is described in the Prospectus,

(vii)   to the Company in connection with the repurchase of shares of Common Stock issued pursuant to equity awards granted under a stock incentive plan or other equity award plan, which plan is described in the Prospectus, or pursuant to the agreements pursuant to which such shares were issued, as described in the Prospectus, provided that such repurchase of shares of Common Stock is in connection with the termination of the undersigned's service provider relationship with the Company,

(viii)   pursuant to a bona fide third-party tender offer, merger, consolidation or other similar transaction that is approved by the Board of Directors of the Company and made to all holders of the Company's capital stock involving a change of control of the Company, provided that in the event that such tender offer, merger, consolidation or other similar transaction is not completed, the Undersigned's Shares shall remain subject to the provisions of this Lock-Up Agreement,

(ix)   in connection with the conversion or reclassification of the outstanding preferred stock into shares of Common Stock of the Company, or any reclassification or conversion of the Company's Common Stock (including the conversion of shares of Class B Common Stock into Class A Common Stock), provided that any such shares of Common Stock received upon such conversion or reclassification shall be subject to the terms of this Lock-Up Agreement,

(x)   by operation of law, such as pursuant to a final qualified domestic order or in connection with a divorce settlement,

(xi)   with the prior written consent of Goldman Sachs & Co. LLC and J.P. Morgan Securities LLC on behalf of the Underwriters,

provided, that (A) in the case of (i), (ii), (iii), (v), (ix) and (x) above, it shall be a condition to the transfer or distribution that the donee, devisee, transferee or distributee, as the case may be, agrees in writing to be bound by the restrictions set forth herein, and there shall be no further transfer of such Common Stock except in accordance with this Lock-Up Agreement, (B) in the case of (i), (ii), (iii) and (v) above, such transfer shall not involve a disposition for value, (C) in the case of (i), (ii) and (iii) above, no filing under Section 16 of the Securities Exchange Act of 1934, as amended (the "Exchange Act"), or other public filing, report or announcement reporting a reduction in beneficial ownership of shares of Common Stock shall be required or shall be voluntarily made during the Stockholder Lock-Up Period (other than any required Form 5 filing), (D) in the case of (iv) and (v) above, no filing under Section 16 of the Exchange Act, or other public filing, report or announcement shall be required or shall be voluntarily made during the Stockholder Lock-Up Period in connection with such transfer or distribution, and (E) in the case of (vi), (vii), (x) and (xi) above, it shall be a condition to such transfer that if any filing under Section 16(a) of the Exchange Act, or other public filing, report or announcement reporting a reduction in beneficial ownership of shares of Common Stock in connection with such transfer or distribution shall be legally required during the Stockholder Lock-Up Period, such filing, report or announcement shall clearly indicate in the footnotes thereto the nature and conditions of such transfer; or

(b)   enter into a written plan meeting the requirements of Rule 10b5-1 under the Exchange Act after the date of this Lock-Up Agreement relating to the transfer, sale or other disposition of securities of the undersigned, if then permitted by the Company, provided that the securities subject to such plan may not be transferred until after the expiration of the Stockholder Lock-Up Period and no public announcement or filing under the Exchange Act shall be required or shall be voluntarily made by any person regarding the establishment of such plan during the Stockholder Lock-Up Period.

For purposes of this Lock-Up Agreement, "immediate family" shall mean any relationship by blood, marriage, domestic partnership or adoption, not more remote than first cousin. The undersigned now has, and, except as contemplated by clause (a) above, for the duration of this Lock-Up Agreement will have, good and marketable title to the Undersigned's Shares, free and clear of all liens, encumbrances, and claims whatsoever. The undersigned also agrees and consents to the entry of stop transfer instructions with the Company's transfer agent and registrar against the transfer of the Undersigned's Shares except in compliance with the foregoing restrictions.

In addition, and notwithstanding the provisions of the second paragraph of this Lock-Up Agreement, if (i) at least 120 days have elapsed since the Public Offering Date and (ii) the Stockholder Lock-Up Period is scheduled to end during a Blackout Period (as defined below) or within five Trading Days (as defined below) prior to a Blackout Period, the Stockholder Lock-Up Period shall end 10 Trading Days prior to the commencement of the Blackout Period (the "Blackout-Related Release"), *provided, that* promptly upon the Company's determination of the date of the Blackout-Related Release and in any event at least seven Trading Days in advance of the Blackout-Related Release, the Company shall notify the Representatives of the date of the impending Blackout-Related Release, and shall announce the date of the Blackout-Related Release through a major news service, or on a Form 8-K, at least two Trading Days in advance of the Blackout-Related Release, and *provided further, that* the Blackout-Related Release shall not occur unless the Company shall have publicly released its earnings results for the quarterly period during which the Public Offering occurred. For purposes of this paragraph, a "Trading Day" is a day on which the New York Stock Exchange and the Nasdaq Stock Market are open for the buying and selling of securities. For purposes of this Lock-Up Agreement, "Blackout Period" shall mean a broadly applicable period during which trading in the Company's securities would not be permitted under the Company's insider trading policy. For the avoidance of doubt, notwithstanding anything to the contrary contained herein, in no event shall the Stockholder Lock-Up Period end earlier than 120 days after the Public Offering Date.

Notwithstanding anything to the contrary contained herein, this Lock-Up Agreement will automatically terminate and the undersigned will be released from all obligations hereunder upon the earliest to occur, if any, of (i) the Company advises the Representatives in writing, prior to the execution of the Underwriting Agreement, that it has determined not to proceed with the Public Offering, (ii) the Company files an application with the SEC to withdraw the registration statement related to the Public Offering, (iii) the Underwriting Agreement is executed but is terminated (other than the provisions thereof which survive termination) prior to payment for and delivery of the Shares to be sold thereunder, or (iv) March 31, 2018, in the event that the Underwriting Agreement has not been executed by such date; *provided, however*, that the Company may, by written notice to the undersigned prior to such date, extend such date for a period of up to three additional months.

In the event that either of the Representatives withdraws from or declines to participate in the Public Offering, all references to the Representatives contained in this Lock-Up Agreement shall be deemed to refer to the sole Representative that continues to participate in the Public Offering (the "Remaining Representative"), and, in such event, any written consent, waiver or notice given or delivered in connection with this Lock-Up Agreement by the Remaining Representative shall be deemed to be sufficient and effective for all purposes under this Lock-Up Agreement.

The undersigned hereby consents to receipt of this Lock-Up Agreement in electronic form and understands and agrees that this Lock-Up Agreement may be signed electronically. In the event that any signature is delivered by facsimile transmission, electronic mail, or otherwise by electronic transmission evidencing an intent to sign this Lock-Up Agreement, such facsimile transmission, electronic mail or other electronic transmission shall create a valid and binding obligation of the undersigned with the same force and effect as if such signature were an original. Execution and delivery of this Lock-Up Agreement by facsimile transmission, electronic mail or other electronic transmission is legal, valid and binding for all purposes.

The undersigned understands that the Company and the Underwriters are relying upon this Lock-Up Agreement in proceeding toward consummation of the offering. The undersigned further understands that this Lock-Up Agreement is irrevocable and shall be binding upon the undersigned's heirs, legal representatives, successors, and assigns. The undersigned hereby represents and warrants that the undersigned has full power and authority to enter into this Lock-Up Agreement. This Lock-Up Agreement shall be governed by, and construed in accordance with, the laws of the state of New York without regard to the conflict of laws principles thereof.

Very truly yours,

_____
Exact Name of Shareholder

_____
Authorized Signature

_____
Title